Privatization Experiences in the European Union

CESifo Seminar Series
Edited by Hans-Werner Sinn

See http://mitpress.mit.edu for a complete list of titles in this series.

Privatization Experiences in the European Union

Marko Köthenbürger,
Hans-Werner Sinn, and John
Whalley, editors

CESifo Seminar Series

The MIT Press
Cambridge, Massachusetts
London, England

MIT Press books may be purchased at special quantity discounts for business or sales promotional use. For information, please e-mail special_sales@mitpress.mit.edu or write to Special Sales Department, The MIT Press, 55 Hayward Street, Cambridge, MA 02142.

This book was set in Palatino on 3B2 by Asco Typesetters, Hong Kong and was printed and bound in the United States of America.

Library of Congress Cataloging-in-Publication Data

Privatization experiences in the European Union / Marko Köthenbürger, Hans-Werner Sinn, and John Whalley, editors.
    p. cm. — (CESifo seminar series)
Includes bibliographical references and index.
ISBN-10: 0-262-11296-5   ISBN-13: 978-0-262-11296-3 (alk. paper)
1. Privatization—European Union countries. I. Köthenbürger, Marko. II. Sinn, Hans-Werner. III. Whalley, John. IV. Series.

HD4138.P77   2006
338.94′05—dc22   2006043325

10 9 8 7 6 5 4 3 2 1

Contents

Series Foreword

This book is part of the CESifo Seminar Series. The series aims to cover topical policy issues in economics from a largely European perspective. The books in this series are the products of the papers and intensive debates that took place during the seminars hosted by CESifo, an international research network of renowned economists organized jointly by the Center for Economic Studies at Ludwig-Maximilians-Universität, Munich, and the Ifo Institute for Economic Research. All publications in this series have been carefully selected and refereed by members of the CESifo research network.

Introduction

Privatization of public enterprises has been at the top on the political agenda over the past two decades. Beginning with the privatization experiments in the United Kingdom and the liberalization of the U.S. telecommunication sector, policymakers around the world began to pay attention to the virtues of privatization. The result was that in many developing and developed countries, policymakers for one reason or another gave way to private incentives in core sectors of the economy. The privatization trend, which was part of a global movement toward liberalization, was fostered within the European Union (EU) by the issuance of various directives by Brussels that set general requirements for limiting public activity in the telecommunications, water, gas, and electricity sectors of EU member states. The policy seemed to be broadly supported by most academic economists on the grounds that market-guided resource allocation is generally superior to central direction or the political process. Yet at first glance, the outcomes of these privatizations seemed to be mixed in terms of actual impact. Phone rates had fallen sharply, and in some countries natural gas and energy costs had fallen more broadly; however, the quality of public transportation had not increased on a broad scale. Most notably, in the United Kingdom—the first European country that significantly privatized network industries—trains seemed to run late and be dirty, and the number of accidents had significantly increased. Actual impact, as widely perceived, and the basis for academic support for privatization were not always fully in tune with each other. In probing the literature, we found few papers on actual ex post evaluation, and the project set itself the task of evaluating impacts and gaining a better understanding of the experiences involved.

This book contains ten chapters on country experiences with recent privatization in the EU and two chapters setting out conceptual frameworks to aid our understanding of the issues and techniques for evaluation. The chapters were originally presented and discussed at two subsequent conferences organized by CESifo, Munich, and the University of Warwick. Most would not have been written had they not been solicited for this book. Academic journals do not lend themselves well to a discussion of national policy experiments. Yet we believe, that experience is more important than all theories in finding out which factors render privatization successful and which are likely to lead to failure.

Before reviewing the chapters, we first provide a brief discussion on what is meant by privatization and how national incentives to privatize core industries evolved in the EU.

I.1   What Is Privatization?

A number of important themes emerge in this book. One is that discussion of privatization proxied by a transfer in ownership rights is too simplistic as a concept to understand both the issues and to evaluate the impact. As Ingo Vogelsang emphasizes in chapter 2, it is necessary to distinguish between changes in ownership (simple privatization), changes in the rules of market participation and conduct (liberalization), and changes in public regulation (deregulation).

The most narrowly defined view of privatization refers to a change in ownership. It may imply a mere relabeling of public activities by bundling them into a state-owned enterprise (SOE). This view has not become an issue in the United States, as the amount of public ownership is traditionally small compared to Europe, where, prior to the 1980s in countries such as Spain, Ireland, Italy, and France, there had been extensive government involvement in many major areas of the manufacturing and service sectors, going well beyond those areas often characterized as natural monopolies such as railways, power utilities, and telecoms. In Europe, it is not uncommon that the bundling of state activity into an SOE is the first step in a more ambitious privatization plan. For instance, the German railway company (Deutsche Bundesbahn) has recently been organized as an incorporated SOE with a public share offering scheduled over the next several years. This notion of privatization is often taken to represent and define European privatization, suggestively inspired by the sales of British Airways stock and of British Petroleum in the United Kingdom throughout the Thatcher years. The reality, however, is that privatization is a more nuanced concept than this. Privatization can equally well (and possibly exclusively) refer to changed rules of conduct and market entry. In this vein, the EU directives on telecommunications do not require a change in ownership. The directives primarily prescribe liberalization of the telecommunication industry, including specific rules of conduct and market entry. The state may still own the previous monopoly firm, but is now required to allow competition with other telecommunication service providers.

Third, privatization may imply a change in regulation—a reduction in state oversight and in constraints imposed on private firms. This concept of privatization may be of particular relevance in countries where distributional considerations or the aim to protect the domestic industry prevalently guide national policy.

For evaluating the policy experiences in the EU, the second view on privatization is the more relevant one. EU privatization of network industries did not necessarily require the state to sell the previous monopoly. Also, as the industries involved feature elements of a natural monopoly, regulation continued to be desirable in general. The states were free to choose the specific modes of regulation in certain network industries out of an EU-determined set of regulatory procedures. Privatization therefore might have involved a change in regulation but not a widespread deregulation of network industries.

I.2   The Directives of the European Union

In the EU the European Commission (EC) had a prime impact on national privatization policies. To foster and coordinate reforms of network industries, the EU has launched a variety of directives related to telecommunication, electricity, and gas and took a more tentative approach with respect to the reform of national railway systems. The two most influential ones are the telecommunications directive and electricity directive.

I.2.1   EU Directive on Telecommunications

Until the early 1980s the European telecommunications market was exclusively regulated nationally. The EC took a stance on privatization policy largely motivated by Article 90 of the EC Treaty, which stipulates the construction of competition-oriented systems in the EU. The involvement was controversially debated as member states feared their national autonomy in danger. In various rulings, however, the European Court of Justice confirmed Brussels's supremacy, which to some extent paved the way for the widespread liberalization of tele-communications markets in the EU. One of the first directives involved the abolition of the incumbents' exclusive right to distribute tele-communication terminal equipment. More substantial changes were successively requested, such as the liberalization of services other than voice telephony in 1990 and the final liberalization of voice telephony and infrastructure provision in 1998.

Despite the formal EU supremacy over member states (with regard to competition policy), it might be surprising that national governments followed the directives. The asset boom in the past decade arguably contributed to the willingness of EU countries to comply with the various EU privatization directives. The need to limit public debt, stipulated by the Maastricht Treaty (prescribing fiscal eligibility criteria for entry into the European Monetary Union), created a vested interest to fuel the public budget by privatization receipts. Such a hypothesized time profile of privatization receipts is supported by actual receipt figures in the past decade that peaked in 1998—a year exhibiting soaring asset prices (see chapter 3 by Belke and Schneider).

I.2.2   EU Directive on Electricity Markets

The second prominent directive relates to the privatization of the EU internal market for electricity launched in 1996. The directive prescribes a restructuring of the national generation, transmission, and distribution of electriticity with the goal of creating a single market for electricity in Europe. The centerpiece of the directive relates to access to national electricity markets. The directive includes specific targets for the opening of national electricity markets. The minimum market opening is roughly 26 percent of the national market by February 1999, 28 percent by February 2000, and 33 percent by February 2003.[1]

Table I.1 provides an overview on the scope of market opening as of 2003. Compliance with the directive is well progressed. The thresholds pertaining to 2003 are implemented in all EU countries, with France being closest to the threshold level.

Table I.1
Overview of market opening, 2003

Country	Market opening	
	Share in 2003 (%)	Size of open market (Tera watt hour)
Austria	100	55
Belgium	80	60
Denmark	100	33
Finland	100	77
France	37	140
Germany	100	490
Ireland	56	12
Italy	66	182
Netherlands	63	64
Spain	100	205
Sweden	100	135
United Kingdom	100	335

Source: Third Benchmarking Report on the Implementation of the Internal Electricity and Gas Market. Brussels, March 2004.

I.3   Linking Privatization to Policy Impacts: General Issues

All of the aforementioned dimensions of change characterize privatization in Europe, but each is likely to have distinct impacts. A transfer of ownership rights (simple privatization) alone may not bring about the desired improvements in prices and service quality. As emphasized in chapter 1 by David Newbery, it is the complementary character between the sale of a monopoly firm and wisely chosen rules of market conduct and entry that is key to the success of privatization. A sale alone without allowing competition will most likely only marginally affect the incentives of privatized firms to lower prices and care about service quality. Reflecting different economic structures and regulatory systems at the time when the various directives were launched, privatization experiences differ sharply in the European countries involved. In Finland, for instance, the picture is one of public divestiture of large state-owned entities that were previously well run, and therefore this resulted in little impact. In Ireland, the combination of telecom privatization with a sharp fall in rates and transportation deregulation with a large fall in airline rates was seemingly a significant factor (along with tax cuts and other changes) behind strong Irish growth in the 1980s and 1990s. In Spain, extensive privatization from the 1960s on is often believed to have been significant in spurring growth by a positive impact on productivity. Power privatizations in the United Kingdom seemingly divested state assets at bargain prices, sharply lowered phone rates, and greatly increased water and sewage fees (which financed new infrastructure investments in those sectors) but also resulted in lowered quality and higher prices for railways. Little economy-wide macro impact occurred in Denmark, as only limited telecoms privatizations were enacted.

There are many closely intertwined difficulties in determining the actual impacts of privatization and in separating out their impacts from other influences on economy-wide performance. Data on changes in output prices and quality changes for products of privatized enterprises needed to assess impacts on consumer welfare are scarce and limited. Assessing impacts on productivity and growth of previously state-owned monopolies due to changes in managerial control, reduced shirking, and other practices is complicated by other nonprivatization influences. Little analysis has been carried out on the indirect effects, such as positive benefits of reduced telecom rates for nontelecom sectors. Furthermore, the impact of privatization on macro performance cannot be easily distinguished from other macro influences. The issue is of particular relevance for Ireland and Spain, which simultaneously with the privatization of network industries experienced a period of tremendous growth due to a catching-up process to other European economies. Relatedly, the impacts of privatization and change of management on asset prices are a key macroeconomic issue at least in the public debate on the success of privatization. Did the rise in the stock price of British Airways after privatization indicate the market valuation of a successful change in ownership, or simply that the assets were sold off too cheaply? One view sees privatization as a success, the other as a natural consequence of the underpricing of initial share offerings in many countries uninformative as to whether privatization had been a success.

Facing the methodological challenges and the diversity of country experiences, the chapter authors were given a well-defined set of criteria by which they were asked to make their country assessments, among which the goals of reducing consumer prices, increasing quantity, and improving quality were deemed the most important ones. The striking feature of privatization in Europe is the sharp diversity in both forms of privatization and experiences by country. The country studies indicate that there are both good and bad elements in their

actual impacts, which provide some important answers to the fundamental policy question of whether privatization in the EU classifies as
a success.

I.4   Country Experiences in a Nutshell

The studies break into two groups. One group is seemingly motivated
by a major pullback in extensive government involvement in manufacturing and services industries in general rather then having a sector-
specific intent. These chapters are by Pablo Arocena on Spain, Sean
Barrett on Ireland, Ansgar Belke and Friedrich Schneider on Austria,
Michel Berne and Gerard Pogorel on France, and Andrea Goldstein on
Italy. Interestingly, a comment was put forward in the conference that
there was perhaps a significant religious factor bearing on privatization experiences in Europe, insofar as where the Catholic church had
extensive influence in the past, more extensive government involvement in economic management was thought both necessary and politically acceptable. In European countries with Weber's Protestant ethic
in place, a more rugged individualism prevailed, and state involvement was less, and, sectorally targeted.

Arocena's discussion of Spain spans the major transformation of
the Spanish economy from the isolationism and near autarky of the
Franco years to the EU-driven integrated and interdependent Spanish
economy of today. He documents the substantial unfolding of state
involvement. He underpins the widespread conjectures that Spanish
privatization was important for the elevated growth performance in
Spain over the past three decades, along with other macroeconomic
factors, such as infrastructure investments. He documents that the privatization of public utilities went along with a reduction in consumer
prices for telecommunication services and water, but elevated the price
for gas. Barrett's discussion of Ireland is the context of the strongest
growth performance in Europe over the past twenty years as Ireland
has changed from a high-unemployment economy with a high share
of taxes to GDP to the other end of the scale, simultaneously moving
from GDP per capita at perhaps 60 to 70 percent of the EU average
to around 110 percent of the EU average. The story often told of this
Celtic Tiger performance is of tax and regulatory policy being the key
to a surge of inward foreign investment coupled with transfers from
the EU budget to Ireland. Privatization's role in Ireland is as much
regulatory as a change in ownership. The entry of Ryanair allowed

Dublin-to-London airfares to fall substantially, and thus spatial connection of management in Ireland to Europe was transformed. Sharp reductions in phone rates allowed Ireland to "competitively talk to the world."

Belke and Schneider discuss privatization in Austria and relate these to experiences in other EU countries. These focus heavily on the macro effects, discussing the proceeds of privatization as well as macroeconomic policy impacts. In line with the Catholic ethic of market mistrust, state involvement in a variety of nonnetwork industries was dominant in Austria. The change of ownership in these industries during the 1990s led to a surge in privatization receipts. Furthermore, case study data support the conclusion that the macro effects of privatization in Austria (similar to other EU countries) are positive, with a strong correlation between the degree of privatization and the country's overall economic performance measured by GDP growth rates.

Italy and France are discussed in the chapters by Goldstein and the joint work by Berne and Pogorel. These are two of the four larger economies in Europe in which government enterprise involvements, especially in financial services, transportation, and utilities, were widespread, but were also accompanied by involvement through significant government-controlled (or involved) manufacturing groups. The picture in these two cases is of change and withdrawal from these arrangements over time, although perhaps less dramatically so than for the other countries. For instance, the electricity market in France is still highly dominated by the national utility EdF (Electricité de France). Implementing the Electricity Directive of the EU is still to come. As a consequence, impacts on performance and overall efficiency of operation seem less clear in these countries. Compliance with the EU's Telecommunication Directive is more advanced in France and Italy, and the increased competition has translated into lower prices of a variety of telecommunication services. However, the price for mobile services in Italy still exceeds that of its European neighbors. The second group of studies cover countries in Northern Europe where privatization experiences largely dealt with industries often regarded as natural monopolies, or what Newbery refers to in chapter 1 as network industries. These are railroads, road transport, airlines, ports, power generation and distribution, water, sewage, and telecoms. At a casual level, country experiences across these sectors seem mixed. Phone rates in Europe have fallen sharply, with the benefits frequently attributed to successful privatization. On the other hand, a frequent complaint of privatization is that trains arrive late, are dirtier, and are in accidents more frequently.

In detail, Henrik Christoffersen and Martin Paldam provocatively (and convincingly) argue that in the Danish story of privatization, the EU directives mattered little (if at all) as the retrenchment of state activity would have been implemented even in their absence. The telecom sector took a remarkable path as—politically inconceivable in other countries such as France—the Danish phone company (Tele Danmark) was sold to a foreign company. In line with other European experiences, consumer phone prices fell in response to the opening of the local market. Furthermore, largely motivated by fiscal considerations, a variety of SOE were sold, including the Copenhagen airport.

Eric van Damme discusses the Dutch case, where scope for privatization was limited due to a historically low state involvement in the economy and privatization measures were necessarily focused on sectors akin to natural monopolies. The Netherlands is one of the few EU countries that implemented the EU directives targeted at these sectors in a timely way. The Dutch telecom KPN benefited from the spur of privatization in European countries by strategically entering into some of these markets. Also, the telecom faced fierce competition for domestic consumers, which gave way to consumer phone prices that were well below those of its neighbor countries.

David Parker discusses the U.K. privatization of the Thatcher years and those that followed. In water and sewage, the main impact seems to have been a sharp rise in rates to consumers, with the proceeds being used to finance infrastructure and quality of service improvements in the sector. One interpretation sometimes advanced here is that this privatization was a way for politicians to escape the political blame that would have followed were public enterprises to remain and rates rise to finance infrastructure. Parker suggests that evidence on weakened railway performance is less conclusive than one might think and that sharp falls in telecom rates indicate success.

Günter Knieps's analysis reveals that privatization in Germany occurred largely in sectors that are akin to natural monopolies. The first wave of privatization taking the form of liberalization in the telecom and electricity market led to a significant drop in consumer prices. In the second wave, entailing a change in the organizational structure, the Deutsche Telekom became publicly listed (with a significant share still owned by the federal government). The railway system moved from a public enterprise to an SOE, which went along with higher consumer orientation, although complaints about service quality and the downsizing of the railway network (by closing unprofitable connections) are also voiced. Knieps concludes that especially in the German privatization, regulating access charges to those parts of network infrastructure, which he characterizes as monopolistic bottlenecks, remains an important task even after full privatization and market opening.

Finally, Johan Willner's portrayal of the Finnish experience provides an interesting contrast to the other studies. He reports a change in management and ownership under privatization, going from one well-functioning structure to another, with little evidence of improved financial performance or cost efficiency despite stronger focus on profits. Indeed, Willner's data suggest that on Finnish stock markets, where minority share holdings in state-owned enterprises are traded, they sometimes do so at a premium to stock in related private enterprise in the same sector, suggesting that the market attached a premium to state ownership and management.

I.5   Concluding Remarks

Privatization in the EU significantly transformed core sectors of the economy such as electricity and telecommunication in ways not anticipated at the early stage of policy implementation. The country studies in this book document the tremendous change in most EU countries that has already occurred or will likely be observed in the near future.

What can one conclude from the studies? As an old Chinese sage once observed, the truth can never be established; it can only be suggested. But there are suggested insights, and these are offered by the chapter authors. One important insight is that the impacts of privatization depend on the form of privatization taken by the countries and are mostly overlooked in the euphory toward privatization by the political and cultural institutions inherent in the countries. An apparent example is Finland, where the inefficiencies of SOEs appeared to be minimal with the consequence of little impact of privatization policies.

Unfortunately, the appropriate metric for success or failure of privatization is an unresolved issue that renders the classification of the various privatization experiences on a success-failure spectrum infeasible. As with other reform policies, the aggregation of efficiency and distributional implications of the reforms to one metric will always be an issue of political controversy significantly guided by the cultural values of the countries involved. Turning to a disaggregated measure of success, an obvious lesson that can be learned from the country studies is that consumers largely benefited from a more competitively organized telecom sector and certainly enjoyed lower electricity prices in many countries.

All in all, the European experience is seemingly one of strong claims of success as seen in the late 1980s, tempered by more realistic claims seen from today. As demonstrated by this book, it is essential to turn to each country experience separately to learn about policy pitfalls and to make up one's own view on which privatization policy is exemplary. The book will thus be essential for any informed discussion on privatization, which will shape tomorrow's policymakers' decisions.

Note

1. The figures are calculated as the ratio of electricity consumption of final customers with a single demand exceeding 40 GWh per year to total final consumption. The threshold is reduced to 20 GWh per year in 2000. In a further three years, the threshold is lowered again to 9 GWh per year.

I Conceptual Issues and U.S. Experiences

1 Privatizing Network Industries

David M. Newbery

The privatization of strategic and network industries is a relatively new instrument of public policy. How that instrument is used will depend on the objectives of the government of the day. Just as tax and public expenditure policies can be used to improve efficiency, redistribute income, or protect local interests such as farming, industry, coal mining or other favored groups, so privatization policies may be molded by a desire to achieve a variety of goals. Standard economic rhetoric lays particular emphasis on increasing efficiency by reducing distortions and improving incentives. In the British case, additional objectives influenced the program (Vickers and Yarrow 1988). The desire for wider share ownership was certainly intended to make reforms hard to reverse. Renationalization would risk alienating the critical middle-class swing voters in the electorate, quite apart from being fiscally expensive. Private ownership was considered one of the better ways of reducing the power of the trade unions, and with it the perceived support for the opposition Labour party. Indeed, creating counterweights to the perceived monolithic unions meant that inadequate attention was given to dispersed control and competition in the early utility privatizations of telecoms and gas.

In other countries, creating national champions or increasing the power of the industrial oligarchy were intended or unintended consequences of the process of privatization. Kornai's (1992) view that privatization was needed to create "real owners" in central and eastern Europe was based on the premise that only by injecting the bacillus of private property into the Soviet body politic would a constituency to support the institutions of capitalism be created. While this view has a certain persuasiveness, it overlooks the historical evidence that efficient and sustainable institutions of capitalism may take a long time to mature with a poor allocation of initial wealth.

In South Africa, privatization was actively discussed before the ending of apartheid as a mechanism to protect white interests and preserve at least the commercial, if not political, structures of predemocratic South Africa. Conversely, the African National Congress stressed the importance of controlling the commanding heights of the economy as an essential component of the political transfer of power (Lipton and Simkins 1993).

Given the wide range of objectives consciously or unconsciously pursued, it would be surprising if all privatizations, and particularly those of network industries, were to achieve similarly high scores along the single axis of improved efficiency. There is also a problem of endogeneity in assessing the success or otherwise of any privatization. Those industries selected for privatization, and those countries pursuing policies of privatization, are unlikely to be a representative sample of industries and countries. Instead, candidates for privatization are more likely to be performing badly by some criteria (losses, inefficiency, labor relations) and are quite likely to improve their performance in response to any coherent attempt to address these problems, so there is likely to be a sample selection bias in studying privatization cases. With these cautionary remarks, we can turn to the evidence to see how far it accords with theoretical predictions of what might be expected of particular types of reform.

1.1. Defining Privatization

The British definition of *privatization* is the transfer of ownership and control by the state (central or local government) to private owners. In practical terms, that means selling at least 50 percent of the voting shares, in most cases with the objective of selling 100 percent, bearing in mind the financial advantages of selling in stages at successively higher prices. Even here the first tranche was invariably more than 50 percent of the shares as an irrevocable commitment to private control. If the state retains control, then the enterprise has not been privatized. This raises an interesting question when state enterprises buy privatized utilities in other countries, like Electricité de France (EdF) buying London Electricity. Does this amount to renationalization? Does London Electricity (now called EdF Energy) count as a private company or a state-owned enterprise?[1]

The issue is important, for figure 1.1 shows that as late as 2000, Austria, Belgium, Finland, France, Germany, Greece, Luxembourg,

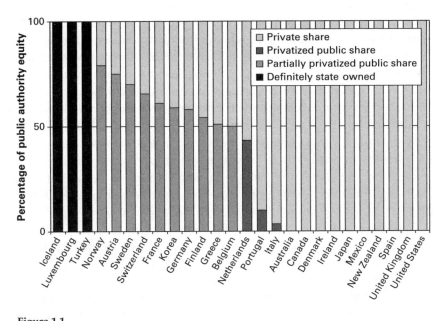

Figure 1.1
Public sector equity share in incumbent telephone operator in 2000

Norway, Sweden, and Switzerland all had above 50 percent public ownership in telecommunications (Schneider and Jaeger 2003).

For wholly regulated utilities, this definitional issue may not raise practical difficulties, especially if it is a wholly owned subsidiary whose debt is not guaranteed by the parent state-owned company. Where state enterprises buy competitive companies abroad (for example, generation companies or mobile phone companies), there would be an obvious concern about state aids in the form of subsidized or favorable access to capital that might distort competition and arouse antitrust concerns. Some governments, and certainly the British government, retained a golden share when privatizing companies. These carried veto rights over subsequent changes of ownership, possibly for a limited period, to ensure that the objectives of dispersed share ownership and possibly ownership by a majority of nationals would be protected. Golden shares could also be used to prevent takeovers by state-owned enterprises abroad, but have been attacked by the European Union as restricting capital market liberalization.

Network utilities such as telecoms, gas, electricity, water, and rail are characterized by a natural monopoly network which is essential for the delivery of network services to final consumers. Most network utilities involve large sunk investments delivering essential services to the mass of the voting population, who are therefore concerned to protect themselves against the unregulated exercise of market power that a natural monopoly makes possible. Those asked to invest in the utility will be concerned that the resulting powerful political lobby will argue for low prices after any investment has been irrevocably sunk, making investment unattractive (Gilbert and Newbery 1996). Although most network utilities were originally built by private investors, they were successfully retained only in private ownership where the institutions of capitalism evolved politically sustainable forms of regulation that protected the interests of both investors and consumers (Newbery 2000).

The default resolution of the conflict between consumers and investors in most countries was public ownership providing access to investment funds and political control over final prices. The natural form of most of these utilities under both public and private ownership was as a vertically integrated franchise monopoly. Final prices were regulated under both private and public ownership at the cost of service (also known as rate-of-return regulation), reinforcing the commitment to protect both owners and consumers from exploitation. Such regulation was inefficient, except in cases where rapid technical progress allowed costs to fall and rate reviews were delayed, allowing prices to remain steady, mimicking the effects of price cap regulation.

1.2   The New Model for Structure and Regulation

Criticisms of the inefficiency of rate-of-return regulation for encouraging gold-plating and cost inefficiency (Averch and Johnson 1962) became cumulatively decisive in the liberalization movement in the United States. In Britain, privatization was primarily driven by more political motives, to "roll back the frontiers of the State" and because "the business of government is not the government of business" (Lawson 1992, 199). The early success of the Thatcher government in privatizing normally commercial activities such as oil, cars, transport, and defense industries raised no obvious regulatory or competitive issues, but the announcement to privatize BT in 1982 inevitably raised the question of how such a network monopoly would be regulated. Stephen Littlechild was commissioned to propose a system of regulation. He saw the task as avoiding the inefficiencies of cost-of-service regulation, creating incentives for improved efficiency while restraining market power, and providing a transitional period of regulation until the industry became competitive (Littlechild 1983, Bartle 2003). Thus was price cap regulation, or RPI-X (Retail Price Index minus the efficiency factor, X), developed and with it the supporting institutions of independent regulation and licenses subject to periodic review.

The emphasis in the earlier utility privatization in Britain was on the transfer of ownership and improved regulation of the natural monopoly network, rather than the pressure for liberalization and competition that drove the very different reforms in America, where utilities were already in private ownership. BT was therefore privatized without restructuring, facing a small competitor with a protected duopoly status that was guaranteed until the duopoly review of 1991. British Gas was privatized in 1986 as a completely vertically integrated utility, owning gas fields in the North Sea (though also buying at the beachhead from other oil and gas companies), owning the high-pressure national transmission system, all storage facilities, all local distribution networks, and the retailing business.

Economists had always been critical of transferring public monopolies into private monopolies, and Littlechild specifically designed price cap regulation as a transitional device to a competitive market that would no longer need regulation. The breakup of AT&T in the United States with the Modified Final Judgment of 1984 exposed the once monolithic Bell telephone company to competition for long-distance calls, although the local Bell Operating Companies retained their franchises. Economists such as Vickers and Yarrow (1988) stressed the distinction between privatization, or the transfer of ownership, and liberalization, the introduction of competition for the network services supplied over the network.

Liberalization would need potentially competitive network services to be able to access the natural monopoly network, and here two models were on offer. The incumbent utility could continue to own the network and also provide network services, but other entrants would be allowed access to the network and could compete with the incumbent. This was the intention with BT and is the standard model for telecoms privatizations in most countries. The more radical solution is to separate ownership of the network from ownership of the network service companies. Such ownership unbundling removes the risk that the incumbent can favor its own network services and impede entry to gain competitive advantage, but risks losing economies of scope between the network and network services. These were arguably considerable in the case of telecoms, where the operator of a switched network has to create end-to-end connectivity and at the same time calculate the cost of the call in order to bill the customer. The switches designed to route and record such information have natural synergies that would take considerable investment and design to replicate at comparable cost in unbundled form.

In contrast, there were no obvious reasons that gas production, gas transport, gas storage, local gas distribution, and retailing should all be provided by the same incumbent, particularly, as in the case of Britain, once the high- and low-pressure pipeline system was mature. The history of the restructuring of British gas is one of fifteen years of regulatory pressure from successive investigations by the Office of Fair Trading and the Monopolies and Mergers Commission (Newbery 2000). Increasingly onerous regulatory conditions were then imposed, finally leading British Gas to accept that it would be commercially prudent to separate first the operation and then the ownership of these various activities.

By the time the government started thinking about privatizing the electricity supply industry (ESI) toward the end of the 1980s, the message that the public did not like private monopolies had become loud and clear. Economists argued that competitive pressures were more likely to deliver cost improvements and hence politically attractive price reductions. The new guiding principle was to restructure to introduce competition where possible, and to simulate as far as possible the effect of competition on the natural monopoly network through price cap regulation. Subsequent privatization acts laid down the duties of regulators to promote competition where possible, and the architects of restructuring were increasingly required to create structures that maximized the opportunities for competition.

This gradual change in emphasis from privatization as purely a transfer of ownership to privatization combined with restructuring to introduce competition took time. The decisive turning point came in 1990 with the restructuring of the Central Electricity Generating Board (CEGB), the vertically integrated generation and transmission company that supplied electricity to England and Wales. The CEGB was divided into four companies: National Grid, National Power, Power-Gen, and Nuclear Electric (the last remaining in public ownership as the custodian of nuclear power stations whose net asset value was extremely uncertain).

The water and sewerage companies of England and Wales, but not Scotland, were also privatized in 1990 with provisions that would allow a modest degree of competition to develop, but retaining the verti-cally integrated structure for the most part. (In some areas, relatively small water-only companies retained their form, with the sewerage services provided by the larger regional companies.) Competition of any form was extremely slow to develop. This was mainly because the cost of moving water any distance is high compared to its value and because the incumbent was responsible for ensuring the specified high-quality standards. Water utilities were therefore reluctant to ac-cept and transport competitors' water without also controlling the management of water from source to final delivery.

The full consequences of the pursuit of competition as the key element of privatization were realized in the restructuring of British Rail from 1994 to 1996. That previously monolithic company was frag-mented into over 100 different companies. The core track company (Railtrack) bought services from a variety of maintenance companies, and the twenty-five train operating companies (TOCs) lease their equipment from three rolling stock leasing companies, which in turn contract out the building and maintenance of these assets. Competition on the rails was considered desirable but difficult, so the alternative of competition for the market was chosen. TOC franchises (typically for seven years) were to be bid, with the best value (least subsidy for specified quality) being awarded in the expectation that this would deliver lower costs and prices. Competition would also be introduced between the suppliers of services and new rolling stock selling to leas-ing companies or, in some cases, directly to TOCs. Early attempts at encouraging competition on the rails were quietly shelved, to reduce the commercial risks facing the TOCs, and because they were clearly more difficult and costly than the likely gains warranted.

The rail accident at Hatfield in 2000 in which four passengers died revealed an alarming gap between the ownership and operation of the network and the critical maintenance needed to ensure its safety and reliability. The subsequent effective bankruptcy of Railtrack, the huge increases in costs of repairing and replacing the network, demon-strated that the initial restructuring had been overly ambitious and had failed to recognize the important synergies between track owner-ship and track maintenance.

1.3 Privatization and Liberalization

Privatization and liberalization are distinct policies, but while it is possible (and regrettably common) to privatize without liberalizing, it is less clear that one can liberalize without privatization. The core network in most cases will remain a regulated natural monopoly and thus not subject to competition. There is no obvious reason that an unbundled core network should not remain in public ownership while network services are privatized. Several countries, such as the Netherlands, have retained the national grid in public ownership while allowing private ownership in generation. Similarly, it is quite common for gas and electricity distribution networks to be municipally owned, with private ownership elsewhere. After the collapse of Railtrack, the British government created Network Rail, a nonprofit distribution public-private partnership, a quasi-commercial public entity that is a compromise between the desire to renationalize and a desire to keep the debt off the public sector's balance sheet. Roads are almost entirely in public ownership, while transport services are almost entirely privately supplied.

The main case for privatizing networks like the grid is that they can be more effectively exposed to profit-related incentives, while at the same time clarifying the nature of regulation and separating the regulatory and ownership functions. The alternative view is that the state can better pursue its interests by direct control through ownership than by indirect control through regulation, which involves an additional principal-agent relationship that introduces a further layer of potential inefficiency. This argument would not apply to a choice between bureaucratic control and the market, which would seem to require independent owners to ensure effective competition and hence rule out state ownership, as discussed below. It does carry some weight when comparing public or private ownership of a natural monopoly, where the issue is primarily of the quality of regulation and incentives under the two forms.

The modern approach (Sappington and Stiglitz 1987) is that the owner is the authority with the residual rights, that is, those rights that are not subject to contract or control. Regulation limits the actions of privatized networks but cannot specify their actions in full detail, leaving considerable discretion to the private owners. In a state-owned enterprise, the state may delegate day-to-day control to the management, who may report to a board that has considerable autonomy, but the state as owner retains the right to intervene directly. Sappington and Stiglitz (1987, 567) argue "that the main difference between the two modes [public and private ownership] concerns the transactions costs faced by the government when attempting to intervene in delegated production activities. The greater ease of intervention under public ownership can have its advantages; but the fact that a promise not to intervene is more credible under private production can also have beneficial incentive effects."

Ownership affects the ability to control the behavior of the utility, so that the objectives of the owner matter. The standard but oversimplified assumption is that private firms maximize profit (subject to regulatory constraints), while state-owned enterprises pursue "the national interest", normally interpreted as maximizing social welfare. In both cases, there is a principal-agent problem to ensure that managers act in the interest of owners, and the private sector typically finds it easier to do this by stock options, although there are precedents for linking managerial pay to profits in state enterprises (Network Rail provides one example, although it is not exactly state owned). In addition, publicly quoted companies are subject to the capital market disciplines of takeover, bank monitoring over debt, and bankruptcy, all of which encourage the pursuit of profit and discourage costly managerial discretion. State-owned networks lack the hard budget constraints associated with bankruptcy, reducing the state's ability as regulator-principal to commit to future penalties. It might be thought that private networks cannot be bankrupted, but Britain forced Railtrack into administration (effectively bankruptcy), underlining the difference between public and private ownership.

State-owned networks have managers subject to monitoring by boards, appointed by the owner, the state, which should be better placed to exercise control as there is no free-rider problem that affects individually small shareholders (Vickers and Yarrow 1988). The argument can be pushed further back to ask whose interests the state represents, and specifically why the state should wish to maximize social welfare. In addition, we need to know what objectives the regulator has and how far these constrain the actions of the private utility. If regulation represents the same interest groups that influence the government, then the differences between public and private ownership are more a function of the form of regulation or oversight. Obvious differences are that privatized networks have more managerial discretion, but are subject only to periodic review, and normally operate within a well-specified regulatory framework (e.g., license conditions, price caps, quality standards, protection against entry, universal service obligations). State-owned networks might have contracts specifying their obligations (as in France), rather like license conditions for privatized networks, but these contracts can be renegotiated in their entirety, while the licenses of privatized networks can often be renegotiated only with the agreement of the utility. The difference is thus one of the degree of commitment to future regulatory or monitoring behavior, and it can be exaggerated—some systems of regulation lack commitment, while some public utilities may be given considerable autonomy and operate on the expectation that this will continue. Well-designed and credible regulation offers the prospect that poorly managed state-owned networks might do better under private ownership, and privatization in that case represents a commitment to placing commercial objectives above other objectives that are better pursued by different policies.

The next question is whether it is possible to sustain competition under public ownership for the network services, where markets offer distinctly different incentives to bureaucratic control. Is privatization a necessary step to market liberalization? The most powerful force for improved efficiency is the incentive to drive down costs combined with safeguards to ensure the desired quality of service. Competitive markets in which consumers make informed decisions between alternative suppliers satisfy both requirements. In competitive markets, firms can increase profits only by driving down costs or improving the attractiveness of their product or service. Competition encourages efficiency and innovation. Effective competition passes on these cost reductions in lower prices.

Public ownership might be compatible with competition either with investor-owned utilities (common in the United States) or between different companies, all of which are state (or municipally) owned. If competition is to deliver efficient outcomes, then participants need to face hard budget constraints and have access to inputs, especially labor and capital, on the same terms. Municipal utilities in the United States enjoy tax-free bond finance and so have a lower cost of capital than investor-owned utilities, while until recently many continental utilities were exempt from company taxation. These distortions can be corrected, but even if they are, state enterprises can borrow at the risk-free government bond rate and hence undercut equally efficient private competitors. They are effectively protected from the threat of takeover or bankruptcy, which lowers the cost of debt, but may reduce the incentives for efficiency. The combination of these various factors means that either the lower apparent capital costs of public ownership are dissipated in lower efficiency (or higher wages for public sector workers), allowing an inefficient equilibrium, or that the public cost advantages make private competition unviable.

The case has been made (Cremer, Marchand, and Thisse 1989; Willner 2003) that if state-owned companies are charged to compete with private companies, they may discipline private competitors, which would otherwise be able to exercise market power (or reduce quality). This is definitely second best, for if both types of firm survive, the publicly owned company must be productively inefficient (excess capital-labor ratios and inefficiently bureaucratic management). The gain then comes from reduced market power or superior quality. This is an indirect form of competition policy, better replaced by structural and regulatory reforms where possible (and privatization offers a unique opportunity for getting this right).

Most examples of competing public utilities appear to be transitional forms evolving out of regional franchises provided by municipally owned utilities. Full competition requires contestable entry (and the possibility of exit), making competition between different state-owned service providers suspect, although different municipally owned companies might be able to compete in each other's markets, as in Norway. At first glance, it is very difficult to see what advantages state or municipal ownership provides for contestable service provision, in contrast to the ability to impose universal service obligations and other social objectives on publicly owned natural monopolies. The one potential argument for retaining public ownership of potentially competitive network services is that it would be difficult to sustain competition that was sufficiently strong to pass on full cost reductions to domestic consumers, while meeting other objectives such as security of supply and universal service obligations.

1.4 Determinants of Successful Utility Privatization

The critical enabling condition of successful utility privatization is whether a system of regulation can be designed that provides good incentives for delivery of services of the right quality while reassuring investors of the profitability of economically justified investments. This issue of credibility is a key stumbling block to privatization in many developing countries, where the reputation of the government for efficient management is low and the regulatory institutions and supporting legal and constitutional protections are inadequate or untested. A number of authors have confirmed this for the electricity supply industry (which, as argued below, is particularly dependent on good regulation).[2] They find that the amount of private investment is positively correlated with institutional factors that support credible reform, such as the protection of property rights, judicial and regulatory independence, and country political risk. The first determinant of success is therefore the extent to which credible regulation is a key determinant of success.

The second determinant of success is whether the network would perform better under price cap or incentive regulation than under the de facto cost-of-service regulation characteristic of the public sector. A price cap has the advantage that it provides incentives for cost reductions (particularly if the cap is set to the efficient level or the average of other comparable companies' cost), and also, if well designed, allows the utility to rebalance prices in line with costs. The main problems with price cap regulation are maintaining the efficient level of quality and providing efficient investment incentives.

The third issue is whether the prices charged under public ownership are sufficient to cover operating costs and a return on any new investment that will be required. Figure 1.2 shows the evolution of prices of British utilities before and after privatization. If prices are above avoidable costs but below long-run marginal costs, then, as with the British water industry, it is possible to increase prices gradually to the

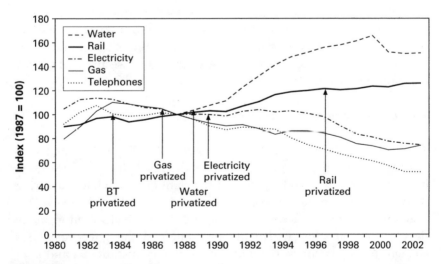

Figure 1.2
Real domestic price of public utilities for the United Kingdom

level at which they can earn a market return on new investment while providing some return to the existing assets. The existing assets will be valued at the return they are allowed to earn, which in the case of British water companies was less than one-tenth of their replacement cost. If, as in much of central and eastern Europe, prices were below avoidable costs, few private owners will be willing to buy them unless they believe that costs can be driven down below the prices they are allowed to charge. One of the constraints affecting the ease, speed, and political support for privatization will be the direction in which prices have to move after privatization to reach competitive levels. In Britain for gas, electricity, and telecoms, competitive prices were lower than the previous prices, and privatizations were popular. In the case of water, prices had to increase and privatization was relatively unpopular, as it was for energy companies in transition and developing countries.

All of these conditions are necessary for success, but may not be sufficient to deliver improved social welfare. That will depend on whether the new structure provides better incentives for efficient operation and investment.

The evidence from the growing number of utility privatizations points to a number of features that make privatization more likely to be socially profitable and other features that raise significant challenges, although not necessarily arguing against privatization. Effective competition with informed consumers is a powerful force to drive down costs and safeguard quality. The major determinant of beneficial privatization is whether the industry is capable of sustaining effective competition and whether the prospects for innovation are promising or minimal. Unbiased competition is more likely if the ownership of network services can be unbundled from the network. If the synergies or economies of scope between the network and the services are very strong, vertical integration has lower costs than an unbundled industry, which may outweigh the benefits from introducing competition. Liberalization without ownership unbundling is an intermediate step that may achieve the best of both worlds but could experience the worst of both worlds.

The next question is whether the market structure created at privatization will allow enough competition to pass on the cost savings in lower prices to final consumers. If the incumbent remains vertically integrated and entrants are allowed to use the network, then the market structure may be so concentrated that continued asymmetric regulation is required, with the risk of distorting competition and losing potential efficiency gains. The ideal set of circumstances is one in which the synergies between network and services are low and there is excess capacity in service provision, with few economies of scale. In that case, it is possible to create a sufficient number of competing service companies while the spare capacity restricts their ability to raise prices above costs. One way of measuring market power is to ask whether, if all other competing service providers operate competitively, the residual largest supplier is required to meet maximum demand, or whether its customers can satisfy demand without its presence. If demand is fairly inelastic, as in electricity, and if the largest producer is required to meet demand, then that largest producer will have substantial market power, at least in periods of high demand.

1.5   The Potential for and Experience of Success for Different Utilities

Perhaps not surprisingly, the order in which the United Kingdom (and many other countries) privatized its utilities is almost the rank order of the likely social benefits of privatization.

1.5.1   Telecoms

BT was the first British privatization in 1984 (Parker 2003), and Wellenius and Stern (1994) demonstrate that reforms were well advanced in developed, transitional, and developing countries by the early 1990s. Galal, Jones, Tandon, and Vogelsang (1994) provide more case studies of telecoms privatizations than any other utility. There are excellent reasons for this popularity. First, regulatory credibility is less of an issue, as the regulatory compact (the utility invests in return for an assurance that it can earn a return on the investment) is almost self-enforcing. The normal problem with regulatory credibility is that regulators (or ministries controlling prices) view the gains from lower prices as greater than the possible future discouragement to investment. If demand is growing strongly, investment needs are high and the public sector finds it difficult to finance such investment, then the balance of advantage shifts toward the utility investors. All of this is true for telecoms, particularly where demand has been suppressed and waiting lists are long.

In addition, international telecoms companies bring managerial and technical expertise lacking in most domestic companies and can credibly threaten to seriously degrade performance if they do not continue to maintain the software and equipment, quite apart from the need of any country to secure interconnection with telecoms companies abroad. Finally, in many countries, telephones are a luxury service, relatively price insensitive, and consequently potentially very profitable, making them attractive purchases. For all these reasons, the costs of reneging on the terms of a telecoms privatization are likely to be far higher than any temporary benefits, reassuring investors. Indeed, the prospect of attractive profits for telecoms companies is partially reflected in the large bids that companies are willing to make for the right to enjoy these profits.[3]

Not only is it relatively easy to sell telecoms companies, but there is a growing belief, supported by evidence, that adequate investment in telecoms infrastructure is critical to economic growth (Roller and Waverman 2001). The previously common structure of placing post and telecommunications under a government ministry is then seen as a recipe for inadequate investment, delayed modernization, and suppressed innovation. Separating out telecoms from post, followed by commercialization and privatization, is the obvious solution to both problems. The main problem with telecoms privatization is thus not one of regulatory credibility or even of convincing governments of its desirability, but rather securing a reasonable proportion of the potentially large gains on offer for the public good. This requires the design of effective regulation and liberalization so that the gains from more efficient operation and investment are translated into lower prices and reduced deadweight loss.[4]

Over time, the cost of long-distance and international calls has fallen far faster than the cost of the local loop (or the "last mile") connecting consumers to the nearest switch or exchange. The relentless operation of Moore's law on switches (halving microelectronic costs every eighteen to twenty-four months) and the rapid increase in capacity with fiber-optic cables have driven down unit costs, compared to the labor-intensive provision of the twisted copper pair in the local loop. Under public ownership (or state regulation in the United States), it was politically attractive to cross-subsidize local calls from the profits on long-distance calls. The situation for international calls was even worse, for each country's single telephone company owned cross-border links up to the midpoint (or border), and so each could separately set the charge for call completion, resulting in prices above joint-profit maximizing levels. As the elasticity of demand for such calls is high (greater than one), the deadweight losses of excessive margins are extremely high compared even to the high profits.

As an example, in 1995 the United Kingdom made 1.025 billion minutes of international calls to the United States at an average price of 55 U.S. cents per minute and an average cost of 8.57 cents per minute (Mason 1998). The price was therefore nearly seven times cost, largely as a result of the international settlement system. The profit on this single route generated by this distorted price was U.S.$481 million per year. The potential consumer surplus of lowering price to cost would have been U.S.$1,050 million at a price elasticity of demand of unity, implying a deadweight loss of U.S.$569 million per year, greater than the profits. These numbers are large, particularly when scaled up by the global telecoms revenue for the United Kingdom (domestic and all international calls, not just those to the United States) of $27.6 billion (WTO, 1998). At plausibly higher elasticities, the deadweight losses would be even higher.

In addition, economies of scope argue for vertical integration between the network and service provision, at least at the regional level (in the United States), and possibly at the national level in geographically smaller countries. Competitors offering long-distance and international calls need access to the local loop, and it was rapidly learned that leaving this to bilateral negotiation between incumbent and entrant would result in either entry deterrence or collusive pricing, even at above profit-maximizing levels (Armstrong 1996, 1998, 2002; Laffont Rey and Tirole 1998a, 1998b; Vogelsang 2003). Access prices therefore need to be regulated, at least until the incumbent fixed-line operator ceases to possess significant market power, as defined by the EC Communications Directives (2002/21/EC, Art. 14). Regulating access pricing is made more complicated by the complexity of the cost structure of telecoms, itself a consequence of rapid technical progress. The British telecoms regulator Oftel worked with industry groups for over a decade to reach agreement on cost modeling and cost allocation, and disputes continue to complicate regulation (Competition Commission 2003). In the United States, tensions between the federal regulator, the Federal Communications Commission (FCC), concerned to create efficient competition, and state public utility commissions anxious to preserve cross-subsidies to local calls and provide various extensions to universal service obligations, have resulted in inefficient regulation. Again, as elasticities are quite high and price-cost margins may be significantly distorted, regulatory inefficiencies can be very costly (Hausman, Tardiff, and Belinfante 1993; Crandall and Waverman 1997).

The inefficiency of public ownership or poorly regulated private ownership does not end with the overpricing of some services. Hausman (1997) argues that one of the most costly consequences of traditional regulation as practiced in the United States is the delay hindering the introduction of new services, caused by concern that these new services might be cross-subsidized from the captive customer base. Hausman gives two examples: voice messaging and cell phones. AT&T originally wished to offer voice messaging in the late 1970s, which the FCC delayed until 1986 and finally allowed in 1988, when it was immediately introduced. The estimated consumer surplus it generated is estimated at U.S.$1.27 billion per year by 1994 (the estimated price elasticity of demand for messaging was −1.6), so the ten-year regulatory delay cost billions of dollars. Hausman further argues that a possible ten-year regulatory delay in introducing mobile phones might have cost consumers as much as $100 billion, large compared with the 1995 U.S. global telecoms revenues of $180 billion.

The consequences of regulatory design are nicely illustrated by the two case studies of Latin American telecoms privatizations in Galal, Jones, Tandon, and Vogelsang (1994). The Chilean company CTC was in private ownership until 1970 and was reprivatized in 1987, but was subject to benchmark regulation from 1977. The benchmark in this case was an ideal efficient model firm used to set the price control. As the price cap is unrelated to the firm's own costs, the incentive effects are more powerful than the standard form of RPI-X price cap developed in Britain, where periodic reviews relate the cap at least in part to the firm's actual costs. This novel approach of incentive regulation, already well established before privatization, avoided many of the problems of securing the potential benefits of privatization. The social cost-benefit analysis of CTC showed present discounted social gains of over 140 percent of base-year revenues, largely secured by domestic consumers. In contrast, the privatization of the Mexican company Telmex failed to secure the productivity improvements for the domestic economy as a result of poorly designed regulation. That regulation was perceived to lack credibility, resulting in underpricing, so that most of the benefits flowed abroad to foreign shareholders, causing an overall loss in present discounted social welfare of 13 percent of base-year revenues.[5]

Wallsten (2002) studied a panel of 200 countries from 1985 to 1999 to examine the impact of sequencing of reform on investment, and a smaller sample to examine the effect of regulatory reform on privatization proceeds. Wallsten found that countries that established separate regulatory agencies before privatization experienced more investment and more penetration of both fixed-line and mobile telephony, and realized higher sales prices. Gutiérrez (2003) also found that sound regulatory governance has a positive impact on telecoms network expansion and efficiency in a panel of twenty-two Latin American countries from 1980 to 1997.[6]

If regulation is inefficient and excessive pricing produces such high deadweight costs, then the obvious solution is to replace regulation by competition where possible. Britain provides an early example of the potential gains from opening up the market. The Telecommunications Act 1981 separated British Telecommunications (later BT) from the Post Office and ended its statutory monopoly over the network. The small company Mercury was licensed in 1982, but BT was privatized in 1984 without restructuring as the sole owner of the network, under the regulation of Oftel. Mercury was licensed as the sole competitor until 1991. The duopoly was reviewed in 1990 and terminated in 1991, with any application for a license thereafter to be considered on its merits. By 1995 there were over 150 operators licensed to compete with BT, including 125 cable TV companies that could offer telephony with cable, of which 80 were actually providing service (Bell 1995). Rapid entry was followed by substantial consolidation, but by 2003 cable companies had more than half the broadband market, with BT supplying most of the rest by Asynchronous Digital Subscriber Line (ADSL).

Progress in creating a competitive market for fixed-line domestic customers has been rather slow. By April 2003, only 5 percent of these customers were using carrier preselection. Oftel reported in its August 2003 survey that 95 percent of U.K. homes claimed to have a fixed-line phone, and only 1 percent had neither a fixed nor mobile phone.[7] Only 23 percent of fixed-line homes were currently using an alternative or additional fixed supplier to BT (normally a cable company), a number that had remained almost unchanged over the previous two years. In areas covered by cable, BT's share was lower, at 64 percent, and cable's higher, at 35 percent. Other operators have only 3 percent of the overall market. About 30 percent of fixed-line subscribers had ever switched their supplier; fewer than had switched gas or electricity suppliers, although switching has been possible in the energy sector only since 1999.

The failure to create a more competitive structure at privatization and the delay in allowing competition led Armstrong, Cowan, and Vickers (1994) to the judgment that "the duopoly policy has been detrimental to development of competition, and its main beneficiary has been BT itself" (240). This does not mean that privatization was undesirable—only that opportunities were lost (though they may not realistically have been available). Galal, Jones, Tandon, and Vogelsang (1994) provide a cost-benefit analysis of the privatization of BT based on data to 1990. They concluded that privatization benefited shareholders, government, and consumers as a whole, though business consumers did substantially better than residential consumers, many of whom may have suffered a net loss. The main sources of these benefits were changes in prices and improvements in the rate of investment once the constraints imposed by state ownership were removed.

Newbery (1997) demonstrated that until 1991, BT's labor productivity did not appear to change compared to the experience of comparable companies elsewhere, though there was a sharp improvement in 1992 after the duopoly review. Martin and Parker (1997) find the same. Boylaud and Nicoletti (2001) use an international database to study the impact of entry liberalization and privatization on productivity, prices, and quality of service in long-distance and mobile telephony in twenty-three member countries of the Organization for Economic Cooperation and Development (OECD) between 1991 and 1997. They find that that both prospective competition (as proxied by the number of years remaining to liberalization) and effective competition (as proxied by the share of new entrants or by the number of competitors) bring about productivity and quality improvements and reduce prices. Perhaps surprisingly, they found no clear evidence that the ownership structure (measured by the state share and years remaining to privatization) affected performance. This is consistent with the view that competition rather than ownership is the key determinant of success, but apparently not with the view that successful pressure for privatization is strongest where performance under public ownership is worst, and where improvements are most likely.[8] If we accept that liberalization requires privatization, then it would be difficult to disentangle these two effects. Gutiérrez (2003) finds that for his sample of Latin American countries, competition (a zero-one variable) is associated with increased efficiency (lines per employee), while privatization appears to enhance investment only when interacted with regulation (whose quality is measured by an index), confirming the importance of both regulation and competition.

Lenain and Paltridge (2003) observe that the U.S. Telecommunications Act of 1996 and the EU Telecommunications Directive of 1997 were indicative of a strong move to open fixed-line telecoms markets to competition. Thus, while only eight of thirty OECD countries had open competition in 1995, twenty-two had by 1998, and all but one (Turkey) had opened its markets by 2003. New entrants have been successful in winning market share in long-distance and international markets, though they were less successful where access to the local loop is required, for example, in broadband. In mobile telephony, almost all countries have three operators, although the fixed-line incumbent often owns the largest mobile company. Mobile phone competition has frequently been sufficiently intense as to warrant little if any regulation, although mobile call termination increasingly is seen as an essential facility requiring regulation (Competition Commission 2003).

The main regulatory issue is for what services competition is sufficiently advanced that ex ante regulation can be replaced by normal competition policy. New Zealand provides an interesting case study of the benefits and limitations of (very) light-handed regulation. De Boer and Evans (1996) estimate that productivity reduced costs annually at 5.6 percent from privatization in 1987 to 1993, and that prices fell, consumer surplus increased, and quality improved with deregulation, although it is hard to know what might have happened under more conventional ex ante regulation. Certainly the incumbent was able to contest and delay interconnection agreements with entrants, resulting in court cases and a ministerial inquiry into telecommunications that reported in 2000.[9] This led to a new telecommunications bill, enacted in December 2001, that created a sector-specific regulator to regulate key services and accelerate dispute resolution (ITU 2002).

Most developed countries are therefore converging on a structure that distinguishes sharply between services experiencing significant market power that require ex ante regulation and potentially competitive services that can be left to normal competition legislation. Increasingly, cost-benefit tests are being used to guide changes in regulatory practice (as in the New Zealand inquiry and by Oftel in deciding on local loop unbundling for broadband, and more recently for regulating mobile phone termination charges; see Competition Commission 2003).[10]

There are also important issues about whether sustainable (unregulated) competition is best ensured by facilities-based competition, or whether enforced unbundling or regulated access makes better use of the economies of scope between network and service, despite the extra cost of more intrusive regulation. Facilities-based competition, in which entrants provide new infrastructure (e.g., cable, mobile towers), offers the prospect that the network (or large parts of it) ceases to be a natural monopoly requiring close regulation, but risks raising costs by duplication. This has been the preferred U.K. approach, where Oftel has been willing to accept some increase in total cost as the price to pay for more intense competition, with the prospect of more vigorous innovation and a swifter move to ending significant market power and asymmetric regulation. The United States, in contrast, has attempted to enforce more access to network components, which has been contested in the courts and has arguably raised costs and retained inefficient forms of regulation.

The rapid evolution of the industry from regulated or state-owned incumbent to an increasingly competitive industry has been largely shaped by the rapid development of technology, and one should not underestimate the role of technical progress in precipitating structural and institutional change.

The conclusion on telecoms privatization is that public ownership is now considered a handicap to innovation rather than the natural source of investment funds, and it is therefore curious that state shareholdings are still significant in several continental countries, as figure 1.1 shows.

1.5.2   Gas

In most countries, private quoted oil companies have been active in gas exploration and production, although some oil companies are state owned, and there are specialized gas companies, the largest of which is the Russian Gazprom. The case for public ownership of gas exploration and production companies is relatively weak on commercial grounds and in the past has normally been justified for energy policy reasons, specifically to ensure security of supply and for the government to gain access to strategically valuable information. BNOC (British National Oil Corporation) was set up by the Labour party in 1976 to develop North Sea oil and was an obvious and early candidate for privatization. The Conservative Manifesto of 1979 promised to review the case for continued public ownership. The Conservatives decided to sell the company in 1982, after fierce opposition from the opposition Labour party and with unfortunate timing, after the price of oil suddenly fell (Lawson 1992). At its height, BNOC produced only 7 percent of North Sea oil, the remainder coming from private or foreign companies, and the necessarily speculative nature of oil and gas exploration makes that part of the industry a poor fit with public ownership.

Gas production, certainly offshore production in the North Sea, is capital intensive, and building a high-pressure gas pipeline system is even more so.[11] Where such developments have been undertaken by private oil and gas companies (the norm outside the Soviet bloc), they have been financed on the back of long-term contracts, although the pipeline system in Britain was developed by the state-owned British Gas. Where the gas industry was publicly owned, the question was how best to restructure and regulate the industry, and where it was already in private ownership, the question was how best to (de-)regulate and liberalize the industry. The case for restructuring the industry is that the long-term contracts that were claimed to be essential to finance gas development and pipelines effectively vertically integrated the industry, often creating de facto monopolies, although they faced competition in final markets from other fuels, notably oil (and electricity in domestic use). As a result, and because there was no obvious international price for gas (unlike oil), gas was frequently either priced at oil parity or markets were segmented, with gas for different uses effectively priced marginally below the cost of the competing fuel. This might be high-priced light fuel oil or electricity in domestic use, down to cheap coal for power generation. Such monopolistic pricing supported by vertical integration restricted the development of gas markets before deregulation and created significant allocative inefficiencies.

Once the gas transmission and distribution network is mature, gas penetration high, and the market developed, this equilibrium is vulnerable to regulatory opportunism, clearly demonstrated in the United States (Newbery 2000). The U.S. gas market is quantitatively and qualitatively different from that anywhere else in its maturity and market structure. Whereas continental Europe was dominated by a small number of mainly state-owned enterprises, the United States had over 8,000 producers, with the 40 largest accounting for 57 percent of 1990 gas production. They were connected to more than 1,600 local distribution companies (LDCs) through 44 major interstate pipeline systems and hundreds of smaller pipeline companies (IEA 1994). Despite the obvious prospect of competition in supply, from 1954 the Federal Power Commission had the power to regulate the wellhead price of gas. The huge inefficiencies that resulted from the imposition of poorly designed regulation during the oil shocks was estimated to have cost consumers between $2.5 and $5 billion per year (Loury 1981, Pierce 1988, Ellig 1991). Worse still, the resulting gas shortages caused by holding prices below market clearing levels encouraged merchant pipeline companies to sign long-term take-or-pay contracts at the height of the oil price boom without the precaution of linking prices to those of oil. As oil prices fell, these contracts became stranded at above-market levels. Between 1972 and 1986 gas demand dropped by 20 percent creating excess capacity in pipeline networks, ideal conditions for the introduction of competition (IEA 1994). Various Federal Energy Regulatory Commission orders from 1984 on finally unbundled and restructured the industry to one of third-party access that facilitated active competition.

Unfortunately, that experience was not exploited when British Gas was privatized as a vertically integrated monopoly in 1986, although Vickers and Yarrow (1988) criticized the failure to introduce competition. Other suppliers had to negotiate access to the pipelines and found it difficult to compete in the downstream market, where British Gas could price-discriminate and undercut competitors. Under intense regulatory pressure, supported by the Office of Fair Trading and by references to the Monopolies and Mergers Commission, British Gas was persuaded to functionally unbundle the competitive services from the natural monopoly networks and then break up the company into competitive and monopoly parts. The latter, Transco, sold off storage activities and finally merged with the already unbundled electricity National Grid Company, consolidating the regulated energy networks in one company.

The British experience demonstrates that the natural monopoly pipes can be efficiently regulated, that investment can be sustained, and that the advantages of regulated third-party access in creating a competitive spot and contract market have been substantial. The huge expansion of gas use in electricity generation has been matched by extensive exploration and development of increasingly hostile sectors in the North Sea, all under private ownership. Thus, in 1970, Western Europe consumed 73 million tonnes oil equivalent (Mtoe) of natural gas, only 13 percent as much as the United States in that year. By 2000, this figure had grown to 413 Mtoe, or nearly sixfold, to 70 percent of the U.S. level.[12]

The case for liberalizing gas has been extensively argued by the European Commission, but progress is handicapped by two significant obstacles. The first is that much of the industry is already in private ownership, so that the restructuring options readily available at privatization are harder to secure, as Britain and the United States demonstrate. The second is that the Continent is heavily and increasingly dependent on gas imports, mostly from politically unstable and distant countries, some of which require transit rights through other unstable countries. Britain and the United States are almost alone in being self-sufficient (at least at present) and having fully restructured their industries. Other countries see gas imports as of major geopolitical concern and are most unlikely to allow the industry to evolve solely in response to market forces and short-term consumer demands. Nor is a competitive downstream industry necessarily the ideal complement to an upstream foreign monopoly as powerful as Gazprom.

Inevitably, then, importing countries are more concerned with energy policy and security of supply than securing the considerable potential benefits of greater gas-on-gas competition. Security is pursued by long-term contracts and geopolitical negotiations, combined with mandatory storage capacity. As Britain shifts from a gas exporter to gas importer within the next five years, these issues will increasingly have to be addressed by the British government. Already the gas interconnector with the Continent has ended the period of gas pricing based on gas-on-gas competition and reestablished the link between gas prices and oil prices, thereby wiping out many of the benefits of earlier U.K. gas liberalization.

The conclusion for gas is that regulated private ownership works well for the natural monopoly transmission and distribution system, but that creating a competitive gas market has been more difficult, particularly where gas is imported from few sources or from monopoly suppliers. Public ownership of production provides some comfort to countries concerned about controlling rent, although taxation and license auctions work well in fiscally competent countries, at least where oil and gas interests have not suborned the political process. Public or municipal ownership in distribution may be somewhat less efficient than private regulated distribution companies. Municipalities are more likely to combine electricity and gas in one company, which may also be less efficient.[13] In addition, municipal utilities are often tempted to use their franchise as a source of rent extraction to cross-subsidize other municipal services. The resulting extra deadweight costs may be no more serious than that caused by the irrationality of much of energy taxation (Newbery 2003b), and smaller than the more substantial deadweight losses caused by the lack of competition in supply and the resulting underutilization of this low-carbon energy resource.

1.5.3 Electricity

In terms of the criteria for successful privatisation and liberalisation, the electricity supply industry (ESI) presents a mixed picture. The evidence is that the potential benefits from introducing competition by full ownership unbundling exceed any synergies of vertical integration in all but the smallest systems, and even there, the single buyer model may be preferable to vertical integration.[14] There is also evidence that well-designed price cap regulation can enhance the performance of the unbundled network without prejudicing investment and quality of service, certainly in moderately independent systems like Britain (Pollitt and Domah 2001). The main problem is the credibility of sustaining competitive wholesale generation markets when new investment is needed and the difficulty of designing efficient markets and good regulation. There are important and largely unresolved issues regarding the interface between interconnected markets operating under different market rules, and there are serious concerns in Europe about the persistence of market power.

The ESI in most European countries worked technically quite well under the previous vertically integrated, largely state-owned structure. Electricity demand is fairly inelastic, so the allocative inefficiencies of mispricing were small. Therefore it should not be surprising that the gains from privatization and restructuring appear modest even when the reforms were carefully done. It follows that imperfect restructuring could result in social losses, a lesson that was available before being underlined by the Californian electricity crisis of 2000.

Just as technical progress has greatly aided the development of competition in telecoms, to the point of making the network natural monopolies contestable, so technical progress in the ESI has reduced the barriers to entry into generation and supply. The development of combined cycle gas turbines (CCGT) makes this the natural choice for new generation, except where gas is not readily available, or local coal or hydro have overwhelming cost advantages. CCGT stations can enter rapidly (two years) and at modest scale (50–500 MW), compared to coal and nuclear stations (five to ten years and 1,000 MW). Gas in mature systems can be delivered closer to the final electricity marketplace more cheaply than electricity, reducing the need for expensive grid investments and reducing the advantages of geography (well-placed coal mines or dams). CCGT technology therefore makes generation more contestable than before and supports liberalization.

These developments helped but did not dramatically change the case for liberalization, which in Britain occurred before CCGT arrived. Generation stations in most of the larger industrialized countries are small compared to the market—the largest one in Britain (one of the largest in the world) had less than 8 percent of total capacity, and economies of scale of coal and nuclear stations fall off rapidly beyond 2 percent of total U.K. capacity. Smaller markets like Belgium are typically interconnected with a wider system, leaving only isolated small countries like Ireland facing a serious problem of indivisibility.

The quantitative evidence on reform experience is not extensive but is growing. Steiner (2001) and Hattori and Tsutsui (2004) examine the impact of regulatory reform on the ESI using panel data for nineteen OECD countries, the latter study using a slightly longer time series (1987–1999). The two studies reach different conclusions about the effect of creating a wholesale market on the industrial price of electricity, probably due to slightly different definitions of regulatory reform indicators. However, they both find that third-party and retail access tend to lower industrial electricity prices and also lower the ratio of industrial to domestic prices, which in many countries represents an improvement in allocative efficiency. Steiner (2001) finds that privatization improves operating efficiency and capacity utilization.

Arocena and Waddams-Price (2001) find that in Spain, public generators are on average more efficient than private generators under the earlier cost-of-service regulation. However, private generators catch up and overtake the public firms once cost-of-service regulation is replaced by price cap regulation, suggesting that private firms are more responsive to the kinds of market signals to be expected with liberalization and good regulation.

U.K. electricity reform provides an excellent example of the benefits of restructuring and the importance of structural decisions. The United Kingdom tried all three possible models: in England and Wales, the Central Electricity Generating Board (CEGB) was unbundled into three generating companies and the grid, the twelve distribution companies were privatised; and a wholesale market—the electricity pool—created. Scotland retained the two incumbent vertically integrated companies with minimal restructuring and constrained export links to England. Northern Ireland adopted the single buyer model with the combined transmission-distribution company NIE holding long-term power purchase agreements (PPAs) with the three independent generating companies.

The subsequent history of competition in England and Wales has been told many times (Newbery 2000, Newbery and McDaniel 2003) and is again a history of regulatory pressure and government and competition authority bargaining to introduce further competition. Briefly, and identifying the key decisions, the companies were privatized with three-year contracts for the sale of electricity and the purchase of coal. These contracts reduced the incentive to manipulate the spot or wholesale price in the market (the electricity pool) that had been created to trade electricity between generators and suppliers. Once these contracts expired, the coal contracts collapsed, the price-cost margin widened dramatically, and the attractive wholesale price induced a "dash for gas." The architects of privatization had anticipated the unsatisfactory market structure and had put in place relaxed regulations on the distribution companies (the regional electricity companies, or RECs) that allowed them to collaborate to set up "independent" power producers that could enter the industry and thus reduce concentration. The persistence of high and growing profit margins caused the regulator to impose a price cap on the two generators that would be lifted only if they sold 6,000 MW of plant (about 10 percent of peak demand). This they did in 1996, but high profit margins persisted and led to calls to reform the wholesale electricity market (Newbery 1998).

Meanwhile, the duopoly generators perceived the risk-reducing attractions of integrating downstream into retailing and proposed merging with RECs. The mergers were referred to the Monopolies and Mergers Commission, which found them against the public interest. The secretary of state then prevented the proposed mergers. Subsequent negotiations traded off horizontal concentration for vertical integration, and by the end of the decade, the generation industry was supplied by the equivalent of eight comparably sized companies (most vertically integrated into supply, which became more concentrated), as well as experiencing excess capacity as a result of excess entry. The resulting collapse of prices finally delivered the benefits of competition that a more competitive initial structure would have produced more rapidly.

Newbery and Pollitt (1997) and Pollitt (1997, 1998) have completed social cost benefit analyses of the three different models, with striking and intuitively plausible results. The restructuring of the CEGB immediately introduced daily competitive price bidding for each power station. All generating companies dramatically increased productivity and drove down costs, including the state-owned Nuclear Electric. The audit of the first five years was that the social benefits amounted to a reduction of costs of 6 percent compared to the counterfactual, equivalent to a 100 percent return on the sales price (when discounted at 6 percent real). These benefits were initially almost entirely captured by companies, for profits rose as costs fell and prices remained stubbornly high until continued and aggressive regulatory intervention forced extensive divestment of capacity. Figure 1.3 shows the gradual erosion of market shares of the two fossil generators, National Power and Power-Gen, as they sold plant and independent power producers (IPPs) entered, taking advantage of the recently developed rapid-build, low-cost gas-fired CCGT technology in the "dash for gas."

By the end of the decade the dominant duopoly had evolved into a relative unconcentrated industry with very competitive pricing. Entrants and incumbents operated efficient CCGT stations, a range of international generating companies bought divested plant, and the modern nuclear stations had been privatized.

Figure 1.4 shows the evolution of the wholesale electricity price. The cost of generating by coal and gas is also shown, so the margin of the price over the short-run avoidable fuel cost is readily seen. The prices are yearly moving averages of the half-hourly wholesale prices or the quarterly fuel prices, and are deflated by the retail price index to the 2001 price level. The line with diamonds gives the Hirschman-Herfindahl index (HHI), defined as the sum of the squared percentage shares of coal-fired plant capacity (which set the price most of the time until 1999) owned by different companies, read on the right-hand scale. An HHI of 5,000 represents a symmetric duopoly, and the initial concentration was somewhat higher than this as National Power was 50 percent larger than PowerGen.

The detailed bidding behavior of each generator is available and allows one to test for the exercise of market power. Sweeting (2001) shows that in the period up to 1994, the incumbents were bidding at less than the profit-maximizing level. Nevertheless, the widening

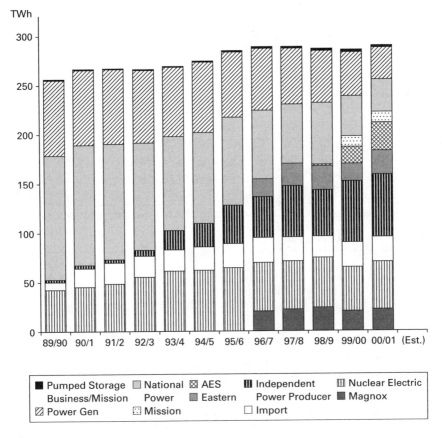

Figure 1.3

Output shares of generators in England and Wales

Note: The order of companies corresponds to the order in the key at the bottom of the graph, but note that Pumped Storage Business/Mission is the very small element at the top and that Magnox is the lowest element on the right five bars, after Nuclear Electric (NE) had been restructured into British Energy (shown as the residual NE in England and Wales), and Magnox. Data on output (as opposed to capacity) by generator ceased to be regularly available with the ending of the pool. The last data available are given in the *Pool Statistical Digest*, February 2001, and relate to the period up to December 2000. The forecast is based on assumptions about the final quarter of the year to March 31, 2001.

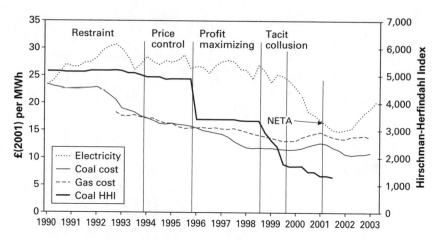

Figure 1.4
Evolution of wholesale prices in England and Wales

price-cost margin led the regulator to impose a price control until plants were divested in 1996. The next period was characterized by individual profit maximization, until further sales reduced concentration but not the price-cost margin. For a brief period until the market collapsed, generators were acting as though they were tacitly coordinating on a higher-priced equilibrium. Once the market had fragmented sufficiently, this became unsustainable and prices collapsed, *before* the New Electricity Trading Arrangements (NETA) were introduced in March 2001. The evidence therefore suggests that the industry must be relatively unconcentrated before the productivity gains are passed on in lower prices. The subsequent recovery in wholesale prices is also interesting. In response to the unattractive prices (whose collapse precipitated the bankruptcy of TXU and the near-bankruptcy of British Energy), generators removed some 8,000 MW of capacity, causing the reserve margin to fall from 30 to 17 percent and tightening the wholesale market to the point that prices could recover. In response to a rise in forward prices, several plants were brought back in time for the winter peak.

Scotland was a different story. In 1990, electricity prices were 10 percent lower than in England, but the lack of competitive pressure meant that by the end of the decade, prices were some 5 percent higher. The very modest benefits of privatization were entirely absorbed by the costs of restructuring, delivering no net benefit. Northern Ireland gives a mixed picture. The long-term PPAs provided powerful incentives for increased plant availability and cost reductions, so that the improved generator performance outstripped that of the CEGB by three times. However, these PPAs retained the benefits with the generating companies. Consumers were able to benefit only by aggressive price reductions on the nongenerating elements of cost, combined with government subsidies to reduce the embarrassing price gap between Northern Ireland and Britain.

The lessons from U.K. electricity restructuring are clear. Increased competitive pressure on generation is needed to reduce costs, and that requires separating generation from transmission and distribution. Whether these benefits will be passed on to consumers depends on the intensity of competition, particularly the number of competitors and the existence of an open access wholesale market. Unrestructured industries, even if privatized, appear to deliver few benefits. Securing efficiency improvements in transmission and distribution requires tough regulatory price controls. Improvements in the first five years under the initial price controls were modest, with most of the price cuts, efficiency gains, and transfers to consumers confined to the second and subsequent regulatory reviews (Pollitt and Domah 2001). The evidence suggests that regulators have to work hard to translate efficiency gains into lower consumer prices.

These economic lessons of liberalization are reinforced by evidence from Norway and other EU countries (see Bergman et al. 1999). Effective competition in generation under private ownership reduces costs and passes those cost reductions through to consumers in price reductions. Effective competition in generation requires regulated third-party access to separately owned networks. This in turn requires ex ante regulation by specialized utility regulators, as competition law alone is inadequate given the special properties of electricity. For cost reductions to be passed through as price reductions, there must be sufficiently many competing generating companies and a well-designed market for the various ancillary and balancing services, as well as adequate capacity. The number of actively competing generators may be increased by improving transmission links, as in the Nordic market (Bergman and von der Fehr 1999). Otherwise, enforcing or encouraging divestiture of plant by the incumbent may be necessary. Contract coverage reduces market power and needs to be encouraged by the regulatory environment while entry barriers should be kept low. The lesson that unbundling is necessary has been taken to heart in restructuring choices around the world, and particularly in the EU.

The European Commission presented its proposals for amending the Gas and Electricity Directives at the European Council in Stockholm in March 2001.[15] The commission pressed for vertical separation, preferably with legal separation of ownership, together with regulated third-party access to transmission, a national regulator, and retail competition. Unfortunately, the Californian electricity crisis of December 2000 raised serious concerns that liberalization could easily lead to supply insecurity, blackouts, and dramatic increases in prices, and slowed the subsequent progress toward agreeing on a revised Energy Directive (Newbery 2003a). This was finally accepted as 2003/54/EC and came into effect on August 4, 2003, in a somewhat attenuated form.

It is probably too soon to tell whether privatizing and restructuring the ESI will deliver sustainable improvements, but it is certainly early enough to say that poor market design and poor regulation can make matters considerably worse, as California demonstrates (Joskow and Kahn 2002). Econometric studies can pick up the effects of reforms and restructuring on prices, investment, and productivity, although the length of time since most reforms occurred is still rather short for the long-run effects to be clearly identified. Cost-benefit studies can identify the net social gains from restructuring, but they are few and far between, as Pollitt (1997) notes, and are also restricted to a relatively short time period.[16]

The major concerns are that reforms have frequently failed to address issues of market power (Newbery 2002, 2003a), but competition may not be sustainable either. There are concerns that the intensity of competition needed to transfer the efficiency gains and fuel price falls through to final consumers will reduce the incentive to invest, prejudicing security of supply. Surplus capacity, of the kind prevalent in Northern Europe, helped liberalization by reducing the risks of shortage and attenuating market power, but generating companies benefit from a shortage of supply. Competition of the kind seen in the very competitive English electricity wholesale market in 2001–2002 only just covered variable costs, which are only half total costs (Newbery and McDaniel 2003). Generating companies therefore delayed investment, mothballed plant, and allowed scarcity to increase, allowing prices to recover. The concern is that the market response may err on the side of too little rather than to much capacity. Yet England and Wales demonstrate that if entry is easy and the market is both concentrated and as a result profitable, excess entry can also occur. Power cuts in the United States, Italy, and Denmark have raised doubts about investment adequacy and effective coordination in transmission. Although this may be a problem in some countries, Britain has invested £16 billion in transmission and distribution since privatization in 1990, or 100 percent of the turnover of the entire industry. Well-regulated network companies can therefore deliver adequate infrastructure investment.

In Europe, the ESI is still very much in a state of transition. Some countries have restructured and privatized: the United Kingdom is the leading example. Some have partially privatized, such as the Netherlands and Spain; some already had extensive private ownership, like Germany, but have extended the private share through mergers and acquisitions. Others are still in the process of restructuring, like Italy and Portugal, while France remains monolithically state owned, and Scandinavia seems committed to the ownership status quo. In many countries, reforms have yet to be seen as obviously beneficial in reducing prices without prejudicing security of supply. Given the potentially small gains on offer, the considerable risks if the restructuring is flawed, and the difficulty of restructuring after privatization, such caution is understandable.

The latest Energy Directive (2003/54/EC which came into effect in August 2003) anticipates full domestic liberalization by January 1, 2007, although this decision is subject to review. This would end the domestic franchise and allow domestic customers the same rights as all other (larger) customers to choose their supplier. On the British model, suppliers would be unregulated and would be able to go bankrupt (and on several occasions have done so). There are considerable doubts whether the costs of liberalization are worth the benefits (Green and McDaniel 1998). The evidence suggests that consumer inertia allows incumbent suppliers to charge 10 percent or more than the median competitor, and the supply margin has risen to 34 percent for domestic customers, compared to the notional 1.5 percent margin allowed when supply was regulated. Marketing costs have risen, but these are largely rent dissipation, suggesting that the social costs of full liberalization exceed the benefits. Ending the franchise could also shorten contract periods and may thereby raise the cost of capital for providing new electricity-generating capacity or investments to find and transport gas.

If a full social cost-benefit analysis shows that unregulated supply competition is inferior to regulated supply, then the case for unbundling supply from distribution is weakened, and in that case distribution companies would retain a franchise and, hence, a local monopoly. The earlier argument for continued public or municipal ownership might then hold. In this case, competitive and private suppliers to the nonfranchise market would be competing with the vertically integrated franchise company. It seems quite likely that the low capital costs of an agile supply business competing for commercially astute customers could survive in competition with a publicly owned distribution and supply company. This argument does not refute the claim that liberalization requires privatization, for the only case for public ownership here is the apparent efficiency of continued monopoly provision. Certainly in Britain it was not taken as an argument for keeping the distribution companies in public ownership, and their performance has improved relative to the counterfactual of continuing under public ownership (Pollitt and Domah 2001).

1.5.4   Water

The typical problem facing publicly owned European water companies is that they have inherited written-down assets of low book value that are in a poor condition to meet the increasingly onerous quality and environmental standards set by the European Commission. Prices that might be justified on the old book value are inadequate to finance the needed investment. On the face of it, this inability to finance activities at market rates of return would seem to be a serious impediment to privatization, although the British experience demonstrates that it can be done. The assets were sold in 1989 for a very small fraction of their modern equivalent asset value with an escalating price cap in place, of the form $RPI - X + K$. The K factor allows for a growing revenue stream to finance the borrowing needed for the ambitious investment program.

Credibility of the regulatory framework in Britain was reinforced by the previous experience of other privatizations and because the evident need for continued recourse to the capital market would keep the regulator honest. The first director general, Ian Byatt, already had a strong reputation for cost-benefit analysis and proper public sector accounting. He commissioned and published a series of papers on the proper measurement of the cost of capital (which can be found on the Ofwat web site). The importance of incentives for efficiency and quality was recognized explicitly in the Water Industry Act 1991. The act anticipates that each water or water and sewerage company will be bench-marked against its peers. To be effective, this requires a sufficient number of independent companies, and the act requires all mergers within the sector above a certain size to be referred to the Competition Commission. They will balance the efficiency gains of the merger (and the consequential reduction in water bills) against the reduction in regulatory information caused by the loss of a comparator. Such price cap regulation has proven effective in driving down costs and improving productivity, at least (as with other utilities) after the first postprivatization periodic review (Saal and Parker 2003).

Water differs from the other utilities discussed so far in that it is costly and difficult to create competition because water has low value to weight and is costly to move across regional boundaries (which were set to coincide with water catchment areas), and because of the difficulty of ensuring quality. Competition is therefore unlikely to be an effective source of efficiency gains, and the case for privatization rests almost entirely on better management in the private sector (through the stock market discipline of takeovers) and on the improvement in regulation made possible by creating an independent regulator.

The downside of British water privatization is that the government no longer has such a stake in resisting increasingly unreasonable EU directives on water quality, few of which would pass any social cost-benefit test. The companies have also become free to speculate in businesses in which they were soon shown to have negligible expertise (hotels being a notable example). The pressure on public owners to ensure that water quality is adequate is likely to be strong if there is any evidence of serious health risks. The advantage of minimizing the cost of delivering potable water by placing it under local authority control, with many other claims on its finance, is appealing, at least to economists. The case for water privatization is therefore weaker than for most other utilities.

1.5.5   Rail

Railway passenger transport is uncompetitive with road (and probably air over longer distances) except in dense urban areas, which includes delivering passengers to those urban areas, and where the infrastructure costs have been largely written off. Freight traffic is marginal except for dedicated loads over moderate to long distances, such as coal and aggregates, where speed is not critical and dedicated rolling stock and handling facilities can be installed. Rail can be made to appear more competitive with road by underinvesting in road and raising the price of road travel through otherwise unwarrantably high road charges and taxes. Commuter travel may be socially desirable by rail, but the economics of very peaky demands are commercially unattractive. As a result, all European railways require heavy subsidies. The ratio of revenues to costs varies from 9 percent in Hungary to 66 percent in Finland, with Britain at 57 percent, compared to the average over sixteen European countries of 39 percent (Nash et al 2002).

The first and arguably fatal problem with privatizing European railways is railway's failure to cover even operating costs (including maintaining the system), and the consequential need for continuing subsidy. Figure 1.5, taken from Smith (2003), shows the cost recovery ratio (the ratio of non-subsidy revenue to total costs) for various European railways. It shows that all railways needed subsidies, and although Britain appears to need the lowest subsidies, these increased after privatization. There are two solutions available: keep the loss-making part in public ownership or feed subsidies into the industry. The first solution, exemplified by Sweden, keeps the rail infrastructure in public ownership and makes it available at marginal cost. Private companies can then use the track (just as roads are state financed but

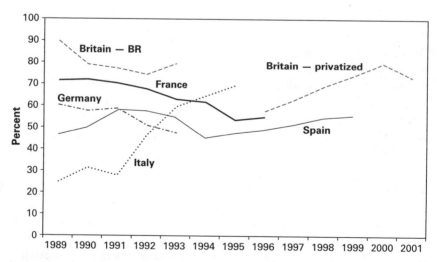

Figure 1.5
Cost recovery ratio, European railways, 1989–2001

road transport is privately provided). Subsidies may still be required for rail users. The second solution was adopted in Britain, where the entire industry was privatized. Railtrack charges the full cost (typically by a two-part tariff), and the track users are subsidized directly, originally via the franchise office, OPRAF. Railtrack's charges were regulated by the Office of Rail Regulation (ORR).

The tension intrinsic in this second solution is considerable. Around the time of Railtrack privatization, the train operating companies (TOCs) bid the amount they would need to run the franchises, and the British government was willing to underwrite these declining subsidies, in part compensated by the sales revenue from Railtrack and in part replacing existing annual treasury subventions. Indeed, over the first five years, the total cost to the government appears to have fallen compared to the counterfactual (assuming the same increase in passenger demand; Pollitt and Smith 2002). The problem arises when franchises are retendered, when the periodic review increases the charges, or between periodic reviews when the rail regulator increases charges to reflect inescapable and unexpected changes in costs, particularly those visited on the industry by the Health and Safety Executive, for example after any rail crash. Clearly, these cannot be passed to the TOCs in full to be recovered from passengers, as only some fares are capped and the remaining fares are already set at profit-maximizing levels, given the competition from road.

The government is particularly unenthusiastic about granting an independent regulator the power to force it to increase payments via OPRAF or its successor, the Strategic Rail Authority (SRA). The fight over who pays for such cost increases is likely to end in tears, particularly if there are dispersed private shareholders, as was the case with Railtrack. These tensions are made worse when naturally optimistic engineers committed to railway excellence underestimate the costs of enhancements (as they always do). Railtrack was effectively forced into bankruptcy when a minor rail accident at Hatfield revealed a large shortfall in the required annual maintenance expenditure, and the full cost of the West Coast Main Line became clearer. That cost had escalated from its original (and presumably wildly optimistic) estimate of £2.5 billion to over £12 billion (against a sales price for Railtrack of less than £3 billion).

Many of these problems would arise when running an existing railway at preprivatization levels of demand and with existing capacity. The problems were greatly amplified by the unexpected 30 percent increase in demand, reversing fifty years of stable or declining rail use and immediately exposing the capacity constraints on the existing system. A regulated utility like Railtrack may be well designed to manage existing assets under a traditional price cap regulatory regime, but not be well suited for managing investments of highly uncertain cost, much of which has extremely dubious benefit-cost ratios.

In the case of the water companies, the existing assets were sold for less than 10 percent of their replacement value, and the regulatory asset base was similarly low relative to future investment needs. However, those investment expenditures were reasonably predictable, relatively standardized, and could be protected though the K factor, which allowed the costs to be recovered from consumers over the succeeding periodic reviews in a sufficiently predictable way that banks could provide bridging finance. None of these benign characteristics holds in the case of railways. Passengers cannot pay the increased cost, long-term guarantees from the government are essentially worthless, and the benefit-cost ratios are doubtful and therefore vulnerable to subsequent close scrutiny by an intelligent Department of Transport, so only the most optimistic engineering-oriented management would consider undertaking such investments.

The existing structure of the British railway industry has been criticized for excessive vertical unbundling. Much of the criticism has been directed to the separation of track from train operation. When new investment is less critical and the number of competing or cousing companies is manageable, the separation of train from track is not necessarily the wrong solution. Provided—and this is a considerable proviso—that the true costs imposed on track by different trains can be properly identified and correctly charged, separation should not reduce the synergies of vertical integration too much. This is important, as under the EC Railway Directive, train operations should be separated from the track to facilitate equal access by different train companies to facilitate efficient intercountry use on the Continent.

The major restructuring failure appears to have been the separation of track from maintenance, and the casualization of the maintenance workforce attendant on that separation. It may be that this problem could have been overcome once a proper asset register and methods of measuring quality have been put in place, combined with sufficiently well-funded and long-lived maintenance companies to provide the necessarily lifetime guarantees for work done. The old BR system had dedicated and experienced maintenance engineers responsible for sections of track with which they became very familiar. This represented a decentralized form of asset register in their knowledge base, enabling timely maintenance. Railtrack has now been effectively absorbed back into the public sector as Network Rail, under an awkward and probably unsustainable ownership, regulatory, and financing structure. Track maintenance activities were taken back into the core network company in October 2003, with the expectation of cutting annual maintenance costs from £1.3 to £1 billion. That would seem to confirm the importance of economies of scope between operation and maintenance for railways.

It remains to be seen whether privatizing parts or the whole of railway industries is a viable and preferable alternative to the very expensive public ownership common in most countries. If it reduces cost (probably by also reducing the network size), then it might be worthwhile. If, as in Britain, it raises the cost of making explicit and legalistic the safety regulations (as with water), and if unbundling loses economies of scope without reducing costs adequately, then the privatization experiment may prove costly.

1.6   Perceptions of Privatization

As a general rule of thumb, privatization is popular provided prices appear to come down or the quality of service improves, or both. Privatization is unpopular with unions when associated with job losses or a fragmentation of union power. High profits and, even more, high pay to the directors attract unfavorable media coverage, although they probably have little effect by themselves unless associated with other unsatisfactory events, such as water rationing caused by drought, power blackouts, or price rises. In Britain, telecoms privatization ended the waiting list for connection, and service quality improved. Long-distance and international calls became dramatically cheaper, and the rebalancing of tariffs adversely affected only a small fraction of the population. Waddams Price and Hancock (1998) estimated that average real domestic telephone bills decreased by £73 from 1984 to 1997, but pensioners lost about £10 and about 1 percent of the population is deterred from having a fixed line because of the higher rental cost.

Figure 1.6 shows the evolution of real domestic prices for gas, electricity, water (after 1987), and telephones, repeating the evidence of figure 1.2, but this time plotted on a log scale so that equal proportional changes in prices are represented by the same vertical

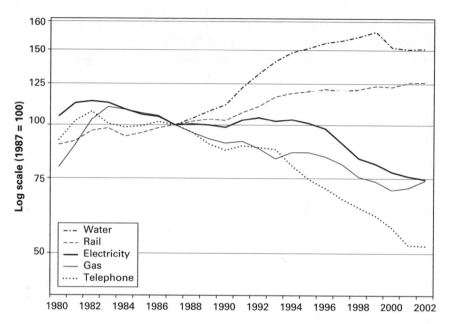

Figure 1.6
Real domestic price of public utilities for the United Kingdom

distances.[17] Gas prices fell steadily until 2000, when Britain connected
to the continental gas grid and its oil-linked prices. In electricity, fuel
costs fell and so (eventually) did real final domestic prices. Although
domestic prices failed to fall (except for those switching) with the
2000–2002 wholesale price fall of 40 percent, because prices did not go
up and consumers could switch, there was remarkably little criticism
of the retailers. In water, because prices rose with no obvious change
in the service, the privatization was relatively unpopular. Railway privatization has been even more severely criticized than it perhaps
merited, but there is a long tradition of complaining about inadequate
and unreliable railway services, and no great conviction that matters
would be much better under public ownership. Certainly the quasi-
privatization of track operations of London Underground was strongly
criticized before it happened, but if, as planned, quality improves, and
the cost is ultimately borne by taxpayers, opposition will probably be
muted.

Figure 1.7 shows the expenditure pattern on utilities across the income distribution, with pensioners separately identified. It is striking
how constant expenditure levels (not shares) are across the bottom

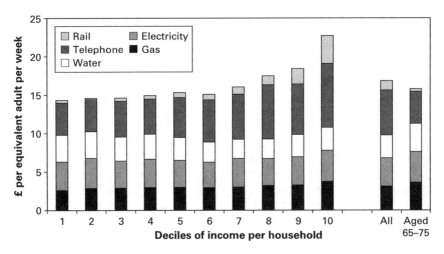

Figure 1.7
Distributional impact of utility prices in the United Kingdom

two-thirds of the income distribution, suggesting that utility price changes act almost like lump-sum taxes or transfers. Indeed, the amount of water expenditure actually falls with income (reflecting the rise in the number of equivalent adults per household with rising income), so that the real price rises here have been particularly damaging from a distributional point of view. The only obviously income elastic services are telephones and rail, but only 13 percent of the population record any expenditure on rail. The fall in the prices of energy has dramatically reduced fuel poverty and on balance outweighs the adverse effects of water price increases.

In Eastern Europe, privatizing electricity and gas required large increases in domestic tariffs, which were understandably unpopular and often resisted by changed governments, to the detriment of regulatory credibility. The main lesson to draw is that how privatization is perceived has a rather tenuous relationship with whether the privatization is judged an economic success, as other costs (such as fuel inputs or environmental requirements) may overwhelm any efficiency gains in affecting the final price that is the prime determinant of popularity.

1.6   Lessons Learned

The main lesson to draw is that the difficulty of meeting the various criteria for successful privatization varies across industries. In telecoms, privatization is almost certainly better than public ownership, but poorly designed privatization is costly compared to a delay followed by a more carefully designed privatization. In gas, the main problem is one of moving the industry toward a more satisfactory market structure, and liberalization may be able to play only a modest role if the industry is already largely private. Electricity was largely publicly owned in Europe and offered important opportunities to move to a better industrial structure—an opportunity that was often wasted. The gains from electricity privatization are modest and the risks of costly choices considerable. In water, the case for privatization is weaker as liberalization is difficult, and regulation is less effective at resisting unreasonable quality standards. Finally, it is even more difficult to privatize railways in a way that both improves performance and reduces the public cost.

Notes

This was originally presented at the CESifo conference on privatization, Cadenabbia, Oct. 31–Nov. 3, 2003. I am indebted to the careful comments of a referee and the editors.

1. The legal answer in Britain at least is that EdF Energy is deemed a private company.

2. Bergara, Henisz, and Spiller (1997), Holborn (2001), Zelner and Hensiz (2000).

3. Thus, GTE bid U.S.$1.8 billion for 56 percent of Puerto Rico Telephone, which has 1.5 million lines, while Tisa bid $1.925 billion, suggesting a price of nearly $2,300 per line (*FT*, 15/7/98). Wellenius and Stern (1994) report bids varying from U.S.$700 per line for the earlier Chile privatizations, up to $3,300 per line for Venezuela in 1991, compared with the cost of building a network of perhaps $1,000 to $1,500 per line. Bids for mobile telephone companies (before the dot-com crash) were three or more times asset value, reflecting the value of the customer base and its associated profit stream.

4. See Noll (1999, 2002) for a discussion of telecoms reform in developing countries and a criticism that too little attention has been devoted to securing a sound regulatory regime and a competitive environment.

5. In both cases social welfare is a weighted sum of the various gains, as explained in Newbery (2000), and these differ from the net change in welfare recorded in the original source. A defense of the sale was that subsequent regulation and policy established the credibility of Mexico in the eyes of the international investment community, enabling substantial and more socially profitable privatizations.

6. This study tests for, and finds, endogeneity; that is, telecoms' performance affects the choice of reforms, as well as the more normally tested effect of reforms on performance. He criticizes Wallsten for neglecting this feedback and thus tending to exaggerate the impact of privatization and regulation on performance.

7. At ⟨http://www.ofcom.org.uk/static/archive/oftel/publications/research/2002/q10fixr1002.htm⟩.

8. The authors note that reverse causality might account for this association, in that low productivity encourages governments to accelerate privatization. They also note that the date of privatization is taken as the first date of sale of any shares, not the date of transfer of control to private owners. See figure 1.1 for the importance of this distinction.

9. At ⟨http://www.teleinquiry.govt.nz/⟩.

10. While cost-benefit analysis is a desirable discipline, in the hands of advocates, it can be distorted to favor the preferred solution, as argued extensively in the evidence presented to Competition Commission (2003) and the subsequent judicial review (Case CO/ 1192/03 High Court before Moses, J, June 27, 2003, para 146).

11. Gas delivered to Western Europe from Russia travels 6,000 kilometers from the wells through pipelines of 1,200 mm diameter.

12. Data from *BP Statistical Review of World Energy* (1980, 2000).

13. Stevenson (1982) compared twenty-five gas and electric utilities with fifty-four single fuel utilities (which therefore had to compete against the other fuel) and found the more competitive were less X-inefficient both statically (taking the capital stock as given) and dynamically (allowing for investment).

14. The single buyer model is one in which a single company, normally owning transmission, signs contracts with all generating companies and sells power to final consumers.

15. COM(2001) 125 final, March 13, 2001, available with the press release and working paper at ⟨http://europa.eu.int/comm/energy/en/internal-market/int-market.html⟩.

16. One problem is that typically a few years after restructuring, mergers and acquisitions change the corporate structure and make it increasingly difficult to reconstruct the aggregated "industry" accounts to compare with the counterfactual under continuing public ownership.

17. That is, the index of consumer prices in the ONS *Monthly Digest of Statistics* is deflated by the retail price index.

References

Armstrong, M. 1996. *Network Interconnection*. Discussion Paper ET 9625. University of Southampton.

Armstrong, M. 1998. "Network Interconnection in Telecommunications." *Economic Journal*, 108, 545–564.

Armstrong, M. 2002. "The Theory of Access Pricing and Interconnection." In M. Cave, S. Majumdar, and I. Vogelsang, eds., *Handbook of Telecommunications Economics*. Amsterdam: North-Holland.

Armstrong, M., Cowan, S., and Vickers, J. 1994. *Regulatory Reform—Economic Analysis and British Experience*. Cambridge, Mass.: MIT Press.

Arocena, P., and Waddams-Price, C. 2001. "Generating Efficiency: Economic and Environmental Regulation of Public and Private Electricity Generators in Spain." *International Journal of Industrial Organization*, 20(1): 41–69.

Averch, H., and Johnson, L. L. 1962. "Behavior of the Firm under Regulatory Constraint." *American Economic Review*, no. 52, 1053–1069.

Bartle, I., ed. 2003. *The UK Model of Utility Regulation: A Twentieth Anniversary Collection to Mark the "Littlechild Report"—Retrospect and Prospect*. Bath: Centre for the study of Regulated Industries.

Bell, A. 1995. "The Telecommunications Industry 1994/95." In P. Vass, ed., *CRI Regulatory Review 1995*. London: CIPFA.

Bergara, Mario, Henisz, Witold J., and Spiller, Pablo T. 1997. "Political Institutional and Electric Utility Investment: A Cross-Nation Analysis." POWER working paper no. PWP-052, University of California Energy Institute, University of California at Berkeley.

Bergman, L., Brunekreeft, G., Doyle, C., von der Fehr, B.-H., Newbery, D. M., Pollitt, M., and Regibeau, P. 1999. *A European Market for Electricity?* London: Centre for Economic Policy Research.

Bergman, L., and von der Fehr, N.-H. 1999. "The Nordic Experience: Diluting Market Power by Integrating Markets." In L. Bergman et al., *A European Market for Electricity?* London: Centre for Economic Policy Research.

de Boer, D. B., and Evans, L. 1996. "The Economic Efficiency of Telecommunications in a Deregulated Market: The Case of New Zealand." *Economic Record* 72, 24–35.

Boylaud, O., and Nicoletti, G. 2001. "Regulation, Market Structure and Performance in Telecommunications." *OECD Economic Studies* 32, 99–142.

Competition Commission. 2003. *Mobile Phone Charges Inquiry*. London: Competition Commission.

Crandall, R. W., and Waverman, L. 1997. *Universal Service: For Whom the Bell Used to Toll*. Washington, D.C.: Brookings Institution.

Cremer, H., Marchand, M., and Thisse, J. 1989. "The Public Firm as an Instrument for Regulating an Oligopolistic Market." *Oxford Economic Papers* 41, 283–301.

Ellig, J. 1991. "Endogenous Change and the Economic Theory of Regulation." *Journal of Regulatory Economics* 3, 265–275.

Galal, A. Jones, L., Tandon, P., and Vogelsang, I. 1994. *Welfare Consequences of Selling Public Enterprises: An Empirical Analysis*. New York: Oxford University Press.

Gilbert, R. J., and Newbery, D. M. 1994. "The Dynamic Efficiency of Regulatory Constitutions." *Rand Journal* 25(4), 538–554.

Green, R., and McDaniel, T. 1998. "Competition in Electricity Supply: Will '1998' Be Worth It?" *Fiscal Studies* 19(3): 273–293.

Gutiérrez, L. F. 2003. "The Effect of Endogenous Regulation on Telecommunications Expansion and Efficiency in Latin America." *Journal of Regulatory Economics*, 23, pp. 257–286.

Hattori, Toru, and Tsutsui, Miki 2004. "Economic Impact of Regulatory Reforms in the Electricity Supply Industry: A Panel Data Analysis for OECD Countries." *Energy Policy* 32: 823–832.

Hausman, J. A. 1997. "Valuing the Effect of Regulation on New Services in Telecommunications." *Brookings Papers: Microeconomics*, 1–38.

Hausman, J. A., Tardiff, T., and Belinfante, A. 1993. "The Effects of the Breakup of AT&T on Telephone Penetration in the United States." *American Economic Review* 83(2), 178–184.

IEA. 1994. *Natural Gas Transportation: Organisation and Regulation.* Paris: IEA/OECD.

ITU. 2002. *Trends in Telecommunications Reform 2002: Effective Regulation.* Geneva: International Telecommunications Union.

Joskow, P., and Kahn, E. 2002. "A Quantitative Analysis of Pricing Behavior in California's Wholesale Electricity Market during Summer 2000." *Energy Journal,* 1–35.

Kornai, J. 1992. "The Post-Socialist Transition and the State: Reflections in the Light of Hungarian Fiscal Problems." *AER Papers and Proceedings* 82, 1–21.

Laffont, J.-J., Rey, P., and Tirole, J. 1998a. "Network Competition: Overview and Non-Discriminatory Pricing." *Rand Journal of Economics* 29(1), 1–37.

Laffont, J.-J., Rey, P., and Tirole, J. 1998b. "Network Competition: Price Discrimination." *Rand Journal of Economics* 29(1), 38–56.

Lawson, N. 1992. *The View from No. 11: Memoirs of a Tory Radical.* London: Bantam.

Lenain, P., and Paltridge, S. 2003. "After the Telecommunications Bubble." Paris: OECD. ⟨http://www/oecd.org/eco⟩.

Lipton, M., and Simkins, C., eds. 1993. *State Owned Market in Post Apartheid South Africa.* Johannesburg: Witwatersrand University Press.

Littlechild, S. 1983. *Regulation of British Telecommunications Profitability.* London: HMSO.

Martin, S., and Parker, D. 1997. *The Impact of Privatisation: Ownership and Corporate Performance in the UK.* London: Routledge.

Mason, R. 1998. "Internet Telephony and the International Accounting Rate System." *Telecommunications Policy* 22(11), 931–944.

Nash, C., Bickel, P., Friedrich, R., Link, H., and Stewart, L. 2002. "The Environmental Impact of Transport Subsidies." Paper presented at the OECD Conference on Environmentally Harmful Subsidies. Paris, November 7–8.

Newbery, D. M. 1997. "Privatisation and Liberalisation of Network Utilities." *European Economic Review* 41(3–5), 357–384.

Newbery, D. M. 1998. "The Regulator's Review of the English Electricity Pool." *Utilities Policy* 7(3), 129–141.

Newbery, D. M. 2000. *Privatization, Restructuring and Regulation of Network Utilities.* Cambridge, Mass.: MIT Press.

Newbery, D. M. 2002. "Problems of Liberalising the Energy Utilities." *European Economic Review* 46, 919–927.

Newbery, D. M. 2003a. "Regulatory Challenges to European Electricity Liberalisation." *Swedish Economic Policy Review* 9(2), 9–44.

Newbery, D. M. 2003b. "Sectoral Dimensions of Sustainable Development: Energy and Transport." *Economic Survey of Europe,* no. 2: 73–93.

Newbery, D. M., and McDaniel, T. 2003. "Auctions and Trading in Energy Markets—An Economic Analysis." In P. Vass, ed. CRI *Regulatory Review 2003.* Bath: Centre for the Study of Regulated Industries.

Newbery, D. M., and Pollitt, M. G. 1997. "The Restructuring and Privatisation of the CEGB—Was It Worth It?" *Journal of Industrial Economics* 45(3), 269–303.

Noll, Roger G. 1999. *The Economics of the Slowdown in Regulatory Reform*. Washington, D.C.: AEI-Brookings Joint Center for Regulatory Studies.

Noll, Roger. 2002. "Telecommunications Reform in Developing Countries." In Anne Krueger, ed., *Economic Policy Reform: The Second Stage*. Chicago: University of Chicago Press.

OJ. 2001. "Proposal for a Regulation of the European Parliament and of the Council on Conditions for Access to the Network for Cross-Border Exchanges in Electricity." *Official Journal* C 240 E, 28/08/2001, 72–78.

OJ. 2002. "Opinion of the Economic and Social Committee." *Official Journal* C 36 E, 08/02/2002, 10–19.

Pierce, R. J. 1988. "Reconstituting the Natural Gas Industry from Well Head to Burner-tip." *Energy Law Journal* 9, 11–57.

Pollitt, M. G. 1997. "The Impact of Liberalisation on the Performance of the Electricity Supply Industry: An International Survey." *Journal of Energy Literature* 3, 3–31.

Pollitt, M. G., and Domah, P. D. 2001. "The Restructuring and Privatisation of the Regional Electricity Companies in England and Wales: A Social Cost Benefit Analysis." *Fiscal Studies* 22, 107–146.

Pollitt, M. G., and Smith, A. J. 2002. "The Restructuring and Privatisation of British Rail: Was It Really That Bad?" *Fiscal Studies* 23, 463–502.

Roller, L.-H., and Waverman, L. 2001. "Telecommunications Infrastructure and Economic Development: A Simultaneous Approach." *American Economic Review* 91(4), 909–923.

Saal, D. S., and Parker, D. 2003. "The Impact of Privatisation on Productivity Growth in the English and Welsh Water and Sewerage Industry." Paper presented at the CESifo Conference, January.

Sappington, D. E., and Stiglitz, J. E. 1987. "Privatization, Information and Incentives." *Journal of Policy Analysis and Management* 6(4), 567–581.

Schneider, V., and Jaeger, A. 2003. "The Privatization of Infrastructure in the Theory of the State: An Empirical Overview with a Discussion of Competing Theoretical Explanations." In E. F. M. Wubben and W. Hulsink, eds., *On Creating Competition and Strategic Restructuring*, Northampton, Mass.: Edward Elgar.

Smith, A. J. S. 2003. "Developments in Financing Britain's Railways: Perspectives from Recent Experience and Comparisons with Other European Models." Mimeo. Cambridge University Judge Institute.

Steiner, Faye. 2001. "Regulation, Industry Structure and Performance in the Electricity Supply Industry." *OECD Economic Studies*, no. 32, 2001/I.

Stevenson, R. E. 1982. "X-Inefficiency and Interfirm Rivalry: Evidence from the Electric Utility Industry." *Land Economics* 58, 52–66.

Sweeting, A. 2001. "The Effect of Falling Market Concentration on Prices, Generator Behaviour and Productive Efficiency in the England and Wales Electricity Market." MIT Department of Economics. http://web.mit.edu/ceepr/www/2001-003.pdf.

Vickers, J., and Yarrow, G. 1988. *Privatization: An Economic Analysis.* Cambridge, Mass.: MIT Press.

Vogelsang, I. 2003. "Price Regulation of Access to Telecommunications Networks." *Journal of Economic Literature* 41, 830–862.

Waddams-Price, C., and Hancock, R. 1998. "Distributional Effects of Liberalizing Residential Utility Markets in the UK." *Fiscal Studies* 19(3): 295–319.

Wallsten, Scott. 2002. "Does Sequencing Matter? Regulation and Privatization in Telecommunications Reforms." World Bank Policy Research Working Paper Series 2817.

Wellenius, B., and Stern, P. A. 1994. *Implementing Reforms in the Telecommunications Sector.* Washington, D.C.: World Bank.

WTO. 1998. *Data on Telecommunications Markets Covered by WTO Negotiations on Basic Telecommunications.* ⟨http://www.wto.org/press/data3.htm⟩.

Zelner, B. A., and Henisz, W. J. 2000. "Political Institutions, Interest Group Competition and Infrastructure Investment in the Electric Utility Industry: A Cross-National Study." Working paper WP 00-03, Reginald H. Jones Center, Wharton School, University of Pennsylvania.

2   Network Utilities in the United States: Sector Reforms without Privatization

Ingo Vogelsang

While sector reforms in network utility industries in the United States were viewed as exemplary and innovative for a long time, the United States has lately been viewed as a laggard (Vogelsang 2003), and confidence in the reform process has been badly shaken in the two main network industries, telecommunications and electricity. Should we change our views of the sector reforms in the light of these recent experiences? This chapter successively addresses these questions: "What happened here?" "Why did it happen?" and "What can be learned for the future and for countries outside the United States?"

The second leitmotif of this chapter lies in the semantics of the title. The British economics literature has established a fairly precise use of the word *privatization* in the context of the reform of network industries (and otherwise). According to this literature, which is best captured in Armstrong, Cohen, and Vickers (1994) and Newbery (2000), the sector reform consists of privatization, liberalization, and (de)regulation. Here, *privatization* means the sale of public enterprises to private shareholders; *liberalization* means the opening of the markets for competition; *regulation* and *deregulation* mean the establishment and reduction of state oversight and of constraints on firms in these industries. In contrast, the U.S. literature takes a very broad view of privatization as anything that increases the scope of markets relative to command and control by governments. This is understandable, since the amount of state ownership in U.S. industries was small to begin with and has changed little under the sector reform movement. Thus, the sale of public enterprises does not deserve to monopolize such a valuable and loaded expression as *privatization*. An analysis of U.S. privatization in the British sense would therefore shed little light on the corresponding non-U.S. experience. Rather, because privatization in network

industries outside the United States involves liberalization and
(de)regulation as main complementary processes, we concentrate on
these aspects of the U.S. experience.[1] Network industries worldwide
have in common that they have gone or are currently going through
major reforms. What differentiates U.S. reforms from those of other
countries is the lack of privatization in the British sense. Although a
sample of one country does not permit statistical conclusions, the concentration on regulatory and liberalization experiences in the United
States in comparison with the European experience can help develop
conjectures about and extract the independent influence of the ownership change.[2]

2.1   The U.S. Regulatory System

Before analyzing regulatory reforms in specific U.S. network industries, it is worth explaining the distinguishing features of U.S. regulation. Particularly distinguishing is the presence of separate regulators
at the federal and state levels with often overlapping responsibilities.
Federal regulators in particular include the Federal Communications
Commission (FCC) and the Federal Energy Regulatory Commission
(FERC); the state regulators are often referred to as public utilities commissions (PUCs). In both cases, regulators are political appointees with
regulatory commissioners at the federal level appointed by the president and at the state level by the governor or legislature or directly
elected by the state voters. Regulators usually have a broad regulatory
mandate for rule making and adjudication, providing substantial regulatory discretion and some independence from the executive branch.
As a consequence, they follow a procedures-oriented approach in
reaching their decisions, and there are established procedures for
judicial review. In most of the history of regulation, there has been
an important role for antitrust policy, the most prominent example
being the breakup of AT&T in 1984. Antitrust or competition policy
can be a substitute for or a complement to regulation. It can be a substitute if it addresses the same issues. In this case, antitrust policy takes
over under deregulation. Antitrust policy becomes a complement if
it addresses issues that regulation cannot address. Typically antitrust
authorities are politically more independent than regulators, because
antitrust rules have to apply to potentially all industries and service
sectors of the economy. Federal antitrust authorities can affect both
federal and state regulation. PUCs are usually multi-industry agencies,

while the FCC and FERC are more industry specific. PUCs exhibit a large diversity among states by virtue of size, method of appointment (elected or appointed commissioners), and institutional history. Some PUCs are viewed as progressive and others as backward, some as independent and some as captured. FCC and FERC are dependent on Congress for legislation and budget. This dependence opens the door for political influence. Because of potentially overlapping duties, coordination problems and disputes arise between federal and state regulators. They are resolved by four methods. First, the regulators can meet in federal court (appellate court or the Supreme Court). Second, so-called federal-state joint boards have been established for coordination problems that require ongoing interaction, such as accounting rules for regulated firms. These boards are dominated by federal regulators, who are the agenda setters and have the last word. Third, through federal preemption, the federal regulators can usurp an issue. Last, federal legislation can redefine the roles of federal and state regulators, as has occurred under the Telecommunications Act of 1996 (1996 Telecom Act) and is currently under discussion for the electricity sector.

Federal and state regulation—each has its comparative advantages. The main advantages of the state level include, in particular, the availability of local information and preservation of local diversity. The large number of different regulations provides a laboratory of the states to find the best solution. State regulators can milk the residents of other states through regulations favoring their own residents (e.g., by opposing local deregulation). In contrast, the advantages of federal-level regulation derive from the need for harmonization and standardization (to reduce undesirable diversity), for the resolution of interstate distributional and compatibility issues, the internalization of externalities across states, and the exploitation of regulatory economies of scale. Dual federal and state regulation cannot just combine the advantages of each regulatory level, as it leads to additional administrative costs, protracted interagency disputes, and misallocations, due to separation of spheres. Dual regulation nevertheless furthers interagency competition, division of labor, and increases in civil liberties.

The general principle behind the division of labor between state and federal regulation in the United States is the differentiation between intrastate and interstate commerce. State regulation is responsible, in principle, for intrastate commerce and federal regulation for interstate commerce. Consequently an individual regulated firm will, in principle, be regulated by state regulators for its intrastate transactions and by federal regulators for its interstate transactions. This straightforward principle is hard to apply to telecommunications for basically two reasons: First, telecommunications transactions can rarely be classified as purely intrastate or purely interstate. Local exchange carriers (LECs), for example, sell access to interexchange carriers (IXCs) for long-distance calls that may or may not cross state borders, depending on choices made by callers (or by recipients, in case of 800 number calls). The question then is whether and to what extent the sale of access is intrastate or interstate telephone traffic. One could hold that this should depend on whether ex post a call can be shown to have crossed state lines. This, however, is hard to verify for incoming switched traffic.

One could also hold that all access is intrastate because it occurs in the local loop and that only the transmission between the IXC's points of presence (PoPs) at both ends can be interstate traffic. Conversely, one could hold that any sale to an IXC automatically becomes interstate.

Second, the same assets are used for intrastate and interstate telecommunications. How then shall costs and regulation of use be divided between federal and state jurisdictions?

These two problems have no unique analytical solutions. Rather, the division of labor between state and federal regulation is complex and contentious. It is based on the commerce clause and the supremacy clause of the U.S. Constitution and is guided by some basic principles.

The commerce clause promotes commerce between the states of the Union. On this basis, federal regulation should affect interstate commerce, while state regulation should be restricted to intrastate commerce. This division of labor is therefore based on the geographic scope of activities ("markets"). The underlying principle is hard to apply to telecommunications and electricity, because transactions are not purely inter- or intrastate and the suppliers use common assets for both types of transactions. As a result, ambiguities and conflicts of interest arise between federal regulators and state PUCs, which are predominantly resolved by federal preemption, according to which the FCC can declare that federal regulation supersedes state regulation if interstate communications or telecommunications is materially affected. The following conditions must be met for preemption to occur:

• Preemption has to be based on statutory regulatory objectives (for example, the 1996 Telecom Act in case of the FCC).

• There has to be a conflict between FCC objectives and PUC regulation.

• Preemption has to be construed so narrowly that no further separation of state regulation is feasible.

The last requirement has led to separations of federal and state spheres via a uniform system of accounts, which is accompanied by a host of cost allocation issues and implies fully distributed costing. Examples of federal preemption include deregulation of telecommunications equipment as an affirmative regulatory act, meaning that federal deregulation did not create a void that state regulators could fill.

Division of labor between federal and state regulators based on the supremacy clause derives its power from the supremacy of the U.S. Congress in defining the respective spheres of federal and state regulators through federal legislation, as has occurred in the Telecommunications Act of 1996, which emphasizes local competition, an intrinsic intrastate issue. Furthermore, the FCC is put in charge of implementing the act. This division of labor is based on harmonization (standardization) and expertise and has meant that the FCC has moved into traditionally local issues. The interpretation was mostly resolved by the Supreme Court in 2002, which has confirmed the expanded FCC role. The FCC now provides general rules, while the PUCs do details and adjudication. In some cases, the FCC has become the decision maker of last resort (interconnection agreements, permissions for local exchange companies to enter long-distance markets). Examples such as these show that regulatory reforms and transitions to a new division of labor between federal and state regulation in the United States are anything but smooth.

2.2   Examples of Reforms: What Happened?

Network utilities have special properties that make them targets of government interference in the form of public ownership, regulation, and antitrust policies. There are economies of scope in supply between different infrastructures and services. Often a natural monopoly of end user access becomes a bottleneck or essential facility for competitors. Sunk costs are most important for access but are by no means negligible elsewhere. Network effects on the demand side include bandwagon effects from network externalities (Rohlfs 2001, Faulhaber 2002). Competition has become feasible due to access and interconnection possibilities and their regulation and through demand growth. On a time line, attempts for network utility reforms in the United States started in a feeble way in the 1950s and 1960s, when microwave transmission for long-distance telecommunications started to play a role and equipment suppliers challenged AT&T's absolute monopoly on telephone sets. The reforms received momentum only in the 1970s, culminating in the liberalization of the airline industry in 1978 and its subsequent total deregulation. Although the liberalization and deregulation movement for competitive industries (airlines and trucking and, to some extent, railroads) was different from network utilities, it affected those by setting an example and jump-starting a movement. In contrast to the United Kingdom, the United States developed no systematic and comprehensive reform approach to its regulated industries. Deregulation and liberalization in a number of industries could therefore start at the same time that social regulation of health and environmental issues took off and grew in a major way.

Rather than providing a full history of network utility restructuring, I will concentrate on a few examples, which reflect my preknowledge and biases. They contain successes and failures, where the failures require specific explanations. This holds particularly for failures that produced essentially no winners.

2.2.1   Telecommunications

General issues
Telecommunications is the quintessential network industry, in which all users are connected with each other by a network of networks. Coming from a vertically integrated monopoly network, the United States has experienced a proliferation of other networks, vertical and horizontal separation of the incumbent AT&T, the emergence of new types of networks, and the beginning of convergence of telecommunications with the communications and information industries. The institutional reform of the sector was at the heart of these changes. From the wealth of reform components, we pick only the deregulation of telecommunications equipment, the liberalization of the long-distance market, and the attempts to introduce competition in local telephony. We thereby touch only marginally on mobile telephony, cable TV, the Internet, and reforms in spectrum assignment and spectrum management.

Deregulation of terminal equipment

Since AT&T (Bell) originally developed the telephone system, it is not surprising that it started out as a vertically integrated company that offered network services along with equipment manufacture. It is also understandable that this lasted beyond its economic usefulness, as long as AT&T maintained a virtual monopoly of telephone services. The vertical integration was reemphasized by rate-of-return regulation that could at least be partially circumvented by producing unregulated along with regulated services. However, because AT&T offered only standardized equipment to its subscribers and since it charged prices well above costs for it, pressure from entrepreneurs arose as early as in the 1950s and 1960s to offer alternative or value-added equipment. AT&T's insistence on network integrity as a defense for its absolute monopoly of equipment dragged out equipment liberalization for about a decade but ultimately was shown to be empty or, at least, easily achievable with less restrictive means, and so equipment was liberalized and totally deregulated by 1980. AT&T was already offering equipment through a separate subsidiary (Western Electric) so that full vertical separation of the network monopoly from equipment manufacturing was not decreed until the AT&T breakup in 1984 (the Modified Final Judgment or MFJ).

Since equipment manufacture is a diverse and potentially competitive industry, the liberalization of the equipment market was an immediate success and has never been questioned since. Consumers and other network providers have enjoyed much more choice and lower prices since then. Looking at Lucent, Nortel, and other equipment manufacturers today, one might, however, get the impression that the liberalization and deregulation of telecommunications equipment was a short-term success and a long-term failure. While this is probably the wrong conclusion, its mere possibility may prevent us from drawing definitive conclusions elsewhere (such as for airlines or long-distance telephony).

Long-distance telephony: Success under vertical separation

Competition in long-distance telephony can originally be pinpointed to the emergence of the microwave technology that confronted AT&T's cross-subsidized price structure. Microwave transmission was used during World War II, but its competitive impact first became clear when large telecommunications users wanted to apply it to their

company-internal telecommunications needs. AT&T was able to prevent this use for about a decade, then its further use for specialized carriers for another decade, and finally its competitive use for the general
public for another few years. What has emerged here is a general pattern for incumbents to use the regulatory process to retard change
they see as against their perceived interest. However, the small victo-
ries achieved this way may lead to an ultimately big defeat—in this
case, the breakup of AT&T in 1982–1984, in which long-distance telephony was separated from the local monopolies.

The MFJ has been the great U.S. experiment with vertical separation
of network monopolists. It was deemed necessary, among other reasons, because local telephony was perceived to be a natural monopoly,
while long-distance services were viewed as potentially competitive.
Since long-distance services need local telephone calls as essential
inputs, the local monopolies had to be providing bottleneck access to
the long-distance companies. This had proved to be contentious and
created conflicts of interest and the accusation of monopolization during the 1970s, leading to the U.S. Department of Justice's lawsuit
against AT&T. The breakup occurred by consent decree.[3] As a result,
the court (Judge Harold Greene) was in charge of its execution and
acted as a third, very powerful regulator (besides the FCC and the
state PUCs). From 1984 on, long-distance telephony developed into an
increasingly competitive industry. AT&T's share in long-distance revenues fell from about 86 percent in 1984 to about 42 percent in 1998, and
simultaneously the Hirfindahl-Hirschman Index (HHI) among long-
distance companies fell from 8,200 to 2,600 (Kaserman and Mayo
2002). Competition was both facilities based and resale based. While
high local access charges initially kept long-distance charges high, they
no longer distorted the competition between other long-distance carriers and AT&T.

The buildup of excess capacity through several full-sized long-
distance networks became obvious even in the 1980s but did not lead
to excessive competition as long as product differentiation and brand
names allowed substantial margins above marginal costs. That episode
is by now history and certainly has been replaced by fierce competition
today. In 1989 AT&T was relieved from rate-of-return regulation and
came under fairly flexible price caps. In 1995 its prices were fully
deregulated. The record of long-distance competition received generally favorable reviews from economists (surveyed in Kaserman and
Mayo 2002), but dissenters, led by MacAvoy (1996), pointed to evi-

dence that oligopolistic network competition might have led to collusive outcomes by the early 1990s. A major reason for the mixed review is that a large percentage of price reductions are explained by steep decreases in access charges that long-distance carriers had to pay local carriers. Thus, while AT&T's average revenues per minute fell by about 69 percent between 1984 and 1998, the average revenues net of access charges fell by only about 44 percent (Economides 2003). The 1990s brought attempts by the long-distance companies to provide local access services to themselves and local end user services to others, and the 1996 Telecom Act played to the desire of the large local exchange companies to reintegrate vertically into long-distance services. This begged the question if vertical separation had caused a severe loss of economies of scope. While no concrete evidence has been found, price and productivity trends in U.S. telecommunications are more favorable before than after the 1984 breakup. Thus, Phillips (2002) finds that real prices of telephone services decreased by 1.27 percent annually during the 1959–1979 period but only by 0.69 percent per year between 1980 and 2000. This may indicate that the vertical relationships between separated long-distance and local exchange carriers were associated with high transaction costs. If the rules had been simply biased against either party, then only one of them would want to integrate vertically. It is thus not clear if vertical separation gave the U.S. telecommunication sector an advantage over countries with continuing integration of their incumbent dominant firms, such as the United Kingdom and the rest of Europe.

The last few years have led to decreasing prices and a deterioration of the profitability of long-distance telephony. The financial outlook of the industry continues to be bleak. In my view, this can be attributed to excess capacity from the fiber-optics revolution combined with commoditization of long-distance telephony, mobile substitution, and the increasingly successful entry of local exchange companies in the long-distance area. Since the networks are sunk, none of these factors is going to disappear soon. Does this mean that long-distance telephony reform has finally become a failure? So far there are no signs that customers will suffer any disadvantages. That could occur only if local exchange companies were able to remonopolize those markets, something that will most likely be prevented by antitrust laws, sunk investments, and mobile competition.

Thus, judged at this point, long-distance competition has been a moderate success. However, the general public perception that competition is responsible for the large price reductions experienced over time is only partially true. Competition revealed the large rent transfers that were contained in long-distance access charges and, hence, these were reduced in the political process.

Local telephony and the 1996 Telecom Act

Like long-distance competition, local competition was also triggered by a combination of price distortion and technical innovation. The price distortion came from the universal service policy of subsidizing local telephone subscriptions (on a flat rate basis) through long-distance access charges. Since those access charges originally were a multiple of the long-run incremental costs of access, they invited local access bypass for larger long-distance users. The technological innovation was the optical fiber ring installed by competitive access providers (CAPs). The fiber rings were later copied by incumbent local exchange companies. So although the CAPs were originally cherry pickers, they helped improve the efficiency of the incumbent networks.

While CAPs were the forerunners of local competition and while attempts of true local competition started in a few states, such as New York and Illinois in the early 1990s,[4] it was the 1996 Telecom Act that was supposed to jump-start local competition in these ways:

• Establish obligations for local resale with a wholesale discount

• Provide various unbundled network elements, with which new competitors could construct networks through leasing arrangements at long-run incremental cost

• Provide reciprocal interconnection arrangements between competing local networks

• Make entry of the large local exchange companies dependent on progress in local competition in their territories (section 271 of the 1996 Telecom Act)

In spite of very pro-competitive enforcement by the FCC and most state PUCs, the big push forward did not happen. Over six years after passage of the 1996 Telecom Act, the new competitors had gained little over 12 percent market share in terms of access lines but less than 10 percent in terms of revenues (ALTS 2003). While this looks like a small gain, it is about the same as in the long-distance market over the 1984–1989 period. However, most local service competitors do not provide their own lines. Over two-thirds of more than 300 competitive local exchange companies operating in 2000 had disappeared by 2003 (ALTS 2003). Some more promising competitors have gone bankrupt, although they may emerge more strongly from Chapter 11 bankruptcy proceedings.[5] Since most local competition takes place in the business market and since local residential markets have traditionally been cross-subsidized by business services and long-distance services, one can conjecture, in the absence of official data, that prices for business users have declined.

What accounts for the slow pace of progress in local competition? The simplest explanation is that local services continue to be priced below cost in many, particularly rural, areas. Second are continuing natural monopoly and bottleneck problems. Third, by making universal service charges explicit, the 1996 Telecom Act helped reduce long-distance access charges, thereby eliminating an incentive for backward vertical integration. Fourth, the FCC's enforcement of the 1996 Telecom Act was legally challenged and therefore partially in limbo until 2002. At the same time, an extreme unbundling policy was demanded by the FCC. This required organizational and network changes that the local exchange companies could drag out. The local collocation required for loop unbundling is costly.[6] All parties underestimated these difficulties. The long-distance carriers underestimated the continuing barriers to entering local markets, even with entry help. And the Bell operating companies underestimated the regulatory hurdles before being able to enter long-distance markets. These hurdles were a direct function of the difficulties of the long-distance carriers to enter the local markets. Universal service policy calls for continuing regulatory interference. Last, continued regulation of end user prices by state PUCs prevented price rebalancing in accordance with costs. This led to a particular failure for competition to develop for residential users. Thus, the failure to establish local competition quickly is itself a combination of regulatory quagmire and genuine entry barriers in the form of high duplication costs under low penetration.

The future of the FCC's entry help to local competitors is in doubt at this time, as the FCC has been switching from a balanced approach toward service and infrastructure competition to favoring more facilities-based competition. The incumbent local exchange carriers are already losing lines to new competitors, mobile services, and broadband Internet. The competitive picture is therefore moving from moderately unsuccessful intramodal local competition to intermodal competition in specific local areas.

Conclusions on telecommunications

In all three examples, the reform took substantial time from the beginning of the events that triggered it. Meanwhile, the incumbent
enjoyed continued monopoly power, something that Owen and Braeutigam (1978) ascribe to the U.S. regulatory process in general.

Telecommunications is the major network industry where technical
change played a crucial role in some reforms, but not obviously in all,
such as telecommunications equipment.

All reforms, however, started from distorted prices that triggered
competition. The early success of long-distance competition and delay
of local competition are probably both explained by the lack of rebalancing of prices as a result of cost reduction in long-distance services
and cost increases in local services. Regulators could therefore potentially have avoided some reforms and accelerated others by pricing
more in line with costs. Why did they not? The lack of price rebalancing in telecommunications in the past is intimately connected with the
policies of state PUCs, which did not want to raise local service prices,
and with the problem of universal service. At the time of AT&T's un-
assailed monopoly position, the interests of the FCC and state regulators virtually coincided, as exemplified by the fact that the FCC
willingly let interstate services subsidize local services. This situation
changed through market entry of new competitors between 1960 and
about 1975. Until then, the FCC had fully backed the alleged cross-
subsidies of the local network through long-distance rates and had
strictly opposed market entry that could have undermined this equilibrium. However, after initially being forced by court decisions into
allowing entry, the FCC changed its position and subsequently favored
further market entry. The ensuing conflict with state regulatory positions made the FCC more active in preempting state regulation.
However, to some extent, cross-subsidization continues, although the
1996 Telecom Act put universal service on a more rational basis. At
the same time, universal service policy has expanded and become
highly complicated.

The U.S. telecommunications sector today provides a bleak picture
from the perspective of investors and telecommunications companies.
Telecommunications carriers are said to face a debt spiral, and investment advisers have, for some time, advised against the competitive
telecommunications segment in a wholesale fashion. The only slightly
brighter spot is the monopolistic segment, consisting of incumbent local exchange and cable television companies. From the customer per-

spective, the picture is somewhat different. In the competitive sector, customers enjoy low prices and ample choice, while prices in monopolistic markets vary by the regulatory impact. Thus, the economists' conclusions need to be differentiated. Current industry profits, or the lack thereof, however, matter for society because they are part of the surplus and are important for future investments.

Looking at the reform history over more than twenty-five years now makes me believe that telecommunications is not an inherently unstable industry; rather, the Internet hype in the late 1990s fostered a unique investment optimism that led to excess capacities and financial failures that will burden the future for some time.

2.2.2   Electricity

General issues

In contrast to telecommunications, the United States has not been at the forefront of electricity market reforms. Rather, these have been led by the United Kingdom, Chile, Argentina, Norway, Alberta (Canada), and Victoria (Australia). The crucial early academic inputs, however, were American. Joskow and Schmalensee (1983) were the first to systematically discuss the vertical economies of the industry, and, starting in the late 1970s, Schweppe proposed real-time pricing that has influenced the specific short-run nodal pricing approach widely used in the United States today and proposed by the FERC as the national standard.[7]

Electricity regulation in the United States, like telecommunications, is divided between federal and state regulation. The federal regulator, the FERC, is responsible for interstate high-voltage transmission and for wholesale transactions, while the state regulators are in charge of retail transactions, low-voltage distribution, and intrastate transmission. In practice, there is an overlap of regulatory reach of both. In case of conflicts, the FERC can use federal preemption to solve conflicts in its favor.

Federal issues

The Public Utility Regulatory Policy Act (PURPA) of 1978 led to independent generation at a time when public utilities had investment problems due to lack of demand growth and nuclear cost overruns and delays. The entrance of small, qualified generation facilities (QFs) was also driven by comparatively high prices received from public utilities as stipulated by the law (claimed to be at avoided costs). At the same time, state PUCs disallowed many new (nuclear) power plants built by traditional electric utilities, while other nuclear plants had huge cost overruns and turned out to be unreliable. As a result of the success of QFs and failure of utility investments in generation, state PUCs started to use competitive bidding for new generation rather than simply license the building of new plants by electric utilities (Watkiss and Smith 1993). The Energy Policy Act of 1992 (EPact) allowed generation competition beyond QFs, but did not allow retail wheeling. Rather, it required third-party access to transmission grids, which formed the basis for FERC orders on open access. Environmental regulation, shorter lead times, and new technical developments favored medium-sized gas-fired power stations over large coal-fired stations, particularly in California.

While restructuring of the electricity industry was largely done by state PUCs, the FERC, until 1999, provided only the conditioning feature of open access transmission. Its Order 888 in 1996 on open access required transmission owners to provide access to others "comparable" to themselves (not as strictly as 1996 Telecom Act in telecommunications). However, through its 1999 Millennium Order, the FERC directly aimed at restructuring the industry by demanding regional transmission organizations (RTOs) to be formed according to some presepecified criteria. This would require transmission owners either to relinquish their managerial power over their assets or divest these assets altogether and become shareholders in a specialized vertically separated transmission entity. Most recently, the FERC has embarked on a standardized market design for transmission markets throughout the United States, but this is still in the rule-making stage.

State issues: The example of California
In the early 1990s California had among the highest electricity prices in the United States. The high costs were due to cost overruns with nuclear plants and long-term fixed price contracts of utilities with small generators. At the same time, the favorable British experience with electricity restructuring seemed to show a way to substantial cost and price reductions. In this situation, California was the first U.S. state to embark on an ambitious electricity sector reform. Rather than learn from the British example, however, the state legislature and public utility commission designed something completely new, using ingredients

that had never been tried before and putting them together to a complicated whole.

California reform design   The California reform design contained a complicated set of ingredients. First, an independent system operator (CAISO) was created to solve the complex real-time problems due to nonstorability of electricity and balancing problems in electricity markets (e.g., loop flow, voltage and frequency control, reserve requirements). Making the entity independent begs the question of its objectives and incentive structure, along with the problematic separation of ownership and control of transmission assets.

Second, a power exchange (PX) was created for daily trades. The use of the PX was obligatory for main public utilities (until the crisis peaked). The two-tier structure of market organization raised the problem of coordination between CAISO and PX. The CAISO was responsible if trades in the PX exceeded transmission capacity (imbalance market). The CAISO chose a two-zone congestion pricing system instead of nodal pricing that would have incorporated the complexity of actual transmission congestion and revealed the true transmission bottlenecks. In 1999, the PX started to run a forward market, which never really took off because the large utilities feared that long-term contracts would be viewed as imprudent (rather than the opposite!), because it could expose them to high prices if spot prices took a dive and because they could then lose their customers to new entrants, which would price low.[8]

Third, the main IOUs (investor-owned utilities, as opposed to municipal electric utilities) had to sell off generation capacity, and they sold virtually all their gas-fired plants to five companies.[9] Although these new companies ended up each owning only 6 to 8 percent of the state's generation capacity, they could exercise market power in the day-ahead markets. This possibility of market power of (noncolluding) firms with small market shares in markets with extremely inelastic demands and lumpy supply is a new discovery from these markets. In particular, Borenstein, Bushnell, and Wolak (2002) estimate that market power increased wholesale electricity prices on average by about 33 percent from June to October 1998 and by almost 100 percent from June to October 2000. In the latter period, this was associated with productive inefficiency of about $350 million, which represents about 4 percent of electricity expenditure.

Fourth, through the restructuring, the main IOUs had essentially become owners of transmission and distribution capacity that were regulated by open access. Their main business therefore was the sale of electricity to final users. Although there was open entry into this marketing business, the IOUs' end user prices continued to be regulated. They had to sell under a carrier-of-last resort obligation at a standard offer price, which was 10 percent below the prerestructuring price. This price reduction was financed partially through low-interest bonds that lowered the utilities' cost of capital and partially through a surcharge on customers of incumbents and entrants until the bonds were fully repaid. Since the resulting total charges were, at the time of restructuring, expected to be considerably above the incumbent utilities' costs, the resulting surplus would be used to pay for stranded costs until those costs would be fully paid off or until April 1, 2002, at the latest (Blumstein, Friedman, and Green 2002). As it turned out, entrants could not effectively compete against the standard offer, at which incumbents had to sell to end users.

Fifth, time-of-day metering and end user peak-load pricing in the United States is underdeveloped, possibly due to overcapitalization under rate-of-return regulation (the Averch-Johnson effect). Demand responses to capacity shortages were therefore minimal, while they could have been achieved through peak-load pricing without an increase in average prices. The lack of demand response enhanced the exercise of market power, which could have been prevented by long-term contracts for electric power in wholesale markets (see Vogelsang 1987, Allaz and Vila 1993, and, for experience in the United Kingdom, Newbery 2000).

To sum up, the California reform design totally concentrated on short-term supply benefits and longer-term demand benefits, while neglecting long-term supply issues and short-term demand responses. The naive expectation was that competitive prices would result at levels well below regulated prices.

Consequences of the California reforms The California reforms worked reasonably well for the first two to three years, during which the wholesale price was below the standard offer price plus surcharges.[10] It nevertheless turned out that downstream competition failed totally as a result of the standard offer by the incumbents, which also benefited from their goodwill and from customer switching costs. In late 1999 and during the course of 2000, adverse issues arose. A severe drought in the Pacific Northwest implied that hydro imports from there had to be cut, resulting in increased generation from gas-fired stations, which resulted in increased gas prices and increased prices for nitrogen oxide pollution permits. Lack of transmission capacity between northern and southern California and between California and eastern states prevented arbitrage opportunities that could have dampened the crisis. On top of all that, a strong economy and hot weather implied increased electricity demand.

During and after restructuring, little new generation and transmission capacity came on stream. The lack of new capacity in California is partially the result of the uncertain and protracted restructuring process that new generators wanted to see completed before committing funds. The PURPA experience in California had shown that electricity supply could be generated outside traditional utilities. However, this usually occurred under long-term contracts. Therefore there existed no empirical basis about how real-time pricing would influence investments (Blumstein, Friedman, and Green 2002). By the end of 2000, the crisis had led to extremely high spot prices, resulting in a liquidity crisis for the two largest IOUs and to their inability to buy all required electricity. In the face of threatened outages and IOU bankruptcies, there was an exceedingly slow fix of the problem. Politicians and regulators either believed the crisis would quickly go away or, more probably, were too timid to respond by adjusting retail prices. The electricity reform had been sold to the public as a way to reduce electricity prices, so stiff price increases did not fit into the political picture. At the peak of the crisis, in February 2001, Governor Gray Davis was quoted as saying, "If I had wanted to increase prices I could have solved the crisis in twenty minutes." Rather, the crisis lasted for another four months, leading to a number of planned power outages and lost production in other sectors, due to interruptible power contracts.

The crisis ultimately was resolved in these ways:

• An increase in supply with the help of long-term contracts, entered into by the state of California, and through the establishment of solvency through state guarantees and the assumption of state ownership of parts of the transmission system

• New generation capacity coming (back) on stream

• Demand management that provided incentives for lower consumption (general price increases coupled with rebates for reduction of consumption well below previous levels)

• A change in the adverse weather conditions and a weakening economy

Conclusion from the California disaster and beyond   The California problems should not distract the view from some positive aspects of electricity reform experience in the United States. One main purpose of the reforms was a reduction in generation costs due to competition. Data indicate that over the 1981–1999 period, partial productivity measures of generation increased in states with competition over states without. For example, plant heat rates fell by 2 to 2.5 percent following vertical separation of ownership. At today's fuel prices, that would translate into about $4 billion savings per year nationwide (Wolfram 2003). Whether these and other productivity changes translate into total factor productivity increases and whether they make up for increased transaction costs is an open question.

While California was having its reform meltdown, other U.S. areas, such as New England, New York, and Pennsylvania–New Jersey–Maryland (PJM), were more successful with a more centralized ISO structure designed to recapture lost vertical integration economies (Wilson 2002). For example, Sutherland (2003) claims that compared to a sample of nonrestructured states, consumers in the five PJM states benefited by almost $3.3 billion (or almost 15 percent of their electricity expenditures) in 2002 alone. Despite the high costs of the crisis to California, the experience suggests that decentralized regulation with a laboratory of the states has worked to some extent. California influenced other U.S. states to restructure, but they did not follow the same model. Thus, the response to the California crisis was twofold: states with ongoing reforms strengthened those to avoid California pitfalls, and other states, with the exception of Texas, postponed or canceled any planned electricity reforms at the state level. In addition, the FERC went in to strengthen precautions against the use of short-term monopoly power in generation and increase interstate transmission coordination and transmission capacity.

Crew and Kleindorfer (2001) see the California electricity crisis as a problem of piecemeal policies, ignorance of experience by others and lack of concern for nuts and bolts. An example of piecemeal policies is the lack of coordination between upstream spot pricing and downstream price caps and default service obligation.[11] Politicians cherish price reductions and abhor price increases. This made them neglect the vertical issues. There was a naiveté in the mandated price reductions for residential consumers. The IOUs faced a truncated price distribution with a possible squeeze. If wholesale prices were high, IOUs would have to supply at the standard offer price. If wholesale prices were low, they would have to compete with entrants at the spot wholesale price plus other costs.

The U.K. experience with market power was totally neglected, possibly because of the small market shares of the various generators in California. In the long run, there is a major difference between the exercise of market power by withholding existing capacity versus restricting capacity investment. The latter is likely only if entry is restricted (e.g., in transmission).

Nuts and bolts were neglected in the lack of peak-load pricing and smart metering (a problem for the United States in general). This was topped by a lack of capacity forecasts, a lack of consideration of low-demand elasticities, and a lack of hedging. At the very least, when selling their power plants at unexpectedly high prices, utilities should have expected high prices for generation (Kahn 2001). Also, economic theory would suggest large effects of forecasting errors in industries with inelastic supply and demand.

An additional aspect emphasized by Joskow (2001) is a coordination failure between federal and state regulation. The divestiture of generation capacity by the formerly vertically integrated utilities implied a switch from state to federal regulation of these capacities. This regulation was not exercised vigorously under the mistaken belief that market power was no problem. Furthermore, the FERC refrained from preempting state regulation on transmission but rather tried to exercise softer influence, while California was uncooperative.

In the end, the disaster was the result of a combination of bad design and delayed regulatory reaction, combined with a stretch of unlikely adverse (and partially correlated) events.

Conclusions on electricity reforms
The main economic benefits of electricity competition are potential cost savings and demand responsiveness in generation, a better mix of generating facilities, and a reduction in markups for final users. The potential benefits also include faster introduction of new technologies. As long as transmission and distribution are natural monopolies, coordination problems among generation, transmission, and distribution are counteracting these benefits. These coordination problems can be solved in the short term through real-time nodal pricing,

provided no market power is exercised by generators (and transmission entities). Long-term investment problems have been dealt with only partially so far. If anything, the high expectations from electricity reforms would have to be fulfilled through investment in cheaper capacity. However, the problem that generation investment can and will lead to boom-and-bust cycles (Ford 2001) has not yet been addressed at all.

In contrast to telecommunications, where cross-subsidies from long-distance services to local services enabled long-distance competition, there are no apparent cross-subsidy issues in electricity. Rather, price rigidity and pricing below full costs in the past caused stranded costs that are reflected in the difference between the historic costs of an incumbent and the forward-looking costs of an entrant. Under continued monopoly, stranded costs would have little significance beyond intergenerational cross-subsidization. However, their very existence was revealed by competitive entry pressure under the then ruling regulated electricity prices.

In contrast to telecommunications, no major technical breakthroughs have occurred in the electricity sector that would explain sector restructuring. Rather, to the extent that technology has played a role, it has been the overestimation of the efficiency of known technologies and the underestimation of their environmental impact that led to a reduction in perceived scale economies in generation. Given the long lead times and long life of power plants, the overestimation led to an overshooting without the possibility of undoing the damage. The new situation made competition in generation appear feasible, but that did not hold for transmission and distribution, where strong natural monopoly properties persisted. Thus, in order to introduce competition in electricity generation, vertical separation of generation from transmission and distribution and/or open access to transmission and distribution grids was required.

2.2.3 Summary of the Experience

The examples in the telecommunications and electricity industries show some strongly positive experiences in markets that have developed competitively through liberalization and almost total deregulation. The mildly positive examples involve separation of monopoly and liberalized competitive areas with deregulation of the competitive parts. In contrast, the failures include liberalization with heavy-handed asymmetrical regulation of incumbents with respect to end users and open access of incumbent networks to competitors.

Liberalization almost invariably started with entrepreneurs who tried to overcome regulatory entry barriers. Under the multifaceted U.S. regulatory system, they were able to get a foot in the door and offer services in some restricted geographic or product spaces. The success of these niche entrepreneurs provided the basis for cost-of-regulation studies trying to extrapolate the benefits from these niches to the whole industry. Eventually, and with the help of new entrants and customer groups envisaging benefits, they were able to convince regulators, courts, and legislators about the benefits of liberalization. Opening the door to competition, however, meant that regulation of the incumbents had to be changed as well. This took two main forms. The first and more straightforward was deregulation of the sector, as it occurred for trucking, airlines, and telephone equipment. The second was asymmetric regulation of the incumbent, which continued to be regulated at the retail level and incurred new regulation for access to its bottleneck facilities.

Not surprisingly, the successes and failures of reforms in network industries are correlated with the time at which they occurred. As a rule, early reforms, such as airlines, telecommunications equipment, and long-distance telephony, have been more successful than later reforms, such as electricity and local telephony. This is natural in the sense that the low-hanging fruits are picked first. However, since foreign experience was largely unavailable (or was not used, as in the case of electricity), U.S. regulators and legislators had to learn how to reform these industries. Later reforms could then benefit from these experiences. That seems to have happened only to a limited extent. On the contrary, the consequences derived from the success of earlier reforms seem to have been the belief that the other fruits were also hanging low.

The examples show that markets work as predicted. Compared to regulation, workable competition in airlines, trucking, and telecommunications equipment has generated substantial net benefits and allowed complete deregulation. Vertical separation of the competitive segment has also been successful in efficiency improvements and deregulation of long-distance telephony (roughly between 1984 and 1996). However, the presence of monopoly upstream or downstream and dominant vertically integrated firms has caused problems in local telephony and electric utilities, where rent transfers have been substantial relative

to efficiency gains. All examples have in common that vertical relationships are paramount to successful competition in network utilities. The
longer-lived and the more sunk the assets employed by incumbents
are, the more likely it is that reforms reflect attempts to undo past mistakes and are therefore more related to a redistribution of rents from
sunk costs than to superior competitive entry. Since long-term contracts are a sunk investment, all of these costs were largely sunk and
therefore not about to change with liberalization (Borenstein 2002).

2.3   Some Explanations for Reforms and Their Success

2.3.1   Why Did Reforms Occur?

While there had been attempts before at reforming regulation and
while regulation has perceivably changed over time, the reforms that
matter for us all started with some liberalization. It was the pressure of
new competitors to be allowed in the market and of customer groups
seeking the benefits of such competition that triggered it all.[12] These
benefits were primarily substantial price reductions compared to those
under regulation without competition. What differed in the various
examples are the reasons for the potential price reductions. In long-
distance telephony, they were technical and demand changes that
lowered costs for entrants and exhibited fewer economies of scale than
the old technologies. This alone would not have sufficed, given that
the incumbents' costs were largely sunk (although demand growth
reduced sunkness). It was the regulatory rigidity of the price structure
that made competition feasible. This rigidity is closely linked with the
balance between federal and state regulation that had been reached at
the time. It was perceived that increases in local rates would have hurt
state regulators more than long-distance rate reductions would have
benefited the FCC. The FCC's procompetitive position emerged only
after court decisions forced it to allow competition, and even then it
continued to help the state PUCs preserve cross-subsidies from long-
distance to local prices via high long-distance access charges.[13] These
state interests continued to frustrate FCC interests. In particular, the
FCC could not preempt states to open local markets to competition because they were entirely intrastate. It took the 1996 Telecom Act to do
this.
   Although technology and demand changes provide a convincing explanation for reforms in telecommunications, they are less convincing

in trucking, airlines, railroads, natural gas, and even electricity. Thus, since commensurate reforms occurred in all these industries, the technical and demand changes can only explain differences (in sequencing, scope, and type) in the various industry reforms. In electricity markets, the reforms were spurred by a sector crisis, due to cost overruns under rate-of-return regulation, the rising impact of environmental regulation, and long-term fuel contracts at high prices. Again, that would not have sufficed without the PURPA and the MFJ experience, which suggested low costs of vertical separation along with the (largely unsubstantiated) belief that competition in generation would work wonders.

The liberalization and regulation reforms in the United States occurred in a time framework and directionality that suggests a reform movement. It would, however, be very coincidental if similar technology and demand-related reasons occurred in the various industries. It would also be surprising if regulatory snafus had occurred at about the same time in these cases, some of which had been regulated for almost a century. Rather, it suggests that something contagious happened that was triggered by events in a subset of the industries. This may well have been the technical change in long-distance telephony that showed feasible competition and provided competitive pressure. This, along with airline and trucking deregulation, has worked as an eye opener for the virtues of competition.

2.3.2 What Explains Success or Failure?

The reforms occur first in industries, where claims for expected efficiency increases from deregulation were strongest and most believable (and where there was a group that has a lot to gain). This particularly holds for industries that are naturally competitive (trucking and airlines) or experience a lot of technical and demand changes (telecommunications). The success in those industries reemphasizes the original claim that is then extrapolated to industries where success is less likely. To the extent that the claims are believed and the results occur with a lag, one might expect overshooting, so that reforms occur where they should not or in arrangements that are not viable (as with the California electricity reforms). The conundrum about the less successful examples is not so much that efficiency gains were absent but rather that the formerly dominant interest groups allowed large rent transfers at their expense. This is explainable only by their loss of political power or a total misjudgment on their part. The former is plausible but does not seem to be the correct reason. First, the losing incumbents in the unsuccessful reforms did not substantially oppose the reforms, as shown by the fact that the California electricity restructuring and the 1996 Telecommunications Act passed essentially unopposed. However, the incumbents agreed only because the reforms were adapted to their perceived needs.[14] This made the reforms exceedingly complicated and opaque. Second, the Supreme Court has been a protector of regulatory assets under rate-of-return regulation.[15] So in my view, the electric utilities and Bell operating companies voluntarily agreed to these reforms but made a big mistake in doing so.

The same kind of euphoria is expressed in the California (and other) electricity reform as in the 1996 Telecom Act. Both promised consumers large benefits from competition while shielding them (for example, by guaranteed prices) from the risks (Kahn 2001). Such euphoria may be necessary to get big reforms started. However, the net efficiency benefits of reforms vary and are not high on average. This implies that care is needed for reforms, and type I and type II errors have to be assessed in detail, where the problem of evaluation lies in establishing a proper counterfactual.

The two main failures, local telephony and California electricity, have in common that retail competition has not been developing, but the reasons are quite different. In the case of local telephony, the local loops as remaining bottlenecks hinder competition, even if loops can be rented from the incumbents. In the California electricity market, it was the artificially low regulated price for the incumbent's services (although that holds to some extent for local telephony as well). The standard offer, along with natural advantages for large users, seemed to guarantee a Pareto improvement, expressed by unanimity in California legislature, with which electricity reform was passed. As with the U.S. Telecommunications Act of 1996, unanimity seems to be a weakness rather than the strength of a piece of legislation because it hints at excessive compromise. The two examples of failures also have in common that the propaganda of reform (the potential entrants) had predicted strong competitive inroads. Such predictions were emphasized by the entrants and not contradicted by the incumbents, leading to a lack of precautions against the effects of forecasting errors.

New entrants have to overcome large hurdles against well-known incumbents with valuable brand names and service reputation. A major problem with the introduction of any retail competition in hitherto monopolistic network industries is that entrants have to overcome switching costs and customer inertia. They therefore need to have either substantially lower costs than the incumbent or face an incumbent's prices that are substantially above its costs. In general in the network industries, the latter seems to be a common phenomenon associated with (often politically motivated) cross-subsidization. In that sense, selective competition gets a head start, as long as incumbents do not respond quickly with price restructuring. Such restructuring, however, is often prevented by regulators or not in the interest of incumbents, which fear goodwill losses from the accompanying price increases. The rigidity of past regulatory pricing has led to a cross-subsidization trap, because regulated monopolists need not change politically popular price structures in response to cost changes. While cross-subsidization creates and maintains powerful interest groups backing the status quo, it also plants the seeds for competition in the form of cream skimming. This seed grows particularly strong if the new technologies lack the strong natural monopoly properties of the old ones, as has happened in long-distance telephony.

The discrepancy between (current) regulated prices and prices envisaged under competition leads to stranded costs, due to overinvestment or investment in inefficient technology and long-term contracts. The reforms start by concentrating on forward-looking costs of new entrants as compared to full historic costs of incumbents and largely neglect that the forward-looking costs of incumbents (because of large sunk-cost elements) are often even lower. When the reform threat becomes real, the incumbents claim stranded costs from past investment, the recovery of which has often been granted in exchange for their agreement to liberalization. Incumbents have such power because they incurred investments in the stranded assets under a rate-of-return regulated regime that entitled them to the expectation of a fair rate of return on the assets. The expected cost reductions from such liberalization are then attributed to liberalization rather than to bad bookkeeping. Network utility reforms are shaped by two seemingly opposing forces: competition, along with liberalization and regulatory persistence. Once the nose of the camel (competition) is in the tent, the whole camel follows (Hogan 2001). In contrast, regulators rarely let go.[16] Full deregulation has occurred only in competitive industries (telephone equipment, trucking, and airlines); in industries with dominant suppliers and natural monopoly characteristics, regulation continues and is influenced by redistributive policies. Those are enhanced by the ability to hide costs and burdens in the regulatory process, while calling it deregulation (Crew and Kleindorfer 2001). Deregulation and liberalization are separate issues, independent of privatization. Thus, deregulation may follow the liberalization process, but it is not an inevitable and definitely not a short-term outcome.

Asymmetric regulation is a widespread consequence of sector reforms that have not led to full deregulation. This regulation comes in two forms. First, bottleneck regulation of access to and interconnection with the incumbent's network enhances the feasibility of competition. Second, end user regulation curbs the incumbent's remaining market power in relation to end users. In both the telecommunications and the electricity industries, end user regulation is now entirely in the hands of state regulators, while bottleneck regulation is shared between federal and state regulators. Since state regulators often pursue social objectives with end user regulation, the resulting prices can be in conflict with competitive objectives pursued by federal regulators. In telecommunications, the 1996 Telecom Act forced many state regulators to accept local competition, but they can still counteract the consequences by continuing cross-subsidized end user prices. In electricity, the California crisis has exposed the most blatant contradictions between such regulated end user prices and competition.

Asymmetric regulation, while necessary, creates problems of equity and efficiency. A problem with all regulatory reforms with the exception of full deregulation is that they increase the regulatory uncertainty perceived by a Bayesian investor. In particular, incentives for investment by incumbents are usually dampened, while investment incentives for entrants can be dampened if bottleneck inputs are provided too cheaply. At the same time, the investment incentives become excessive in the nonbottleneck areas. Whether this type of regulation has had any influence on the current telecommunications sector crisis with excess capacities in fiber optics is an open question.[17] In the United States the problem with end user regulation is exacerbated by the fact that it is largely controlled by state PUCs, which want to maintain the traditional patterns of cross-subsidies in spite of liberalization. This holds particularly for residential electricity and local telephony. The influence of state regulation is therefore decidedly mixed in accelerating and retarding reform. Acceleration occurs through "progressive" PUCs (with much to gain from competition); delay occurs through lack of uniformity in solving an issue that requires nationwide change (rate rebalancing for Bell system).

Performance-based regulation has increased pricing flexibility in some areas and thereby been conducive to liberalization if only as a concession to make incumbents willing to accept sector reforms. The impact of amending or replacing rate-of-return regulation by incentive regulation (price caps) is somewhat similar to privatization in the British sense: both increase short-term efficiency incentives. However, both rate-of-return regulation and public enterprises had been commitment devices against expropriation and therefore have shielded sunk, lumpy investments (Newbery 2000). The 1970s and 1980s showed that both devices no longer worked. Rate-of-return regulation prevented innovative investment and was associated with the nuclear cost overruns, while public ownership dried up investments in British Telecom. The further problem with U.S.-style rate-of-return regulation is that it is not compatible with competition because it reduces the incumbent's cost-reducing incentives and its pricing flexibility.

2.3.3 Conclusions on Explanations

Reforms have occurred largely because of price rigidities under regulation. Prices became out of line with costs because of political will and because of market changes occurring through innovations, swings in world market prices, new environmental regulation, and the like. Since reforms have to overcome the opposition of former beneficiaries, they occur only with a lag. Once successful reforms occur, the former rent transfers are revealed. This makes potential competitors look for similar situations in other industries or industry segments. Reforms then become contagious. The reforms were staggered because the underlying reasons date at different times. Tipping toward reforms usually occurs when competitive pressures of actual and potential entrants become sufficiently high. This pressure makes it impossible for incumbents and other beneficiaries of the past to claim that there were no implicit rent transfers. Reforms fail because early successful reforms have raised expectations about what competition can achieve. The successful reforms have increased the political value of favoring competition. This leads to the political belief in future reform success and the willingness to enter into compromises that win over otherwise losing groups of the reforms. A strong example is the standard offer to residential customers in the failed California electricity reform. In the cases of failed reforms, the hurdles may be too high to achieve competition, and that combines well with the inability of regulators to let go. It also appears that the failed reform cases did quite badly in their application of performance-based regulation.

2.4   Conclusions: The New Learning?

2.4.1   Learning for the United States

Only a few years ago, a chapter on sector reform in U.S. network utilities would have looked different and would have come to entirely different and substantially more optimistic conclusions. In this assessment, I may have become victim of the very cognitive biases that I accuse policymakers of. However, the past few years provide crucial data points for Bayesian updating.

What lessons can be learned from the U.S. experience in avoiding mistakes and going for successes? Since (with the possible exception of postal services) there are no further network industries to be reformed, the advice can be directed only at improvements in the already reformed industries. By now, it is clear that new reforms will be approached more carefully for some time. In the U.S. electricity industry, the restructuring in a number of states has been postponed or scrapped. Those in which reforms took place will now have to show long-term benefits before others are going to follow.

Is total deregulation the answer to failed reforms, as some authors like Crandall (1999) suggest? It may well be. The question, however, is, "When and where?" Since successful reforms have been associated with deregulation, one might be tempted to suggest deregulation as a solution to reform problems or as a way to avoid such problems altogether. Benefits from total deregulation include an obvious simplicity and a lack of mistakes from contradictions in a reform packet. They also potentially include the commitment power of deregulation. However, the short-term irreversibility is also the greatest danger because total deregulation will work only if competition is either sustainable from the beginning or if its emergence over time cannot be prevented by the incumbent (or if there are no rents, such as in U.S. railroads). It is obvious that competition worked in the successful reform cases. How can one know that it will work in others? Normatively one could suggest a two-step procedure. If competitive pressure emerges, one should liberalize while simultaneously eliminating regulatory distortions. The problem with this suggestion is the positive issue that regulatory distortions benefit certain groups that would not give them up without fight. Making the implied subsidies explicit is rarely going to help because the benefiting groups would not get the necessary political support once it is clear that they receive these benefits. Thus, it appears that competition is the necessary discovery process for regulatory distortions as well as efficiency enhancing in its own right. As the economic theory of regulation has brought out, wealth distribution is more important for understanding economic policies than efficiencies. The proper place for efficiency is to aid distributional policies. While voters behave with reasonable rationality, the outcomes can be quite inefficient. Part of this is due to lack of information by all parties and asymmetric information. Competitive pressure exerted on a regulated monopolist reveals otherwise hidden rents that are captured by winning interest groups. Once this occurs, the paying groups no longer remain passive and put their political weight against the old regulatory regime. Thus, although efficiency in the traditional economic sense may not be improved by the resulting reforms, the political efficiency will be.

2.4.2   Lessons for Other Countries

Lessons for other countries could be learned from institutional setups or from the specific policies and problem solutions. On the institutional side, the United States has a long tradition of two-level regulation by federal and state commission. This setup could provide lessons for the relationship between the European Commission and national regulatory authorities (NRAs) in Europe. Considering the more recent performance of U.S. regulatory reform in telecommunications and electricity, however, makes one wonder if U.S.-style regulation would carry advantages for Europe. Clearly, the U.S. approach has, over a long time, demonstrated substantial adaptability to new situations without requiring major new legislation. In a way, regulatory innovations are endogenous to the system. However, this changed with the exogenous 1996 Telecom Act and with state legislations to restructure electricity sectors. With the 1996 Telecom Act, U.S. telecommunications regulation at least partially moved from the old separations model of regulation to a new delegations model. Under the separations model, the division of labor was based on the geography of interstate versus intrastate commerce. This led to cost separations and other policies that created or maintained cross-subsidization and was not compatible with competition and liberalization. In the electricity sector, state-induced restructuring created competition and, from the perspective of state regulators, involuntary shifts in responsibility from state PUCs to the FERC. Since these changes, the authority of federal regulators and the relationship between federal and state regulators have suffered, suggesting that it takes a long time before the regulatory and legal procedures reach a new equilibrium. For some time, this has reduced the commitment power necessary for credible regulation.

The U.S. regulatory system is quite unsystematic when it comes to the coordination of problem areas with different regulatory histories. This becomes particularly clear when comparing the EU Telecommunications Directives with the U.S. telecommunications policies. The EU Telecommunications Directives set clear and common standards for the prerequisites of regulation for all parts of the telecommunications sector. They are based on the definition of relevant markets and the persistence of market dominance. The definition of markets and the analysis of market dominance are left to NRAs, which also determine the remedy should regulation be required. The EU Commission keeps the right to veto NRA decisions on market definitions, market analysis, and remedies against the adverse consequences of market dominance. However, it does not act as a regulator. The EU model is therefore based much more on delegation than on separation. Although the resulting outcomes are likely to be quite similar, the United States gets there through a very different process. As Marcus (2002) has pointed out, the European approach is logical and elegant. That does not mean it is superior to U.S. regulation. At the same time, recent history puts doubt on the superiority of the U.S. regulatory approach. In such a situation, it becomes important to recognize that a wholesale adoption of the U.S. approach would be impossible for Europe. The main distinguishing features of the U.S. regulation are (1) distinct regulatory authority at the federal and state levels, (2) the possibility for federal preemption of state regulation, (3) a broad regulatory mandate for the federal regulator, and (4) strong implementable rules for the legality of the regulatory process. It is hard to see how another country could hope to mimic the U.S. regulatory system by successfully copying one of these distinguishing features without also copying the rest (Vogelsang 1994).

Concerning policies and problem solutions, many of the network industries in other countries face problems that are similar to those of the United States. Those foreign industries that have not been reformed yet might learn from the U.S. experience. Since most countries with a comparable institutional, geographic, and economic endowment already have reformed their network utilities, they may only be able to learn for future adjustments and reforms of reforms.

In some cases, other countries have done better and have better prospects than the United States. A California electricity disaster is unlikely to happen anywhere else. The prospects for competition in local telephony are not much brighter elsewhere than in the United States, but that seems to be the nature of the beast. Generally European countries seem to have less distorted local telephone charges and less extreme universal service policies than the United States (Cherry and Bauer 2002). Compared to the United States, this would improve prospects for unbiased competition, although geographic rebalancing is still way off.

One major learning is not to expect Pareto improvements from reform. Rather, there will be winners and losers. This will make reforms that do not benefit the dominating interest groups politically more difficult. In that respect, privatization in the British sense provides an additional instrument because the sale price for the public enterprise can be used to benefit otherwise losing groups. A major problem, however, is that the one-time opportunity of privatization has already occurred in most cases.

While privatization allows a clean slate, vertical separation or horizontal divestiture—although each would often be beneficial—is difficult to achieve with it. Separation requires enough time, cooperation of management, and market values for the firm's assets.

The U.S reform examples and their discussion yielded some answers to my initial question about sector crises. The crises should influence our approach to current and future reforms. In particular, imitating U.S. regulatory reforms may appear less warranted for other countries than it was just a few years ago.

Notes

1. Some sale of public enterprises has occurred in the U.S. railroad industry (Conrail, which was nationalized in the early 1970s to save it from the Penn Central bankruptcy), and some municipal electric utilities have been sold. In contrast, some public enterprises have expanded, when municipal utilities moved into telecommunications.

2. Bortollotti et al. (2002) provide evidence that regulatory changes are more important than ownership changes in explaining the performance of restructured telecommunications sectors.

3. The other main basis for the suit was the vertical problem of equipment manufacturing. The name *Modified Final Judgment* resulted, because it legally was drawn up as a modification of AT&T's 1956 consent decree.

4. For the history of this local competition, see Vogelsang and Mitchell (1997).

5. As done in official statistics, we treat broadband access as separate from local telecommunications. Broadband access is characterized by intermodal competition, with cable TV companies having over 60 percent of the market and incumbent local exchange companies about 30 percent, competitive local exchange companies about 3 percent, and satellite TV the rest.

6. Collocation means that competitors can locate their own equipment in the switching offices of the incumbent and thereby interconnect more directly, for example, before a call reaches the incumbent's switch.

7. This work culminated in Schweppe et al. (1988) and Hogan (1992).

8. This adverse selection problem of hit-and-run entry is worth further study. It can be resolved by back-to-back contracts so that end users interested in stable prices would have to commit to long-term contracts as a condition for load-serving entities to sign long-term contracts with generators.

9. Vertical separation provides market estimates for stranded costs (Kahn 2001).

10. In fact, San Diego Gas and Electric, the smallest of the three main IOUs, managed to pay back its stranded costs in time to escape the standard offer price in 2000, only to find out that its severe price increases were revoked by the California regulators.

11. This ignores earlier bad U.S. experience with price moratoria analyzed in Isaac (1991).

12. The breakup of AT&T was additionally triggered by its desire to get into other markets, such as the computer business (in which it failed miserably).

13. For a discussion of other possible explanations, see Vogelsang (1994).

14. Barbara Cherry (personal communication to the author, November 17, 2001) stated that interest groups concentrate on their perceived most important items of a reform and neglect others that may turn out to be important.

15. Sidak and Spulber (1997) question this under the heading of "deregulatory takings."

16. This is the tar baby effect claimed by Kahn (2001). It is based on McKie (1970) and, to some extent, Owen and Braeutigam (1978).

17. Favoring this view are Hausman and Sidak (forthcoming).

References

Allaz, B., and Vila, J. L. 1993. "Cournot Competition, Forward Markets and Efficiency." *Journal of Economic Theory* 59, 1–16.

ALTS. 2003. "The State of Local Competition 2003." Association for Local Telecommunications Services, April. http://www.alts.org.

Armstrong, Mark, Cowan, Simon, and Vickers, John. 1994. *Regulatory Reform: Economic Analysis and British Experience*. Cambridge, Mass.: MIT Press.

Blumstein, Carl, Friedman, L. S., and Green, Richard J. 2002. "The History of Electricity Restructuring in California." Working paper CSEM WP 103, University of California Energy Institute, August.

Borenstein, Severin. 2002. "The Trouble with Electricity Markets and California's Electricity Restructuring Disaster." *Journal of Economic Perspectives* 16(1), 191–211.

Borenstein, Severin, Bushnell, James B., and Wolak, Frank A. 2002. "Measuring Market Inefficiencies in California's Restructured Wholesale Electricity Market." *American Economic Review* 92(5), 1376–1405.

Bortolloti, Bernardo, D'Souza, Juliet, Fantini, Marcella, and Megginson, William L. 2002. "Privatization and the Sources of Performance Improvement in the Global Telecommunications Industry." *Telecommunications Policy* 26, 243–268.

Cherry, Barbara A., and Bauer, Johannes M. 2002. "Institutional Arrangements and Price Rebalancing: Empirical Evidence from the United States and Europe." *Information Economics and Policy* 14, 495–517.

Crandall, Robert W. 1999. "Managed Competition in U.S. Telecommunications." Working paper no. 99-1, AEI-Brookings Joint Center for Regulatory Studies, Washington, D.C., March.

Crew, Michael A., and Kleindorfer, Paul. 2001. "Regulatory Economics: Twenty Years of Progress?" *Journal of Regulatory Economics* 21(1), 5–22.

Economides, Nicholas. 2003. "Telecommunications Regulation: An Introduction." New York: Stern School of Business, New York University, ⟨http://papers.ssrn.com/paper.taf?abstract_id=465020⟩.

Faulhaber, Gerald. 2002. "Bottlenecks and Bandwagons: Access Policy in the New Telecommunications." In Martin E. Cave, Sumit K. Majumdar, and Ingo Vogelsang, eds., *Handbook of Telecommunications Economics*. Amsterdam: North Holland/Elsevier.

Ford, Andrew. 2001. "Waiting for the Boom: A Simulation Study of Power Plant Construction in California." Mimeo. Program in Environmental Science and Regional Planning, Washington State University.

Hausman, Jerry A., and Sidak, J. Gregory. Forthcoming. *The Breakdown in the Telecommunications Industry under Deregulation: The Failure of Good Intentions*. Cambridge: Cambridge University Press.

Hogan, William W. 1992. "Contract Networks for Electric Power Transmission." *Journal of Regulatory Economics* 4, 211–242.

Hogan, William W. 2001. "Electricity Restructuring: Reform of Reforms." *Journal of Regulatory Economics* 21(1), 103–132.

Isaac, Mark R. 1991. "Price Cap Regulation: A Case Study of Some Pitfalls of Implementation." *Journal of Regulatory Economics* 3, 193–210.

Joskow, Paul L. 2001. "California's Electricity Crisis." *Oxford Review of Economic Policy* 17(3), 365–388.

Joskow, Paul L., and Schmalensee, Richard. 1983. *Markets for Power*. Cambridge, Mass.: MIT Press.

Kahn, Alfred E. 2001. "The Deregulation Tar Baby: The Precarious Balance between Regulation and Deregulation, 1970–2000 and Henceforward." *Journal of Regulatory Economics* 21(1), 35–56.

Kaserman, David L., and Mayo, John W. 2002. "Competition in the Long Distance Market." In Martin E. Cave, Sumit K. Majumdar, and Ingo Vogelsang, eds., *Handbook of Telecommunications Economics*. Amsterdam: North Holland/Elsevier.

MacAvoy, Paul. 1996. *The Failure of Antitrust and Regulation to Establish Competition in Long-Distance Telephone Services*. Cambridge, Mass., and Washington, D.C.: MIT Press and AEI Press.

Marcus, J. Scott. 2002. "The Potential Relevance to the United States of the European Union's Newly Adopted Regulatory Framework for Telecommunications." OSP working paper no. 36, Office of Strategic Planning and Policy Analysis, Federal Communications Commission.

McKie, James W. 1970. "Regulation and Free Markets: The Problem of Boundaries." *Bell Journal of Economics and Management Science* 1, 6–26.

Newbery, David M. 2000. *Privatization, Restructuring, and Regulation of Network Industries*. Cambridge, Mass.: MIT Press.

Owen, Bruce M., and Braeutigam, Ronald. 1978. *The Regulation Game: Strategic Use of the Administrative Process*. Cambridge, Mass.: Ballinger.

Phillips, Almarin. 2002. "What It Was Like, What Happened, and What It's Like Now: Developments in Telecommunications over Recent Decades." *Journal of Regulatory Economics* 21(1), 57–78.

Rohlfs, Jeffrey. 2001. *Bandwagon Effects in High-Technology Industries*. Cambridge, Mass.: MIT Press.

Schweppe, Fred, Caramanis, Michael, Tabors, Richard, and Bohn, Robert. 1988. *Spot Pricing of Electricity*. New York: Kluwer.

Sidak, J. Gregory, and Spulber, Daniel F. 1997. *Deregulatory Takings and the Regulatory Contract: The Competitive Transformation of Network Industries in the United States*. Cambridge: Cambridge University Press.

Sutherland, Roy. 2003. "Estimating the Benefits of Restructuring Electricity Markets: An Application to the PJM Region." Center for the Advancement of Energy Markets, September. ⟨http://www.caem.org⟩.

Vogelsang, Ingo. 1987. "The Role of Contracts in International Coal Trade." In D. Wood, ed., *The Changing World Energy Economy*. Papers and Proceedings of the Eighth Annual North American Conference of the International Association of Energy Economists, MIT, November 19–21, 1986, May 1987, pp. 264–269.

Vogelsang, Ingo. 1994. "Federal Versus State Regulation in U.S. Telecommunications." Wissenschaftliches Institut für Kommunikationsdienste, discussion paper no. 134.

Vogelsang, Ingo. 2003. "The German Telecommunications Reform—Where Did It Come From, Where Is It, and Where Is It Going?" *Perspektiven der Wirtschaftspolitik* 4(3), 313–340.

Vogelsang, Ingo, and Mitchell, Bridger M. 1997. *Telecommunications Competition: The Last 10 Miles.* Cambridge, Mass., and Washington, D.C.: MIT Press and AEI Press.

Watkiss, Jeffrey D., and Smith, Douglas W. 1993. "The Energy Policy Act of 1993—A Watershed for Competition in the Wholesale Power Market." *Yale Journal on Regulation* 10, 447–492.

Wilson, Robert. 2002. "Architecture of Power Markets." *Econometrica* 70(4), 1299–1340.

Wolfram, Catherine. 2003. "How Might Restructuring Affect the Efficiency of Electricity Generation in the U.S.?" CSEM working paper, University of California Energy Institute, Berkeley, April.

II

European Experiences

3   Privatization in Austria: Some Theoretical Reasons and Performance Measures

Ansgar Belke and Friedrich Schneider

Privatization has been a key element of structural policy reforms in most European Union countries including Austria during the past decade. Governments undertaking privatization have pursued a variety of objectives: achieving gains in economic efficiency, given the extensive prevalence of poor economic performance of public enterprises in many countries and limited success with their reform; and improving their fiscal position, particularly when governments have been unwilling or unable to continue to finance deficits in the public enterprise sector. In addition, budgetary-constrained governments facing fiscal pressures have sometimes privatized mainly to finance fiscal deficits with the privatization proceeds.

The issues of privatization (and sometimes deregulation) have been reviewed in a large literature that has emphasized its potential efficiency gains.[1] Hence, we provide some theoretical reasoning as to why privatization is useful as well as profitable for an economy, and empirically present the extent of privatization in Austria and other European Union countries. In order to assess the impact of privatization in Austria on economic performance, we observe cash flows, the employment performance, and the stock exchange ratings of the privatized formerly state-owned enterprises.[2]

3.1   Reasons for Privatizing Public Enterprises

For at least a century, economists have employed economic theory to explore the implications of profit maximization by private firms operating in private property contexts. Only since the late 1960s have empirical studies been undertaken dealing with the behavior of publicly operated firms.[3] Since then, a large number of studies on the activities of public or private enterprises have focused on how public firms differ from their private equivalents.

Basically they use two approaches. One is the property rights approach, which concentrates on the differences in the ease of capturing the economic surplus of a resource and the rights to direct an asset's use—alter its claims from or transfer its claims among existent and potential owners. This approach explores the differences in incentives between public and private agencies caused by variation in the ability of owners to monitor management and the problems that emerge when the goals of "owners" and their agents, "managers," diverge.[4] Numerous studies have tested this proposition and found that public enterprises are less efficient than private ones.[5] The second approach, called the *public choice approach*, concentrates on political coalitions and their effect on input usage and reward or product characteristics (or both). The public choice approach, which also includes the theory of bureaucracy (Niskanen 1971, 1975), appears to provide a broader analysis than the property rights approach. It assumes that politicians, bureaucrats, and managers of public enterprises are selfish utility maximizers subject to constraints.[6] In this approach, it is assumed for a politician, for example, that he acts selfishly in order to reach his ideological or personal goals under the constraint not to lose the next election. Since staying in power is the most important constraint (or even sometimes a goal) for a politician, he will also use public utilities for his own selfish goals.

3.2   Privatization in Austria

3.2.1   *Privatization in Small, Open Economies*

Table 3.1 shows that the amount of privatization in eleven small, open economies in Europe was quite moderate at the beginning of the 1990s, with the exception of Belgium. The Belgium government privatized public utilities in 1993 and received proceeds of U.S.$956 million, roughly 30 percent of all privatization proceeds of the economies in table 3.1 and figure 3.1. The second highest privatization proceeds in 1993 were in the Netherlands with U.S.$780 million, followed by Portugal, which had a quite ambitious privatization program over the years 1993–1998, with privatization proceeds over U.S.$12 billion between 1993 and 1998. A number of well-known public utilities in Portugal, including the power plant EDP, the highway system BRISA,

Table 3.1
Privatization proceeds in small, open economies, 1993, 1995, 1997, 1998, and 2000

Privatization proceeds in small open economies

Country	1993 $ million	in % of total	Rank	1995 $ million	in % of total	Rank	1997 $ million	in % of total	Rank	1998 $ million	in % of total	Rank	2000 $ million	in % of total	Rank
Austria	142	4	7	1.035	9	4	2.020	17	2	2.935	12	5	2.083	11	3
Belgium	956	29	1	2.681	22	2	1.562	13	3	1.467	6	7	—	—	—
Denmark	122	4	8	10	0	9	45	0.5	8	4.502	18	2	111	1	8
Finland	229	7	6	363	3	7	835	7	5	1.999	8	6	1.827	10	4
Ireland	274	8	4	157	1	8	293	3	7	4.864	19	1	1.458	8	5
Island	10	0	9	6	0	10	4	0	10	129	0.5	10	—	—	—
Netherlands	780	24	2	3.993	33	1	831	7	6	335	0.5	9	310	2	7
Norway	—	—	—	521	4	6	35	0.5	9	28	0	11	1.039	6	6
Portugal	500	15	3	2.425	20	3	4.968	43	1	4.271	17	4	3.256	18	2
Sweden	252	8	5	852	7	5	1.055	9	4	172	1	8	8.082	44	1
Switzerland	—	—	—	—	—	—	—	—	—	4.426	18	3	—	—	—
Total	3,265	100		12,043	100		11,648	100		25,128	100		18,166	100	

Source: Own calculations with Belke and Schneider (2004, table 3.2).
Note: — = Null or insignificant.

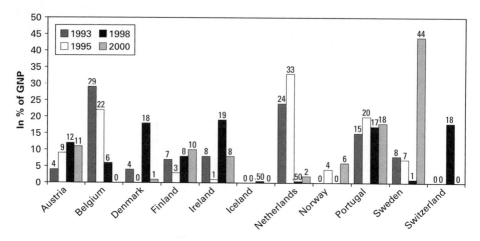

Figure 3.1
Privatization proceeds in percentage of GNP in small, open economies, 1993, 1995, 1998, and 2000 (current prices and exchange rates)

and cement factories ZINPOR, have been privatized. In Austria privatization proceeds also have been quite large. In 1998 the Austrian government privatized firms with proceeds of U.S.$2.94 billion. In Austria, the sale of a 25 percent share of the public telecom was the biggest deal, with proceeds of U.S.$2.33 billion. Starting at rank 7 in 1993, Austria steadily improved its performance in percentage of total privatization proceeds in small, open economies, peaking in 1997, and at the end of the sample, ranked third out of eleven of these economies. However, one should not overemphasize this pattern, since in general, the amount of privatization proceeds in small, open economies increased between 1993 and 1998. In 1993 proceeds reached U.S.$3.26 billion and in 1998 U.S.$20.246 billion.

Figure 3.1 shows the privatization proceeds of these economies in relation to GNP. The dominant position of Portugal over time is clear, followed by the Netherlands and Belgium, which display enormous privatization proceeds in 1993 and 1995. In Austria, the privatization proceeds as a percentage of GDP over the years are the average of the economies under consideration. However, we detect no systematic correlation between the degree of openness of an economy and its privatization intensity. In general, this makes external impacts on the speed and intensity of privatization less plausible.

However, we will show in section 3.3 that this was not the case for Austria. At most, the announcement of the launch of the euro seems to have hastened the privatization wave in Europe. In general, privatization and the proceeds from privatization were a considerable and policy-relevant issue in the 1990s for the small, open economies.

3.2.2   Privatization in Austria

Among industrialized countries now awaiting further privatization, Austria is characterized by historically strong government interventions. Large parts of the manufacturing and the electricity sector were nationalized after World War II, in part to safeguard the country's economic independence after German occupation and in part to finance the reconstruction of destroyed large-scale industries. Jointly with public ownership in telecommunication, transport, and banking, this generated one of the largest public sectors in Europe.[7]

As a whole, Austria's economy has been characterized by a relatively important state-owned industry, a lack of capital funds due to the comparatively small company size, and a predominantly bank-based investment system. In 1998, Austria had a 17 percent market capitalization relative to GDP, an even lower valuation ratio than Italy (30 percent) and Germany (39 percent) (Boutchkova and Megginson 2000). The globalization and Austria's accession to the EU have revealed structural problems in this system. Those sectors of the Austrian economy protected from international competition, like telecommunication, energy supply, and food industries, had to be integrated in the internal market. As a consequence, restructuring programs have recently been launched focusing on liberalizing and privatizing Austria's economy. In addition, joining the European Union represented a structural break for Austria with respect to the incentives to delay necessary deregulation and privatization because it was now much less attractive to use public utilities and industries for reelection purposes.[8]

The Austro-Keynesian era of stabilization policy, which lasted from the beginning of the 1970s to the mid-1980s, can be viewed as an attempt of direct employment policy in public utilities and the public industrial sector, mainly in the basic (e.g., steel) machinery and chemical industries. In a sense, relatively large budget deficits and a continuously increasing debt-to-GDP ratio have often been excused in the past by pointing to the fight against unemployment. The primary goal of this type of short-term policy in private goods markets was to stabilize employment and real income in the nationalized industry and, by means of the Austria-specific interindustrial relations and the multiplier process, in the private sector as well. To achieve this political target, various steps were taken by the public management: the maintenance of the greatest possible level of production in the face of diminishing prices and demand; the greatest possible hoarding of employees even when rationalization measures (dismissals) were required (resulting in unemployment on the job); an overdimensioned propensity to invest (primarily with regard to the income effect of investment); an expansionist wage and fringe benefits policy with respect to buying power (causing high labor costs); and the financing of firms' deficits out of the federal budget.

With regard to the social and reelection problems arising from unemployment and low incomes, the direct employment policy in public industrial firms intended to smooth the inevitable adjustment process to the rising requirements of global competitiveness in the long run. This stabilization policy immediately had substantial effects on the public industrial firms' productivity, thriftiness, and profitability, thus reducing international competitiveness and augmenting deficits in the short run (Nowotny 1982). Nonetheless, production and employment could not be maintained permanently at a high level, because the rationalization measures could not be postponed any longer. Since the mid-1980s, the Austro-Keynesian stabilization policy has been increasingly criticized for its long-term efficacy. Finally, the troubling rise of the financial losses of state-owned firms in the iron and steel, chemical, machinery, and vehicle industries caused a shift in public opinion and economic policy. The amounts of subsidies to public industrial firms covering deficits and financing investment were limited to a fixed total and to the period until 1989. This change of policy emerged when the government realized that due to the critique of the opposition, mass media, and private entrepreneurs, as well as the public's fear of tax increases, a majority of voters would no longer tolerate subsidies to public industrial firms. In this sense, the repercussion from the voter to the government worked quite well in Austria. Prior to this change, politicians had formed coalitions with the management of the relatively big and locally concentrated public firms in order to secure the subsidies that rendered inefficiencies possible and served local constituencies. Moreover, there have been powerful shop stewards who at the same time were members of the legislating National Council and succeeded in financing the expansionist enterprise policy out of the federal budget.

At the end of the 1980s, there was a turnaround in the Austrian policy with respect to the public industrial sector and public utilities. A considerable privatization took place in the 1990s, and enterprises were used much less for reelection purposes, partly due to the fact that after joining the European Union and the deregulation of former monopolies into competitive markets, it was much less attractive to use public utilities and industries for reelection purposes. Between 1993 and 1998 the privatization of Austrian state-owned industrial firms and state-owned utilities reached over U.S.$6 billion (Belke and Schneider 2004). These dramatic changes in Austrian policies gained momentum in the middle of the 1990s; some authors even speak of "New Austrian public policies" (Clemenz 1999, p. 1). Although substantial privatization took place, the privatization potential in Austria remains quite large. In most cases, the Austrian government kept substantial shares of partly privatized enterprises. Considering the federal, state, and community levels and including all public utilities, there is a privatization potential of 45 billion euros, from which the federal government owns 62 percent, the city or state of Vienna 13 percent, all other states (e.g., Upper and Lower Austria) 14 percent, and the communes (without Vienna) 11 percent. The privatization proceeds of the federal government, from 1999 to 2001, are presented in table 3.2.

Table 3.2
Privatization proceeds in Austria (federal government), 1999–2001

Year	Public enterprise	Proceeds (millions of euros)
1999	Privatization of 9.4% of the Austrian Tobacco AG	6.8
2000	100% PSK (Postal Bank)	969.5
	24.4% Telecom (to Telecom Italia)	763.8
	100% State Printing Office	2.2
		1,742.3
2001	17.38% Airport Vienna AG	54.1
	41.1% Austrian Tobacco AG	582.2
	100% Dorotheum	55.6
	100% Strohal Rotary Printing	21.1
		713.0
Sum	**1999–2001**	**2,455.3**

Source: Ministry of Economic Affairs (2002).
Note: These are the most recent available figures.

In 1999, 9.4 percent of the Austrian tobacco industry was privatized, which brought 6.8 billion euros. On February 28, 2000, the Austrian federal government authorized the minister of finance to issue the privatization mandate to the Österreichische Industrieholding AG (OeIAG), the Republic of Austria's holding and privatization agency, at the annual general meeting on May 17, 2000. In accordance with the mandate, OeIAG was required to transfer 100 percent of the following companies or interests in companies to completely new shareholders, strategic partners, or the general public: Österreichische Staatsdruckerei GmbH, Dorotheum GmbH, Print Media Austria AG, Flughafen Wien AG, Österreichische Postsparkasse AG, Telekom Austria AG, and Austria Tabak AG.

In carrying out this privatization mandate in the interest of the Austrian people, the OeIAG had to "obtain the maximum revenue possible, taking into consideration the companies' and Austria's interests" (OeIAG 2003). It is important to note that the OeIAG depends on rulings issued by the Republic of Austria. A second phase envisaged at that time involves examining the possibility of even further privatization. In the meantime, the OeIAG has already privatized more companies or parts of companies, including Österreichische Staatsdruckerei GmbH, Dorotheum GmbH, Flughafen Wien AG (17.4 percent), Österreichische Postsparkasse AG, Austria Tabak AG, Print Media Austria AG, and Telekom Austria in compliance with the privatization mandate of the federal government. In 2000, 100 percent of the postal bank was privatized, with proceeds of 970 million euros. Also 24 percent of the state-owned telecom utility was privatized in an initial public offering, with proceeds of 763 million euros. In sum, in 2000, 1.742 million euros of privatization proceeds were achieved. The next year, 41.1 percent of the Austrian tobacco state-owned utility was privatized, which brought proceeds of 582.2 million euros. In sum, from 1999 to 2001, 2.455 billion euros of privatization proceeds were achieved. This sizable sum helped the Austrian government reduce the federal debt. Some Austria-specific features deserve significantly more attention.[9]

3.2.3 *Backlogs of Privatization and Their Elimination by the Recent Center-Right Coalition*

Observers often claim significant backlogs of privatization in Austria. One example is the privatization of the two largest Austrian banks, which became a long-lasting and cumbersome process from 1987 on.

The problem was mainly due to political quarrels and arguments of the usual "too-big-to-fail" kind and by itself would justify a separate public choice analysis (Aiginger 1999, Belke 2000, EIRO 2002).[10] However, privatization gained momentum under Austria's center-right coalition government, which came into power in February 2000, and was mainly intended to help to balance the budget (the so-called Austrian Null-Defizit target). We take this episode as evidence in favor of the hypothesis that the democratic repercussions from voters who fear tax increases if privatization is postponed any longer to the government functions in Austria today as well as in the past. Hence, one necessary condition for the emergence of politically motivated privatization cycles is still given, especially in Austria. Obviously, the new government, including the FPÖ, has initiated a comprehensive reform process, including extensive privatization. It claims that Austria has successfully privatized the majority of its large manufacturing firms and will continue privatization in order to consolidate the budget. Following the successful sales of the postal savings bank, Oesterreichische Postsparkasse AG (PSK), to the banking group BAWAG, and of stakes in the Vienna airport, Vienna's famous auction house (the Dorotheum), and cigarette manufacturer Austria Tabak to Gallagher Group of the United Kingdom, and the privatization of all hospitals in Upper Austria in 2001, further privatization in 2002 was hoped to be successful. The biggest Austrian privatization in history was the sale of Telekom Austria to Telecom Italia for 1.979 billion for a 25 percent minority holding. A fourth mobile license was sold to Germany's Telekom Service GmbH & Co. KG for 98 million.

The accuracy of our diagnosis of significant backlogs in the Austrian process of privatization is underscored by a study confirming that the German civil law tradition negatively affects the probability of privatization. Bortolotti, Fantini, and Siniscalco (2001) cannot reject empirically the hypothesis that countries like Austria, as opposed to common law countries, seem particularly reluctant to privatize. Moreover, Austria was not able to maintain its position in the top group in the current international employment ranking by the Bertelsmann Foundation. This gives some additional support to the main hypothesis of this chapter: that governments always time privatizations with an eye on their impacts on the performance of the labor market and thus on reelection probabilities. It states that the Austrian economy and the labor market are burdened by high state intervention manifesting itself in abundant government outlays and a high degree of regulation.

However, the new government is endeavoring to trim the state and the administration extensively (Bertelsmann Foundation 2002). In the same vein, the Austrian Reform Commission (Ausgabenreformkommission) has tested the performance of government institutions and has recommended that the state confine itself to certain central tasks.

Finally, the importance of headquarters which are surrounded by high-value services and R&D generating higher incomes is emphasized quite often (see, e.g., Aiginger in Austrian Parliament 2000). According to his reasoning, too few headquarters are located in Austria. With the goal of condiorating this deficiency, one of the objectives of the privatization of Voestalpine AG declared during the extraordinary general meeting of the OeIAG on April 7, 2003, was that the decision-making headquarters of privatized former state-owned enterprises (SOEs) be located in Austria. Most striking and in strict accordance with the partisan view of privatization described later, the decision-making headquarters of the company to be privatized shall be maintained in Austria if possible through the creation of Austrian core shareholders (OeIAG, 2003).

3.3   Economic Consequences of Privatization in Austria

For Austria, aggregate productivity gains have not come primarily from intersectoral resource shifts. The contribution of these shifts between two-digit SIC sectors to aggregate productivity change is quite small for Austria.[11] Hence, a further promising candidate for explaining movement in the Austrian productivity time series is ownership, that is, privatization. Both, the microeconomic and case study data are supportive of the positive effects of privatization over time on growth and employment (see, e.g., Davis et al. 2000, Megginson and Netter 2001). These results reflect geographical diversity and are representative of a range of privatization experiences in developing and transition economies. They hold for EU countries but are less pronounced for transition and developing countries. The microeconomic evidence indicates that private firms are operationally more efficient than those held by the state, particularly in competitive industries.[12] A strong correlation between privatization and growth is also found for EU countries. However, and consistent with the growth literature, privatization is likely serving as a proxy in the regressions for one or more missing variables that may be characterized as a favorable regime change. Public enterprises often seek to maintain employment, and they benefit from staff budget constraints. Consequently, there is a concern that privatization may lead to increased unemployment.[13] Also, empirical evidence suggests that aggregate unemployment tends to downsize following privatization (although an identification problem might arise with respect to Austria due to the fact that the country's period of main privatization efforts is superimposed by its EU entry).[14] However, particular groups of workers may still be adversely affected. In general, there are good theoretical reasons for privatization; moreover, the proceeds from privatization, if used in a clever fashion in the areas of education, technology, and infrastructure, can increase the welfare of such countries. The main reason is that the classical public good argument still applies for these areas. However, is this generally positive picture also applicable to the Austrian case? What are the economic consequences from the privatization program for the Austrian economy from 1990 on?

It should first be mentioned that in the same period, that is, together with the privatization, a considerable amount of EU deregulation and liberalization (telecom, gas, electricity, and other service markets) initiatives took place. Due to the opening of competitive markets in these areas and the gained efficiency of privatized enterprises, considerable price reductions could be observed and an additional growth of 0.1 to 0.32 percent per year took place over the period 1996 to 2001.[15] The origin of this additional growth was due to price reductions in the telecom (−25%), gas (−12%), and electricity (−13%) sectors, resulting in cheaper input factors for users and increased purchasing power for consumers.[16] In the case of the partly privatized Austrian Telekom, solely the stifled competition and the EU directive add to the observed effects on prices and the quality of output. Such an analysis is limited to the extent possible for the now totally privatized VOEST, a steel mill, which today works in a totally different context, compared to 1985, when it was a 100 percent public enterprise. We will not show the financial data for this firm, because in the past, its products and production technology were totally different than they are today. Hence, we refrain from giving performance measures and convey only a rough indication of the performance of Voestalpine Stahl AG for the time span 1993 to 1997. Its operating income rose from a 71 million Austrian shilling (ATS) deficit to 3.2 billion ATS profits in 1997. However, even this impressive increase in performance cannot be attributed to a change in ownership rights in the sense of a statistically corroborated causality relationship (Nowotny 1998).

There are additional reasons to be very careful and not overemphasize the results. One is that the choice of firms for privatization has
been far from random, which might lead to an upward bias, that is, to
better-than-average performance results from privatization (Carlin
et al. 2001). Second, the effect of an ownership change might be quite
different for different performance measures. Third, there might be
additional influences behind the suspected impact of privatization on
Austrian economic performance. For instance, legal reforms with respect to antitrust laws and competition policy and the abandonment
of price regulations took place in Austria within the same period. In
Austria, privatization came as a self-enforcing package with more
prudent fiscal policies, liberalization, and deregulation.[17] Hence, the
following analysis of the macroeconomic growth and employment
contribution of privatization and its impacts on profitability of firms in
general has to be conducted with these caveats in mind.

3.3.1   Labor Market Impacts

We start with a discussion of the (un-)employment impacts of privatization in Austria, because this seems to be the politically most
highlighted aspect of privatization there. For member countries of the
Organization of Economic Cooperation and Development (OECD),
among them Austria, current privatization receipts cannot be rejected
empirically as having a significant diminishing effect on the unemployment rate (implementation, new entry in the market) but a positive
effect on the previous period's unemployment rate (announcement,
restructuring). A potential explanation for this pattern might be that
when privatization, and thus restructuring, is announced, firms feel
inclined to operate more efficiently. If privatization is implemented,
there is new market entry, which increases labor demand and lowers
unemployment (Katsoulakos and Likoyanni 2002). Similar results can
be found, for instance, in Megginson and Netter (2001) and some other
studies for developing countries. However, we do not want to push
our interpretation of the Austrian case much further in view of the
fact that the studies cited above do not give fixed effects estimates of
the idiosyncratic privatization impact in Austria. If the analysis is
limited to the employment performance of Austrian firms after privatization, the general picture changes, and one cannot reject the hypothesis of no change in employment after privatization. This is at least
valid for Austria's early privatizations of Austria Microsystems, Aus-

trian Airlines, Böhler-Uddeholm, Energieversorgung Niederösterreich, Flughafen Wien Schwechat, Flender, Immotrust, OMV, Voestalpine Eisenbahntechnik, Voestalpine Technologie, Voestalpine Stahl, and Voith which took place from 1987 to 1995 (Schaffhauser-Linzatti 2003). Moreover, in some cases, production capacities were shifted toward foreign countries in the wake of privatization—in the case of Austria, especially to Central and Eastern European countries (see, e.g., the Semperit AG)—which might overlap with the otherwise positive employment impact in Austria and create some empirical identification problems.

We should focus not only on the employment and growth impacts of privatization in Austria but also on the effect of privatization on the development of capital markets. New share listings on the Vienna stock exchange can directly create some net new wealth and a limited number of additional high-skilled jobs, but the main economic benefit from more efficient and liquid capital markets arises from the financing opportunities and monitoring possibilities these markets deliver. Moreover, efficient capital markets foster economic growth and grant individual firms the ability to fund investment opportunities they otherwise would have to forgo (see, e.g., Belke, Fehn, and Foster 2003). Hence, privatization appears valuable in view of whatever direct role it has played in promoting the highly underdeveloped stock market development in Austria (through new share offerings), and for the indirect role it might had also in Austrian bond market development (Megginson and Netter 2001).

3.3.2 Impacts on Corporate Performance

Evidence is more ambiguous with respect to the impacts of privatization on corporate performance in general. Some studies point to the absence of a clear and unambiguous effect of changes in ownership on the economic performance of the affected firms and the economy in general. Evidence that privatization enhances performance has not in all cases emerged from the Austrian data. For instance, Schaffhauser-Linzatti (2003) studied the change in the operating and financial performance of the Austrian firms Austria Microsystems, Austrian Airlines, Böhler-Uddeholm, Energieversorgung Niederösterreich, Flughafen Wien Schwechat, Flender, Immotrust, OMV, Voestalpine Eisenbahntechnik, Voestalpine Technologie, Voestalpine Stahl, and Voith, which were either partly or fully privatized between 1987 and

1995. Using accounting data prior to and after the privatization, she measures the change in efficiency, profitability, capital structure, investment behavior, and employment (number of employees) for inflation- and business cycle–adjusted data. While profitability (the return on turnover, the return on equity, and the return on total capital) and efficiency (alternatively measured as sales per employee, return per employee, and staff costs per employee) display significant change between the period of state ownership and privatization, the other measures exhibit no significant change. Hence, she concludes that the Austrian privatization program was not that successful as compared to other international experience. Reasons for these quite unexpected results are the small sample included in this study, the partial instead of total privatization of most of the enterprises, and the structure of the management. Here, the number of members of boards of directors was kept almost constant, so there were only a few possibilities for introducing new management techniques and new leadership of privatized Austrian firms. Moreover, after privatization, there was on average a decrease in salaries of board members by 2.6 percent, indicating either a lack of incentives after privatization or salaries that were too high before privatization.[18] Gugler (1998) aims to add to the knowledge about the effects of privatization on the economic performance of former SOEs in Austria. He assesses ownership structure (e.g., concentration) and the relative importance of the investor categories banks, the state, families, and domestic and foreign firms on the basis of a sample of 600 of the largest nonfinancial corporations. Balance sheet data, internal rates of return calculations, and regression estimates show that not only ownership concentration but also the identity of the large, controlling shareholder is relevant to efficient governance of corporations. While foreign control increases profitability state control is particularly detrimental to shareholder wealth maximization (see also Clemenz 1999).

With respect to the capital market, it must not be forgotten that the "New Austrian" privatization policy significantly enhanced the role of the Vienna stock exchange itself.[19] This can be highlighted by two measures. First, during the period 1992 to 1997, around 45 percent of the total volume of new issues on the Vienna Stock Exchange consisted of issues by the OeIAG. Second, shares of privatized enterprises were responsible for 34.5 percent of the turnover on this stock exchange in 1997 (Nowotny 1998). Another important question is whether privatization has had a significant impact on the performance of the shares.

From 1993 to 1997, the performance of shares of privatized enterprises was significantly better than the trend increase of the Vienna Stock Exchange as a whole (Nowotny 1998). The relative importance of share issue privatizations (SIPs) in Austria can be read off from their relative position among Austrian firms in terms of the single firm's market capitalization as a percentage of the entire national market's year-end 1999. In Austria, privatized companies are the second most valuable firms (Megginson and Netter 2001). Worldwide, large SIPs played a key role in the growth of capital markets almost everywhere, especially because they are generally among the largest firms in national markets. Davidson (1998) investigates one-, three-, five-, and ten-year market-adjusted returns for these SIPs from five European countries (Austria, France, Italy, Spain, and the United Kingdom) through March 1997. After a long period of underperformance, averaging 1 to 1.5 percent per year, he concludes that SIPs outperformed European market averages during the previous twelve months.

3.3.3   Impacts on the Performance of ATX Stocks

We now focus on two recent individual examples of Austrian privatization: the Vienna Airport and Telekom Austria. At this stage of analysis, we dispense with using benchmarks (e.g., the trend of the Vienna Stock Exchange or the ATX as a whole) and also neglect potentially missing factors (e.g., an overlap with speculative bubbles). The main issue we tackle is whether we are able to observe an increasing profitability of privatized firms, that is, an increased value of the shares, after privatization at the Vienna Stock Exchange. This view is certainly not corroborated with respect to Vienna Airport, but it cannot be excluded for Austrian Telekom (see figures 3.2 and 3.3). Note that the date of complete privatization of Vienna Airport was March 2001. Its starting price at the Vienna Stock Exchange (closing) was 37.9 euros, and its price in April 2001 rose to 39.1 euros. In the last two-thirds of the sample, the trend development of the airport shares was significantly negative. However, a totally different picture emerged from trade in Telekom shares, which started in Vienna and New York on November 21, 2000. At the beginning, the 75 percent shareholder OeAIG announced a share price of 123.8 ATS respectively around 9 euros. However, the price of Telekom shares (closing) fell immediately after the first privatization issue to a price of 6 euros in order to recover again and increase with a positive trend.

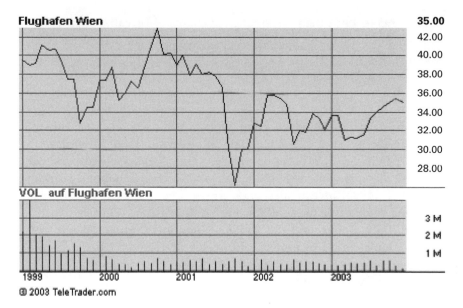

Figure 3.2
Performance of shares of Vienna Airport at the Vienna Stock Exchange
Note: VOL = trade volume. Flughafen Wien = Vienna Airport.
Source: Vienna Stock Exchange (2003).

In order to arrive at a more systematic picture and build more solid conclusions, we finally compare the change of performance of the eleven (partly) privatized Austrian firms to the change of performance of their international competitors within the same industrial sector from December 30, 1994, to November 22, 2000.[20] The performance of Austria's early privatizations is measured as a first step as the development of share prices and as a second step as the dividend yield, each time in relation to a benchmark. The results for share prices are displayed in table 3.3.

Within the sample and expressed in dollars, four of eleven Austrian stocks underperformed the Morgan Stanley international sectoral indexes (MSCI). However, this has to be traced back to a significant extent to the strong dollar versus the euro. Only four of eleven shares—those of Austria Tabak AG, Böhler-Uddeholm AG, VA Stahl AG, and the Verbundgesellschaft—displayed better performance than their international counterparts, although in the cases of Austria Tabak and Böhler-Uddeholm, only marginally (1 and 7 percent, respectively).[21] The only Austrian stock that experienced significantly better per-

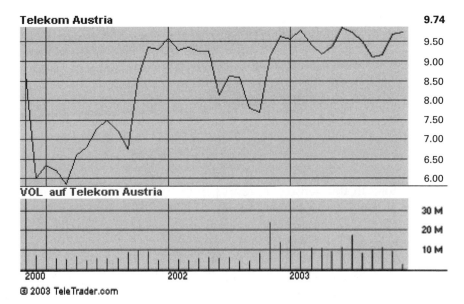

Figure 3.3
Performance of shares of Telekom Austria at the Vienna Stock Exchange
Note: VOL = trade volume. Flughafen Wien = Vienna Airport.

Table 3.3
Performance of privatized ATX quotations

Austrian stocks	Change of perfor-mance	MSCI Index	Change of perfor-mance	Com-parison of perfor-mance
AMS AG	+20%	Electrical & Electronics	+411%	−
AUA	−44	Transportation—Airlines	+35	−
Austria Tabak AG	+2	Beverages & Tobacco	+1	+
Bank Austria AG	−36	Banking	+39	−
Böhler-Uddeholm AG	−46	Metals—Steel	−53	+
EVN AG	−31	Utilities—Electrical–gas	+34	−
Flughafen Wien AG	−12	Transportation—Airlines	+35	−
OMV AG	−14	Energy Sources	+99	−
VA Stahl AG	−19	Metals—Steel	−49	+
VA Tech AG	−68	Machinery & Engineering	−22	−
Verbundgesellschaft	+49	Utilities & Gas	+34	+

Source: Sachsenhofer (2000).
Note: A plus sign means performance of Austrian stocks is better than the Morgan Stanley MSCI Industrial Sector Index (MSCI), ⟨http://www.mscidata.com⟩. A minus sign means that performance of Austrian stocks is worse than the MSCI. Performance is measured as the development of share prices.

formance than the index of the metal and steel sector is VA Stahl. Moreover, in only three of the eleven cases of privatized Austrian firms did the shares increase their initial values and, hence, improve their performance (AMS AG, Austria Tabak AG, and Verbundgesellschaft).

If one looks at the sectoral disaggregation of the performance revenues from privatization, it becomes obvious that shares of the steel sector (Böhler-Uddeholm and VA Stahl AG) clearly outperformed the international sectoral index for metals and steel. Just the opposite is true with respect to the transportation and airlines sector. Here, the AUA and the Vienna Airport AG underperformed their international competitors. In this sense, our results from figure 3.2 for the Vienna Airport shares are corroborated again.

With respect to the utilities and the electrical and gas sector, the picture is mixed for Austria. On the one hand, the international index outperformed the EVN share. On the other hand, the price of the Verbundgesellschaft share experienced the highest price growth (49 percent) of all eleven Austrian ATX shares considered here and performed better than the international electrical and gas sector benchmark. Hence, privatization in the Austrian metals and steel sector appears to be more efficient than privatization in the transportation and airlines sector. The result with respect to the utilities and the electrical and gas sector is ambiguous.

However, our assessment of the benefits of privatization in Austria changes significantly if dividend yield is investigated instead of share prices as a measure of profitability of privatization. Table 3.4 summarizes the pattern of dividend yields of early privatized Austrian firms in the first year after going public (if shares were issued after June 30, in the following year). This table reveals that in the first year of comparison, only two of eleven Austrian firms had a higher dividend yield than their European competitors.[22] Only the Austrian Tabak AG (3.83 percent) and the VA Tech AG (2.18 percent) earned higher dividend yields than their most important European counterparts.

The pessimistic results change if we focus on a more recent business year. Here, the profitability gains of privatization seem to have materialized to a larger extent. Hence, we conclude that there is a time-to-build effect at work. Table 3.5 displays a systematic comparison of the Austrian dividend yields from the business year 1999 with those of their international competitors. According to this analysis, the dividend yields of six of eleven Austrian firms (Austria Tabak AG, Bank Austria AG, Böhler-Uddeholm AG, OMV AG, VA Stahl AG, VA

Table 3.4
Dividend yields gained by privatized ATX quotations (first year of comparison)

Austrian firm	Divi- dend yield	European competitor	Divi- dend yield	Com- parison of dividend yields
AMS AG	1.46%	ST Microelectronics SA	0%	+
AUA	3.09	British Airways PLC	4.93	−
Austria Tabak AG	3.83	Altadis SA	2.49	+
Bank Austria AG	0.87	Deutsche Bank AG	2.32	−
Böhler-Uddeholm AG	3.25	ThyssenKrupp AG	5.18	−
EVN AG	2.12	RWE AG	3.14	−
Flughafen Wien AG	1.81	British Airports Authority PLC.	2.56	−
OMV AG	3.98	Royal Dutch Petroleum Co.	6.23	−
VA Stahl AG	3.11	Usinor SA	5.96	−
VA Tech AG	2.18	Asca Brown Boven Ltd.	1.77	+
Verbundgesellschaft	5.25	Scottish Power PLC.	0	+

Source: Sachsenhofer (2000).
Note: A plus sign means that the dividend yield of the Austrian firm is higher than that of the international competitor. A minus sign means that the dividend yield of the Austrian firm is lower than that of the European competitor.

Table 3.5
Dividend yields gained by privatized ATX quotations, 1999

Austrian firm	Divi- dend yield	European competitor	Divi- dend yield	Com- parison of dividend yields
AMS AG	0%	ST Microelectronics SA	0.06%	−
AUA	2.71	British Airways PLC.	6.03	−
Austria Tabak AG	4.38	Altadis SA	3.52	+
Bank Austria AG	1.82	Deutsche Bank AG	1.37	+
Böhler-Uddeholm AG	4.37	ThyssenKrupp AG	3.83	+
EVN AG	1.82	RWE AG	3.19	−
Flughafen Wien AG	4.64	British Airports Authority PLC.	4.77	−
OMV AG	2.49	Royal Dutch Petroleum Co.	2.48	+
VA Stahl AG	3.69	Usinor SA	3.60	+
VA Tech AG	1.83	Asea Brown Boven Ltd.	1.54	+
Verbundgesellschaft	0.83	Scottish Power PLC.	5.43	−

Source: Sachsenhofer (2000).
Note: A plus sign means that the dividend yield of the Austrian firm is higher than that of the international competitor. A minus sign means that the dividend yield of the Austrian firm is lower than that of the European competitor.

Tech AG) outperformed those of their international competitors. This extraordinary performance made Austrian shares of privatized firms more attractive to investors.

For four Austrian companies (Bank Austria AG, Böhler-Uddeholm AG, OMV AG, and VA Stahl AG), a clear time trend toward higher dividend yields emerges. As it was already the case in our comparison of the relative share price performances of Austrian firms (table 3.3), a clear sectoral pattern again emerges. Dividend yields of shares of the Austrian metals and steel sector (Böhler-Uddeholm and VA Stahl AG) were lower in the first year of comparison and higher in 1999 than the yields of their international competitors. In contrast, the firms from the Austrian transportation and airlines sector had lower dividend yields in both cases (AUA and the Vienna Airport AG). With respect to the utilities and the electrical and gas sector, the picture is again mixed for Austria. While the Verbundgesellschaft reached a higher dividend yield at least in the first year of comparison than its main U.K. competitor, the dividend yield of EVN AG in both years of comparison was lower than that of the German RWE AG.

We cautiously conclude that both the performance and the dividend yield measures point to the same result. Especially the Austrian metals and steel industry gained profitability by privatization, while this seems not to be the case for the Austrian transportation and airlines sector. According to figure 3.3, the same positive assessment might be valid with respect to Telekom Austria. With respect to the Austrian utilities and the electrical and gas sector, evidence is ambiguous. Since the dividend yields of the eleven privatized Austrian firms in 1999 outperformed those of their international competitors, the underperformance of the shares of these eleven ATX quotations cannot be explained by lower dividend yields. What else might be the reason for the observed underperformance of privatized Austrian firms? First, the Austrian capital market seems to be quite weak due to the fact that the Vienna Stock Exchange is still small. Second, state ownership of (partly) privatized Austrian firms is still rather high. Third, the role of Austria's financial market has remained marginalized up to now. Hence, the varieties of possibilities to sell public assets as a constitutional element of privatization are severely limited (EIRO 2002). Finally, by selling underpriced shares in the domestic retail market, the Austrian government might intend to attract the median voter, shaping a constituency interested in the maximization of the value of financial assets and averse to redistribution policies to the left (Perotti 1995,

Biais and Perotti 2002).[23] In fact, for Austria, there is evidence that the mean underpricing of initial public offerings of former SOEs is 6.5 percent for the period 1984 to 1999, which was dominated by government participation of the ÖVP and a sample of seventy-six cases (Aussenegg 1997).

From this point of view, especially in Austria, there is clear evidence of strategic privatization as a rational strategy to raise the probability of the success of market-oriented coalitions in future elections.[24] We now turn briefly to the potential impacts of privatization on the public sector fiscal stance.

3.3.4   Impacts on the Public Sector Fiscal Stance

Although the redemption of public debt itself is not a good reason to privatize,[25] we address the fiscal effects and impacts of privatization on public budget deficits and public debt. The reason is that the budgetary impacts seem to be important incentives for Austria's more recent move toward privatization. Katsoulakos and Likoyanni (2002) conducted an econometric analysis applying country-level panel data of twenty-three OECD countries, among them Austria, for the period 1990 to 2000, analyzing the impact of privatization on the public deficit and the impact on public debt. They show that privatization receipts are not significantly correlated with budget deficits for the whole OECD sample, Austria included. They also identify a statistically significant and negative relation between privatization receipts and public debt for the whole OECD sample, which again includes Austria. However, any sound assessment of budget impacts of privatization in Austria should consider that especially in this country, a higher number of sales is not correlated with higher proceeds (Bortolotti, Fantini, and Siniscalco 2001; see also Belke and Schneider 2004).

3.4   Summary and Conclusions

Privatization has been a key element of structural reform in EU countries including Austria, and proceeds from privatization have been substantial in most of these countries. Gross receipts that can be transferred to the budget are affected by actions prior to sale, the sales process, and the postprivatization regime. An evaluation of the potential uses of privatization receipts or proceeds should reflect the implications for government net worth and their macroeconomic impact.

Insofar as government net worth is concerned, proceeds from privatization do not often indicate that the government is better off. Privatization has longer-term implications in terms of revenues forgone and expenditures that will not be made in the future, and government decisions on the use of proceeds should reflect this intertemporal effect. Government net worth will rise to the extent that private sector ownership leads to an increase in efficiency and the government shares in this gain.

The macroeconomic effects of privatization depend in part on whether receipts and proceeds are from domestic or foreign sources, the degree of capital mobility, and the exchange regime. Broadly, the effects of a decrease in the deficit financed by privatization receipts would be similar to those resulting from a debt-financed fiscal expansion. Both the economic recovery and privatizations lead to receipts that can be used to lower the deficit. The use of proceeds to reduce external debt provides an automatic neutralization of what may be substantial capital inflows associated with privatization. The reduction of domestic debt may have an impact on domestic stability. Redemption and interest payments become lower by collecting privatization receipts. Hence, privatization takes some of the strain off the budget and the capital market by lower interest rates. This in turn increases efficiency, which tends to improve prospects for the labor market as well after some restructuring period.

This chapter has shown that there are good reasons for privatization in general, although this strategy raises some opportunity costs, and that privatization proceeds under certain circumstances can enhance the welfare of these countries. With regard to Austria, we are skeptical about whether Austria's privatization potential has been exploited fully and whether the speed of privatization, although quite sizable, has been sufficient. However, future prospects for quick and full privatization in Austria are rather gloomy, although economic theory (Alchian and others) and empirical evidence suggest that only full privatization, as opposed to partial privatization is successful with respect to economic performance in the long run (Boardman and Vining 1989, 1991). However, as long as politicians interfere with this process, there will be no straight development toward full privatization. This assessment is all the more valid with an eye on the Austrian habit of appointing former members of the Austrian government as CEOs at the Austrian privatization agency OEIAG, and the state is still determined to keep a strategic stake in the latter. According to the statute of the

Österreichische Industrieholding AG, "Austrian interests must be protected as follows: ... the creation and maintenance of secure jobs in Austria, ... maintenance of the decision-making headquarters of the company to be privatized in Austria" (Österreichische Industrieholding AG 2003). One glimmer of hope is that Austrian finance minister Karl-Heinz Grasser did not reiterate in December 2003 that the state would sell its entire remaining stake in Telekom Austria, despite some calls to keep a blocking minority. The state privatization agency OeIAG, charged by the government with selling off most of Austria's industrial holdings, holds 47 percent of Telekom and is now charged by the center-right government with selling it by late 2006. This seems to be extremely important, since otherwise a continued holding would only slow Telekom Austria in adapting to a fast-moving telecoms market.

Notes

We are grateful to an anonymous referee for valuable comments and to Rainer Fehn, Andreas Freytag, Eduard Hochreiter, Marko Koethenbuerger, Hans-Werner Sinn, and John Whalley.

1. Surveys of the privatization literature are provided in Megginson and Netter (2001), Boes and Schneider (1996), and Bartel and Schneider (1991), and a summary of the earlier discussion is given in Borcherding, Pommerehne, and Schneider (1982).

2. Since politoeconomic aspects relating to income distribution and ideology play an important role in explaining the way, the extent, the speed, and the economic effects of privatization, they have to be considered as well. See extensively Belke and Schneider (2004).

3. See, for instance, Borcherding, Pommerehne, and Schneider (1982) and Boes and Schneider (1996).

4. The first approach was developed by Alchian (1961, 1965) and more recently by Baron and Myerson (1982), Grossman and Hart (1983), and MasColell, Winston, and Green (1995).

5. Compare the studies by Boes and Schneider (1996), Schneider (1997, 2002), and Schneider and Hofreither (1990). These results are so well known that they are not reported here.

6. Compare Schneider and Frey (1988), Bartel and Schneider (1991), Pardo and Schneider (1996), and Schneider (2002).

7. See among others Aiginger (1999). Nowotny (1998) discusses different meanings of privatization in the context of Austria.

8. See Clemenz (1999) and Nowotny (1998) on Austrian public enterprises as instruments of economic and social policy as a means of avoiding labor market hysteresis (theory of cooperative economics, or *Gemeinwirtschaft*).

9. A further comprehensive and informative source of the history of privatization in Austria is found in Clemenz (1999).

10. Astonishingly and perhaps due to the specific Austrian phenomenon of politically motivated decision making even in business affairs, neither the unions nor the Works Council of Bank Austria opposed the bank takeover by the Bavarian HypoVereinsbank. See EIRO (2002).

11. Carlin et al. (2001) document for the case of Austria that between-sector movements accounted for 6.5 percent of the total between 1991 and 1996—1.1 percentage points out of a total increase of 17.4 percentage points. In this sense, Austria is entirely typical of market economies.

12. This was especially the case in Austria.

13. However, employment losses often appear to be widely exaggerated. For instance, the Communist party of Austria (2003) argues that the number of employed in the Austrian electricity sector since the start of the "liberalization efforts" has already shrunk from 33,000 to 22,000. If one uses the EU as a benchmark, this number will probably be further reduced to 16,000.

14. See extensively Belke and Schneider (2004) on the relationship between the institutional environment of the Austrian economy (e.g., its EU and the EMU entry) and the speed of privatization in Austria.

15. Our calculations are based on an econometrically estimated simulation model.

16. Average price reduction for the period 1996–2001.

17. Nowotny (1998) describes the "Austrian experiment" of privatization more deeply, differentiating with respect to the character and form of privatization in terms of change in ownership, change in regulation, corporatization, liberalization to activities promoting efficiency and competition within the government, and change in competition. Privatization does not necessarily imply a withdrawal of the state from economic policy. The government still has to define the conditions for an efficient activity of enterprises and to meet precautionary measures against market failure—measures in the area of competition policy and antitrust law as well as in environmental policy. See Nowotny (1998, 46).

18. However, Schaffhauser-Linzatti and Dockner (1999) conclude that there was no significant change between the period of state ownership and privatization with respect to efficiency, leverage, investment behavior, and output. Instead, they identify a significant change for profitability and employment. See also Clemenz (1999, 21).

19. See Nowotny (1998, 43). Nevertheless, the role of the Vienna stock exchange was still limited until eastern enlargement of the EU.

20. However, if quotation starts later than on December 30, 1994, we refer to the first trading day. Telekom Austria is not included in the sample because it was not privatized until after the end of the sample considered here.

21. The result for Austrian Tabak becomes even more ambiguous if one takes into account that there were rumors of a takeover of the OeIAG shares of Austrian Tabak by the German Reemtsma group after November 22, 2000.

22. In 1994, ST Microelectronics SA did not exist, and the Scottish Power PLC was not founded earlier than 1991. Hence, we do not attach too much importance to the results for AMS AG and the Verbundgesellschaft in table 3.4.

23. Biais and Perotti (2002) show that privatizing governments that cannot commit to absentism are still able to reduce investors' perceived probability of future interference by allocating underpriced shares to median class voters. Hence, the number of shares of the SOE initially sold and the associated underpricing will increase with the degree of income inequality of the privatizing country.

24. However, left-wing governments also embark on privatization but mostly when fiscal conditions deteriorate (as in Italy). See Bortolotti and Pinotti (2003), and Jones et al. (1999). Aussenegg (2000) compares the characteristics and the price behavior of case-by-case privatization initial public offerings and private sector initial public offerings in Poland over the first nine years after the reopening of the Warsaw Stock Exchange in April 1991. He finds evidence that the Polish government is market oriented, trying to build up reputation for its privatization policy over time by underpricing, selling a high fraction at the initial offer, and underpricing more when selling to domestic retail investors.

25. See Clemenz in Austrian Parliament (2000).

References

Aiginger, Karl. 1999. "The Privatization Experiment in Austria." *Austrian Economic Quarterly* 4, 261–270.

Alchian, Armen A. 1961. *Some Economics of Property Rights.* Santa Monica, Calif.: Rand.

Alchian, Armen A. 1965. "Some Economics of Property Rights." *Il Politico* 30(4), 816–829.

Aussenegg, Wolfgang. 1997. "Short and Long-Run Performance of Initial Public Offerings in the Austrian Stock Market." Working paper no. 24, Austrian Working Group on Banking and Finance, August, Vienna.

Aussenegg, Wolfgang. 2000. "Privatization versus Private Sector Initial Public Offerings in Poland." *Multinational Finance Journal* 4, 69–99.

Austrian Parliament. 2000. *Parlament Industrieausschuss, Parlamentskorrespondenz/02/ 13.04.2000/Nr. 199.* Vienna.

Baron, M., and Myerson, P. 1982. "Regulating a Monopolist with Unknown Costs." *Econometrica* 50, 911–930.

Bartel, Rainer, and Schneider, Friedrich. 1991. "The 'Mess' of Public Industrial Production in Austria: A Typical Case of Public Sector Inefficiency?" *Public Choice* 68(1), 17–40.

Belke, A. 2000a. "Too Big to Fail: Bankenkonkurs und Wählerstimmenkalkül." In D. von Delhaes, K.-H. Hartwig, and U. Vollmer, eds., *Monetäre Institutionenökonomik, Schriften zu Ordnungsfragen der Wirtschaft*, Stuttgart: Lucius & Lucius.

Belke, Ansgar, Fehn, Rainer, and Foster, Neil. 2003. "Venture Capital Investment and Labor Market Performance—A Panel Data Analysis." In Christian Keuschnigg and Veas Kanniainen, eds., *Venture Capital, Entrepreneurship and Public Policy.* Cambridge, Mass.: MIT Press.

Belke, Ansgar, and Schneider, Friedrich. 2004. "Privatization in Austria: Some Theoretical Reasons and First Results About the Privatization Proceeds." CESifo working paper no. 1123, Munich, January.

Bertelsmann Foundation, ed. 2002. "International Employment Ranking." Guetersloh, Germany: Bertelsmann Foundation Publishers.

Biais, Bruno, and Perotti, Enrico. 2002. "Machiavellian Privatization." *American Economic Review* 92, 240–258.

Boardman, Anthony E., and Vining, Aidan R. 1991. "The Behavior of Mixed Enterprises." *Research in Law and Economics* 14, 223–250.

Boes, Dieter, and Schneider, Friedrich. 1996. Private Public Partnership: Gemeinschaftsunternehmen zwischen privaten und der oeffentlichen Hand. *Zeitschrift fuer Unternehmens- und Gesellschaftsrecht* 25, 519–543.

Borcherding, Thomas, Pommerehne, Werner W., and Schneider, Friedrich. 1982. "Comparing the Efficiency of Private and Public Production: The Evidence from Five Countries." *Zeitschrift fuer Nationaloekonomie/Journal of Economics* 89 (Suppl. 2), 127–156.

Bortolotti, Bernardo, Fantini, Marcella, and Siniscalco, Domenico. 2001. "Privatisation Around the World—New Evidence from Panel Data." *Nota di Lavoro 77.2001* (working paper), Fondazione Eni Enrico Mattei, Venice.

Bortolotti, Bernardo, and Pinotti, Paolo. 2003. "The Political Economy of Privatization." *Nota di Lavoro 45.2003* (working paper), Fondazione Eni Enrico Mattei, Venice.

Boutchkova, Maria K., and Megginson, William L. 2000. "Privatization and the Rise of Global Capital Markets." *Financial Management* 29, 31–76.

Carlin, Wendy, Fries, Steven, Schaffer, Mark E., and Seabright, Paul. 2001. "Competition and Enterprise Performance in Transition Economies: Evidence from a Cross-country Survey." CEPR discussion paper no. 2840, Centre for Economic Policy Research, London.

Clemenz, Gerhard. 1999. "Privatization, Liberalization and Deregulation—The Austrian Experience." Paper presented at the ISNIE-Conference 1999, *Session: Public Policies and Industrial Structures*, Washington, D.C., September 17–19.

Communist Party of Austria. 2003. "E-Wirtschaft in globaler Kapitalhand." ⟨http://www.kpoe.at/bund/archiv/antiprivatisierung/ewirtschaft.htm⟩.

Davis, Jeffrey, Ossowski, Rolando, Richardson, Thomas, and Barnett, Steven. 2000. "Fiscal and Macroeconomic Impact of Privatization." IMF *occasional paper 194*, Washington, D.C.

Economist. 2003. "Don't Sell Our Family Silver! Austrians Are Still Reluctant Free-Marketeers." September 4.

EIRO. 2002. "Comparative Study Questionnaire on 'Industrial Restructuring: the Impact of Variations in Forms of Corporate Governance.'" Ireland: European Industrial Relations Observatory. ⟨http://www.eiro.eurofound.ie/2002/09/word/AT0207203S.doc⟩.

Grossman, S., and Hart, O. 1983. "An Analysis of the Principal-Agent Problem." *Econometrica* 51, 7–45.

Gugler, Klaus. 1998. "Corporate Ownership Structure in Austria." *Empirica* 25, 285–307.

Jones, Steven L., Megginson, William L., Nash, Robert C., and Netter, Jeffry M. 1999. "Share Issue Privatizations as Financial Means to Political and Economic Ends." *Journal of Financial Economics* 53, 217–253.

Katsoulakos, Yannis, and Likoyanni, Elissavet. 2002. "Fiscal and Other Macroeconomic Effects of Privatization." *Nota di Lavoro 113.2002* (working paper), Fondazione Eni Enrico Mattei, Venice.

Megginson, William L., and Netter, Jeffry M. 2001. "From State to Market—A Survey of Empirical Studies on Privatization." *Journal of Economic Literature* 39, 321–389.

Niskanen, W. A. 1971. *Bureaucracy and Representative Government.* Chicago: *University of Chicago Press.*

Niskanen, W. A. 1975. "Bureaucrats and Politicians." *Journal of Law and Economics* 18(4), 617–643.

Nowotny, Ewald. 1982. "Nationalist Industry as an Instrument of Stabilization Policy." *Annalen der Gemeinwirtschaft* 51(1), 41–57.

Nowotny, E. 1998. "Privatization, Deregulation, Reregulation—Experiences and Policy Issues in Austria." *Journal for Institutional Innovation, Development, and Transition* 2, 35–49.

Österreichische Industrieholding AG. 2003. OEIAG—Österreichische Industrieholding AG. ⟨http://www.oeiag.at/english/OeIAG/privatisierung.shtm⟩.

Pardo, José Casas, and Schneider, Friedrich. 1996. *Current Issues in Public Choice.* Cheltenham, U.K.: Elgar Publishing Company.

Perotti, Enrico. 1995. "Credible Privatization." *American Economic Review* 85, 847–859.

Sachsenhofer, Susanne. 2000. "Performance und Dividendenpolitik privatisierter ATX-Werte." *Diplomarbeit Universität Linz.* Institut für betriebliche Finanzwirtschaft.

Schaffhauser-Linzatti, Michaela. 2003. Ökonomische Konsequenzen der Privatisierung in Osterreich: Eine empirische Analyse anhand boersennotierter Aktiengesellschaften." *Zeitschrift für Betriebswirtschaft* 73(1), 49–71.

Schaffhauser-Linzatti, Michaela, and Dockner, Engelbert. 1999. "The Financial and Operating Performance of Privatized Firms in Austria." Mimeo., University of Vienna.

Schneider, Friedrich. 1997. "Deregulierung und Privatisierung als Allheilmittel gegen ineffiziente Produktion von oeffentlichen Unternehmen?" In Wieviel Staat, wieviel Privat?, *Sammelband der Arbeitsgemeinschaft der wissenschaftlichen Wirtschaftspolitik*, pp. 33–59. Vienna: OeGB Verlag.

Schneider, Friedrich. 2002. "Privatisierungen und Deregulierungen in Oesterreich in den 90er Jahren: Einige Anmerkungen aus Sicht der neuen politischen Oekonomie." In Hartmut Berg, ed., *Deregulierung und Privatisierung: Gewolltes—Erreichtes—Versaeumtes? Schriften des Vereins fuer Socialpolitik* (Neue Folge, Band 287), pp. 89–120.

Schneider, Friedrich, and Frey, Bruno. 1988. "Political Business Cycles: A Survey." In Thomas Willet, ed., *Inflation and the Political Business Cycles.* Durham, N.C.: Duke University Press.

Schneider, Friedrich, and Hofreither, Markus F. 1990. *Privatisierung und Deregulierung in oeffentlichen Unternehmen in westeuropaeischen Laendern: Erste Erfahrungen und Analysen.* Vienna: Manzsche *Verlags-und Universitaetsbuchhandlung.*

Vienna Stock Exchange. 2003. Österreich/Börse Wien, Aktien. ⟨http://vlbg.rdg.ttweb .net/_frm/index.asp⟩.

4   Privatization in Denmark, 1980–2002

Henrik Christoffersen and
Martin Paldam

Denmark is an advanced welfare state and widely perceived as semi-socialist. However, no private company has been deliberately nationalized in the last 125 years, and few Danish businesses outside the network industries were built as state-owned enterprises (SOEs). Table 4.1 gives a survey of the status of privatization in 2003 and a brief look back and forward. The topic of privatization in Denmark has not received much attention. In fact, until now, there was not even a list of what has been privatised in Denmark.[1]

According to the leading index of economic freedom, Denmark is a typical Western country and is not particularly socialist (see figure 4.1). The detailed data show that the public sector is relatively large, and that the "freedom" score is above average in other fields. That applies to the sections of the index dealing with ownership, freedom of trade, and finance. Denmark is a large welfare state characterized by relatively strict capitalism. For a long time, it differed from the German welfare state model, which was supposed to have more regulation and less public welfare expenditure, but the two models have converged.

Figure 4.1 shows that Denmark has moved toward a more liberal economy. Part of this process is the increased freedom of international capital movements and other deregulation, which will not be discussed here, but part of it is also privatization and outsourcing. We use the usual definitions: *privatization* is when the ownership of production units changes from public to private.[2] *Outsourcing* is when goods and services provided to people by the public are bought in the market, normally after competitive bidding. This is mainly done by the local authorities.

This chapter examines the historical background, the politics of privatization and the actual cases. It also addresses the gradual process of outsourcing production of public goods in the municipal sector.

Table 4.1
Survey of production ownership and delivery

Sector	Status	Change, 1980–2002	Plans	Experiences
Primary sector	Private, except 2/3 of forests	Marginal	None	None
Trade and finance	Over 99% private	Small privatizations	None	See sections 4.1.1 and 3
Manufacturing	Over 99% private	Small privatizations	None	See sections 4.1.1 and 3
Service production[a]	Over 99% private	Small privatizations	None	See sections 4.1.1 and 3
Housing	Private, cooperative subsector	None	Cooperative[b]	Not discussed
Network industries	Public share about 70%	10% privatization	More expected	Discussed
Electricity, heating often included	Mixed state/municipal/private—no dominating owner	Some shares sold	More to be sold	Not discussed
Water	Municipal and private	Marginal	None	No study
Natural gas net[c]	SOEs, state plus other public	None	May be sold	See section 4.1.3
Telephone	Private	Privatized	None	See section 4.3.1
Railroads	Main lines SOE; some side lines outsourced	Outsourced January 2003	Main line may be sold	See section 4.3.2
Bus lines	About 80% private	20% privatization	More to be sold	See sections 4.3.2 and 4.4.3
Post	Public	Postal bank sold	Plan to sell rest	See section 4.3.2
TV and radio	Main stations public, most other stations private	None	Second station just sold	Political fight,[d] not discussed
Airline	SAS is SOE; 30% by other companies all private	SAS structure is made privatizable	Shares may be sold	See section 4.1.3
Airports	Two largest private, most smaller local public	Most shares of Copenhagen Airport sold	Last shares may be sold	See section 4.3.2
Roads	All public, no tolls			Not discussed
Giant bridges	SOEs, financed by tolls	Both opened	Next private	See section 4.1.3

| Core public sector[e] | 20% outsourced in old "special" arrangements[f] | *Weak trend toward outsourcing* | New government for free choice of public and private production | About 20–30% cost savings; see section 4 |
| Auxiliary services | 60% outsourced | | | |

[a] Service sector outside the traditional public sector.
[b] Plans are being made to make social flats semiprivate and eventually in some cases private. The proceeds will to be used to build more flats.
[c] Gas production is private, but gas pipelines are public.
[d] Control of media is very political, and the left has preferred public, while the right has pushed for private ownership. The result has been complex compromises.
[e] Core services are the ap 80 percent of public services that people demand (e.g., education, health care); non-core services are the auxiliary inputs in production that people normally disregard.
[f] Primary health care is done by "semiprivate" practitioners; some special clinics are private too. Ten percent of primary and secondary education is nonprofit private schools, and many kindergartens and old people's homes are run by nonprofit private organizations. Little is run as business.

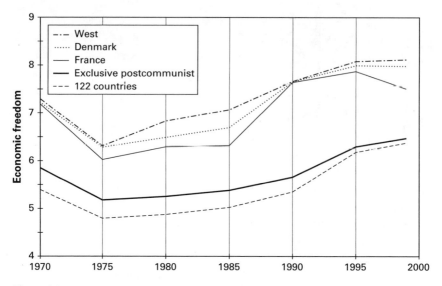

Figure 4.1
Economic freedom ratings in Denmark, 1970–1999
Note: Numbers from the Fraser Institute data set. These data measure the degree of regulation in the economies, so that 10 is the perfect laissez faire. The classical socialist economy of the Soviet type was 1.5. Paldam (2003) and Gørgens, Paldam, and Würtz (2003) discuss the index. The data contain fewer observations in the beginning than the end and have been extrapolated backward for consistency in six groups. Part of the liberalization since 1990 is due to the transition from socialism. Hence the line "exclusive postcommunist" countries.

4.1   Development of Denmark's Economic System

Denmark deviates somewhat from the average Western country by combining a relatively large welfare state with a relatively capitalist system, both in the sense of relatively strict private property rights and (for a long time) unusually free trade.[3] We discuss how the system originated (based on Paldam 1991) and then turn to recent trends.

4.1.1   Origin of the System: Extreme Liberalism until the 1920s

A large welfare state reduces incentives and needs relatively strict capitalism for efficiency. Also, in small countries those who are in the elite know each other, so a sharp division of powers and free trade is important. These arguments seem not to have played a political role in Denmark. However, three historic trends are important.

First, Denmark was unusually liberal in all respects during the "liberal century" (1818–1914), especially from 1870 to 1901, when a prolonged constitutional fight paralyzed political decision making.[4] The financial sector developed during the period of political paralysis and was fully private, but cooperative institutions such as saving banks and (bond issuing) mortgage funds were important. The mortgage bonds were sold on the market, so real estate was (and still is) in private hands—also financially. The cooperative sector has gradually grown to appear much as normal business. The public sector share was constant at about 9 percent of GDP, as in the world's most liberal country today (Hong Kong); it was below the OECD average as late as 1960. The Danish welfare state thus started from an unusually low point in the 1920s.

Second, until 1950, Danish exports were largely agricultural, processed in the cooperative sector of the farmers. To get access to export markets for agricultural goods, tariffs on other products were low. Also, the old trading and shipping business strongly favored free trade.

Third, industry developed in the same way during the liberal century without public support and protection and with no natural base. It was mostly light industry for the home market, but it gradually turned to the world market. It is marked by a low level of concentration in the sense that no firms dominate. The biggest firm since the 1930s has been the shipping-trading conglomerate Maersk, which conducts most of its activity abroad. It is a family company with one key owner, who just turned ninety.[5]

Socialists wanting to take control of the commanding heights of capitalism have had a hard time finding these heights. Consequently, few proposals to nationalize have made the political agenda, and the few that happened were at the border with normal business.[6]

4.1.2   The Welfare State and the Big Compromise after 1920

The Social Democratic party was the largest political party between 1924 and 2001, but it did not obtain a majority even with the parties of the (divided) left wing. This caused the small center parties, notably the Radical party, to be pivotal in Danish politics. The center parties were against socialism but for social responsibility (i.e., the welfare state). This led to a big compromise: the left obtained the welfare state and the right obtained rather strict capitalism. Polls over the years have demonstrated how the consensus around this solution has increased. In addition, the precarious political balance in the country since the 1930s has led to a tradition of cross-center agreements on the big issues.

The only significant case of a rust-belt industry—old heavy industries in distress—is shipyards; Denmark used to have a dozen. Here a financial subsidy existed, much as everywhere else, but the state never took over, and when the shipyards failed, they had to close; today only one major shipyard is left. In addition the state owned shares in a small metal recycling factory that recently went bankrupt.

4.1.3 Special Cases: Companies with a Special License and New Semicommercial SOEs

Two major Danish private industries have operated with a highly profitable public license. They were allowed to keep the monopoly profits without much pressure or political discussion.

The Danish Alcohol Monopoly was the only firm allowed to distill alcohol between 1923 and 1973.[7] However, import was always free, though liquor taxes were levied in a way favoring Danish schnapps. The monopoly was revoked in 1973, and the tax has been made more even-handed. Also, the distillery has been sold (by DANISCO) to a Swedish company (the Swedish State Liquor Monopoly).

Since 1932, a group of farmers and the Danish Sugar Company (now part of the DANISCO conglomerate) have had a highly profitable license system, which is now part of the EU sugar arrangement. It forces consumers to buy sugar at a price about twice the world market price. The sugar company and the farmers split approximately 150 million euros of income due to the price difference. (The Danish crown is fixed to the euro. For easy comparison, all prices are given in euros.) The drugstore licensing system is worth mentioning too. It was a closed system for a long time with a set number of controlled pharmacies. It ran (and still does) a lobby, but a process of liberalization has started.

The SAS airline is jointly owned by Denmark, Norway, and Sweden. It operated under a route licensing system like other national airlines, generating high fares and amazingly large rents in the form of excess costs. European air traffic is being gradually liberalized by the EU; the SAS corporate structure has been streamlined, and hard budget constraints have been introduced. SAS has had to cut costs—during the past three years by no less than 50 percent. Sector analysts seem to believe that some fat remains to be cut.

Finally, seven new large state-owned enterprises (SOEs) have been formed, five of them in natural gas. In the early 1970s, natural gas and oil were found in the Danish parts of the North Sea. The exploration and production are private. A large majority in the Parliament decided that the oil and gas should be used to make Denmark self-sufficient in energy.[8] With this aim, six (now four) SOEs were established by law in 1972. The largest was DONG, building and owning the national gas grid costing about 5 billion euros, while the local net and sale were given to five (now three) regional companies.[9] The decision to launch these companies was based on a compromise in the Parliament, where it was decided that natural gas was a viable production for the country, so the large subsidy necessary was hidden as a tax rebate (for "environmental" reasons). Now the net has been written sufficiently down that the companies are almost viable, and they may be sold.

A similar case is the SOEs that are running two new giant bridge-tunnel complexes, both spanning waters of about 22 kilometers: the Great Belt Bridge, built between 1982 and 1994 between the islands of Funen and Zealand, and the Oresund Bridge, built from 1995 to 2000 between Zealand and southern Sweden. Both were deemed too big and too uncertain for business. The first bridge is commercially successful, but the second is not, so a special cross-subsidization arrangement has been made. A third giant bridge is now in the negotiating stage: the Fehmern Belt bridge, to connect Zealand to Germany. It appears that it may be built by a private company.

4.1.4 The Rise and Stabilization of the Public Share

Between 1958 and 1973 the public sector increased from about 23 percent of GDP to about 50 percent, or 27 percentage points over just fifteen years. The expansion was equally divided between an increased production of (nondefense) public goods and increased redistribution. The expansion was very smooth, and even when it was fully financed by taxes, it caused a period of rapid growth. It created the welfare state, but it ended up in a relatively large crisis.[10] The expansion had to be stopped, and since the early 1980s, the share has been almost constant—just above 50 percent of GDP.

Denmark is highly dependent on foreign trade, with trade shares of about 40 percent of GDP.[11] All responsible decision makers know that national competitiveness is crucial.[12] Hence, it is important that the share of the public sector is controlled and not permitted to rise too much above the level in the EU and other main trade partners.

The dynamics of public sector growth and the demand of the public for increased service has made it a constant problem to prevent the growth of the public sector share. The ability of politicians to control program costs is influenced by the fact that the share of the population that depends on the public sector is now about 60 percent.[13] The strong upward drift in public spending, and the pressures on the decision makers to prevent the drift, have caused pressure to privatize at the two relevant margins. On the one hand, the public sector has wanted funds in the short run to finance the public sector, and, on the other hand, it has wanted to reduce costs. Privatization of the last few ordinary SOEs—in particular, the telephone company (Tele Denmark)—has generated public income, and outsourcing has provided some savings. Because of increasing public budget surplus in recent years, the cost argument has now become the most weighty argument for further privatization.

The Danish story of privatization is much as it is in other EU countries. We have found few indications that pressure from the EU mattered for most of the decisions in any of the cases, but it is likely that the zeitgeist of liberalization has contributed. It is, as always, difficult to substantiate.

4.2   Politics and Values: The Ownership Issue

Most economists see competition as the key to efficiency, so the question about any privatization is how it affects competition. Property rights theories claim that ownership matters more for efficiency.[14] Marxist theory considers the ownership to the means of production the basic factor shaping society, and hence the central political issue. Consequently, the ownership issue is complex and can easily be politicized. This may still happen in Denmark, but it has not yet, for two reasons: the largest privatizations have been carried out by the center-left, and private ownership is in accordance with the values of a large majority of the population.

4.2.1   Privatization and Party Politics

When the lists of privatizations in the appendix are compared with table 4.2, it appears that most were done under the center-left government of Poul Nyrup Rasmussen.

The reasons for the privatizations seem to have been largely fiscal. Since Tele Denmark and Copenhagen Airports were already SOEs, why not sell the shares? As the sales were done by a center-left government, neither the parties to the right nor the trade unions could protest,

Table 4.2
Danish governments during the last quarter-century

	Prime minister	Composition
February 1975– September 1982	Anker Jørgensen	Social Democratic (minority)
September 1982– January 1993	Poul Schlüter	Conservative/Liberal coalition, with various small parties
January 1993– November 2001	Poul Nyrup Rasmussen	Social Democratic/Radical coalition
November 2001–	Anders Fogh Rasmussen	Liberal/Conservative coalition

so the sales were largely uncontroversial. Most of the media space devoted to the sale of the phone company discussed the high price obtained. The current liberal/conservative coalition has undertaken to sell more. The sales planned are mostly in the network industries (see table 4.1). It appears that few decisions have been made yet.

4.2.2   An Index of Attitudes toward Public versus Private Ownership

The World Value data set covers ownership by the item, "*Do you support private/public ownership of business?*" Ronald Inglehart (1997), who headed the group developing the survey, argues that the question shows people's attitudes on the ideological socialism/capitalism axis. The answers are on a ten-point scale, from 1-strong support for private to 5-neutral, to 10-strong support for public. Category 11 is "don't know." Figure 4.2 is a visual survey of the cumulative distributions of the ten answers for selected countries. Only between 5 and 10 percent answered "don't know," so the issue is salient for people.[15]

We have drawn the answers for some countries as a cumulative curve. A high curve (toward the northwest) points to high support for private ownership, while a low curve (toward the southeast) points to high support for public ownership. The straight neutrality line from (0,0) and (10,100) divides capitalist (above) values from socialist ones (below). Twice the area above the line in percentage of the area of the full square is a (Gini type) score for the amount of capitalist values. If the area is below the line, it points to socialist values. Nearly all the curves discussed are above the axis, and we have hence scaled the cumulative area above the axis as positive (for capitalist values). The area below the axis is thus negative (for socialist value).[16]

The scores for all available developed countries are given in table 4.3. The two waves of the World Value survey are from 1990 and 1999,

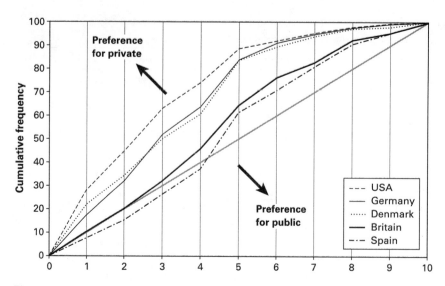

Figure 4.2
Private versus public ownership for five countries, 1990

but for nine of the countries, intermediate waves are available too. Only the first wave includes Denmark, but table 4.3 shows that these values change slowly in most of the countries.

Capitalist values dominate in all twenty-two countries, though only marginally in Spain, but strong socialist segments of the population appear in both Asia and Latin Europe. With such a divided population, the curve has an S shape, so it is important to consider the whole curve.

Denmark has one of the highest capitalist values. Only the United States, Canada, Switzerland, and Austria are more capitalist, while Finland, Australia, Iceland, and West Germany are close to Denmark.[17] The remaining fourteen countries all have more socialist values.

4.3   The State Sector: Twelve Privatizations and Fifteen Dubious Ones

As listed in the appendix the Danish state formally sold a business twenty-seven times from 1980 to 2002. Table 4.A1 lists twelve genuine privatizations, while table 4.A2 covers fifteen dubious cases. In the genuine cases, a normal operating company was sold to the private sector for the market price. In the dubious cases, a company was terminated by a sale of some assets, or the sale was of a noncommercial

Table 4.3
Capitalist value scores for twenty-two developed countries, in increasing order

Country	Wave	Score	Country	Wave	Score
Spain	90	9.8	Britain	98	14.6
Japan	90	10.0	South Korea	96	17.7
Britain	90	17.0	Japan	95	17.8
South Korea	90	17.6	Norway	96	24.9
Northern Ireland	90	20.2	Sweden	96	25.6
Netherlands	90	27.0	Finland	96	31.4
Italy	90	27.6	West Germany	97	34.0
France	90	27.7	Australia	95	38.9
Norway	90	28.1	Switzerland	96	48.2
Portugal	90	29.4	USA	95	52.6
Sweden	90	29.4	Last wave—Eurobarometer		
Ireland	90	33.1	Britain	99	18.0
Belgium	90	34.0	Portugal	99	20.3
Iceland	90	37.5	Northern Ireland	99	24.4
Denmark	**90**	**41.1**	Germany	99	26.0
West Germany	90	41.5	Netherlands	99	26.9
Finland	90	42.3	Ireland	99	30.3
Austria	90	47.1	Finland	99	30.4
Canada	90	48.1	Italy	99	32.2
United States	90	52.1	France	99	34.2
Different waves			Iceland	99	41.9
Spain	96	5.9	Austria	99	47.5
Taiwan	95	11.0			

Note: The two main waves are from 1990 and 1999 for Europe only. Seventeen countries have more than one observation. The average change is −0.6, so we are dealing with rather stable attitudes.

character. In addition, a couple of SOEs went bankrupt and were liquidated, without a sale of assets.[18] When all twenty-seven SOEs privatized are sorted by revenue, a skewed distribution results. One privatization accounts for 76 percent of the revenue, and sixteen cases added provide less than 1 percent. The total revenue corresponds to 3 percent of GDP for the middle year, 1990, but it is only 0.15 percent per year for the two decades considered. Below, we look at the cases in order of size. We start with the large one.

4.3.1   Tele Danmark

In November 1990 the four regional Danish phone companies were merged to form TDC. Then they lost their monopoly and finally were sold to the U.S. company Ameritech (now SBC) for 4.2 billion euros in 1998. Now a number of new operators are competing in the market, though TDC is still by far the largest operator. Also, much competition has emerged from the mobile phone market. The Danish phone companies were typical SOEs, while TDC is a private U.S. company. Everybody expected the new company to be both leaner and meaner than the old SOE. However, TDC decided to start operations with as few changes as possible and even put two former ministers of finance in charge. The chairman of the board is a former Social Democratic minister of finance (just retired) and the CEO is a former Conservative minister of finance.[19]

The increase in competition has caused prices to fall, so the company has been under a profit squeeze, and it has reduced personnel by 15 percent—first by not replacing those who were retiring and then by a round of layoffs. Analysts assume that the state obtained a rather good price.

The CPI price index for telephoning has fallen by 20 percent relative to the general index between 1998 and 2003, mostly due to a large drop in long-distance fees. However, the composition of teleservices consumed has changed in the period, and experts disagree about the average savings; the gain for the average family, they say, is probably larger. The story is thus fairly typical of the many privatizations of phone companies that have taken place throughout the world during the past two decades.

Politically, the privatization took place under a Social Democratic government and with little opposition in the Parliament. Also, it seems that the personnel in the company recognized that they could do nothing to prevent the privatization, so the whole process appeared to take place in a calm atmosphere.

4.3.2 Four Middle-Sized Cases

The next three privatizations are also all at the border to the traditional public sector: the Public Pension Insurance Institute, Copenhagen airports and the postal bank.

The first case is the pension system for civil servants. It worked as all other such systems do and was sold to a private company, Baltica A/S, in 1990. As the assets and liabilities are easy to assess, the sale went smoothly, and caused little debate. Also, no effects on the efficiency of the company have been reported.

Kastrup Airport in Copenhagen is the country's main international airport and also for the SAS airline. In 1990 Kastrup was merged with the much smaller Roskilde Airport and turned into an SOE. Thus far,

66 percent of the shares have been sold to many investors on the Copenhagen Stock Exchange. The main reason for the sale was fiscal, and little has changed in the way the airports run.[20]

The third case is the postal bank, which was made an SOE in 1993 when 52 percent of the shares were sold. In 1995, the remaining shares were sold, and the PostBank (in Danish GiroBank) merged with a savings bank Bikuben to become BG Bank. Later BG Bank became part of the largest banking company in the country, Danske Bank, but it continues as BG Bank.

Finally two small cases relate to the potentially large case of the Danish Railways, DSB. One is the colorful case of Combus, a public bus corporation formed by DSB, to compete with private bus companies. It did so by large-scale underbidding at tenders for bus lines. When it later had to run the lines it won, it did so with a large deficit. When the government enforced a hard budget constraint, the company went bankrupt after a much discussed scandal. Its remaining assets were sold for 15 euros. In 2002 a number of train sidelines in Jutland, which had been run by DSB, were outsourced. Even though DSB made a very low bid, the British company Arriva was chosen. In January 2003, Arriva started to run the train service. It took almost half a year before the service worked as well as it had before, but now customers' satisfaction is as high as before (perhaps even higher). It has been reported that the effect of introducing competition in railways has greatly enhanced the efficiency of DSB.

DSB has been formally broken into smaller units—tracks, goods transport, ferryboats—and some or all of these parts may be privatized. While the division is being carried out, it has not yet been decided whether the sales will be made.

4.3.3 Remaining Cases

Datacentralen was a data processing company that served the public sector. It was moderately successful and was sold in two installments to the (much larger) U.S. company CSC, one of the largest data processing companies in the country. The Export Credit Insurance SOE was sold to a major international concern in the field. Both sales seem to have followed normal business practices, and the prices reached appear to have been reasonable.

Most of the other remaining cases are empty or failed SOEs that were sold for next to nothing. Most are small, little-known companies.

The Construction Machine Station was an SOE created to help small contractors in the building sector in 1948 as a Marshall Aid project. It started well, but it was not a dynamic enterprise, and when it was finally sold, the feeling was that it had outlived its usefulness.

Five small consultancy services had branched off from larger public entities and obtained an independent life. They were sold to the market. One of these is the Internet facility developed by Uni-C, the university computer net. A sad case is the research-heavy computer pioneer, Regnecentralen. At one stage, it looked promising as a producer of technologically advanced small mainframes, but it always lacked commercial acumen and gradually lost its considerable human capital to university computer departments.

The final case is a popular amusement park that for a long time (allegedly since 1583) existed in the Royal Deer Park (established 100 years later). In 1997 the state decided to sell its interest in the holding company running the park at a nominal amount to the association of the owners of the stalls.

4.3.4 Cases Connected to Greenland

Within the Danish Kingdom is the microstate Greenland with 56,500 inhabitants. It has home rule and an economic system where the public owns virtually everything. Historically, it was a traditional less developed country with hunting and gathering instead of agriculture until the early 1950s,[21] when Danish politicians decided to change the colony to a "normal" Danish county by huge transfers of funds. The idea was to provide Danish institutions at the same standard as much as conditions permitted. The transfers have amounted to about 15 billion euros thus far.

Greenland obtained home rule in 1979, but the flow continues, and it now amounts to 8,700 euros per capita per year. The subsidy is not given to the individual Greenlander, but to the home rule government. The transfer is a bit larger than Greenland's production would be in the absence of the transfer. This has created a very strange economy, where virtually all business is in the form of heavily subsidized or protected SOEs, a price level 50 percent above the Danish one, and a huge public sector (collective consumption is no less than 55 percent of GDP, as explained in Paldam 1997). Five of the dubious cases are from Greenland.

The biggest of these cases is Kryolitselskabet Øresund, which generated a privatization revenue of about 100 million euros. It was an SOE that ran a mine for the rare mineral cryolite (sodium aluminum fluoride) at Ivigtut in Greenland from 1870 to 1987, when the deposit was exhausted. Cryolite was the first catalyst in aluminum refining, and the company was thus profitable, accumulating considerable assets (in Copenhagen). The surplus of the company corresponded to the deficit of the colony of Greenland, until extensive subsidization started in the early 1950s. However, all cryolite ore was accounted for in the early 1980s, and the company assets were sold to the insurance company Hafnia in 1985.

The remaining cases occurred in the late 1970s, when Greenland home rule was established. In addition to the cases mentioned, many public firms were donated to the new home rule authority. The Royal Greenland Trading Company and the stock of public housing (virtually all housing in the towns) were thus donated to Greenland. The state "lost" a great deal of Danish property, but it was not privatized.

In order to gradually turn the economy into a normal market economy, the home rule authority has converted its business activities into SOEs, and vague plans exist to gradually privatize these SOEs. Thus far, only one privatization has occurred, as the main chain of shops has been sold. However, most of Greenland's SOEs operate with large subsidies or heavy protection and with cost levels far exceeding the competitive ones, so they will be difficult to sell. Also, the boards of the SOEs are dominated by local politicians, and examples are plentiful that political considerations hold sway. Even when most of the SOEs have Danish management, they operate much as SOEs everywhere else do.

4.4   Privatization in the Municipal Sector

The Danish municipal sector is unusually large and powerful.[22] It is forbidden to run and subsidize business in the traditional private sector. However, municipalities do run many small business-like activities at the border between the sectors. Some privatizations have been made, but no central authority has kept track of what has happened.

4.4.1   The Municipal System and The Formal Nationalization of Nonprofit Organizations

Local public utilities have traditionally been a main task for the municipalities. Supply of water, gas, and electricity was organized as municipal activities in most urban municipalities during the liberal century up to the 1920s. From their formation in the 1840s, municipalities were responsible for primary schools and social security, but private non-profit schools have been an important part of national cultural life, not least because of a tradition of religious freedom. They enroll about 10 percent of each age cohort. In social security, private charity played an important role during the liberal century, but gradually the municipalities became involved. The modern local government system in Denmark came about through two reforms.

First was a system of economic equalization payments between rich and poor municipalities established in the 1930s. At the same time, stronger central government norms for service provision passed parliament, when the Social Democratic party achieved ascendancy. However, charitable organizations were still allowed to provide public services.

The second round of institutional local government reforms took place around 1970 when 1,300 municipalities were amalgamated into 275 new units and 14 counties were established with the same institutional and democratic status as the municipalities.

These reforms took place during a period of rapid growth of public expenditures, as married women entered the labor market earlier and stronger than in other European countries (except Sweden). The municipalities became the replacement of the family in child care. The belief in the modern welfare state was strong, and it took full control over the production and distribution of welfare services. Consequently it became decisive for municipalities and counties to exploit economies of scale in the service area fully, and large units were needed.

After the structural reform, a local nationalization process took place in Danish local government. The private school sector survived because of its cultural importance, although the economic conditions were reduced, but almost all social institutions run by charity organizations or profit-seeking organizations became public systems.

4.4.2   Increasing Outsourcing as a Means to Control Costs

Research from many countries as surveyed by Borcherding, Pommerehne, and Schneider (1982) and Domberger and Jensen (1997) shows that the same goods and services are cheaper by a cost difference of 20 to 30 percent on average if bought on the market than if they are produced by a public monopoly organization.[23] These results have been confirmed by Danish studies by Kristensen (1983), Christoffersen, Paldam, and Würtz (2000), and Blom-Hansen (2003). The knowledge of these facts spread much before they were analyzed and documented, and a new market orientation has arisen in the municipal sector since the early 1980s.

The cost difference of 20 to 30 percent might be interpreted as an income transfer to those selected by the municipalities. However, it seems that the choice of recipients is rarely deliberate, so it is more appropriate to consider this cost difference as the margin of monopoly rents the municipal bureaucracies have been able to consolidate as inefficiency. One should probably see the increasing market orientation of the municipalities as an attempt to reduce that rent. In more concrete terms, three main reasons lie behind it.

First, the new market orientation may be a response to the increasing economic pressure on the welfare state in late 1970s, when public budget deficits exploded after fifteen years with immense public growth and after the economic recession that accompanied the oil crisis. A new Conservative-Liberal government in 1982 stopped further public growth and started a program for bringing in market forces to raise efficiency. A core point here was to urge local governments to take up outsourcing in service production.

Second, the fixed costs and economies of scale in the production of local and regional public services have become a more important factor in the cost function. The use of experts and automatic administration systems as a response to increasing requirements contributes to explaining this change in cost structure. Small municipalities become squeezed by the increasing fixed costs, and they can escape the higher unit costs by bringing in private producers.

Third, liquidity pressures urge municipalities and counties to let private investors contribute to financing capital equipment, building stock, and other capital assets. This perspective has become more relevant as central government regulation of local government economic activity now focuses on total spending, including investment spending.

4.4.3   Outsourcing: Nonpartisan Local Decisions and National Politics

Statistics are available for the amount of outsourcing since 1993. They show that approximately 11 percent of municipal production is accomplished by private companies; the data show a significant upward trend, though the net change during the period has been less than 1 percentage point.[24] The core areas such as schools and hospitals are still staffed by municipal or county employees, but marginal activities are often done by private companies. Typical examples are the cleaning of public buildings, regional bus lines, repair of public roads, trash collection, park maintenance, cafeterias in public institutions, and fire engines and ambulances. In such areas, between 30 and 70 percent appears to be outsourced.

Christoffersen and Paldam (2003) analyzed the amount of outsourcing, which is largely an effect of modernity. It is largest in municipalities near main towns with large shares of modern industry and less in traditional rural municipalities. Economic pressure on the municipality increases outsourcing, while the share of population dependent on the public sector decreases outsourcing. Partisan politics was irrelevant.

While the proper privatizations discussed in section 4.3 have caused little public controversy, outsourcing has sometimes been fiercely resisted by stakeholders. The most notorious case is the municipal bus company of the town of Esbjerg, which lost the contract to a private company, Ribus. This caused a prolonged and—for Denmark—fairly violent blockade of the central garage of the new operator. However, the private company prevailed.

The former Social Democratic government did push for outsourcing, but at several of the annual meetings of the party, controversy emerged on the issue, and the party maintains that outsourcing should not be allowed in core areas, notably the hospital sector. The current Liberal-Conservative government has free choice between public and private suppliers of public goods as a much advertised policy, but in practice, outsourcing has dropped. At present there are only a couple of small private hospitals in the country, and no school is run for profit.

4.5   Conclusions: A Typical Story?

The main message from this story is that the international wave of privatizations in the 1980s and 1990s has been reflected in the Danish economy; that is, some network industries have been privatized and liberalized. This has been met with little public resistance as it was mainly done by the center-left. Privatization has been a minor political issue in Denmark as there has been little to privatize. This has historical reasons, as discussed, and it was demonstrated that the structure of ownership is well in accordance with the values and attitudes of the population.

Total privatization revenue amounts to approximately 3 percent of the GDP of the median year (1990) of the period considered, so per year it is 0.15 percent. As taxes amount to 50 to 52 percent of GDP, this is about 0.3 percent of the public revenue, but 76 percent came from the privatization of the phone company.

Even when the sales revenue is small, seen in perspective, it was big for a couple of years, and this may be the main motive. Another motive may have been to unload awkward responsibilities from the state.

With the slowly but steadily increasing pressures to finance the welfare state, new privatizations are being discussed and will probably be approved. The only ones possible are social housing and some of the network businesses: the postal service, the railroads, the public part of the utilities, and the natural gas companies. All of these are already under discussion, but the government is slow to act because these are natural monopolies, which may be problematic to run as private companies. However, one may argue that they are not running impressively well now.

Appendix: Privatizations by the Danish State, 1980–2002

These lists were compiled by checking all acts to the Financial Committee of the Parliament, which should consider all deliberate reductions in public assets. Hence, the lists should be complete. They are divided in two parts: dubious cases and the genuine privatizations.

Table 4.A1 contains the twelve genuine privatizations. They are in chronological order. When the sale is done in several rounds, they are put together, so that only the first round is in chronological order. The odd-looking change in public shares in item 6b is a posting made in connection with the company reorganization before the sale.

Table 4.A2 contain fifteen dubious cases, which appear under the heading privatizations in the acts. Most are of two types: cases where an SOE has failed and is closed, but contains assets of some value, which applies to cases 3, 4, 5, 6, 7, 8, 10, 11, 12, and 15. In nearly all of these cases, the activity of the company has de facto ceased, and in only one of the cases (8) do valuable assets remain. In cases 1, 2, and 9, the company was sold to or given away to a foreign public body, including the home rule authority of Greenland. The last two are case 13, where a commercially valuable but small activity in a research

Table 4.A1
State sale of shares and assets in firms, 1991–2002: Genuine cases

Company	Danish name	Year	State share	Method of sale	Revenue (millions)
1 Junker Industries	do	1989	37/0	Direct sale	7
2 Construction Export Consulting	Byggeeksportrådet A/S	1989	51/0	Direct sale	0.02
3 Construction machine station	Byggeriets Maskinstation A/S	1990	68/0	Block sale	6
4 Civil Servants Life Insurance	Statsanstalt. for Livsforsikring	1990	100/0	Direct sale	574
5 Postal Bank 1 of 2	GiroBank A/S	1993	100/49	Open bidding	98
b 2 of 2	—	1996	49/0	Direct sale	100
6 Phone Monopoly 1 of 3	Tele Danmark A/S	1993	94/90	?	11
b 2 of 2	—	1994	90/*	Reorganization	121
c 3 of 3	—	1998	*/0	Direct sale	4,237
7 Copenhagen Airports 1 of 3	Københavns Lufthavne A/S	1994	100/75	Open bidding	95
b 2 of 3	—	1996	75/51	Open bidding	148
c 3 of 3 pt	—	2000	51/34	Open bidding	132
8 Export Credit Insurance 1 of 2	EKR Kreditforsikring A/S	1995	100/75	Direct sale	10
b 2 of 2	—	1997	—	Sale of assets	37
9 Data processing company 1 of 2	Datacentralen A/S	1996	100/25	Direct sale	46
b 2 of 2	—	1999	25/0	Direct sale	17
10 Standard and testing company	DEMKO	1996	100/0	Direct sale	4
11 Travel bureau	Skandinav. Reisebüro GmbH	1998	100/0	Direct sale	0.9
12 Railroad consultancy service	Banestyrelsen Rådgivning	2001	100/0	Direct sale	10
Total					5,654

Note: In these cases a normal operating company was sold to the private sector. Italics indicate a break in the time line. The "*" in the State share column means that no data are given in the records.

Table 4.A2
State sale or discharge of shares and assets in firms, 1990–2002: Dubious cases

	Company	Danish name	Year	State share	Method of sale	Revenue (million euros)
1	Eurochemie	Eurochemie	1983	–/0	Capital reduction	1.5
2	Nuuk fish industry, Greenland	Godthåb fiskeindustri	1985	41/0	Write off	0
3	Sawmill in public forest	Centralsavværket	1985	–/0	Symbolic sale	0
4	Land surveyor IT service	Landinspektorernes EDB	1985	–/0	Write-off	0.02
5	Mestersvig Mine, Greenland[a]	Nordisk Mineselskab	1985	–/0	Capital reduction	0.6
6	Windmill production	Dansk Vindteknik	1985	–/0	Capital reduction	0.7
7	Production of biogas turbine	Scanenergi	1985	–/0	Capital reduction	0.3
8	Cryolite Mine, Ex-Greenland[a]	Kryolitselskabet Øresund A/S	1985	50/0	Sale of share	97
9	Greenland travel bureau	Grønlands Rejsebureau	1986	33/0	Sale to home rule	0.1
10	Environmental products[b]	Naturdan A/S	1991	/0	Write off	0
11	Computer production company[c]	A/S Regnecentralen af 1979	1992	/0	Direct sale	0.07
12	Transport of hazardous waste[b]	Danfragt A/S	1996	33/0	Direct sale	0
13	University Internet service	UNI-C's internetaktiviteter	1997	—	Sale of assets[e]	1
14	Amusement park holding company	A/S Dyrehavsbakken	1997	50/0	Insider sale	0.03
15	Bankrupt public bus company[d]	Combus A/S	2001	100/0	Direct sale	0
Total						101

Source: Budget acts.
Note: Column 4 shows state share of equity before and after. The cases are termed dubious because they do not concern normal operating companies or are noncommercial sales.
[a] Assets (including financial) left in Copenhagen after exhaustion of mine. The Ivigtut mine was run by a company in Copenhagen having expensive real estate and accumulated funds as well.
[b] These companies were almost empty at the time of the closing.
[c] Regnecentralen was established to produce mainframes, and it developed away from world standards.
[d] Combus was established as a competitive company participating in the outsourcing of bus lines. It did win many contracts, but at prices below production costs, and went bankrupt.
[e] The exact sales revenue is secret.

institute was sold, and case 14, where a very old and legally complex ownership problem was solved.

Notes

The data in the appendix were collected from the Ministry of Finance by Martin Junker Nielsen (of the ministry) and Christian Friis Binzer (AKF), by going through 20 years of records. We have discussed the cases with Anders K. Balling of the ministry and several colleagues. Søren Risbjerg Thomsen helped with the World Value Survey data. We are grateful to Jürgen Jerger and other discussants at the CES-ifo conferences in Munich and Cadenabbia, as well as Jens Blom-Hansen and the anonymous referee.

1. If possible, we refer to published material. Especially when it comes to the results of privatizations, few studies exist. Consequently much of the information reported is based on newspaper articles and private information. In these cases, we use terms such as "it is reported that" or "it appears that."

2. In Denmark mainly by the state, and in the form of the sale of shares in SOEs. Sometimes, but not always, the change from being an administrative branch to becoming an SOE is a step on the way to privatization. We use the strict definition of a change of ownership.

3. If the average rate for effective protection could be calculated for all countries for the nineteenth and twentieth centuries, Denmark would probably take the gold medal—or at least the one of silver—for free trade.

4. From 1866 to 1901 the king kept a government of the right (the old feudal group) in power, while the majority in the Parliaments' first chamber became increasingly dominated by the farmers. They rejected all proposals from the government and managed to prevent the king from signing the law approved by the Parliament. Most public sector decision making thus stopped for almost half a century.

5. The company was formed by a captain owning a couple of ships and his son, who was an extraordinarily able businessman, as was his son, who has just resigned (in the age of 90). The next generation will not manage the company, and the corporate structure has been changed accordingly.

6. From 1840 a dozen private railways were launched. Most of the new railways failed and were therefore taken over by the public sector. In 1885 the public railways were merged into one company (DSB, which still exists). A similar story can be told about a number of harbors. The only borderline nationalization in the twentieth century has been the pilot service in the Danish sealanes.

7. Retail sale of products containing alcohol has always been free in Denmark, contrary to the situation in the other Nordic countries. The alcohol tax has been halfway between the Swedish and the German one.

8. It would have been commercially better to sell the gas to foreign companies that already had pipelines nearby. However, at that time, the two future energy sources appeared to be either atomic energy or Arab oil. To obtain energy security, it was decided to reserve the Danish North Sea oil and gas for national uses.

9. The regional companies are partly owned by the municipalities, and they have a rather poor reputation as for generating incomes and granting perks to local political elites.

10. Both the expansion of the golden 1960s and the crisis after 1973 were strong in Denmark relative to the similar trends throughout Western Europe.

11. Exports and imports of goods and services in percentage of GDP.

12. Competitiveness has two margins. Externally it means that domestic goods can compete with foreign in the market; internally it means that the tradables sector can compete with the nontradables sector for resources.

13. Christoffersen and Paldam (2003) term this the *welfare coalition*. It is the share of those who work in the public sector plus those who receive an income-compensating social payment in some part of the year.

14. A collection of the main articles is found in Pejovich (1997). See also the long essay in Pipes (1999).

15. See Inglehart, Basañez, and Moreno (1997). The data used are from the home page of the project. We disregard the "don't know" and start the cumulative curves (0,0). The curve thus ends at (10,100) per definition. Points for answers 1 to 9 are nontrivial. The area between the curve and the straight neutrality line from (0,0) to (10,100) measures excess capitalist values if the area is above the line or excess socialist values if the area is below the line.

16. From the other chapters in this book, it is obvious that motives other than ideological ones exist to nationalize or create public firms; see, e.g., the chapters on Finland and Spain.

17. The survey is done separately from the (former) DDR. It was even more capitalist than West Germany in 1990, when the easterners wanted to be Westernized, but it was much less capitalist in the latest wave, as many have developed second thoughts, and a wave of *ostalgia* (formed by "east" and "nostalgia") has swept the area of the late DDR.

18. This applies to the Military Uniform Factory and the Naval Shipyard, which were transformed from military institutions into SOEs in the early 1980s but never privatized. The Military Uniform Factory went bankrupt in 1996 in a rather spectacular way and was liquidated, and the Naval Shipyard was closed too, though in a less spectacular way.

19. His description of events is that the process changing the company was planned during his own tenure as minister of finance in the Schlüter government, as a reaction to the EU Green Book (see EU 1987) on telecommunication. Hence it would make the process truly nonpolitical.

20. The second airport in the country is Billund Airport. It has remained private as it started as the company airport of LEGO and gradually developed into the main airport in Jutland. The public Aarhus Airport is losing passengers due to its poor location, which local politics has made it impossible to change.

21. As much as such comparisons make sense, Greenlanders (an Inuit/Eskimo people) had an African standard of living and a widely dispersed population.

22. Three levels exist in Denmark: state, 45 percent; county, 8 percent; and municipality, 45 percent. The percentages show the share of total expenditures they administrated in 2001. Local governments have the right to impose income taxes as well as land taxes, within certain limits.

23. The distribution of cost differences has a large variance and is an upward skew. In about 10 percent the cases, the public producer is cheaper, but at the end of the tail, large

cost differences appear. Public producers sometimes diverge into remarkable inefficiency before the system reacts. In Denmark the most famous case of such divergence is the postal letter sorting facility (Postterminalen) between 1970 and 1985.

24. Another 10 percent is done by nonprofit nongovernmental organizations (NGOs) under municipal control. Thus, 10 percent of the schools are non-profit NGOs, of which some are Catholic or Islamic.

References

Blom-Hansen, J. 2003. "Is Private Delivery of Public Services Really Cheaper? Evidence from Public Road Maintenance in Denmark." *Public Choice* 115, 419–438.

Borcherding, T. E., Pommerehne, W. W., and Schneider, F. 1982. "Comparing the Efficiency of Private and Public Production: The Evidence from Five Countries." *Zeitschrift für Nationalökonomie* 89 (suppl. 2), 127–156.

Christoffersen, H., Paldam, M., and Würtz, A. 2000. "Public versus Private Production and Economics of Scale." *Public Choice*.

Christoffersen, H., and Paldam, M. 2003. "Markets and Municipalities: A Study of the Behavior of the Danish Municipalities." *Public Choice* 114, 79–102.

Domberger, S., and Jensen, P. 1997. "Contracting Out by the Public Sector: Theory, Evidence, Prospects." *Oxford Review of Economic Policy* 13, 67–80.

EU. 1987. Towards a Dynamic European Economy, Green Paper and the Development of the Common Market for Telecommunication Services and Equipment. Brussels.

Gørgens, T., Paldam, M., and Würtz. 2003. "How Does Public Regulation Affect Growth?" Working paper, Department of Economics, University of Aarhus.

Inglehart, R. 1997. *Modernization and Postmodernization: Cultural, Economic and Political Change in forty-three Societies.* Princeton, N.J.: Princeton University Press.

Inglehart, R., Basañez, M., and Moreno, A. 1997. *Human Values and Beliefs.* Ann Arbor: Michigan University Press.

Kristensen, O. P. 1983. "Public versus Private Provision of Governmental Services: The Case of Danish Fire Protection Services." *Urban Studies* 20, 1–9.

Paldam, M. 1991. "The Development of the Rich Welfare State of Denmark." In M. Blomström and P. Meller, eds., *Diverging Paths: Comparing a Century of Scandinavian and Latin American Economic Development.* Baltimore: Johns Hopkins University Press.

Paldam, M. 1997. "Rent Seeking and Dutch Disease: An Essay on Greenland." *European Journal of Political Economy* 13, 591–614.

Paldam, M. 2003. "The Economic Freedom of Asian Tigers: An Essay on Controversy." *European Journal of Political Economy* 19, 453–478.

Pejovich, S. 1997. *The Economic Foundations of Property Rights: Selected Readings.* London: Edward Elgar.

Pipes, R. 1999. *Property and Freedom.* London: Harvill Press.

5   Privatization and Public Ownership in Finland

Johan Willner

In addition to infrastructure industries and public services, there has been public ownership in Finland in banking and manufacturing as well. It contributed 18 to 22 percent of industrial value added (and 12 to 15 percent of industrial employment and 23 to 30 percent of exports), as compared to 14 percent in Austria, 11 percent in Britain, 7 percent in Germany, 6 percent in Sweden, and 1 to 2 percent in the United States (World Bank 1995, Parker 1998).

Many state-owned companies have now been sold, but Finland has no privatization program. The government requires public control of some companies (in energy, aviation, alcohol, broadcasting, lotteries, and football pools), whereas others (mainly in the forest and metal industry) are seen as investment objects that can be sold (and merged). There will be minority ownership in an intermediate group (including producers of chemicals, basic metals and associated technology) because of its strategic importance (Omistuspohjan laajentaminen 2002). As for public services and infrastructure industries, private provision is increasing, but mostly through competition.

As the Ministry of Trade and Industry does, I shall define a company as *state owned* when the state owns at least 50 percent and as *associated* when the proportion is lower (and if there is no government-appointed supervisory board; Kaisanlahti 2001). *Privatization* means a reduction below 50 percent.

5.1 Public Ownership in Finland

In the literature, public ownership is usually analyzed in the context of a natural monopoly or a mixed oligopoly (Cremer, Marchand, and Thisse 1989; De Fraja and Delbono 1989; Willner 1999). But underdeveloped capital markets, short-term or risk-averse investors, and low private returns on investments have been mentioned as other reasons for public ownership (Rees 1984).

The explanations for public ownership in infrastructure industries and public services were the same in Finland as elsewhere, but industrialization provided the rationale in most other cases. Most manufacturing companies were therefore created (often by nonsocialists) rather than acquired, as a complement to conventional industrial policy (Miettinen 2000, Pohjola 1996).[1] In addition, some private investments were financed by the central bank, partly to reduce the interest margins within the banking sector (Knoellinger 1935), which meant that it could be described as a mixed oligopoly.

A growing wage share in the 1950s was believed to jeopardize growth. Public ownership is often seen as associated with a wage premium (Cremer, Marchand, and Thisse 1989), but the authorities saw increased state ownership as a way to sell wage moderation to the unions. Nationalization was ruled out, so the investments were directed toward new and existing state-owned companies (Kekkonen 1952).[2]

The first state-owned companies produced paper and pulp (Enso-Gutzeit and Veitsiluoto), basic metals (Outokumpu), fertilizers and other chemicals (Rikkihappo and Typpi, later merged as Kemira), banking services (the postal savings bank Postisäästöpankki), wines and spirits (Alko),[3] and, after the war, transport equipment (Valmet, Vanaja and Sisu), steel (Rautaruukki), oil products (Neste), paper machines (Valmet), and cars (the joint venture Saab-Valmet). Most of these were organized as limited companies, so as to be flexible and not dependent on the state budget (contrary to Britain and Ireland).

State-owned companies were supposed emphasize profitability, as in the private sector, but their objectives also included social welfare, public service, and the environment (Aura 1962a, 1962b) or support to other industries through cheap freight services and energy. A relatively stronger emphasis on growth as late as the period 1986 to 1989 (Miettinen 2000) is likely to have worked as in a mixed oligopoly. The commercial emphasis may now be even stronger than among private firms, at the expense of technological development (Miettinen 2000). But the fact that the proportion of female board members in listed state-owned companies is planned to increase from 25 percent (as compared to 7 percent among private plc's) to 40 percent may reflect some remaining wider objectives ("Outokumpu minskar skulder" 2002, Valtionyhtiöiden ... 2003).

As Rees (1984) points out, the performance of a public enterprise must be judged according to its objectives—in this case, industrialization and growth. GDP per capita increased in Finland by a factor of 8.7 from 1913 to 1998, as compared to 4.6 in Germany, 3.8 in Britain, 6.0 in Sweden, 5.2 in the United States, 5.6 in China, and 14.7 in Japan (Maddison 2001). Causality is difficult to prove without counterfactuals, but such growth seems to contradict the so-called Washington consensus that urges developing countries to privatize and liberalize (Stiglitz 2002).[4] The numbers are consistent with the positive effect of the size of the public enterprise sector (not the public sector) in Fowler and Richards (1995).[5]

Critics of public ownership usually refer to high costs (but see section 5.3), but sometimes also to dynamic inefficiency, including low R&D (Bös and Peters 1991). But low R&D follows from assuming that the state is unable to hire a competent and appropriately paid manager. Less is known if such restrictions are not imposed. State-owned companies in Finland have, for example, been high R&D spenders, and there is indirect evidence of entrepreneurial dynamism.

For example, Enso was an internationally significant producer with several forest industry plants abroad, and Stora-Enso is now second largest in the world (Statsbolagen 1990, 1996; Statsbolagen och intressebolagen 2001). Outokumpu has divested its mines and is now third largest in steel (after Thyssen Krupp and Arcelor), a world leader in stainless steel and supraconducting materials, and a provider of machinery and technology including water treatment plants ("Lågkonjunkturen hot mot nya satsningar" 2002, 2003b, Outokumpu Technology 2002). Rautaruukki has experienced a similar shift from steel to technology, like Kemira, which is now focusing on environmental cleaning and biotechnology, in addition to a wide range of chemicals in more than thirty countries. Metso (formerly Valmet) is emphasizing automation and is a world leader in paper machines (Statsbolagen och intressebolagen 2001).

Nokia, which was first known for paper tissues, tires, boots, cables, and light bulbs and later mobile phones, has never been state owned. But a highly innovative state-owned producer of defense equipment, Televa, made cables, digital switches, and mobile phones for the domestic market and the Soviet Union and was merged with Nokia's electronics division in 1981. This became Telenokia, which produced a completely digital exchange (DX 2000) in 1982 and the world's first mobile car phone in 1984 (Kasvio 1997, Moen 2002). Low charges and fast digitalization (second only to France) within the public P&T administration may also have contributed to Nokia's success (Björkroth and Willner 2003).

5.2   Privatization and Its Motives

Despite a stronger market orientation in the 1980s, privatization did not enter the agenda until a coalition government issued the blueprint Visio yksityistämisestä Suomessa (1991). The recession prevented its right-wing successor from selling shares until 1994, so most privatizations took place from 1995 to 2003 after a swing to the left. The state will remain a big owner according to the present coalition, but further divestiture is not ruled out (Ajankohtainen näkemys 2003).

Some companies were sold (and acquired) before the 1990s, but the privatizations from 1994 onward signify a policy shift. The most important examples are Enso (1998), Sisu (1997), Valmet (1996), Rautaruukki (1997), and Leonia (2000). Despite a state ownership of less than 50 percent, Outokumpu is still dominated by public sector organizations (like Rautaruukki until 1998). Corporatization has, on the other hand, created new state-owned companies, as in postal services, railways, and telecommunications. There are now thirty-one state-owned and eighteen associated companies (the most important are listed in Table 5.1, together with predecessors and completely privatized firms).

The motives for privatization in Finland are not completely clear. The policy documents are not very revealing, and there have been few debates. The 1991 blueprint described state-owned companies as fairly efficient (see also section 5.3), but mentioned the need for sales revenues and mergers (in contrast to the emphasis on cost cutting and competition in public services). Mixed markets were ruled out as unsound, as was public sector dominance.

Some policy documents also mention the reduced need to intervene in favor of industrialization (Kääriäinen 1994, Valtion yhtiöomistuksen historia 2001, Miettinen 2000), or they no longer see any valid strategic and sociopolitical need for public ownership (Salminen and Viinamäki 2001). International competition and a need to react swiftly are also seen as calling for privatization (through mergers), like the difficulties in using state ownership for policy purposes in, for example, telecommunications (Valtion yhtiöomistuksen historia 2001, Kääriäinen 1994, Miettinen 2000, Salminen and Viinamäki 2001). State ownership is now seen as reducing the access to venture capital (in contrast to the the earlier view).

Table 5.1
Privatization and remaining public ownership: Banking and manufacturing (percentages)

Company	1990	1996	2003	Minimum ownership
Alko-Yhtiöt (alcoholic beverages, production and trade)[a]	100.0	100.0		
Alko Inc. (retail trade)			100.0	
Altia (production and wholesale trade)			100.0	50.1
Finnair Oyj (aviation)	70.0	60.9	58.4	50.1
Fortum (energy production, oil refining)			60.8	50.1
Neste (oil refining)	98.0	83.6		
Ivo Group (energy production)	95.6	95.6		
Kemijoki (energy production)	77.3	78.2	67.0	51.0
Kemira (chemicals)[b]	100	72.3	56.2	15.0
Kone (lifts and escalators)			4.7	0.0
Partek Corporation (engineering)		30.2		
Oy Sisu Ab (vehicles, defense equipment, components)	97.7			
Metso Corporation (metal engineering)			11.5	0.0
Valmet Oy (metal engineering)	79.8	20.3		
Outokumpu Oyj (metals and technology)[c]	57.5	40.0	39.6	10.0
Patria Industries (defense materials and technology)			73.2	50.1
Rautaruukki Corporation (mining and metals)	86.8	68.9	40.1	20.0
Sampo plc (banking and insurance)			40.4	0.0
Postipankki Oy (subsequently Leonia Oy; banking)	100.0	100.0		
Stora Enso Oyj (forest industry)[d]			11.2	0.0
Enso Oy		35.2		
Enso-Gutzeit Oy	50.3			
Veitsiluoto Oy	88.8			
Vapo (peat, timber, biotechnology)	100.0	100.0	66.7	50.1
Oy Veikkaus Ab (football pools and lotteries)	100.0	100.0	99.6	—

Sources: Statsbolagen 1990, 1995; Statsbolagen och intressebolagen 2001, 2002; Valtionyhtiöt ja osakkuusyhtiöt, 2003. Ministry of Trade and Industry press releases (2.8.1996 and 18.9.1996).
[a] The subsidiary Arctia (hotels and restaurants) now belongs to the Scandic chain.
[b] A failed privatization attempt was made in 2002.
[c] The Finnish Social Insurance Institution owns 12.3 percent of the shares, so the majority of the shares are still directly or indirectly in public ownership.
[d] Enso was still indirectly in public ownership 1996 through the Finnish Social Insurance Institution until being merged with Stora Ab in Sweden in 1998.

The authorities refer to globalization in the case of manufacturing and traditional public sector industries (Kohti tehokkaampaa ja laadukkaampaa julkista taloutta 2002, Salminen and Viinamäki 2001). The EU directives that require the commercial production of goods and services to be subject to competition apply to both infrastructure industries and many public services. But state-owned manufacturers such as Enso and Valmet were exposed to international competition before being privatized, and the EU has no policy on ownership.

However, the official motives are not completely convincing. Public ownership may no longer be the only alternative, but this does not make privatization necessary. Also, there was a public sector surplus when the first blueprint was commissioned. Lower wealth just reduces the state's credit-worthiness and future dividend incomes. Some divestiture made entry into the European Monetary Union easier, given the public debt that was later caused by the depression in the 1990s, but this cannot explain the extent of privatization.

As for other motives, political influence can be reduced without privatization. Regulated utilities may in fact be less independent after privatization than universities and central banks or Finland's listed state-owned companies. Raising funds through the stock market does not necessarily require lost control. Mergers may not increase corporate performance.

This difficulty of finding convincing official motives might suggest opportunistic reasons such as electoral gains. But there is no evidence of public pressure in favor of privatization, and a Gallup Finland poll on local services suggests even the opposite ("KTV:n kysely" 2003).[6] This may explain why there is no privatization program, why privatization is not an election theme, and why the authorities use the euphemism "broadened ownership base". But voter inertia may create a temporary monopoly and hence allow a policy that is based on ideology or fashion, as in the report that wants to reduce the "size and significance of the public sector" and describes privatization as "linked to the value and norm climate of society and to the nature of the political administrative system, power hegemonies and corresponding issues" (Salminen and Viinamäki 2001, 56).[7]

5.3   The Industrial Sector: Revenues, Restructuring, and Financial Performance

Like public ownership, privatization must partly be evaluated according to what it was meant to achive. Mergers and high revenues would then be more important criteria than changes in cost efficiency and financial performance.

As divestiture and widespread ownership are not ends in themselves as in Britain, shares are sold only at a satisfactory price. The proceeds from 1990 to 2000 were about 9.650 million euros or 6.6 percent of the GDP in 2000, and more than the EU and OECD averages of 4.2 percent and 0.2 percent (Schneider 2003).[8] This has not reduced the state's dividend incomes, which amounted to about 669 million euros in 2002 despite a decade of divestiture ("Statligt ägande under lupp" 2003a). But Sonera's share price fall (see section 5.4) led to a postponement and hence lost sales revenues. Also, the parliament blocked the privatization of Kemira in 2002 because of doubts about the buyer.

The proceeds have been used to reduce public debt and to fund R&D in universities, the Academy of Finland, and Industry Investment Ltd. (Valtioneuvoston..., 2000). Industry Investment is a state-owned venture capital company that promotes the realization and commercialization of innovations by investing in private equity funds and regional or venture capital funds, with an emphasis on information and communications technology (ICT). It also invests directly, sometimes in partnership, in promising companies like Finlux, which is specializing in nonflammable television sets (Industry Investment 2001).

As for industrial restructuring, Stora Enso was created by merging Veitsiluoto, Enso-Gutzeit, and later Stora in Sweden; Metso by merging Rauma with parts of Valmet; and Fortum by merging IVO group and Neste. Leonia became part of Sampo. A number of large and often international players thus emerged, but the mixed international experiences of mergers suggest a risk for future disappointments (see Tichy 2001, Mueller 2001).[9] It has turned out that Fortum and perhaps Metso will split ("Tor Bergman fick sparken" 2003c).

Low cost efficiency may lead to privatization elsewhere, but might even lead to a postponement in Finland. To compare cost efficiency or profitability is nevertheless relevant because of their relatively larger role in other countries. Also, the stronger emphasis on profits just before privatization rules out sources of change in social welfare other than cost efficiency. The wider objectives among public firms until the late 1980s might, on the other hand, suggest lower performance in earlier periods. Few comparisons of of cost efficiency or productivity are available, so table 5.2 focuses on operating profits and net income as percentages of turnover in mixed industries, on which data are available from the mid-1980s onward.

Table 5.2
Operating profits and net income as a percentage of turnover in state-owned and private companies

State owned	Operating profits	Net income	Private	Operating profits	Net income
Metal engineering					
Valmet	6.9%	3.2%	Rauma-Repola	8.2%	1.9%
Forest industry					
Enso-Gutzeit	16.0	11.7	Kymmene	18.0	13.1
Veitsiluoto	14.9	5.8	Metsä-Serla[a]	14.4	8.0
			Metsä-Botnia	19.2	13.4
			Metsäliiton Teollisuus[b]	13.5	10.0
			A. Ahlström	11.7	6.4
			Yht. Paperitehtaat	14.3	10.5
Steel					
Rautaruukki	18.2	13.1	Ovako Steel	15.1	8.4
Electricity generation					
Imatran Voima	33.7	9.9	Teollisuuden Voima	56.1	30.8
			Pohjolan voima	17.7	7.1
Banking[c]					
Postipankki	10.9	7.3	Kansallis-Osake-Pankki	15.1	9.6
			Suomen Yhdyspankki	17.5	11.9

Source: The numbers are calculated from Suomen Yritysten ... '89 (1988).
Note: Operating profits are as a percentage of turnover, 1985–1987, and net income is as a percentage of turnover, 1986 to 1987.
[a] OP refers to 1986–1987.
[b] OP and NI refer to 1985 only.
[c] The figures are percentages of interest incomes, 1986–1987.

Some state-owned companies performed slightly better and others slightly worse than their private counterparts in the 1980s, so table 5.2 does not support any simplistic views on ownership.[10] However, differences in financial performance are now even less likely than in the 1980s to reflect objectives because of the stronger emphasis on profits in state-owned firms. The remaining state-owned and associated companies do not perform as well as Nokia but are better than average among the other listed companies, as shown in table 5.3.

The macroeconomic turbulence, the gradual change of objectives, and subsequent mergers make it difficult to isolate possible ownership effects, so it may be too early for a verdict. Table 5.4 nevertheless presents operating profits as a percentage of net sales before and after the most important cases of lost state control for the years before priva-

Table 5.3
Average financial performance among listed companies in Finland, 1997–2002

	Profit-ability	Net result	Dividend yield	P/E ratio
All listed companies in Finland	9.5%	5.8%	2.1%	26.7
All listed companies except for Nokia	7.6	4.3	3.3	18.0
State-owned and associated companies	7.8	4.4	2.7	20.4

Source: Statsbolagen och intressebolagen 2002.

Table 5.4
Operating profits as a percentage of net sales before and after privatization

	1987–1990	1998–2001	1999–2002
Enso-Gutzeit/Stora Enso	11.31%	12.26%	11.33%
Outokumpu	9.41	5.72	6.45
Rautaruukki	12.29	4.46	2.89
Sisu/Partek	5.94	5.08	NA
Valmet/Metso	1.10	4.29	4.96
Veitsiluoto/Stora Enso	11.52	12.26	11.33

Sources: 1987–1990: Balance sheet information from Statsbolagen 1987, 1989, 1990. 1998–2002: As presented in Statsbolagen och intressebolagen 2000, 2001, 2002.

tization entered the agenda (1987–1990), the most recent period (1999–2002), and for 1998–2001, which like 1987–1990 consists of three years of high economic activity followed by the first signs of a recession.

The lack of easily detectable ownership effects is also illustrated by a case study of Enso (including predecessors) and two leading private competitors just before and during privatization. The state's holdings were reduced below 50 percent in Enso 1992, but it remained in control until 1997; other public sector owners meant dominant public ownership until the merger with Stora in Sweden in 1998. As table 5.5 suggests, there is little evidence of early ownership effects.

Although little is known about cost efficiency, dramatic improvements would be surprising given the comparisons of financial performance in tables 5.2 to 5.5. It is often argued that competition may be more important than privatization, and most companies met competition long before being sold.[11] The same collective agreements have applied to both public and private firms, so wage costs may have been roughly equal in both types. Managerial mobility between public and private firms may be another reason (see Estrin and Pérotin 1991). But some studies from the United Kingdom, Italy, and Austria suggest

Johan Willner

Table 5.5
Financial performance in the forest industry 1990–1998

	Enso		Metsä-Serla		Kymmene	
	Profitability	P/E ratio	Profitability	P/E ratio	Profitability	P/E ratio
1990	14.5%	20.6	5.3%	<0	18.0%	16.3
1991	11.5	<0	9.3	<0	13.7	<0
1992	15.9	<0	9.3	<0	13.7	<0
1993	22.9	16.7	16.9	62.8	17.3	<0
1994	20.3	5.7	15.5	9.3	17.9	8.9
1995	23.5	2.9	24.0	3.1	20.5	4.1
1996	17.6	8.2	13.6	21.0	17.1	11.2
1997	17.8	7.2	17.7	9.7	21.1	7.0
1998	17.8	30.3	17.9	5.5	26.7	6.3

Source: Wikman (1999).
Note: Enso-Gutzeit became Enso in 1995, and Stora Enso in 1998. Kymmene became UPM-Kymmene in 1996. Profitability refers to operating profits as a percentage of turnover.

that Finland's experiences of limited ownership effects are not unique (Martin and Parker 1997, Fraquelli and Erbetta 2000, Schaffhauser-Linzatti and Dockner 2001).

As for performance comparisons in mixed markets, surveys of the literature such as Megginson and Netter (2001), Borcherding, Pommer-ehne, and Schneider (1982), Millward (1982), Boyd (1986), and Willner (2001) do not overlap completely, and they reach different conclusions. Taken together, they suggest that public ownership is not necessarily inferior, in particular if the output is fairly homogeneous (as also in some infrastructure industries; see section 5.4). This is consistent with some theoretical models and may also apply to industries where privatization requires regulation of price or quality, or both (Pint 1991, De Fraja 1993, Willner 2003, Laffont and Tirole 1991).

Successful public ownership may seem surprising, given the belief that the lack of profit-seeking owners leads to managerial slack or distorted objectives because of selfishness in all social roles. But some still controversial research suggests that the way in which we behave in an organization is to some extent endogenous (Fehr and Schmidt 1999, Fehr and Fishbacher 2002, Frey 1977), and this can affect the quality of governance. Finland gets the highest unweighted average of 199 countries of such governance indicators as government effectiveness, regulatory quality, and control of corruption (Kaufmann, Kraay, and Mastruzzi 2003). This may help to explain Finland's economic growth (Jalilian, Kirkpatrick, and Parker 2003) and ability to use state ownership, at least if the quality of governance was otherwise similar in the 1920s and 1930s, despite some political instability.

The leading ICT companies have not changed ownership, and no major changes in performance have taken place, so privatization cannot explain Finland's recent growth. Also, there have been no changes in labor market policy and the emphasis on profits after privatization, so significant changes of social welfare are unlikely. But so far, privatization has achieved its aims, without falling productivity and deteriorating financial performance. Good preprivatization performance seems to be a success factor, which suggests the paradox that privatization may work best if there is no need to privatize.

5.4   Public Sector Reform: Costs, Quality, and Consumer Benefits

Few providers in public services and infrastructure industries have been sold, but private provision has increased through competition, with the aim to cut costs (in contrast to banking and manufacturing). In local services, private provision has increased more under left-wing authorities, probably as an alternative to cuts (Granqvist 1997). Electricity and telecommunications were not completely noncommercial in the 1990s and are therefore affected by EU directives on competition. But the process is scarcely caused by the directives, because the authorities are not reluctant to liberalize (and they are lobbying the EU in favor of, for example, more railway deregulation).

International evidence suggests that public ownership is not inferior in infrastructure industries such as water and electricity (Boyd 1986; Willner 2001, 2003; Saal and Parker 2000). Most water companies in Finland are likely to remain municipal or supramunicipal, but some companies use private subcontractors. Also, some rural districts have private (noncommercial) providers (Hukka and Katko 2002).

The electricity industry is being liberalized. Supply and production became separated from transmission and distribution in 1995, and since 1998 there has been competition even for households. Half of the electricity is produced by the state-owned Fortum and by Teollisuuden Voima (which is owned by several private companies), and partly by nuclear plants. The remainder is dominated by local and often municipal producers. Some regions are now supplied by Vattenfall (from Sweden). The market is regulated by the Energy Market Authority under the Ministry of Trade of Industry. All types of plants have been described as fairly productive. Total factor productivity increased by

5.8 percent between 1994 and 1996, but there was no significant increase from 1996 to 1998. Finland's participation (with Sweden and Norway) in Nordpool may also have made pricing more efficient. But full liberalization and Cournot competition might not reduce prices and increase welfare (Kopsakangas-Savolainen 2003, Sulamaa 2001).

Telecom Finland was corporatized in 1994 and separated from the PT administration and listed as Sonera in 1998. The gradual deregulation from 1987 to 1993 led to dominance in long-distance calls by Sonera, Finnet (a group of former often municipal providers), and Telia (owned by the Swedish state). The ICT crisis and participation in the German auctions for universal mobile telecommunications services (UMTS) caused problems for the otherwise successful incumbent. The Finnish state owned 100 percent until 1998, 52.8 percent until the merger with Telia in 2002, and now 19.1 percent.[12] Fixed long-distance daytime calls became cheaper by 10 percent after the first step of liberalization in 1987 (and by 11 percent off-peak), but by 47 to 73 percent because of digitalization and other technical progress during the old system before 1987 (Björkroth and Willner 2002, 2003), which may therefore have achieved similar results (see also Sung 1998 and Taylor and Taylor 1993 on the United States). The industry is regulated by the Finnish Communications Regulatory Authority (FICORA).

The railways became a state enterprise in 1990 and were corporatized as VR Group in 1995. Privatization is unlikely, but some profitable freight operations and suburban commuter services may become tendered. Finland's railways do not necessarily offer much scope for improvement, as VR Group has already the highest ratio of revenues to costs (66 percent) among sixteen European countries (chapter 1, this volume). Corporatization has led to higher ticket prices and threats of service cuts, but productivity was higher in Finland than in the United States or Europe in the 1980s as well, with an annual growth of 2.3 to 3.8 percent (Lehto 1991, 1997a). A cautious strategy might therefore be motivated, also in the light of the mixed British experiences (see chapter 1, this volume).

The delivery of greater parcels and business mailings may be subject to competition in the future, but Suomen Posti (which became a limited company in 1994, separated from the telecommunications in 1998, and listed in 2001) will probably also remain in public ownership. Corporatization has led to increased profit margins, these have been achieved partly through service cuts, for example, by 40 percent fewer post offices (Lehto 1997b).

One operator has been privatized and a VR Group subsidiary has in fact expanded, but otherwise there have been few changes in the organization of rural and intercity bus services. The municipal market share shrank by contrast in regional and urban services (from 85 percent to 65 percent in Helsinki), and two suburban municipal operators outside Helsinki were acquired by large foreign companies. Costs fell by 14 to 30 percent (depending on whether tendering costs are included) and ticket prices by about 15 percent. Pay, working conditions, and job security deteriorated (as they did in Britain; see White 1990). The amount of sick leave increased, and the legal proceedings caused by redundancies were expensive. Many private operators have been merged, and some efficient but small firms were unable to organize bids and had to quit.[13] But frequency, tariffs, route network, and rolling stock are still regulated (and services were often cut in advance), so passengers are less affected by competitive tendering than in some British regions with stronger operator autonomy (Haatainen 2000, Kähkönen 2001, Kohtamäki 2000, Mäkeläinen and Pirttinen 2000, White 1990).

Public and private health care have always coexisted in Finland, and the private sector now includes some specialized hospitals as well. The private market share has increased since the 1980s because of public sector underfunding. Medivire, which served state employees, was acquired by the investment company MB-Funds in 2000 and is now Finland's largest occupational health care company (Statsbolagen och intressebolagen 2002, 2003; "MB Funds lead..." 2002). A local hospital has also been sold to a voluntary organization. Otherwise there has been mostly reorganization, including competition between public sector providers, without privatization. Some studies suggest subsequent productivity increases of 0.5 to 5.2 percent (Kohti... 2002, Hjerppe and Luoma 1997).[14]

Property maintenance in the state sector was separated from property management after being transferred to Engel Group Ltd. in 1994 and privatized in 1998. Of 3,200 permanent employees or civil servants, 1,500 were given notice and 600 transferred as so-called new employees with lower pay (Salminen and Viinamäki 2001). Press reports suggest a deterioration of staff welfare and service quality (HS, 30.11.1997).[15]

As for the municipal sector, Kähkönen (2001) evaluates some cases of competitive tendering and increased private provision in Helsinki. School cleaning was rationalized (1991–1993) and subject to competitive tendering (1994–1997), but there is again in-house provision (since 1998) because of lower quality and 14 percent higher costs. Meals on wheels were tendered in 1993, 1995, 1997, and 1999 and wintertime street maintenance (with a stable market share of 35 percent for private contractors) in 1996. Net costs fell by about 18 percent (partly because of lower wage rates and younger staff among the entrants) and 7 to 10 percent, respectively, but there is evidence of lower customer satisfaction and quality.[16]

We may conclude that most observations of reduced costs have occurred in labor-intensive services, which conforms to experiences in other countries (as surveyed in Willner 2001, 2003) or to other chapters in this book.[17] But this does not necessarily imply causality, given the rationalization of the railways and postal services without privatization or substantial competition. The Finnish public sector is comparatively efficient, and the productivity increase was sometimes even higher in core public sector activities that were not subject to competition, such as land survey offices (10.4 percent), tax offices (0.9 percent), and employment offices (26.0 percent) (Kohti...2002, Hjerppe and Luoma 1997).

But the consumers of public services and their employees have often been worse off (while there have been few changes in manufacturing). Lower consumer satisfaction can be consistent with the quality distortions under profit maximization in models such as Spence (1975), not least because of cost cutting related to objectives that are difficult to monitor (Holmström and Milgrom 1991), in which case competition might not help.[18] Also, further consolidation in low-elasticity industries like electricity and telecommunications can mean increased profit margins and hence high welfare losses in the future.

To understand the potential trade-off associated with privatization, suppose that a welfare-maximizing public monopoly with user charges is replaced by an unregulated n-firm Cournot oligopoly. The output and price levels are x_1, x_0, p_1, and p_0; quality changes are ignored. The (absolute value of the) postprivatization price elasticity of demand is η. Long-run marginal costs are c and kc under private and public ownership. The costs of duplication are negligible.

Suppose first that the cost difference $(k-1)c$ depends on wages and working conditions, so that $(k-1)cx_0$ represents internal rent capture and is part of the total surplus, like the profits. Total welfare can then be higher after privatization only by reducing the profit margin below $(k-1)c$, that is, if $p_1 < kc$. It is well known that p_1 can be written as

$\eta n c/(\eta n - 1)$, so the reform improves welfare if $k > \eta n/(\eta n - 1)$. This condition is very stringent if η is low and the competitors are few, as often in former public monopolies. For example, η is about 0.35 in electricity generation in Finland (Kopsakangas-Savolainen 2003). A five-firm oligopoly (or an oligopoly with the Herfindahl index of 0.2) would have to reduce marginal costs by 57 percent in order to beat a welfare-maximizing monopolist, because marginal costs would have to be higher in the public monopoly by a factor of 2.33.[19]

However, competition authorities emphasize consumer welfare rather than a surplus (Lyons 2002). A lower price then always means a higher consumer surplus, so the rule $k > \eta n/(\eta n - 1)$ also applies, even if $(k - 1)c$ would represent waste rather than internal rent capture. So $\eta = 0.5$ would require costs to be higher by factors 3.0 and 1.25 in the public monopoly before a three- and ten-firm oligopoly yields higher consumer welfare.

5.5   Conclusion: Lessons to Be Learned

Finland's state-owned manufacturing sector is larger than in most other countries, despite some divestiture that is partly motivated by ideology and conformism and partly by a desire to fund R&D, secure entry into the EMU, and encourage mergers. Privatization has achieved its aims, not least because the companies that were sold were fairly well run. So far, there is no evidence of substantial changes in efficiency or financial performance. But some of the mergers have already been questioned. Also, a return to earlier wider objectives may be difficult.

As for public services and infrastructure industries, the reforms have in most, but not all, cases led to reduced costs, but this may be caused by competition rather than private provision. In addition, productivity has increased in unreformed activities as well. Social welfare may have changed either way, given that consumers and employees have in some cases been worse off.

Finland's experiences can be interpreted in two ways. A number of successful companies were created and sold at a high price when no longer needed. Also, many public services are cheaper to run. But privatization in Finland can alternatively be seen as a social experiment comparable to mending an engine that is not broken, and the lower costs in public services may at least to some extent represent a transfer rather than an efficiency gain.

Notes

I am grateful for comments by Stefan Voigt and other participants in the CESifo-seminars Privatization Experiences in the EU, Munich, January 10–11, 2003, and Cadenabbia, November 1–2, 2003; by the editors and referees; by seminar participants at Birmingham Business School; and by colleagues at my department. I am solely responsible for remaining errors.

1. However, these companies often had a comparative advantage in expanding to sectors where state ownership was not necessary (Aura 1962a). State ownership was also preferred to foreign ownership and was also supposed to reduce the influence of the then powerful Swedish-speaking minority (Pohjola 1996).

2. Urho Kekkonen was first prime minister and later president of Finland, 1956–1981.

3. Alko was, however, established for paternalistic reasons.

4. Such growth is not necessarily inconsistent with the property right theory, insofar as more cost-efficient alternatives (see, however, section 3) were not available.

5. Overcapitalization may have reduced the growth in output per employee in both public and private firms between the 1970s (Pohjola 1996) and the 1990s, when shareholder value got higher priority (Ali-Yrkkö and Ylä-Anttila 2001).

6. Public resistance made the parliament decide against selling Alko's production and wholesale trade.

7. Fashion matters also elsewhere: "Certainly, for a small open economy such as the Netherlands it would be difficult to ignore developments elsewhere in Europe. Thus, the Dutch privatization programme can be described as a 'curtsy to the times' rather than the result of a positive, grand design to revitalise the economy" (Hulsink and Schenk 1998, 255).

8. The revenues were 8,600 million euros for the period 1991–2002 (Statsbolagen och intressebolagen 2002).

9. Domestic concentration can of course be offset by increased international competition but can also thereby increase (Neumann, Böbel, and Haid 1985; Sugden 1983).

10. The performance among similar public and private firms was roughly similar before the crisis in the 1990s, as also in a pre-privatization comparison of listed companies (Valtionyhtiöt . . . 1989, Julkiset . . . 1996).

11. Finnair and Kemira also performed reasonably well (with percentage net incomes of 11.5 percent and 9.1 percent), but market power can then not be ruled out.

12. Telia-Sonera's mobile call division had to be sold because of the merger.

13. Other repercussions include a bus manufacturer being sold to Volvo in and partly relocated to Poland, because of concerns about customer stability.

14. International experiences of public and private provision are mixed (Willner 2001) partly because the public sector often provides a low-budget service for those who are uninsured. Also, costs per capita tend to be higher in countries dominated by private provision (Böckerman 1997, Puoskari and Taimio 2002).

15. For example, Engel Group lost all tenders while still state owned, until it learned to leave as much dust in the corridors as the competitors (HS, 30.11.1997).

16. Net costs include the costs related to the tendering process.

17. Insurance may be a notable exception (see von Ungern-Sternberg 1996).

18. For example, frequency is the most important quality dimension in urban bus transport. More far-reaching bus deregulation than in Finland meant reduced quality, including coordination, in most regions in Britain (Tyson 1990, White 1990, Oldale 1997). Deregulation in such cases may also require appropriate procedures for maintaining socially desirable routes that were previously cross-subsidized.

19. We might alternatively assume free entry so that firms enter until profits per turnover reach some given level r. As $r = 1/n\eta$, we get $n = 1/r\eta$, so we would get the condition $k > 1/(1 - r)$. A norm of $r = 0.05$ would yield $k = 1.05$, whereas $r = 0.3$ would mean $k = 1.43$.

References

Ajankohtainen näkemys. 2003. Ministry of Trade and Industry. ⟨http://www.reputation.fi/ktm/ajankohtaista/⟩.

Ali-Yrkkö, Jyrki, and Ylä-Anttila, Pekka. 2001. "Globalisation of Business in a Small Country—Does Ownership Matter?" Discussion paper no. 779, Research Institute of the Finnish Economy.

Aura, Teuvo. 1962a. "Valtion liiketoiminta." In Teuvo Aura, ed., *Talous ja yhteiskunta. Puheita ja puheenvuoroja.* Kuopio.

Aura, Teuvo. 1962b. "Hyvinvoinnin rakennuspuita." In Teuvo Aura, eds., *Talous ja yhteiskunta. Puheita ja puheenvuoroja.* Kuopio.

Björkroth, Tom, and Willner, Johan. 2002. "Deregulation and Corporate Behaviour: An Analysis of Long-Distance Telecommunication Charges." Paper presented at the Twenty-Ninth Earie conference, Madrid, September 5–8.

Björkroth, Tom, and Willner, Johan. 2003. "Liberalization and Technical Change in Finland." In Willem Hulsink and Emiel F. M. Wubben, eds., *On Creating Competition and Strategic Restructuring. Regulatory Reform in Public Utilities.* Cheltenham: Edward Elgar.

Böckerman, Petri. 1997. "Kuntapalvelujen kilpailuttaminen." In Eero Lehto, ed., *Monopoli vai kilpailu? Yksityistäminen, sääntely ja kilpailurajat.* Helsinki/Juva: Atena.

Borcherding, Thomas E., Pommerehne, Werner W., and Schneider, Friedrich. 1982. "Comparing the Efficiency of Private and Public Production: The Evidence from Five Countries." *Zeitschrift für Nationalökonomie* (Suppl. 2), 127–156.

Bös, Dieter, and Peters, Wolfgang. 1991. "Privatization of Public Enterprises: A Principal-Agent Approach Comparing Efficiency in Private and Public Sectors." *Empirica* 18, 5–16.

Boyd, Colin W. 1986. "The Comparative Efficiency of State Owned Enterprises." In Anant R. Negandhi, ed., *Multinational Corporations and State-Owned Enterprises: A New Challenge in International Business.* Greenwich, Conn., and London: Research in International Business and International Relations, JAI Press.

Cremer, H., Marchand, M., and Thisse, J. F. 1989. "The Public Firm as an Instrument for Regulating an Oligopolistic Market." *Oxford Economic Papers* 41, 283–301.

De Fraja, Giovanni. 1993. "Productive Efficiency in Public and Private Firms." *Journal of Public Economics* 50(1), 15–30.

De Fraja, Giovanni, and Delbono, Flavio. 1989. "Alternative Strategies of a Public Enterprise in Oligopoly." *Oxford Economic Papers* 41, 302–311.

Estrin, Saul, and Pérotin, Virginie. 1991. "Does Ownership Always Matter?" *International Journal of Industrial Organization* 9(1), 1–170.

Fehr, Ernst, and Fischbacher, Urs. 2002. "Why Social Preferences Matter—The Impact of Non-Selfish Motives on Competition, Cooperation and Incentives." *Economic Journal* 112, C1–C33.

Fehr, Ernst, and Schmidt, Klaus M. 1999. "A Theory of Fairness, Competition and Cooperation." *Quarterly Journal of Econmics* 114(3), 817–868.

Fowler, P. C., and Richards, D. F. 1995. "Test Evidence for the OECD-Countries, 1965–1985: The Relationship between the Size of the Public Enterprise Sector and Economic Growth." *International Journal of Social Economics* 22(3), 11–23.

Fraquelli, Giovanni, and Erbetta, Fabrizio. 2000. "Privatisation in Italy: An Analysis of Factor Productivity and Technical Efficiency." In David Parker, ed., *Privatisation and Corporate Performance*. Aldershot: Edward Elgar.

Frey, Bruno S. 1997. "On the Relationship between Intrinsic and Extrinsic Work Motivation." *International Journal of Industrial Organization* 15(4), 427–440.

Granqvist, Nina. 1997. *Privatisering i princip och praktik. En studie av privata inslag i de finländska kommunernas verksamhet.* Åbo: Åbo Akademis förlag.

Haatainen, Jaana. 2000. "Bussiliikenteen kilpailuttamisen vaikutukset palveluihin ja niiden laatuun." In Timo Aarrevaara, Jaana Haatainen, Risto Harisalo, and Jari Stenwall, eds., *Kilpailuttaminen joukkoliikenteessä—Kilpailuttamisen vaikutusten kartoittaminen*. Tampere: Tampereen Yliopisto, Hallintotieteen laitos.

Hjerppe, Reino, and Luoma, Kalevi. 1997. "Finnish Experiences in Measuring and Promoting Productivity in the Public Sector." Discussion paper 150, Government Institute for Economic Research, Helsinki.

Holmström, Bengt, and Milgrom, Paul. 1991. "Multi-Task Principal-Agent Analyses: Incentive Contracts, Asset Ownership and Job Design." *Journal of Law, Economics and Organization* 7, 972–991.

Hukka, Jarmo J., and Katko, Tapio S. 2002. "Water Privatisation—Panacea or Pancake?" Mimeo., Tampere University of Technology.

Hulsink, Willem, and Schenk, Hans. 1998. "Privatisation and Deregulation in the Netherlands." In David Parker, ed., *Privatisation in the European Union: Theory and Policy Perspectives*. London: Routledge.

Industry Investment. 2002. *Annual Report 2001*. Helsinki.

Jalilian, Hossein, Kirkpatrick, Colin, and Parker, David. 2003. "The Impact of Regulation on Economic Growth in Developing Countries: A Cross-Country Analysis." Mimeo.

Julkiset noteeratut yhtiöt. 1996. Lahti: Opstock, Oko-Osuuspankit.

Kaisanlahti, Timo. 2001. Corporate Governance in State-Owned Companies. Ministry of Trade and Industry Finland, Studies and Reports 11. Helsinki.

Kopsakangas-Savolainen, Maria. 2003. "Quantity versus Price Competition in the Finnish Electricity Markets." *Finnish Economic Papers* 16(2), 51–60.

Kääriäinen, Seppo. 1994. "Omistuspohjan laajentamisesta voimaa teollisuuden kehittämiseen." *Uudistuva teollisuus, valtionyhtiöt ja yksityistäminen*. Helsinki: Kauppa- ja Teollisuusministeriö.

Kähkönen, Liisa. 2001. *Kilpailuttamisen kustannusvaikutukset Helsingin kaupungin bussiliikenteessä, kotipalvelun ateriapalveluksessa, katujen kunnossapidossa ja koulusiivouksessa*. Tutkimuksia 2001:5. Helsinki: Helsingin kaupungin tietokeskus.

Kasvio, Antti. 1997. "Finland's Road to the Information Society." Paper prepared for the Finnish Sociological Congress.

Kaufmann, Daniel, Kraay, Aart, and Mastruzzi, Massimo. 2003. "Governance Matters III: Governance Indicators for 1996–2002." Mimeo, World Bank.

Kekkonen, Urho. 1952. *Onko maallamme malttia vaurastua?* 2nd ed. Helsinki: Otava.

Kohtamäki, Vuokko. 2000. "Bussiliikenteen kilpailuttamisen taloudellisista vaikutuksista." In Timo Aarrevaara, Jaana Haatainen, Risto Harisalo, and Jari Stenwall, eds., *Kilpailuttaminen joukkoliikenteessä—Kilpailuttamisen vaikutusten kartoittaminen*. Tampere: Tampereen Yliopisto, Hallintotieteen laitos.

Knoellinger, Carl-Erik. 1935. *Jämförande studier rörande kreditväsendets organisation med särskild hänsyn till konkurrensen mellan affärsbanker och sparbanker*. Åbo: Åbo Tidnings- och Tryckeri AB.

Kohti tehokkaampaa ja laadukkaampaa julkista taloutta. 2002. Valtiovarainministeriön työryhmä, VM128:00/2001. Ministry of Finance. Keskustelualoitteita nro 70, Valtionvarainministeriö [Ministry of Finance]: Helsinki.

"KTV:n kysely: Peruspalvelut halutaan pitää kunnallisina." 2003. *Helsingin Sanomat*, June 24.

Laffont, J.-J., and Tirole, J. 1991. "Privatization and Incentives." *Journal of Law, Economics and Organization* 7, 84–105.

"Lågkonjunkturen hot mot nya satsningar." 2003b. *Hufvudstadsbladet*, June 19, p. 12.

Lehto, Eero. 1991. *Valtionrautateiden tuottavuus 1945–1989*. Tutkimuksia 36. Helsinki: Työväen Taloudellinen Tutkimuslaitos.

Lehto, Eero. 1997a. "Kilpailuako rautateille?" In Eero Lehto, ed., *Monopoli vai kilpailu? Yksityistäminen, sääntely ja kilpailurajat*. Helsinki/Juva: Atena.

Lehto, Eero. 1997b. "Postipalvelut ja markkinamekanismi." In Eero Lehto, ed., *Monopoli vai kilpailu? Yksityistäminen, sääntely ja kilpailurajat*. Helsinki/Juva: Atena.

Lyons, Bruce L. 2002. "Could Politicians Be More Right Than Economists? A Theory of Merger Standards." Revised CCR working paper CCR 02-1, University of East Anglia.

Maddison, Angus. 2001. *The World Economy: A Millennial Perspective*. Paris: OECD.

Mäkeläinen, Ulla, and Pirttinen Susanna. 2000. "Bussiliikenteen kilpailuttamisen henkilöstövaikutukset." In Timo Aarrevaara, Jaana Haatainen, Risto Harisalo, and Jari Stenwall, eds., *Kilpailuttaminen joukkoliikenteessä—Kilpailuttamisen vaikutusten kartoittaminen*. Tampere: Tampereen Yliopisto, Hallintotieteen laitos.

Martin, Stephen, and Parker, David. 1997. *The Impact of Privatisation. Ownership and Corporate Performance in the UK*. London: Routledge.

"MB Funds Lead the Acquisition of Medivire." 2002. MB Funds, press release, February 11. ⟨http://www.mbfunds.com/tiedotteet/⟩.

Megginson, W. L., and Netter, J. M. 2001. "From State to Market: A Survey of Empirical Studies on Privatization." *Journal of Economic Literature* 39, 321–389.

Miettinen, Topi. 2000. "Poikkeavatko valtionyhtiöt yksityisistä?" Discussion paper no. 730, Research Institute of the Finnish Economy.

Millward, R. 1982. "The Comparative Performance of Public and Private Ownership." In Lord E. Roll, ed., *The Mixed Economy*. London: Macmillan.

Moen, Eli. 2002. *Globalisering og industripolitiske straegier. En sammenligning av Finland og Norge*. Oslo: Makt- og demokratiutredningens rapportserie, Nr. 41.

Mueller, Dennis C. 2001. "Rethinking EU Merger Policy." Paper presented at the Fifth Annual EUNIP Conference, Vienna.

Neumann, M., Böbel, I., and Haid, A. 1985. "Domestic Concentration, Foreign Trade and Economic Performance." *International Journal of Industrial Organization* 3, 1–19.

Oldale, Alison. 1997. "Local Bus Deregulation and Timetable Instability." Working paper, Economics of Industry Group, London School of Economics.

Omistuspohjan laajentaminen. 2002. Ministry of Trade and Industry. ⟨http://www.reputation.fi.ktm/tilastot/⟩.

"Outokumpu minskar skulder." 2002. *Hufvudstadsbladet*, Nov. 29, p. 11.

"Outokumpu Technology Awarded Two Turnkey Projects." 2002. Outokumpu Technology. Press Release, October 11. ⟨http://www.outokumpu.com/corporat/info/⟩.

"Palkka putosi jatyöt lisääntyivät." 1997. *Helsingin Sanomat*, Nov. 30, p. E2.

Parker, David, ed. 1998. *Privatisation in the European Union: Theory and Policy Perspectives*. New York: Routledge.

Pint, Ellen M. 1991. "Nationalization vs. Regulation of Monopolies: The Effects of Ownership on Efficiency." *Journal of Public Economics* 44(2), 131–164.

Pohjola, Matti. 1996. *Tehoton pääoma. Uusi näkökulma taloutemme ongelmiin*. Porvoo: WSOY.

Puoskari, Pentti, and Taimio, Heikki. 2002. *Suomen julkisen sektorin tila ja tulevaisuuden näkymät*. Tutkimuksia 86. Helsinki: Palkansaajien Tutkimuslaitos.

Rees, Ray. 1984. *Public Enterprise Economics*. 2nd ed. London: Weidenfeld and Nicholson.

Saal, David S., and Parker, David. 2000. "The Impact of Privatization and Regulation on the Water and Sewerage Industry in England and Wales: A Translog Cost Function Model." *Managerial and Decision Economics* 21(6), 253–268.

Salminen, Ari, and Viinamäki, Olli-Pekka. 2001. "Market Orientation in the Finnish Public Sector: From Public Agency to Privatised Company. Research reports 2/2001, Ministry of Finance and University of Vaasa, Helsinki.

Schaffhauser-Linzatti, Michaela M., and Dockner, E. J. 2001. "The Financial and Operating Performance of Privatized Firms in Austria." Mimeo. University of Vienna.

Schneider, Friedrich. 2003. "Privatisation in OECD Countries: Theoretical Reasons and Results Obtained." *Journal of Institutional Comparisons* 1, 24–29.

Spence, A. Michael. 1975. "Monopoly, Quality, and Regulation." *Bell Journal of Economics* 6, 417–429.

"Statligt ägande under lupp." 2003a. *Hufvudstadsbladet*, May 23, p. 11.

Statsbolagen 1987, 1889, 1990, 1995. 1988, 1990, 1991, 1996. Annual reports for the state-owned companies. Ministry of Trade and Industry.

Statsbolagen och intressebolagen 2000, 2001, 2002. 2001, 2002, 2003. Annual reports for state-owned and associated companies. Ministry of Trade and Industry.

Stiglitz, Joseph. 2002. *Globalization and Its Discontents.* London: Allen Lane/Penguin Books.

Sugden, Roger. 1983. "The Degree of Monopoly, International Trade, and Transnational Corporations." *International Journal of Industrial Organization* 1, 165–188.

Sulamaa, Pekka. 2001. *Essays in Deregulated Finnish and Nordic Electricity Markets.* Helsinki: Taloustieto OY.

Sung, Nakil. 1998. "The Embodiment Hypothesis Revisited: Evidence from the Local U.S. Local Exchange Carriers." *Information Economics and Policy* 10(2), 219–236.

Suomen yritysten taseet ja taustat '89. 1988. Kajaani: Startel Oy.

Taylor, William E., and Taylor, Lester D. 1993. "Postdivestiture Long-Distance Competition in the United States." *American Economic Review* 83, 185–190.

Tichy, Gunther. 2001. "What Do We Know of the Success and Failure of Mergers?" *Journal of Industry, Competition and Trade* 1(4), 347–374.

"Tor Bergman fick sparken." 2003c. *Hufvudstadsbladet*, September 26, p. 10.

Tyson, W. J. 1990. "Effects of Deregulation on Service Co-ordination in the Metropolitan Areas." *Journal of Transport Economics and Policy* 24(3), 283–295.

Valtioneuvoston periaatepäätös valtion omaisuuden myynnistä vuosina 2000–2003 saatavien tulojen käytöstä. 2000. Ministry of Trade and Industry.

Valtion yhtiöomistuksen historia. 2001. Ministry of Trade and Industry. ⟨http://www.reputation.fi/valtion_omistajapolitiikka/⟩.

"Valtionyhtiöiden hallituksiin löytyy päteviä naisia." 2003. Ministry of Trade and Industry. Press release, March 14. ⟨http://www.reputation.fi/ktm/⟩.

Valtionyhtiöt ja osakkuusyhtiöt. 2003. Ministry of Trade and Industry.

Valtionyhtiöt markkinataloudessa. 1989. Liiketaloustieteen tutkimuslaitos, Helsinki.

von Ungern-Sternberg, T. 1996. "The Limits of Competition: Housing Insurance in Switzerland." *European Economic Review* 40(3–5), 1111–1121.

White, Peter J. 1990. "Bus Deregulation: A Welfare Balance Sheet." *Journal of Transport Economics and Policy* 24(3), 311–332.

Wikman, Daniel. 1999. "Privatisering av offentligt ägda företag—en studie om privati-seringen av Enso Oy." Master's thesis, Åbo Akademi University.

Willner, Johan. 1999. "Policy Objectives and Performance in a Mixed Market with Bargaining." *International Journal of Industrial Organization* 17(1), 137–145.

Willner, Johan. 2001. "Ownership, Efficiency, and Political Interference." *European Journal of Political Economy* 17(4), 723–748.

Willner, Johan. 2003. "Privatization: A Sceptical Analysis. In David Parker and David Saal, eds., *International Handbook of Privatisation*.

World Bank. 1995. *Bureaucrats in Business: The Economics and Politics of Government Ownership*. Oxford: Oxford University Press.

6   Privatization Experiences in France

Michel Berne and
Gérard Pogorel

The approach used in this chapter is twofold. First, a general introduction to the specific features of French privatization policies is set out; then their impact is studied using the example of France Telecom, the incumbent telecommunications operator, with additional information about other significant firms. Because France has no dramatic examples of privatization policies, the interesting part of the story lies in the change of perspective that has led this country to stop being a champion of nationalization and to manage partially privatized firms within the framework of liberalization in Europe.

6.1   Nationalization and Privatization: A Historical Perspective

6.1.1   Nationalization Policies

French privatization cannot be understood without a long historical perspective. Before privatization, France lived through a long period of nationalization and built a doctrine about the coexistence of the private and the public sectors. Public services were traditionally provided by state-owned monopolies.

Private companies were nationalized in France in three major periods:

• At the end of the nineteenth century for some railways and the telephone. The PTT were created in 1889 by the merger of the state administration of Posts and Telegraphs and the privately held Société Générale des Téléphones. The resulting PTT administration existed until 1991.

• Before and after World War II, for the railways, the central bank, the energy producers, the major banks, and the car manufacturer Renault. Some were still state owned in 2003.

• In 1981–1982, the socialist government (F. Mitterrand was president of the Republic) nationalized all the largest industrial companies and banks remaining in private hands. Most of them returned to the private sector before 2000.

The rationale behind these various moves can be summarized as follows. First, some private companies were in poor financial health or provided substandard services (examples are railways, telephones, steelmakers, and computer manufacturers).

Second, some firms were thought to be too powerful or strategic to remain private companies: their resources and policies had a large impact on economic policies as a whole (e.g., banks, energy, transportation, defense). So in order to have a free hand for its economic and social policy, the government concluded it had to own the largest companies in the country. This was especially crucial after World War II, when the infrastructure had to be rebuilt as fast as possible, but it also inspired the nationalization policy of 1982. However, the debate between proponents and opponents of nationalization in 1982 looked like theology to the respected political commentator André Fontaine (1981). Fontaine predicted a limited impact on industrial firms but more on banks. Indeed, as Jacques Attali (1994), special assistant to President Mitterrand from 1981 to 1991, put it bluntly much later, "Had we not nationalized banks, banks would have been extremely hostile to all reforms. Maybe the Left has not transformed them into allies . . . but we have at least weakened and neutralized a potential 'enemy.'" We can add that the government wanted to use these firms as examples of well-run companies with advanced social policies.

Third, there was a special case with Renault. Because Louis Renault, then head of the company, had collaborated with the occupying German forces during World War II, his property was seized.

Starting with Colbert, the mercantilist finance minister of Louis XIV in the seventeenth century, French governments have slowly built a doctrine of a mixed economy, blending powerful public services; large state-owned companies in heavy industries, energy, transportation, and finance; and small private companies. Nationalization was just one part in a global policy including five-year economic plans, price controls, export management, and technology management (Cohen 1992). The peak of this policy can be found during the period when the Socialist party and its allies ruled France (1981–1986). At that time, the total public sector (central and local government plus state-con-

Table 6.1
Employment in public firms in France

	Employees (thousands)	% of total wage earners	% of total active population
1947	1,152	9.9	5.8
1960	1,108	8.3	5.6
1970	970	6.0	4.5
1980	1,088	6.0	4.6
1983	1,852	10.3	7.8
1988	1,355	7.2	5.6
1991	1,763[a]	9.1	7.0
1994	1,505	7.7	6.0

Source: Chabanas and Vergeau (1996), based on figures provided by INSEE.
[a] In 1991, La Poste and France Telecom abandoned their administrative status and became state enterprises; this move added 430,000 employees to the total.

Table 6.2
Companies controlled by the state

Year	Number of firms controlled	Employees in France (millions)	Share of total wage earners
2000	1,500	1.1	5.3

Source: INSEE, *Répertoire des entreprises contrôlées majoritairement par l'Etat.*
Note: The figures in tables 6.1 and 6.2 cannot be compared due to changes in statistical methodology.

trolled companies) represented 21 percent of production, 23 percent of wages earners (tables 6.1, 6.2), 28 percent of GDP, 30 percent of exports, and 49 percent of gross capital formation (Mamou 1996).

6.1.2   The Case for Privatization: Major Factors

It became clear over time that this situation could not go on forever for four major reasons.

First, besides the theoretical critics of state ownership of firms, basically resting on the theory of incentives, the French state behaved like a weak and erratic "shareholder," hesitating between the maximization of short-term financial or political benefits and a laissez-faire approach, which was supposed to let the state firms develop as they wished, in spite of the bureaucratic control of their activities. Several audits of state management of public firms can be found, most recently a report of the National Assembly (Diefenbacher 2003). In particular, the national telecom operator has long suffered from these vagaries (Bonnetblanc 1985; Bertolus, Cedro, and Del Jesus 2003). Adverse effects of poor state control can be felt by the firms themselves, by the treasury, and by other French investors.[1] One radical way to solve the problem was privatization. Another was to manage state investments better. In 2003, the Ministry of Finance created a state agency, Agence des Participations de l'Etat, to bring more consistency and vision to the management of state holdings (Barbier de la Serre 2003, Minefi 2003). In 1999, the total value of shares retained by the state amounted to 400 billion euros.[2] The French state is a major player on the Paris Bourse (now called Euronext).[3]

Second, the coexistence of state-run and private companies (as in the car industry since 1945 and the telecom industry more recently) is awkward and could prevent nationalized companies from expanding freely at home and abroad; any expansion by a state-owned firm causes the public sector to grow, even without any new nationalization measure.

Third, although they can boast an outstanding technical record (see section 6.2 for examples), state monopolies suffered from time to time from traditional problems of high prices, low regard for customers, and a bureaucratic attitude (see Giraud 1987 for the case of telecommunications). They also engaged in uncontrolled and costly expansion policies because of weak government control.

Fourth, a major liberalization and privatization drive started internationally in the 1980s, and France followed the trend. Media provide a good example: even the promoter of the public sector and major architect of nationalization, President Mitterrand, opened the broadcasting sector to private operators starting in 1982. This paved the way later for the privatization of the largest public TV channel, TF1. Although European competition policy does not demand privatization, it imposes severe restrictions on government intervention in the economy (like state aid); at the same time, deregulation policies (telecom, electricity, railways) allow new entrants—private companies that nearly automatically complain about the former state-owned monopoly and lead to difficulties with the European Commission.

6.1.3 Privatization Time Line

Privatization in France took place in several phases depending on the following factors:

• The outcome of legislative elections, the most crucial factor. In France, the prime minister represents the party winning the legislative elections (National Assembly, dominant part of the parliament) and sets the political agenda.[4] The center-right parties (led by the Rassemblement pour la République, since 2002 called Union pour un Movement Populaire) initiated the privatization drive in 1986, but are cautious regarding the privatization of public services. The Socialist party (the major component of the political left in France) after the nationalization episode of 1982 has offered diverging opinions about the management of state firms, and in 2003, this question was still a matter of internal debate in the party. As stated frankly by Henri Emmannuelli, one of the pillars of the Socialist party, "The opinion varies depending on whether we are in the majority or in the opposition" (Le Cœur and Macke 2003).

• Prices on the Paris Bourse (see figure 6.1 for the CAC 40 index over the period 1986–2003) are important as to the timing of privatization but have a limited impact on privatization decisions.

• European deregulation policies (so far particularly in the Telecom sector, but energy is the next on the list).

• Sector evolution like technical innovation, alliances, and globalization. The management of public entities may ask the government to privatize their firm in order to pursue their development plans. For

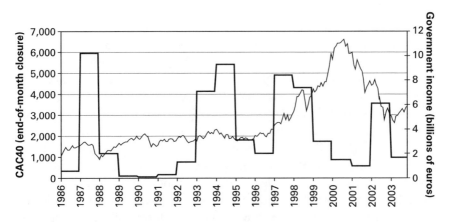

Figure 6.1
Stock market index and gross government income
Source: Minefi (2003).
Note: The CAC40 was initiated on January 1, 1988. For earlier dates, a "rebuilt" index found at ⟨www.bnains.org⟩ has been used. Dates given are for January 31 of each year.

Table 6.3
Privatization framework

1982	Nationalization law (February 11, 1982): Five major industrial firms, forty-one banks and finance groups
1986	Privatization law (July 2, 1986): Privatization of all companies nationalized after 1982 plus twelve others (mostly insurance, banking)
1986	Privatization law for TF1 (major public TV channel)
1989	"Hard-core" shareholders dismemberment act
1993	Privatization act (July 19, 1993): Privatization of thirteen additional groups, including Air France, Renault, SEITA, SNECMA, and Usinor-Sacilor
1997	IPO France Telecom
2003	Creation of Agence des Participations de l'Etat (State Agency for Public Firms Control)

Source: Adapted from Loiseau (2002).

example, Christian Blanc, then CEO of Air France, resigned in 1997 when Prime Minister L. Jospin refused to privatize the national airline.

The size of the state budget deficit also provides a permanent incentive to privatize state firms, as France has constantly experienced budget deficits since 1981. Proceeds from the sales of assets are welcome to finance various types of expenses that would be impossible to fund given the budget situation.

After five years of Socialist government, the center-right parties were in power again in 1986–1988 and started dismantling the enormous state sector (table 6.3). They benefited from favorable conditions on the Paris Bourse, at least until the minor 1997 stock crash. The Socialists came back to power in 1988 with a fragile majority in the National Assembly. They enforced a policy that was then was dubbed "neither-neither" (*ni-ni* in French): no privatization made by the previous government was overturned, but no further privatization was allowed. Limited operations happened nevertheless. The Socialists lost the general elections in 1993, and more privatization was decided on by Prime Minister Edouard Balladur. In 1995, Jacques Chirac won the presidential elections as well as the legislative elections, and additional privatization took place. In 1997, the president called for legislative elections and lost them to the Socialists. After some hesitation, the new prime minister, Jospin, went on privatizing state firms on a large scale. Finally, in 2002, Jacques Chirac won the presidential elections, and the right won the legislative elections (table 6.4).

Since 2002, the center-right government of Jean-Pierre Raffarin has made clear he favors privatizing state-owned companies. In his general policy address to the National Assembly in July 2002, the prime minis-

Table 6.4
Major IPOs and sales of shares by the state

Year	Industry	Services	Banking and insurance
1986	Saint-Gobain		
1987	CGCT, Compagnie Générale d'Electricité	TF1, Havas	Paribas, Compagnie financière de Suez, Société Générale, Crédit du Nord, CCF
1988	Matra		Caisse nationale de crédit agricole
1993	Rhône-Poulenc		BNP
1994	Elf-Aquitaine		UAP, Société Lyonnaise de Banque
1995	SEITA, Pechiney, Usinor-Sacilor		
1996			AGF
1997	Bull	France Telecom	
1998	Thomson-CSF (now Thalès)		CIC
1999	Dassault	Air France	Crédit Lyonnais
2000	Thomson Multi-media, EADS		
2002		Autoroutes du Sud de la France	
2003	Thomson, Dassault Systèmes		

Sources: Loiseau (2002), Minefi (2003).

ter said: "We have a pragmatic approach to the state's role in the economy. As such, we will analyse capital release and privatization projects case-by-case, taking particular account of companies' interests and the potential for alliances and development. This policy can only be envisaged over the full length of the term. In general, the state's aim is to withdraw from the competitive sector unless specific strategic interests make this undesirable" (Raffarin 2002).

One can add that the unsatisfactory government budget situation is a strong incentive to sell and raise funds. However, this government has been very pragmatic in its approach:

• Selling when favorable conditions appeared (for example, Crédit Lyonnais, sold over a weekend to Crédit Agricole in 2003 after some hectic bidding).

• Taking into account the long-term interests of the companies (as in the Air France–KLM merger decided at the end of 2003, which has lowered the share held by the state below 50 percent).

• Trying to "renationalize" companies in deep trouble. Such a rumor circulated regarding France Telecom in 2002 when the operator was close to financial breakdown. Considerable financial aid to France Telecom was given through other means. A bolder move was the attempt to rescue Alstom, the troubled electric and transportation equipment manufacturer, in the summer of 2003. The French government wanted to buy 300 million euros of Alstom shares. But this plan was not approved by the European authorities, and the government had to devise a different plan for Alstom.

6.1.4 Privatization Income

The large number of firms sold and their size make privatization profitable for the government. An evaluation commission (Commission des Participations et des Transferts) created in 1986 estimates the value of the companies being sold. The minister of economy decides on the actual sale price (higher than the price floor price set by the commission) and the sale method: on the stock market to a single investor or a group of investors by mutual agreement, or an auction.

The funds obtained in the sale are housed in a special account (Compte d'affectation des produits de cession), which is also used when the state-owned companies need fresh capital and loans, in particular before they are sold. Figure 6.2 shows the annual balance of this fund.

According to Minefi (2003), the gross privatization income from 1986 to July 2003 amounted to 65.8 billion euros, used in the following way:

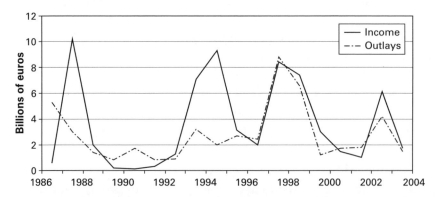

Figure 6.2
Privatization gross income and public sector outlays
Source: Minefi (2003).

• 9 billion to reduce the public debt (mostly between 1986 and 1988)

• 1.6 billion allocated to a special pension fund set up to ease the impact of demographic transition on the French pension system

• 50.5 billion allocated to the firms as equity

• 4.7 billion for the regular state budget (in the early 1990s)

Depending on the methodology used, other figures can be presented. As an example, France Telecom generated 12.3 billion euros of gross privatization income between 1986 and 2003 (excluding dividends and interests on loans, for example). When the state allowed the firm to benefit from an increase in capital of 9 billion euros in 2003, this sum was provided by a state-owned financial holding called ERAP. ERAP borrowed money to provide the amount required. This is not, from a formal point of view, an outlay by the state and therefore is not deducted from the gross income given above. Using this methodology, the Ministry of Finance found that only six major firms showed a negative balance (gross income minus outlays) over the period 1986–2003: Air France, Bull, Crédit Lyonnais, Société Marseillaise de Crédit, Thomson, and Usinor. All these companies have survived very difficult times.

As can be expected, different figures have been computed by other sources. Table 6.5 shows independent estimates from Mauduit (2002).

Whatever the computations made, from figures 6.1 and 6.2 and table 6.4, we can conclude that until 1997, privatization policies were conducted by the right only, while the left abstained. After 1997, the left adopted a more pragmatic approach and privatized major companies. We will see below how the initial public offering (IPO) of France Telecom played a major role in this policy change.

Table 6.5
Gross privatization income, 1986–2002: Major phases

Government	Coalition in power	Dates	Income (billion of euros)
Chirac	Right	1986–1988	13
Balladur	Right	1993–1995	17
Juppé	Right	1995–1997	9.4
Jospin	Left	1997–2002	31

Source: Mauduit (2002), based on Baert (2000) and Orange and Rocco (1999).
Note: More than 6 billion euros had been spent in 1983 in the major nationalization plan.

6.2   Impact of Privatization

6.2.1   *Changes of Ownership*

Two very different cases can be distinguished regarding changes of ownership. Some companies were swiftly and totally privatized (the smaller ones or the industrial firms nationalized in 1982), but a large number of state-controlled companies went through a long and sometimes painful privatization process: after a partial IPO, the state gradually sold additional chunks of shares until its participation became nil or reduced to a "golden share" (*action spécifique*). In a few extreme cases, this last step has not been possible yet because of legal problems (as we will see in the case of France Telecom) or because of the poor financial health of the company (as for Bull, the troubled computer firm).

The legal privatization framework includes a mention in the French Constitution: "The law determines the rules of nationalization of firms and the transfers of ownership of firms from the public sector to the private sector" (article 34) (Legifrance 1958). Therefore, three acts have been passed, covering the standard cases. One of them, voted in 1986, determines the procedures (JO 1986b), while the two others, voted in 1986 and 1993, list the operations to be conducted (JO 1986a, 1993). For the largest companies, a special privatization act is needed to prepare the operation. A government decree is enough for smaller firms.

Moreover, all large public firms have hundreds, and sometimes thousands, of subsidiaries. Sales, joint ventures, and creations are part of the normal development of businesses: therefore, a special system has been set up to allow dynamic changes in the public sector referred to as "respiration". Most subsidiaries of state-owned firms as well as local public services (*sociétés d'économie mixtes locales*) since 1993 can be sold under two simple declarative procedures (Minefi 2003). From July 1993 to July 2003, 324 sales involving 159,622 employees were performed under the "respiration" system; from July 2002 to July 2003, 18 sales were performed, involving 2,555 employees.

If we take the case of France Telecom, the full privatization process required three steps. (See table 6.6.) The first was the transformation of the PTT administration into two parastatal entities called EPIC: Industrial and Commercial Public Entities (see box 6.1). This was done by an act voted on July 2, 1990 (JO 1990a), creating La Poste and France Telecom. A large-scale public debate was organized beforehand by the

Table 6.6
France Telecom (FT) time line

Year	Regulation	France Telecom (FT)
1987	European Green Book	
1990	French Post and Telecom Acts	FT becomes a parastatal firm
1993	European decision: full competition in 1998	Alliance with Deutsche Telekom (Atlas)
		Government decision to use an IPO for FT
1995		CEO: Michel Bon
1996	French telecom acts	Alliance FT-Deutsche Telekom-Sprint (Global One)
1997	ART (regulatory agency) created	FT becomes a private firm at year-end
		Initial public offering
1998	Full competition in Europe	Pensions plans "returned" to the state (5.7 billion euros)
1999		Second tranche offered (FT)
2000	UMTS auctions (United Kingdom, Germany)	IPO, Wanadoo
		Conflict with Deutsche Telekom
2001		Global One and Orange purchased
		IPO, Orange
2002		Severe financial crisis and bailout
2003		CEO: Thierry Breton
	New European regulatory package	Full privatization of FT possible
2004	French telecom act	Orange shares buyout
	French telecom act	Wanadoo shares buyout

Box 6.1
EPIC

An EPIC (*Etablissement public à caractère industriel ou commercial*) is a state entity with mixed features. It belongs to the state system: its mission is defined by law and cannot be easily extended (this is called the "specialty principle"); it cannot default financially as it benefits from state backing; it does not always pay taxes like a normal company; it has a board nominated by the state, and all its main decisions have to be approved a posteriori. But it also conducts quasi-normal commercial operations, can enter partnerships, and can own subsidiaries. Variations exist in the actual statute of the many EPICs found in France. From 1991 to 1996 France Telecom was a *exploitant public* (state-owned operator), a special kind of EPIC (Minefi 1991).

Ministry of PTT to prepare the move (Prévot 1989). The unions were satisfied by the guarantees offered that personnel would remain mostly public servants and that no further change was prepared, except for another act voted on December 29, 1990 (JO 1990b). This act introduced the changes needed by the new European regulatory regime following the 1987 Green Book on telecommunications (European Commission 1987). However, more changes were soon needed to cope with the decision, taken in 1993 at the European level, to have full competition in 1998 in the telecommunication sector. The French government, pushed by the top management of France Telecom, decided to make an IPO of the company in 1995. The change of statute was mainly justified by the international ambitions of France Telecom, after several promising deals abroad (Argentina, Mexico, and above all a strategic alliance with Deutsche Telekom and Sprint). However, the IPO was delayed by protests by trade unions and many other social problems at that time. In 1995, after the elections, a new CEO was named (Michel Bon) with a clear mandate to manage the change of statute and the IPO. To prepare the introduction of full competition in 1998, a second telecommunications act was passed in 1996 to transpose European directives.

As a companion to this July 26, 1996, telecom regulation act (JO 1996a), another act was also adopted in 1996 transforming the parastatal entity France Telecom into a quasi-standard private company (JO 1996b). Moreover, in 1997, France Telecom paid 5.7 billion euros to the state as a lump sum to be used to pay the extra costs of the pensions of its retiring civil servants: the government was happy to receive funds lowering the budget deficit, while France Telecom was happy to get rid of a sizable pension debt looming in the future.

These changes opened the way for the second step in the privatization process, the IPO of France Telecom in 1997. The IPO was planned for the spring of 1997, and a lengthy internal communication process took place to overcome the strong opposition of the unions despite the government's promise that the state would keep control of the firm. But the center-right Juppé government lost the legislative elections and was replaced by the Jospin government (Socialist). The new prime minister asked for a "social audit" of the whole process (the Socialists were traditionally against privatization) but finally gave the green light to the IPO, understanding that the government was unable to finance the development of France Telecom in the new international competitive context (Bertolus, Cedro, and Del Jesus 2003).

Table 6.7
Shareholders of France Telecom (percentages)

	December 1997	January 1999	December 2002	September 2003
State (direct and indirect)	75	63.6	56.5	58.89
General public and investors	22.5	31.2	32.1	34.9
Owned by France Telecom	—	—	8.3	4.29
Deutsche Telekom	—	2.0	—	—
Employees	2.5	3.2	3.1	1.92

Source: France Telecom.

The IPO took place in the fall of 1997 and netted 29 billion euros. The state kept 75 percent of the capital; 4 million individual shareholders asked three times the number of available shares and finally got 10.55 percent of the capital. Financial institutions obtained 11.95 percent (they had asked twenty times the number of available shares) and 70 percent of the personnel of France Telecom bought 2.5 percent. A second public offering took place in 1998 and netted 9 billion euros.

As shown in table 6.7, the percentage of France Telecom owned by the state has not decreased regularly. In 2002–2003, the government had to rescue France Telecom, then in dire financial straits due to its enormous debt (see section 6.3 for details). On this occasion, part of the state participation was allocated to a state-owned financial holding company, originally devoted to the oil sector, ERAP. In October 2005, the state held 31.69 percent of the capital of France Telecom.

The last step will happen when the state sells its last share of France Telecom. In 1997, more than 80 percent of France Telecom personnel were civil servants, and a decision by Conseil d'Etat, the government counsel and higher administrative court, had made it clear that civil servants could work in a private company only if the government still held the majority of shares directly or indirectly and the company was in charge of a public service (Conseil d'Etat 1993). France Telecom met the two conditions. However, in 2003, two changes occurred. On one side, the new European telecom regulatory package was enforced, demanding that universal service be tendered. Therefore, France Telecom could, in theory, lose universal service. On top of that, the Raffarin government (center-right) opened the way to a sale of more France Telecom shares, a move designed to fill the state coffers as well as to free France Telecom from government control (useful for the international expansion of the firm). A law was adopted by parliament at the

Table 6.8
Share of capital owned by foreign investors, 2003

Firm	Sector	Year of IPO or privati-zation	% owned by foreign investors	% owned by U.S. investors
Vivendi (previously CGE)	Media	1987	67.7	35.4
Total	Oil and gas	1994	58.0	35.0
Aventis (previously Rhône-Poulenc)	Pharmacy	1993	56.0	35.0
Alcatel (previously CGE)	Telecom equipment	1987	50	NA
Saint-Gobain	Building materials	1986	48	31
BNP Paribas	Bank	1987	45	NA
Renault	Automobile	1996	26	NA
Thomson	Electronics	2000	20	NA
Thales (previously Thomson CSF)	Defense electronics	1998	15	NA
France Telecom	Telecommunications	1997	11	3
TF1	TV channel	1987	28.1	12.5

Source: Ducourtieux (2003), based on a survey conducted by Georgeson Shareholder.
Note: France Telecom and TF1 figures for 2002.

end of 2003 (Mer 2003, JO 2004). It allowed the 104,000 civil servants still working at France Telecom at that time to remain in the company until they retire.

6.2.2   Who Owns the Privatized Firms?

One major concern of the French government was to keep control of the companies while selling their capital, or at least to prevent the privatized companies from falling into foreign hands. During the first privatization phase (1986–1988), the government tried to set up stable groups of investors (in French, *noyaux durs* for "hard core"). This decision generated a long controversy about the choice of these friendly and stable investors; it was modified in 1989 (JO 1989). There were a limited number of potential investors in France, which led to a fairly high level of "consanguinity" between all the groups, with the largest banks playing a major role in the process. As shown in table 6.8, the percentage of foreign ownership has nevertheless grown to very high levels for some companies. In an extreme case, in 2003, the Canadian firm Alcan launched an offer for Pechiney, so the latter would no

Table 6.9
Private shareholders in privatized companies when the shares were sold

Firm	Sector	Share-holders (millions)	Year
France Telecom	Telecommunications	6.7	1997–1998
Paribas	Bank	3.9	1986
Elf Aquitaine	Oil and gas	3.5	1986–1994
Rhône-Poulenc	Chemicals and drugs	3.0	1993
BNP	Bank	2.8	1993
Air France	Airline	2.4	
Société Générale	Bank	2.3	1987
CGE (now Alcatel, Alstom, and Vivendi)	Telecom equipment, water distribution	2.3	1987

Source: SBF, Bourse de Paris (INSEE 1999).

longer be under French management. One can safely conclude that the economic globalization has dealt a fatal blow to any dreams of national independence that might have inspired French governments in the past.

Another impact was the creation of a large class of small share-holders, tempted by the IPO of blue-chip stocks. As shown in table 6.9, the largest groups of private shareholders were to be found in banks, large industrial firms, and France Telecom. The France Telecom IPO generated a tremendous interest from the general public, who were severely rocked by the incredible rise and precipitous decline of the price of the share in later years. (Details about the financial performance of privatized companies are found in section 6.4.) However, private investors have remained highly interested in shares of privatized companies as proven by the various other IPOs (Observatoire 2003). Employees of privatized companies also massively bought the shares reserved for them by law (at very sweet prices). But as France Telecom staff members soon understood, it could be a risky investment: they saw the value of their shares fall precipitously (by a factor of 10) between 2000 and 2002 (de Tricornot and Picquet 2002).

6.2.3 Changes in Regulation

France does not have a long tradition of independent regulators: direct intervention by the administration was deemed enough to regulate the existing strong monopolies. For example, the central banker, Banque de France, created in 1800 as a private entity, had been nationalized in

Table 6.10
Sector regulation in France: Main bodies

	Sector	Year Created	Remarks
AMF (Autorité des Marchés Financiers)	Finance	2003	Merger of the Commission des Opérations de Bourse and two other state bodies
ART (Autorité de Régulation des Télécommunications)	Telecommunications	1997	Independent regulatory authority; became ARCEP (Autorité de Régulation des Communications Electroniques et de la Poste) in 2005
Banque de France	Banking	1800–1993	Bank, 100 percent owned by the state
CRE (Commission de Régulation de l'Energie)	Electricity and gas	2000	Regulator; the electricity transport network (RTE) is being separated from EdF, the state-owned electricity producer
CSA (Conseil Supérieur de l'Audiovisuel)	Radio and TV broadcasting	1989	Independent regulatory authority
RFF (Réseau Ferré de France)	Railways	1997	Regulator and owner of the main railway network; carries the network debt

1936 but obtained its full independence only in 1993. With the arrival of new entrants following deregulation in most sectors, new bodies were set up (table 6.10). A good example is provided by the broadcasting regulator Conseil Supérieur de l'Audiovisuel (CSA), which was preceded by two short-lived and controversial bodies. Most of these regulators are independent regulatory authorities (Conseil d'Etat 2002). But there is at least one special case: in the railway industry, the network has been transferred to Réseau Ferré de France, a state company (EPIC), that manages the network and regulates rail transport. It receives tolls from the state company, SNCF, and any other users. RFF decides on network expansion, subcontracts construction work and pays SNCF for network maintenance.

The Autorité de Régulation des Télécommunications (ART) provides a good example of the problems encountered. It was set up in 1997, one year before the sector was fully deregulated, so it has limited experience; it shares with CSA the regulation of converging services. Moreover, radio spectrum allocation is decided in a two-stage process supervised by the interministry Agence Nationale des Fréquences (ANFR). And finally, it faces a formidable incumbent, France Telecom, formally under the control of the Ministry of Economy, Finance and Industry. As we will show, France Telecom embarked on an ambitious development plan following its IPO. This plan failed, and a controversy rose in 2002 about government control of the company. Obviously, France Telecom has been able to decide on its own in many instances, but one should stress that government control is weak for a structural reason: as the promoter of competition policy, it cannot closely monitor France Telecom, or it would be accused of ruining competition. (Diefenbacher 2003).

6.2.4   Changes in Competition

Privatization does not appear to be a key ingredient in changes in the competitive situation in France. Deregulation is the key factor, and privatization of any state-owned firm can only help as it clears the way for a normal competitive situation. It is indeed a very awkward situation when the state is at the same time promoting competition and the owner of the largest market player. Furthermore, the situation is quite different in the network industries and in the other sectors. In the latter case, competition is the normal way to run markets, and barriers to entry tend to be lower. In network industries, barriers to entry can be extremely high for economic reasons—the so-called natural monopoly problem, or the related "essential facilities" problem. There could as well be legal reasons such as licensing, but the current deregulation process taking place in Europe is slowly eliminating this last obstacle. Therefore, the privatization of a state monopoly will give various results depending on these elements as shown by the contrasted situation of airlines and telecommunications. Until the arrival of low-cost companies in the twenty-first century, Air France kept a strong grip on the French market and all moves to create a viable competitor to the flag carrier failed, as testified by the attempts of British Airways, Swissair (with Air Lib), and several independent companies.

On the other hand, France Telecom has steadily lost market share to its competitors: at the end of 2002, it held less than 50 percent of the mobile market and 64 percent of the long-distance market. It has kept 81 percent of the local telecommunications market, but the unbundling of the local loop is progressing fast, as shown in table 6.11.

An indirect impact on competition comes from privatization. When a firm leaves the state sector, it undergoes a drastic change in its corporate culture and usually becomes more aggressive on the market and

Table 6.11
Market share of new entrants: Telecommunications in France

	1996	1997	1998	1999	2000	2001	2002
Long distance, fixed (% revenue)	—	—	2.0	19.3	32.8	36.0	35.7
Local, fixed (% revenue)	—	—	—	—	—	3.2	19.1
Mobiles (% users)	42.1	47.0	50.5	51.3	51.8	51.9	50.0
Asymmetric digital subscriber line (ADSL) (% users)	—	—	—	—	—	14	29
Unbundled lines (% main lines)	—	—	—	—	—	0.001	0.02

Source: France Telecom annual reports; ART and calculations by the authors.

Table 6.12
Major state-owned companies in France, 2003

	Sector	Sales in 2002 (billion euros)	Profits in 2002 (million euros)	Employees (2002)
Air France	Airline	12.7	120	71,500
Areva	Nuclear industry	8.3	240	50,100
DCN	Shipyard (navy)	2.2	118	13,300
EdF	Electricity (utility)	48.4	480	172,000
France Télécom	Telecommunications	46.6	−20,700[a]	240,100
France Télévisions	Television channels	2.3	53	6,200
GdF	Natural gas	14.6	840	37,900
GIAT	Army vehicles, weapons	0.8	−118	6,200
La Poste	Postal services	17.3	34	325,000
SNECMA	Aerospace	6.5	106	39,000
SNCF	Railways	22.2	63	182,800

Source: Company information.
[a] Including 18.2 billion euros in exceptional items (amortization and provisions).

more flexible in its management. These points will be expanded when we address the performance of privatized companies.

6.3   Sector Issues

Several reasons explain why some sectors have been privatized faster than others (table 6.12).

First, the existence of competition makes public management complicated. In the case of the car manufacturer Renault, the government was simultaneously the owner of the largest car company and was regulating the industry. Any move by the government regarding technical standards or competition policy, for example, had conflicting impacts on its two missions.

Second, some companies had been state owned briefly in the 1980s. Privatizing them was easier than the public services under public management for decades.

Third, European deregulation accelerated privatization schemes: in telecoms and air transport, deregulation has taken place and national companies have been at least partially privatized. Deregulation was under way in rail transport, energy and postal services at the end of 2003. No concrete privatization moves were made in early 2004, but they are being performed in the electricity and gas sectors in 2005.

Fourth, it is always easier to privatize profitable companies (table 6.13). The Juppé government had planned to sell the then unprofitable company Thomson for 1 French franc in 1996. The Privatization Commission refused the decision, and it was postponed.

Fifth, at the same time, it is more difficult to explain why well-run entities need to be privatized (why change a good system?). Opponents to the privatization of efficient firms like France Telecom first, and later of EDF, stress the risks associated with a change in ownership and management. On the contrary, privatizing poorly run entities is more readily acceptable.

Sixth, strong union presence hinders privatization. The major trade union, Confédération Générale du Travail (CGT), a former close ally of the French Communist party (PCF), is opposed to privatization in principle. It is very strong in some public companies like the electricity producer EdF. In more recent years, a new union (SUD) was created from parts of other unions. SUD is radically opposed to privatization. It is a minor but highly vocal stakeholder in the railways and telecoms.

Finally, timing plays a great role in privatization. Governments decide on a tentative calendar that will be followed—or not, depending on election outcomes, stock exchange levels, economic outlook, and other factors. For example, the capital of Snecma, a major aviation equipment manufacturer, was planned to be opened by the Jospin government (before 2002). Finally, the move was completed in 2005 by the Raffarin government. Poor conditions on the Paris Bourse explain the delay.

At the end of 2005, state-owned firms could be found in four major categories:

Table 6.13
Privatization status of major state-controlled companies, 2005

	% state owned	Status	Remarks
Air France	18	SA, on full privatization track	Government share below 50 percent when Air France and KLM merge
Areva	95	SA	Part of the capital is held indirectly by state entities (CEA, EdF) The public buy not shares but "investment certificates"
DCN	100	SA since 2003	Alliances being signed
EdF	85	EPIC, on privatization track	Affected by European deregulation
GIAT	100	SA	Evolution blocked due to poor financial results
France Télécom	31	SA	Full privatization possible after new law is adopted
France Télévisions	100	SA	No official privatization plans
GdF	80	EPIC, on privatization track	Affected by European deregulation
La Poste	100	"Exploitant public"	Affected by European deregulation
SNECMA (now SAFRAN)	31	SA, on privatization track	Following 2004 merger of SNECMA with SAGEN
SNCF	100	EPIC	No privatization plans

Source: Company information.
Note: The normal legal status for large business firms in France is Société Anonyme (SA). SNCF, EdF, and GdF are EPIC. The legal form of La Poste is unique, but it is close to an EPIC.

Public services. Privatization follows European Union deregulation policies, usually with some delay. The case of EdF, the electricity producer, is discussed below. SNCF, the national railways, provides rather decent service, but it is in very poor financial condition and trade unions are very active. No privatization plans are possible.

Defense and other strategic industries. Privatization or at least transformation of state administrations into standard companies is a must to participate in the construction of the new European defense industry. GIAT Industries produces weapons and armored vehicles. It has existed as a firm since 1990, but its financial problems are such that any further move is impossible. In contrast, DCN (Direction des Constructions Navales, the former navy shipyards) was transformed into a firm in 2003 and is in good shape. SNECMA, a major aviation engine producer, has merged in 2005 with publicly held electronic equipment manufacturer SAGEM.

TV and radio. In 1987, the first state channel, TF1, was privatized and sold to the Bouygues group. It is still the market leader, with about one-third of the total audience and half of the national TV market. France Télévisions is the holding company managing the remaining state TV channels, notably France 2 and France 3. Although rumors surface regularly as to the privatization of one or several of these channels, the government had no official plans at the end of 2005. TF1 had lodged a complaint in 1993 with the European Commission about some state aid to the public TV sector, but the commission approved the aid in 2003.

Miscellaneous firms. Among others are Charbonnages de France (coal mine, which is closing down); Française des jeux (the lottery); and toll highways.

An interesting example of the difficulties of privatization policies for public services is EdF at the end of 2003. On one side, European deregulation policy means that competition has arrived at the French market. The French government is fighting to slow the move at the European level. On top of that, EdF, as an EPIC, benefits from the financial guarantee from the state, a clear advantage when it has to borrow money. From a fiscal point of view, it also benefits from special tax deductions. As a result, in 2003 the European Commission believed that EdF benefited from an undue competitive advantage, and it declared its intention to ask the operator to pay back to the state more than 1 billion euros (mostly unpaid taxes) and to press for a change of statute. On the other side, EdF would like to be able to meet new competition; it would like to supply other energies, reform its specific pension plan, and cut jobs. But it is prevented by law from expanding outside the electricity sector, and the main trade union, CGT, blocked a change in the specific pension plans of EdF-GdF employees in early 2003. So both the firm's management and the French government plan a change of statute and a slow move to competition, a policy that would solve most of EdF's problems. Despite CGTs total opposition to a change of statute, EdF was partially privatized in November 2005, the state retaining 85 percent of the shares at this time.

6.4   Performance measures

It is extremely difficult to give clear and objective performance measures for French privatization. However, we will look at three major areas for performance: prices, productivity and cost structure, and finance.

6.4.1   Prices

In competitive areas like cars and banks, prices are market oriented and price controls very limited. The situation is different for public services. Their tariffs must be approved by the relevant ministries: La Poste has to beg to increase postage stamps prices; EdF has to do the same for electricity tariffs. When a firm is partly privatized and operates in a partly competitive environment, it is in an interesting situation.

If we look at the emblematic case of France Telecom again, we can see its retail prices decreasing in general and significant marketing efforts taking place (ART 2003, France Telecom 2003a). These moves follow a complex tariff rebalancing strategy where local call prices and subscription fees increase while long-distance call prices decrease, as shown in table 6.14. It would be very difficult to assume that these results are due to privatization. More likely, deregulation in the tele-

Table 6.14
Residential prices, France Telecom (including VAT)

Peak hours before any discounts	1984: Time per unit	1995: Time per unit	1998: Fixed charge plus tariff per second	2000: Fixed charge plus tariff per second	2003: Fixed charge plus tariff per second
Local call (3 minutes)	1 unit per call: 0.098 euros	1 unit per 3 minutes: 0.113 euros	0.113 euros	0.157 euros	0.157 euros
National call (3 minutes)	1.48 euros	1.02 euros	0.52 euros	0.36 euros	0.21 euros
Monthly access charge	7.17 euros[a]	6.95 euros	10.37 euros	11.74 euros	13 euros
Retail price Index	100	137	143	146	154

[a] In 1984, the monthly rental included the supply of a telephone set.

com sector and competition from new entrants explain most of the changes. Moreover, France Telecom (like all other state companies) has to get its main prices approved by the ministers in charge of telecommunications and the economy. From 1997 to 2000, a minimum decrease in prices had been imposed by the Ministry of Economy (−9 percent per year in 1997–1998 and −4.5 percent per year in 1999–2000). These figures apply to a selected basket of basic services. The required decrease is much higher than inflation rates. On top of that, France Telecom has to submit most of its price changes to ART. ART's opinion is public but not binding. For example, France Telecom submitted 108 tariff decisions to ART in 2002 for approval, resulting in 64 favorable and 17 unfavorable recommendations (ART 2003). ART is especially careful about predatory pricing by France Telecom, so it might not approve tariffs that are too low. In some well-publicized instances, France Telecom got the ministers to approve very low tariffs despite negative opinions from ART, but these decisions were eventually cancelled when the competitors complained. Therefore, France Telecom is walking a tightrope: if its prices are too high, it will lose market share; if its prices are too low, they will not be approved. Quality of service has not changed significantly since privatization and so far has not been an issue for regulators. The only exception has been customer relations for the entire French mobile and broadband access sector.

Regarding the highly sensitive issue of interconnection prices, France Telecom, an operator with significant market power (SMP), has had to publish a price list (*Catalogue d'interconnexion*) every year since 1997 and get it approved by ART. The goal for France Telecom is to squeeze its competitors between high interconnection prices and low retail prices: therefore, every fall a battle starts between ART and the incumbent.[5] As table 6.15 shows, interconnection prices have significantly decreased as a result of this annual review system. However, tariffs are only one part of the problem; France Telecom can also use many

Table 6.15
Interconnection prices in France

Euros per minute	1998	1999	2000	2001	2002	2003
Local	0.928	0.707	0.667	0.616	0.579	0.5734
Simple transit	1.948	1.537	1.356	1.252	1.051	1.0092

Source: ART.
Note: Average price for a basket of interconnection services.

Table 6.16
Cost structure of selected items for France Telecom (millions of euros)

	1996	2002
Sales	23,059	46,630
	(100%)	(100%)
Personnel costs	6,664	10,240
	(29%)	(22%)
Commercial and administrative costs	5,046	12,579
	(22%)	(27%)
R&D costs	820	576
	(3.6%)	(1.2%)
Financial costs (net)	814	4,041
	(3.5%)	(8.7%)
Income tax	702	2,499
	(3.0%)	(5.3%)
Net income	321	−20,736
	(9.1%)	(−44.5%)

Source: France Telecom annual reports.
Note: Figures in parentheses are percentage of sales.

other tactics to delay or make it more difficult for its competitors to obtain interconnection when they want it and how they want it.[6]

6.4.2   Productivity and Cost Structure

Privatization introduces changes in cost structures for a number of reasons (table 6.16):

• Starting and stopping activities is easier. International expansion is also easier. In the case of France Telecom, a few years after privatization, the firm has been completely transformed through its tremendous international expansion.

• There is more flexibility in human resources management in all its components: hiring, compensation, and promotion.[7]

• After privatization, specific tax systems disappear (usually leading to higher taxes).

France Telecom: Cost structures
Comparing selected figures for France Telecom is not easy because of its transformation from a national to a global company and also because of many changes in accounting methods during the period

studied. However, several facts clearly appear from table 6.16 comparing the 1996 and 2002 situations:

• On the whole, personnel costs have decreased in percentage of sales. However, this is the result of many changes.

• Commercial costs have increased. France Telecom does not always publish details about these costs, but they always show (except in 2002) significant growth linked to the development of the mobile and Internet sector in a competitive environment. In particular, they shot up from 5.2 to 7.3 billion euros between 1999 and 2000. The percentage of administrative costs compared to sales, as far as it can be assessed from the figures provided by France Telecom, has been kept at its pre-privatization level.

• R&D costs have been drastically cut.

• Income tax is difficult to figure out in such a diversified group. However, France Telecom published detailed figures in 1998 for other taxes, such as local taxes. After the end of its specific regime, the 1997 IPO cost France Telecom more than 300 million euros in additional taxes in France (mostly local taxes, excluding income tax) in that year.

It is difficult to disentangle the impact of growth, international expansion, competition, and changes in accounting methods. But it is clear that deregulation has had a major impact on marketing and commercial costs, while privatization has had relatively minors impacts on R&D costs and tatxes.

France Telecom: Personnel costs and labor productivity
If we look at the figures of France Telecom in France as shown in table 6.17, the number of employees has decreased from 160,700 to 141,100 between 1996 and 2002 while the sales per employee increased from 138,000 euros in 1996 to 194,000 euros in 2002. This ratio increased on average 9.4 percent per year, well above inflation levels (about 1.5 percent per year over the period), and well above changes in output.

Indeed, as shown in figure 6.3, labor productivity has grown a great deal. In 1997, each employee of France Telecom had to care for 207 main lines and 10 mobile lines. In 2002, he or she had to care for 241 fixed lines, plus 136 mobile lines and 28 Internet customers.

Many attempts have been made to give a more precise vision of productivity changes, using DEA or similar methods. The results obtained

Table 6.17
Labor and output, France Telecom in France

	Employees	Fixed lines (thousands)	Mobile lines (thousands)	TV cable (thousand lines)	Internet (thousand customers)
1996	160,700	33,200	1,560	663	18
1997	155,500	33,700	3,081	705	106
1998	155,000	34,000	5,450	754	495
1999	152,300	34,056	10,051	709	1,016
2000	148,900	34,114	14,311	769	1,831
2001	145,300	34,151	17,823	824	3,001
2002	141,100	34,066	19,216	854	3,924

Source: France Telecom annual reports; calculations by the authors.

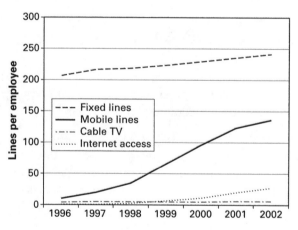

Figure 6.3
Labor productivity: France Telecom in France
Source: France Telecom annual reports.

depend on the quality of the figures and the methods used. Using Data Envelopment Analysis (DEA) and statistics provided by OECD, France Telecom appeared to be 85 percent "efficient" in 1998 compared to the best European telecommunications operators (Pentzaropoulos and Giokas 2002). However, our own efforts to replicate and expand these results using more recent figures have failed due to the absence of consistent data on a national basis in the latest *Communications Outlook* (OECD 2003).

Privatization is only one cause of this increase in labor productivity, the two main ones being the development of new services (like mobiles) and the age structure. In France, France Telecom has rather old employees (the average age was 44.4 years in 2002), mostly civil servants hired in the 1970s and 1980s. Starting in 1996, a large number of employees have retired, with additional incentives provided for early retirement (22,000 early retirees between 1996 and 2002). Hiring new employees has followed a stop-and-go process.

Before 1992, most employees belonged to a civil service "rank," linked to the competitive exam they passed but with a tenuous link to the job they held. This archaic system was replaced by standard job descriptions and promotion systems (leading to an average 7 percent increase in wages). Increased competition and technological progress also forced redeployments in the staff structure. For example, in 2002, 9,500 employees were retrained and most of them transferred to customer relations, information systems, and multimedia (France Telecom 2003a, 2003b). Full privatization should make these changes easier to implement, but trade unions are concerned.

Finally, privatization made it easier to give additional compensation to top management. As expected in a former state administration, salaries were modest for executives, and no stock options were available. The three largest subsidiaries of France Telecom—Orange (mobile), Equant (data), and Wanadoo (Internet)—have set up various stock option plans representing, respectively, 2.3, 3, and 2 percent of the capital of the firms in 2002. Regarding the compensation of the chief executive officer, while Michel Bon (a former high civil servant, graduated from ENA) got around 0.37 euros million per year, his successor, Thierry Breton (an electrical engineer, formerly CEO of Thomson), obtained 1.25 million euros in 2002.

6.4.3 Innovation

French public services have long had a reputation for innovation and technical prowess.[8] All these innovations were possible because tariffs were set by the state and were based on large-scale cross-subsidies between services, at least during the launch of the new services or production tools. European regulation, as it opens public services to competition, prohibits cross-subsidies from regulated to unregulated activities as detrimental to competition. Moreover, the state had a long-term view of technical innovation and financial performance so that payback periods could be long. In privatized firms, private shareholders are more impatient about financial rewards, less enthusiastic about technical innovation (Munari 2002), and unable to deal with social and political controversies (as EdF with nuclear energy, dealing with environmental issues).

The case of France Telecom again provides interesting insights. France had major successes in the 1970s in the development of digital switching and videotex (Berne 1997).[9] A less successful, and very costly, venture was launched in cable television in 1982 (Plan Cable). Most of these innovations came from the renowned research center, CNET (Centre National d'Etudes des Télécommunications), founded in 1944 as a national research institution dealing with fundamental research coupled to a traditional operator R&D center. Following the IPO of France Telecom, CNET was renamed France Telecom R&D and completely refocused on internal needs, mainly for the development of new services (France Telecom 2003a). Costs figures for R&D, provided in table 6.16, show a steep decline as a percentage of sales.

6.4.4 Finance

Financial indicators, like profits, debt ratios, and stock prices, provide another set of measures of performance. Again, methodological reasons could flaw the results. Because public firms are privatized only when they are profitable, one has to be very cautious about financial results. As shown in the annual report on state firms published by the Ministry of Finance (Minefi 2003), the financial health of the public sector is poor, and now that the government has privatized nearly all the profitable companies, it is mostly stuck with the unprofitable ones. One positive impact of the privatization process for firms is that it forces the government to make them profitable (debt reduction, fresh capital, restructuring). Thomson, Air France, Usinor, and Crédit Lyonnais have all gone through difficult times: yet after some painful years, they have been privatized as soon as they were in good shape and since then (at least until 2003) have developed normally.[10] Share prices incorporate both general trends on the stock exchange and the situation of each company. Table 6.18 shows that the results are quite mixed, and sometimes very disappointing when the company is in deep trouble, like Bull. But investors are normally eager to buy shares of privatized groups (Observatoire 2003).

Again, the case of France Telecom is interesting, as shown in table 6.16 and figure 6.3. After its IPO, France Telecom expanded very fast,

Table 6.18
Return for investors, selected privatized companies

Company	IPO date	Initial stock price (euros)	Adjusted stock price, October 31, 2003 (euros)	% change
BNP	1993	18.30	45.6	147
Renault	1993	25.15	56.9	126
Usinor-Sacilor	1995	13.11	12.3	−6
Bull	1997	5.49	0.80	−84
Thomson Multimedia 1	1999	10.73	18.10	69
Thomson Multimedia 2	2000	53.90	18.10	−66
France Telecom 1	1997	24.03	20.08	−13
France Telecom 2	1998	51.59	20.8	−60
Wanadoo	2000	19.00	6.4	−66
Orange	2001	9.5	9.5	0

Source: Figaro (2003).

particularly abroad and in new sectors (mobile, Internet, television). When it bought Orange from Vodafone in 2000 at a price of 43.2 billion euros, 80 percent was paid in cash because issuing new stock would have lowered the share of the state below 50 percent, a move forbidden by law. France Telecom had to borrow massively for this purchase and those following, including the subsequent universal mobile telecommunications systems (UMTS) auctions.[11] Although overall operational results were quite acceptable at group level (table 6.19), some of these purchases failed to produce financial returns (for example, the purchase of MobilCom and its UMTS license in Germany), and servicing the debt was nearly impossible. At the same time, issuing new stock was doomed to fail because of the low level of stock prices due to the economic crisis and the telecom bust. The rescue plan devised in 2002 called for 15 billion euros of fresh money (9 billion euros provided by the state through ERAP), debt refinancing of 15 billion euros, and 15 billion euros of savings. The first of these three measures was investigated in 2003 by the European Commission as a possible infringement of the regulation of state aid, but eventually cleared.

Regarding stock prices (figure 6.4), the introduction price for France Telecom shares was 24.03 euros, and after one trading day it was up to 31.5 euros; the share peaked at 219 euros on March 2, 2000, then fell to an all-time low of 6.94 euros on September 30, 2002. In October 2003 the price was around 21 euros. The IPOs of Orange and Wanadoo, the

Table 6.19
France Telecom at a glance

	1996	1997	1998	1999	2000	2001	2002
Group turnover (billion euros)	22.9	23.4	24.6	27.2	33.7	43.0	46.6
Profit (billion euros)	0.3	2.3	2.3	2.8	3.7	−8.3	−20.7
Long-term debt (billion euros)	16.3	15.4	13.1	14.6	61.0	60.7	68
Employees (group)	164,700	165,000	169,100	174,300	188,900	206,200	240,100
Employees (France)	160,700	155,500	155,000	152,300	148,900	145,300	141,100
Fixed—France (% of sales)	88	82	77	70	55	46	40
Fixed—abroad (% of sales)	1	2	3	9	16	16	20
Mobiles (% of sales)	7	11	15	17	26	34	36
Internet (% of sales)[a]	4	5	5	3	3	4	4

Source: France Telecom annual reports; calculations by the authors.
[a] Includes videotext and directory revenues.

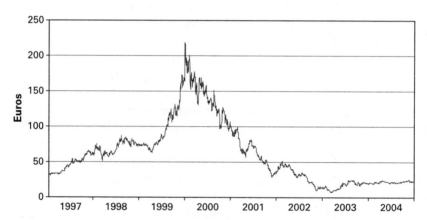

Figure 6.4
France Telecom share price on the Paris Bourse (Euronext)

two major subsidiaries of France Telecom, have not fared better, as shown in table 6.18.

6.5 Conclusions

6.5.1 *The Changing Role of Ideology*

The privatization process in France has been heavily loaded in terms of ideology, as had been the case for nationalization itself. The reluctance to privatize was especially high due to the combination of three political ideologies:

• The socialist ideology states that "people" or state ownership is in all cases superior to private ownership

• The "Dirigiste" (Colbertiste), Bonapartist, and Gaullist tradition, which highlights the superior knowledge and vision of the state

• A Christian-inspired social doctrine that advocates public property in the name of the public good and social solidarity

This combination resulted not only in nationalization but in provisions for public ownership to be written in the 1946 Constitution, as the government coalition was composed of those three political forces. Until the early 1980s, combination was popularly supported. The radical changeover in ideology and reality in the United States and the United Kingdom did induce, but with some delay, changes in French political doctrines. It combined with the disastrous economic situation, which followed the phase of nationalizations performed by the "Union of the Left" coalition (1981–1986) to pave the way for the protracted, and not yet completed, privatization process.

6.5.2 *Perception of Privatization Policies*

Privatization is now widely accepted in principle. However, unions and social forces are often fighting successfully to oppose them as much as they can in order to preserve special workers' and social conditions in the public sector. It often takes heralding imperious strategic moves, as in the Air France–KLM merger case, to assuage this reluctance.

It has to be said that the show of exuberance, and reluctance to comply with governance and information transparency rules, has not helped to promote the image of private corporations.

6.5.3   Lesson to Be Learned?

The implementation of sound governance rules for the private sector seems to go hand in hand with the promotion of the privatization process. The succeeding French governments have learned the hard way that privatization is a slow process and that one should pay as much attention to corporate governance of partially privatized firms as to privatization moves. As an example, the IPO of France Telecom was a resounding success in 1997; the results of the company were disastrous in 2001 and 2002, and not only because of the burst of the telecom bubble. Another sad example is provided by the computer manufacturer Bull: the state has long been unable to bring the firm back to profit, despite massive injections of public money (much disliked by the European Commission, as expected). It eventually succeeded through a drastic downsizing.

6.5.4   Reaction to EU Directives

EU directives have played an important role in the evolution of economic ideologies and realities. In many cases, French governments have taken advantage of them to promote internal policies they actually supported without daring to say so. We know that no directive can be taken without the explicit agreement of member country governments. "Brussels-constraining demands," however, have often been invoked by French governments as imposing on them to take not-so-popular or even unpopular measures and decisions. It is a well-established principle that European policy is neutral regarding the ownership of firms. However, European policy promotes competition in most sectors. These changes have deep impacts on state firms. Actually, they cannot survive in the new, deregulated environment without drastic changes. Probably privatization is the only way for them to meet the challenges of deregulation. After France Telecom and Air France, the government has decided to offer EdF and GdF in an IPO. After France Telecom again, EdF will be a testbed for the success of privatization a vital service, a well-run company, sensitive technologies, huge investments in the long term, and deregulation constraints.

Notes

1. In the case of a large, partly state-owned company listed on the stock exchange, any poor performance will have two impacts: on stock price indexes and on financing conditions.

2. On September 30, 2002, it was down to 17 billion euros, and on September 9, 2003, it was up to 40 billion euros. Changes in the market value of France Telecom explain most of these enormous changes. See section 6.4 for details.

3. Not on a day-to-day basis, but its assets are still massive, and any move will have an impact on the market.

4. The prime minister has to share part of his power with the president of the Republic, elected in separate presidential elections. But for privatization matters, the prime minister decides.

5. The European Commission has published a directive on the topic, as well as benchmarks.

6. Not all central exchanges are opened to interconnection, for example.

7. Besides productivity and costs, privatization challenges the traditional management of human resources. One should note that a large variety of cases exist among state-owned public services. Most of these entities used special statutes for their employees and manage them in a bureaucratic way. Since privatization, they have followed standard human resources policies for private firms. A second major change deals with the choice and compensation of CEOs and top managers, again following standard business practice.

8. To name a few examples, EdF has conducted an outstanding program in nuclear energy; rail transport has been transformed by the introduction of the TGV high-speed train by SNCF; and Air France, jointly with British Airways, operated the supersonic Concorde aircraft.

9. With 7 million Minitel terminals and around 26,000 services in 1995 at the peak of the system.

10. Out of the 1,000 largest firms in the world (listed by *Business Week* by market value in May 2003), forty-eight firms were French. There were twenty-three privatized firms in the list. Among them, with their world rank: Total (24), France Telecom (57), BNP (74), Vivendi (186), Saint-Gobain (291), Alcatel (338), TF1 (617), and Thales (756) (Business Week 2003).

11. UMTS is the European version of the third mobile generation.

References

ART. 2003. *Rapport public d'activité 2002*. Paris: Autorité de Régulation des Télécommunications.

Attali, J. 1994. "Les nationalisations ont sauvé notre industrie." *Capital*, no. 35, August, 116–117.

Baert, D. 2003. *Comptes spéciaux du Trésor et entreprises publiques*. Paris: Assemblée nationale, October 2003.

Barbier de la Serre. 2003. *L'Etat actionnaire et le gouvernement des entreprises publiques*. Paris: Ministère de l'Economie, des finances et de l'industrie, February 24.

Berne, M. 1997. "French lessons: The Minitel Case." In H. Kubicek, W. H. Dutton, and R. Williams, eds., *The Social Shaping of Information Superhighways*. New York: Saint Martin's Press.

Bertolus, J. J., Cedro, J. M., and Del Jesus, T. 2003. *Qui a ruiné France Telecom?* Paris: Hachette.

Bonnetblanc, G. 1985. *Les télécommunications françaises: Quel statut pour quelle entreprise*, Paris: La documentation française, Collection scientifique et technique des télécommunications.

Business Week. 2003. "The Global 1000." *Business Week*, July 14.

Chabanas, N., and Vergeau, E. 1996. *Nationalisations et privatisations depuis 50 ans*. Paris: INSEE.

Cohen, E. 1992. *Le colbertisme "high-tech."* Paris: Pluriel.

Conseil d'Etat. 1993. *Avis no. 355 255 du 18 novembre 1993*. Paris: Conseil d'Etat.

Conseil d'Etat. 2002. *Rapport public 2001, Les autorités administratives indépendantes*. Paris: Conseil d'Etat.

De Tricornot, A., and Picouet. 2002. "Les actionnaires salariés ont perdu 29% de leurs avoirs en 2002." *Le Monde*, October 4.

Diefenbacher, M. 2003. *Rapport de la Commission d'enquête sur la gestion des entreprises publiques afin d'améliorer le système de prise de décision*. Paris: Assemblée nationale, July.

Ducourtieux, C. 2003. "La France s'ouvre de plus en plus aux fonds anglo-saxons." *Le Monde*, July 29.

European Commission. 1987. *Green Book on the Development of the Common Market of Tele-communications Services and Equipment*. Brussels: European Commission.

Figaro. 2003. "Le grand bal des privatisations continue d'animer le marché." November 20.

Fontaine, A. 1981. "La querelle des nationalisations." *Le Monde*, November 15. As reported in: *La Cinquième République*, Paris: Le Monde, 1995, pp. 127–128.

France Telecom. 2003a. *Rapport d'activité 2002*. Paris: France Telecom.

France Telecom. 2003b. *Bilan social 2002*. Paris: France Telecom.

Giraud, C. 1987. *Bureaucratie et changement. Le cas de l'administration des télécommunications*. Paris: L'Harmattan.

INSEE. 1999. *Tableaux de l'économie française 1999–2000*. Paris: INSEE.

JO. 1986a. Loi no. 86–912 du 6 août 1986 (dite Loi de privatisation). *Journal Officiel de la République Française*, Paris.

JO. 1986b. Loi no. 86–793 du 2 juillet 1986. *Journal Officiel de la République Française*. Paris.

JO. 1989. Loi no. 89–465 du 10 juillet 1989 (dite Loi de "dénoyautage"). *Journal Officiel de la République Française*. Paris.

JO. 1990a. Loi no. 90–568 du 2 juillet 1990 relative à l'organisation du service public de la poste et des télécommunications. *Journal Officiel de la République Française*. Paris.

JO. 1990b. Loi no. 90–1170 sur la réglementation des télécommunications. *Journal Officiel de la République Française*. Paris.

JO. 1993. Loi no. 93–923 du 19 juillet 1993 dite "Loi de privatisation." *Journal Officiel de la République Française*. Paris.

JO. 1996a. Loi no. 96–659 du 26 juillet 1996 de réglementation des télécommunications. *Journal Officiel de la République Française*. Paris.

JO. 1996b. Loi no. 96–660 du 26 juillet 1996 relative à l'entreprise nationale France Télécom. *Journal Officiel de la République Française*. Paris.

JO. 2004. Loi no. 2003–1365 du 31 décembre 2003 relative aux obligations de service public des télécommunications et à France Télécom. *Journal Officiel de la République Française*. Paris.

Le Cœur, P., and Macke, G. 2003. "France Telecom: les députés autorisent le gouvernement à engager la privatisation." *Le Monde*, 7 December. www.lemonde.fr.

Legifrance. 1958. Constitution de la République Française. ⟨http://www.legifrance.gouv.fr⟩.

Loiseau, H. 2002. *1985–2000: Quinze années de mutation du secteur public d'entreprises*. Paris: INSEE, July.

Mamou, Y. 1996. "La saga des privatisations." *Le Monde*, November 19.

Mauduit, L. 2002. "En France les privatisations ont rapporté 70 milliards d'euros." *Le Monde*, April 9.

Mer, F. 2003. *Projet de loi relatif aux obligations de service public des télécommunications et à France Télécom*. ⟨http:www.senat.fr/dossierleg/pjl02-421.html⟩.

Minefi. 1991. *Les grands principes de l'EPN*. ⟨http://www.finances.gouv.fr/reglementation/instructions_comptables/M91⟩.

Minefi. 2003. *L'Etat actionnaire, Rapport 2003*. Paris: Ministère de l'économie, des finances et de l'industrie.

Munari, F. 2002. "The Effects of Privatization on Corporate R&D Units: Evidence from Italy and France." *R&D Management* 32(3), 223–232.

Observatoire. 2003. *Observatoire des privatisations/1ère vague*, 2003, Paris: TNS SOFRES Finance. ⟨http://www.tns-sofres.com/etudes/comfi/080403_privatisation.htm⟩.

OECD. 2003. *Communications Outlook*. Paris: OECD.

Orange, M., and Rocco, A. M. 1999. "Nationalisations-privatisations: l'Etat gagnant." *Le Monde*, July 17.

Pentzaropoulos, G. C., and Giokas, D. I. 2002. "Comparing the Operational Efficiency of the Main European Telecommunications Organizations: A Quantitative Analysis. *Telecommunications Policy* 26(11), 595–606.

Prévot, H. 1989. *Rapport de synthèse remis par Hubert Prévot à Paul Quilès, Ministre des Postes, des Télécommunications et de l'Espace*. Paris: Ministère des Postes, des télécommunications et de l'Espace.

Raffarin, J. P. 2002. "General Policy Address." July 3. ⟨http://www.premier-ministre.gouv.fr⟩, Nov. 2003.

Suard, P. 2002. *L'envol saboté d'Alcatel-Alsthom*. Paris: France-Empire.

Tribune. 2003. *La Tribune de l'économie*. Paris.

7 Privatization of Network Industries in Germany: A Disaggregated Approach

Günter Knieps

Network industries are typically characterized by different (sub)parts that strongly complement each other. A large spectrum of different historically grown organizational and institutional structures can be observed, each solving the relevant coordination problems in an institutionally different way. For example, although airport owners, airline companies, and air traffic control agencies can only jointly guarantee well-functioning air traffic, they have been organizationally and institutionally separated from the beginning of commercial air traffic. In contrast, it has only been in recent years that an increasing trend toward vertical open network provision of railroad systems, telecommunications networks, and electricity systems can be observed. The traditional vertically integrated railroad systems are gradually opening to allow access for alternative service suppliers on European railroad networks. Moreover, a strong tendency toward competition within telecommunications networks can be observed, including service competition and competing network carriers.

In order to provide a differentiated picture of the institutional reforms in network industries, it seems useful to differentiate the following network levels:

Level 1: Network services (e.g., air traffic, railway traffic, truck transport, shipping, production and resale of electricity or gas, telecommunications services)

Level 2: Infrastructure management (e.g., air traffic control, railway traffic control)

Level 3: Network infrastructure (e.g., airports, railway infrastructure, transportation and distribution networks of electricity or gas)

The term *privatization* has been applied in different ways. In the broadest sense, privatization refers to the introduction of market-oriented institutional reforms. This includes the sale of publicly owned assets as well as the deregulation of product markets. Privatization played an important role during the transition process of East Germany (e.g., Sinn and Sinn 1991).[1] The focus of this chapter, however, is on network industries.

In this chapter, the role of liberalization and privatization in German network industries is considered for each network level successively, with particular emphasis on the impact of these institutional reforms on the market performance of network services.[2] The topical question to what extent remaining sector-specific regulation is still necessary shifts the focus to the vertical problems of the required access of network services to infrastructure management and network infrastructure. Remaining reform potentials therefore also include the vertical perspective of nondiscriminatory access to infrastructures complementary to the network service level. However, this does not imply the necessity of an end-to-end regulation.

7.1 The Liberalization Process of Network Services in Germany—Level 1

7.1.1 The EC Initiatives

When the debate on the possibilities of privatization and deregulation started in the late 1970s and early 1980s, the primary focus was on network service level. Therefore, this reform process has been strongly interrelated to the EC policy of liberalizing European service markets.

The debate on the deregulation of transport services in Europe was focused not only on airlines, trucks, and ships; the role of (potential) entry on European railway networks was also seriously considered. One precedent was set by Foster Yeoman, a stone producer in the United Kingdom, which in 1986 purchased its own American diesel locomotives from General Motors for its aggregate trains. In 1989 the EC commissioner, Karel van Miert, argued in favor of private suppliers of train services. In 1991, the Council of the European Community issued regulation 1893/91 on the establishment of railway undertakings or railway rolling stock undertakings in the EC, based on a proposal by the Commission of the European Community.

A cornerstone for the take-off of the development toward competition in European telecommunications markets was the Commission of the European Communities' British Telecom decision in 1982 and its confirmation by the European Court of Justice in 1985. According to this decision, British Telecom should no longer be permitted to forbid the high-speed forwarding of telex messages between foreign countries by competitive agencies in Great Britain. The procedural setting of this case was most unusual because the Italian government, not British Telecom, appealed against the commission's decision. Moreover, the British government intervened, taking sides not with the Italian government but with the commission. The important message of the British Telecom case was that the Commission of the European Community was able to apply the Treaty of Rome's competition rules to the European telecommunications administration based on the public law of the different member countries.[3]

Since then, the commission has initiated a wide-ranging discussion of the possibilities of completing the common internal market for telecommunications in the European Community. Obviously, this effort was strongly related to the commission's endeavor to complete the common market by 1992. The Green Paper on the Development of the Common Market for Telecommunications Services and Equipment, issued by the commission in June 1987 (European Commission 1987)—proposed that the provision of terminal equipment as well as enhanced telecommunications services be liberalized within and between the member countries.[4] Basic services (mainly voice telephony) as well as the largest parts of the physical networks could still be monopolized by the national telecommunications administrations;[5] however, arguments concerning the public interest of such a monopoly should periodically be investigated.

It is already well known from normative microeconomic theory, as well as from U.S. experience (e.g., Müller and Vogelsang 1979; Windisch 1987; Horn, Knieps, and Müller 1988), that legal entry barriers, administrative price setting, and prohibition of cabotage are nothing but a publicly sanctioned monopoly or cartel agreement, and therefore counterproductive from the economic welfare point of view.

Consequences of active and potential competition in the markets for network services are the abolishment of monopoly rents with a subsequent reduction of tariff levels, increasing incentives for cost efficiency, optimization of service networks, more rapid reaction of prices to changes in the cost and demand structure, and increasing price-quality options. From a normative point of view, these beneficial effects of entry deregulation and price liberalization are not only to be expected for the markets for network services in Germany, but also for all other countries in liberalizing network services.

Nevertheless, the reform process of liberalizing network services was strongly path dependent. Compared to the U.S. deregulation and U.K. privatization movements in the 1980s, the respective developments in Germany have been quite inconspicuous. Several reasons may be noted. Among other things, there is the long tradition of *Gemeinwirtschaftslehre*, favoring regulation and public enterprises, and the institutionalized role of trade unions opposing privatization and deregulation (Vogelsang 1988). After all, the liberalization process took nearly two decades, until 1998. In fact, the provision of letter services is still monopolized, and the provision of local public transport cannot seriously be called competitive.

7.1.2   Liberalization of Different Network Service Markets in Germany

Transportation markets
Tariffs for truck transport in Germany have been liberalized since January 1994,[6] but it was only after 1998 that entry restrictions by licenses and cabotage prohibitions completely disappeared. The tariffs of the German shipping market were also liberalized in January 1994. Entry and exit were traditionally liberal for ships under German flag, and cabotage prohibitions for foreign ships have been gradually liberalized since 1993.

The European airline market was liberalized by the so-called three liberalization packages in 1987, 1990, and 1992, gradually liberalizing airline tariffs and market entry for international flights. In accordance with EU liberalization policy, the German airline market has been liberalized since 1998. Whereas navigation and truck transport services were always provided by private firms, the German national airline company, Lufthansa, was completely privatized in 1994. Entry deregulation of the airline market, however, was not combined with non-discriminatory access rules to airports. In 1993 the EU adopted the International Air Transport Association (IATA) guidelines under Council Regulation No. 95/93, based on the grandfather rights of incumbent airlines.

Regarding the railway sector, on January 1, 1994, the Bahnstrukturreform (railway reform) was enacted, based on the report of the

Regierungskommission Bundesbahn, which was appointed by the government in 1989 (e.g., Ewers 1994; Boss et al. 1996; Knieps 1996). The transition from a public enterprise to a firm under private law in the form of a joint stock company can be considered a formal privatization (rather than a real privatization by sale of publicly owned assets) because the state is still the sole owner of the Deutsche Bahn AG. Separate branches for infrastructure, commodity transportation, passenger long-distance transportation, and passenger local transportation have been established. The Deutsche Bundesbahn and the Deutsche Reichsbahn, its counterpart in East Germany, suffered from large amounts of debt. The first step of the privatization process thus consisted of liquidating debts and providing new capital. A major goal of privatization was entry deregulation of train services in the context of the liberalization of European transport markets. Accounting separation between service level and infrastructure level was considered a necessary precondition.

German telecommunications reform
The first step of the German telecommunications reform was a law passed on July 1, 1989,[7] restructuring the traditional Deutsche Bundespost (DBP) into three independent enterprises—postal services, telecommunications services, and financial services (Postbank)—which were then privatized. For telecommunications, the public enterprise DBP Telekom was transformed into the privatized Deutsche Telekom AG in 1995. Although the state still holds about 43 percent of the shares, privatization can be considered to be not only a formal one, because a significant part of the shares are traded at the stock exchanges. Moreover, the government has no golden shares, aiming to ensure that ordinary residential telephone service would continue to be made available as widely as before privatization.[8]

Privatization of the former Deutsche Bundespost was accompanied by entry deregulation in two steps. Under the strong influence of the European Commission's Green Paper on the Development of the Common Market for Telecommunications Services and Equipment of June 1987 (European Commission 1987) partial entry deregulation was introduced in European countries. There were controversial debates on the costs and benefits of global entry deregulation. The obstacles to comprehensive entry deregulation did not, however, exclude the possibility of partial entry deregulation. Partial deregulation included free entry into terminal equipment supply and into value-added network services (VANS) on the basis of the physical network provided by the network monopolist.

The Green Paper on the Liberalisation of Telecommunications Infrastructure and Cable Television Networks issued by the commission in October 1994 (European Commission 1994) again strongly influenced the process of liberalization of European telecommunications. The Full Competition Directive of March 13, 1996, demanded that member countries permit free entry into all areas of telecommunications.[9] The new telecommunications laws allowing overall market entry were enacted by the national parliaments during 1996, coming fully into effect on January 1, 1998.

Reform of the German electricity market
The liberalization of European electricity markets is based on the EU directive concerning a common electricity market of February 1997 (Directive 96/92/EC), setting a two-year target for implementation into national legislation. Germany implemented the directive in April 1998 with the modified Energy Act (Energiewirtschaftsgesetz, EnWG). The aim is to achieve competition at the generation stage as well as at the retail stage. Before that, the electricity sector had been characterized by fully integrated monopolies stabilized by an exemption from the general prohibition on cartels. The supraregional electricity networks are mainly in private ownership.[10] On the local and regional levels, active participation of municipalities can be observed.[11]

In contrast to the other European countries, in Germany privately negotiated frameworks (referred to as association agreements) arranging the conditions for network access have been applied. However, implementing the amendment of the EU directive, which entered into force in July 2003 as Directive 2003/54/EC, the revision of the German energy law has been passed in the meantime, introducing sector-specific ex ante regulation.[12] The former regulatory agency for telecommunication and postal services has been transformed into the Federal Network Agency, additionally responsible for gas, electricity, and railroad regulation.

7.1.3   Impact of the Liberalization of Transportation Services on Market Performance

An early survey of the impact of the liberalization of services in different network industries was provided by a study of the Kiel Institute for

World Economics in 1996 (Boss et al. 1996). This study demonstrates that the gradual opening of network service markets has had a positive impact on the performance of markets for network services. Significant price reductions due to tariff flexibility could be observed in German inland shipping, whereas entry has always been free (Boss et al. 1996). After entry, deregulation of truck transport prices decreased, service quality increased, and industry efficiency improved. Large price reductions due to tariff liberalization could be observed in truck transport; during the first year after liberalization, prices decreased on average by 24 percent below the lower tariff borderline of the former regulated long-distance transport tariff (Boss et al. 1996). It has been estimated that in Germany prior to liberalization, regulation accounted for excess costs of 30 to 40 percent for long-distance truck transport. Increasing competition promoted innovation and encouraged firms to improve their services and develop a wide range of specialized transport services (Boylaud and Nicoletti 2001).

Entry of new airlines to service national lines in Germany started gradually in 1988 (Aero Loyd, Germanwings) and has increased since 1991 (Boss et al. 1996). Since the European single aviation market in 1997, airline tariffs for international flights within Europe are no longer governed by the price cartel of the IATA Airlines.[13] According to an OECD study, there is clear evidence that overall efficiency and the rate of occupancy of aircraft seats tend to increase and average fares tend to decrease due to competition; however, only if constraints on airport access are relaxed can the simultaneous liberalization of the domestic and regional market and international (long-distance) routes result in full network optimization and cost efficiency (Gönenç and Nicoletti 2001).[14]

As a consequence of airline deregulation in Germany, product differentiation increased, a large number of different tariffs were established, and the application of yield management was increased. The growing importance of yield management can be illustrated by the pricing strategies of low-cost carriers such as Ryanair, Germania, Germanwings, and Hapag-Lloyd (e.g., Klophaus 2003, Schleusener 2003). The pricing strategies of these newcomers are heterogeneous (see Schleusener 2003). Product differentiation is also strongly dependent on the type of airport the airlines serve. Ryanair, for example, is concentrating on regional airports, with a consequent focus on tourists with high price sensitivity but low time preference. This group of customers is also willing to accept long travel distances to the airport. In contrast,

Germania is focusing on price-sensitive business customers. As a consequence, it serves national and international airports; for example, flights are offered between Frankfurt International Airport and Berlin Tegel. On this route, Germania is competing directly with the traditional incumbent Lufthansa, as the Bundeskartellamt's recent competition decisions on predatory pricing demonstrate.[15]

Active competition on the German railroad market is focused on commodity transportation within Germany as well as local passenger transportation. Entry into cross-border transportation can rarely be observed; cabotage on foreign networks within other EU countries does not exist. Competitive subscriptions for subsidies for local passenger transportation take place only to a limited extent (e.g., Aberle and Eisenkopf 2002).

7.1.4   Impact of the Liberalization of the Telecommunications Markets on Performance

The partial deregulation of the telecommunications sector resulted in free entry into terminal equipment supply and value-added network services, employing the physical network of the DBP Telecom monopoly.[16] Moreover, in addition to DBP Telecom, two alternative mobile communications providers were licensed. Although the voice telephony market was still monopolized, long-distance tariffs were falling by about 20 percent during the period 1996 to 1998. Between 1989 and 1994 tariffs for households had already been decreasing by 9.3 percent (Boss et al. 1996). This indicates not only the technological process in the telecommunications sector, but also the increasing instability of partial entry deregulation. Due to the tendency to mix voice and data communications services, it became increasingly difficult to differentiate between legally protected voice telephone services and competitive value-added network services (Knieps 1989).

Since the complete entry deregulation of the telecommunications market in 1998, massive private investments in alternative long-distance infrastructures have been undertaken, and in this area there is now both active and potential competition. Currently there are a large number of competitors with their own country-wide long-distance networks in Germany. Although the markets for long-distance telecommunications services are still frequently characterized by economies of scale and economies of scope, there is nevertheless active and potential competition.[17] Since overall free entry became possible, the performance of the German long-distance telecommunications market has shown strong improvement: this includes a large number of service providers, providing an increasing scope of services, entry of several network carriers, and strongly decreasing prices for long-distance calls (Gabelmann and Groß 2003, Stumpf and Schwarz-Schilling 1999, Immenga et al. 2001, Brunekreeft and Groß 2000, Monopolkommission 2001).

The price level for long-distance voice telephony decreased substantially during the first years of the global entry deregulation. The development of the price index for long-distance services that is reported by Statistisches Bundesamt 1999 and is part of the consumer price index in Germany fell by more than 40 percent between February 1998 and April 1999. A more differentiated view is provided in figure 7.1.

After global entry deregulation, three types of providers of long-distance voice services emerged: the traditional incumbent Deutsche Telekom; alternative network providers (nationale Vollsortimenter),

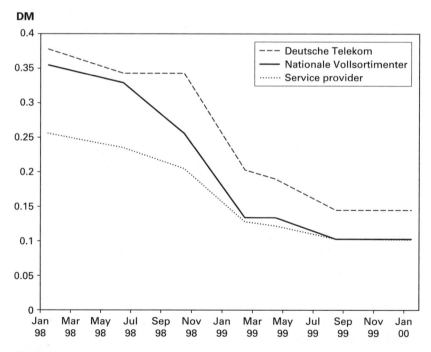

Figure 7.1
Average prices for the three types of providers
Source: Gabelmann and Groß (2003, p. 116).

which invested heavily in infrastructure; and switch-based service providers, which invested little in infrastructure. During the competition process, differences in the price-setting behavior of the different types of firms could be observed. The intense price competition in the winter of 1998–1999 not only reduced the overall level of prices but resulted in a convergence of prices. The Internet and printed media were full of price information, agencies also provided information, and the providers themselves advertised aggressively with price as the decisive variable in long-distance telecommunications (Brunekreeft and Groß 2000).

The overall development can be summarized as follows (Brunekreeft and Groß 2000): Deutsche Telekom lowered its average price by 62 percent, the alternative network operators by 66 percent, and the service providers by 52 percent between February 1998 and April 1999. In April 1999 the service providers charged on average only 32 percent of what consumers had had to pay to Deutsche Telekom for comparable services sixteen months earlier.

After the initial period of strong price decline during 1998–1999, prices began to stabilize. The price for foreign calls was still 36.5 percent lower in 2001 as compared to 2000 and then became stable. In contrast, prices for local access and local calls remained stable (Monopolkommission 2001).[18]

The strong decline of prices for long-distance voice telephone services in Germany since global entry deregulation is summarized in figure 7.2. These price developments are by no means unique; similar developments can be observed in other European countries.

Whereas Deutsche Telekom held 100 percent of the market share for voice telephony before global entry deregulation, the market share of the competitors strongly increased during the period of competition. The competitors' market share (share of traffic volume in minutes) for national long-distance calls, including regional calls, increased from 10.3 percent in 1998 to 34.7 percent in 2001; the market share for international calls increased from 20 percent in 1998 to 51 percent in 2001 (Monopolkommission 2001).[19]

7.1.5 Impact of the Liberalization of the Electricity Retail Services on Market Performance

The deregulation of the electricity market focused strongly on the role of retail competition. In contrast to most other EU countries, Germany

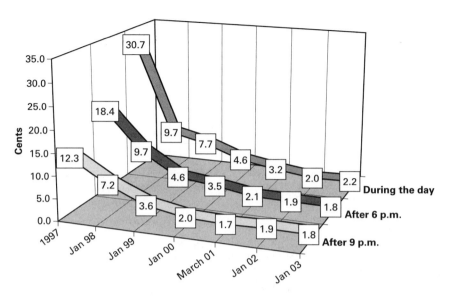

Figure 7.2
Minimal tariffs for national-long distance calls in fixed networks, January 9, 2003
Source: Jahresbericht 2002, Marktbeobachtungsdaten der Regulierungsbehörde für Tele-
kommunikation und Post, p. 23.

opted for complete eligibility from the beginning of liberalization in
April 1998. The development of retail competition focusing on the
large group of small domestic and commercial end users is indicated
in figure 7.3.[20]

The price developments are divided into incumbents' prices (owner
of the distribution network) and entrants' prices (owner of distribution
networks in other areas or pure retailer). Around August 1999, retail
competition started reducing the price level significantly. The lowest
price level was reached in the spring of 2000. Incumbents reacted
immediately. However, since then, entrants have left the market or
increased their prices. As a consequence, prices have risen continuously (Brunekreeft 2003). These developments are shown in figure 7.4.

The price developments until the summer of 2000 were considered
an indication of the success of the liberalization of German electricity
markets. The large-scale entry of large retail companies (e.g., Yello)
and the subsequent price drop attracted substantial media attention.
After entrants increasingly left the retail markets and prices increased
again, public attention shifted to the role of access to electricity networks. In particular, the complaint was that due to excessive access

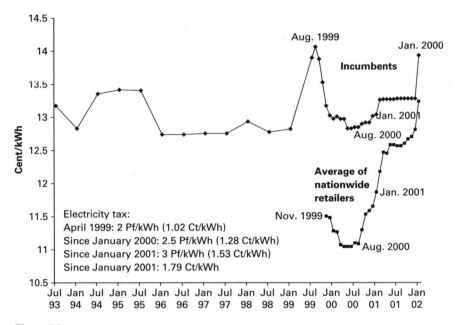

Figure 7.3
Development of electricity prices for residential users (with an annual consumption of 3.500 kWh)
Source: Brunekreeft (2003, p. 220) based on Brunekreeft and Keller (2000, p. 23).

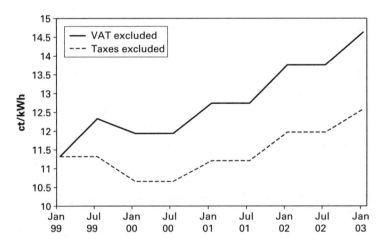

Figure 7.4
Price development in German electricity retail markets
Source: Eurostat, various years.

charges, the price levels of competitive retailers did not guarantee market survival (Brunekreeft 2003).

7.1.6 Provision of Universal Services

The objective of universal service provision by means of subsidization has been of no relevance for the provision of truck transport services or shipping; furthermore, it was of minor interest for airline transportation markets. However, subsidization of telecommunications, postal services (especially first-class mail), train services (in particular local traffic), and public transport (ÖPNV) is still politically relevant.

The major reason that global entry deregulation—including voice telephone services as well as network infrastructure—was introduced only in 1998 (nearly twenty years after the slow beginning of deregulation in the early 1980s) was the provision of universal services at socially desired tariffs by means of cross-subsidization.

In the German telecommunications sector, the political process was dominated by a silent coalition between the Deutsche Bundespost (DBP) and its unions, on the one hand, and small and peripheral users, on the other hand. The DBP and its unions were interested in the monopoly, which could be legitimized and supported politically only by the subsidies it provided for the large majority of small and peripheral users at the expense of business users.

Some way had to be found to compensate small and peripheral users for the losses they would incur in the case of complete entry deregulation. Only such an arrangement could secure their support on the issue of telecommunications deregulation. In order to make free entry into all parts of telecommunications politically acceptable, it was proposed to split the silent coalition between the telecommunications administration and small users by setting up a universal service fund (Blankart and Kneips 1989). The purpose of this fund was to keep the traditional subsidy of the small users stable, changing only the way it was financed from internal to external subsidization. In order to make sure that the small users do not oppose deregulation, it seems to be important to guarantee the price level of the traditionally internally subsidized services as upper boundary (social contract pricing).

Under a universal service fund, every chosen supplier of a subsidized service has the right to obtain an external subsidy, financed out of this fund. The amount of subsidy depends on the difference between the incremental costs of providing the socially desired services and the social contract prices. The competition for subsidies also reveals the actual burden of the universal services and the minimum costs of traditionally internally subsidized services. It cannot be expected that the traditional carrier is necessarily the most cost-effective supplier if new firms with cost-saving technologies (e.g., mobile telephone and microwave systems) enter the market. Therefore, the bidding for the subsidized markets may strongly reduce the volume of subsidies required. In particular, an increase of the universal service fund to finance the traditionally internally subsidized services can be excluded as long as the scope of universal services is not extended (Blankart and Knieps 1989).

One possibility of financing the required subsidies would be the public budget. This is still the case in public transport; for telecommunications and postal services, however, the concept of an entry tax has been proposed, which all suppliers of lucrative activities (incumbent and competitors) would have to pay. The concept of a universal service fund was introduced in the new German telecommunications law enacted in 1996 (as well as in many other European countries). The concept was also introduced in the new postal law.

No universal service fund has yet been implemented in Germany. In contrast, in the United States, a universal service fund was established. The size of this universal service fund became rather large, because not only the traditional cross-subsidized narrowband services in rural areas, but also cost-intensive new services, including broadband Internet access for schools and libraries, as well as health care providers, were included.[21] Contributions to the federal universal service support mechanisms are determined using a quarterly contribution factor calculated by the Federal Communications Commission (FCC). For example, projected program support for the fourth quarter 2003 was $1.6 billion (schools and libraries, $0.55 billion), which was related to total projected collected interstate and international end user telecommunications revenues of $18.6 billion for the fourth quarter of 2003, resulting in a proposed contribution factor of 0.092.[22]

The instrument of a competitive bidding procedure for subsidized public transportation services (transparent and nondiscriminatory subscription procedures) was implemented legally during the reform of the railway services. Today the implementation of the public service contract focusing on ex ante bidding for subsidies from the public budget, instead of ex post, ad hoc subsidy requirements, is the leading concept in EU transportation policy (although its implementation in practice does not always seem to be an easy task).

7.2   Reform of Infrastructure Management—Level 2

The importance of coordination and allocation activities of network capacities varies strongly among network industries. Although the liberalization of network services increases coordination efforts, truck transport and shipping has rarely been coordinated in the past, but the current implementation of toll collection in Germany for heavy trucks shows the increasing importance of infrastructure management for road traffic also.

In contrast, air traffic control has a long tradition in infrastructure management. It is well known that air transport services require not only airports and planes but also air traffic control systems. Air traffic control systems not only have the task of guaranteeing traffic safety but are also responsible for an efficient allocation of airspace capacity. Although airport owners, airlines, and air traffic control agencies can guarantee a well-functioning air traffic only by working jointly, they are organizationally and institutionally separated.

The permanent control and coordination of traffic is also necessary for train services. Train control systems are therefore the decisive link between rails and stations, on the one hand, and the supply of train services, on the other hand. This coordination effort depends on the number of trains, the sequencing of faster and slower trains, and their speed, but is not influenced by the number of train companies that are active on a certain railroad network. Moreover, the cost of train control does not increase when train control systems are organizationally separated from the tracks. The scheduling and operating of trains, as well as the repair of rails, has to be coordinated by train control systems regardless of whether they are vertically integrated with the tracks and station infrastructure. Recent technological developments in advanced train control systems and high-speed computers have provided ample opportunities to automate many functions in scheduling and operating railroads. Thus, train traffic control systems are developing toward highly software-oriented technical systems with a large potential of transborder-oriented scale. Similar to air traffic control, possibilities arise for an integrated Europe-wide train traffic control system, harmonizing train schedules and coordinating train movements on a Europe-wide scale. Compared with the current train coordination policy, which is strongly geared to the national or regional levels, large efficiency benefits can be expected.

The strong national orientation of the capacity management of track capacities was caused by the traditional national railroad monopolies. Transborder orientation within the International Union of Railways (UIC) has been minimized with respect to standardization (Knieps 1995). Therefore, optimization is strongly limited to national railroad systems. A long-term objective could be the founding of a European train traffic control agency responsible for the coordination of Europe-wide train services. Such a development could be strongly stimulated by separating train control from national rail infrastructure policies.

Although air traffic control in Europe is much more integrated than train traffic control, the allocation of airspace is in the competence of the individual countries. Eurocontrol has no final authority; its board, the permanent commission, is composed of the transport ministers of the member countries. National boundaries and the objective of retaining the sovereignty of the individual countries have led to arbitrary inefficient horizontal divisions. According to a study by Eurocontrol (2002), the cost of delays due to air traffic flow management is estimated to be between 2,500 and 3,600 million euros (total airspace user costs and cost of passengers). In the meantime, reform proposals by the European Commission are focusing on the creation of a single European upper airspace by merging the current national regions (European Commission 2002).

In Germany, formal privatization of the air traffic control organization into Deutsche Flugsicherungs GmbH/DFS took place in January 1993. The cost of this organization has to be covered (similarly to Eurocontrol) by user charges. The efficiency effects of formal privatization are not known (Boss et al. 1996). Whereas until 2000, revenues were sufficient to cover costs, in 2001 and 2002 a deficit of 33.380 million euros and 21.466 million euros, respectively, occurred (Deutsche Flugsicherung 2003).

Since traffic control systems are natural monopolies, which need public authority to define the scope and borderlines of the control areas, selective free entry into the control business is not feasible and would lead to disaster. Nevertheless, competitive bidding to find the most efficient traffic control agency for a well-defined control area can be expected to work.[23] If bidding took place Europe-wide, a process of competition among institutions would occur. As a consequence, the agency with the most innovative software and control system might also be successful in providing traffic control services in other countries.

Since the liberalization of the electricity sector, the coordination between electricity generation and transmission has become increasingly important.[24] In the meantime, in continental Europe, transborder high-voltage transportation by means of transborder interconnectors as well as the evolution of markets for balancing power (Regelenergie) have become major issues. Due to the important role of system externalities (based on Kirchhoff's laws, which state that it is the characteristic of electricity to seek the path of least resistance), there seems to be a large coordination potential of transborder electricity flows between European countries, which has been rather unexploited (Zimmer 2004). Coordination efforts also play a role in telecommunications, for example, in standardization, telephone numbering, and spectrum allocation. Such efforts to define and allocate property rights should, however, be differentiated from permanent control and the coordination of traffic flows.

7.3   Reforms of Allocation of Network Infrastructure Capacities— Level 3

The more the aim of liberalizing network services succeeded (e.g., entry deregulation, price deregulation), the more the focus of EC directives as well as the national sector-specific laws shifted to the problems of access to network infrastructure.

7.3.1   The Reform Process

In Germany a telecommunications law, together with a decree on special access, was passed in 1996. Since 1998 a new telecommunications law has allowed global market entry. Taking into consideration the EU review process, German national communications law had been under review and a revised law was enacted in June 2004.[25] A German energy law was passed in 1998. In contrast to all other European countries German legislation opted for allowing negotiated third-party access within the association agreements for network access. The revision of this law has been passed in the meantime, introducing sector-specific ex ante regulation.[26] The German railroad reform of 1993 is currently also under review, focusing on the introduction of sector-specific access regulation. Grandfather rights to airport slots are also under attack in the context of the current review of the EU Council Regulation No. 95/93 on allocation of airport slots from 1993, which at that time did not allow market-based instruments such as slot exchange and slot auction (Boyfield 2003).

In contrast to the provision of network services, state ownership of the infrastructure level still plays an important role in Germany. Highways are owned by the state, and German railways are only formally privatized. Airports are to a large extent owned by the state, but increasingly private capital is attracted. Since 1997 the heavily used (congested) airports in Düsseldorf and Frankfurt, and subsequently in Hamburg and Hannover, have been partly privatized (Teilprivatisierung) (Brunekreeft and Neuscheler 2003).[27] Since private capital can be raised only if risk-equivalent interest rates can be expected, privatization shifted public attention to the cost-covering possibilities of access charges to the infrastructure.

Infrastructure of telecommunications networks is mainly owned by private firms (although the state still owns a large part of the shares of Deutsche Telekom). Private shares have a strong tradition in electricity and gas networks. The long-distance networks for gas transportation are owned by private firms. On the local and regional levels, this picture changes due to the active participation of municipalities.

Vertical separation in terms of ownership between the different network levels did not occur in German network industries, regardless of ownership structure (private or public), before the liberalization process started. However, in the railroad sector, there has been an intense controversy on the issue of separating railway infrastructure from railway services and not only formally privatizing the service companies of the Deutsche Bahn AG (Knieps 1996, Wissenschaftlicher Beirat beim Bundesministerium für Verkehr 1997). This has not yet been resolved.

7.3.2 Remaining Reform Potentials

The reform potentials on the level of network infrastructure and the remaining regulatory problems center around the basic question of whether the providers of network services need access to a network infrastructure with characteristics of a monopolistic bottleneck (Knieps 1997). Remaining reform potentials therefore center around the vertical perspective of nondiscriminatory access to infrastructures complementary to the network service level. However, this does not imply the necessity of an end-to-end regulation including the competitive segments.

The conditions necessary for a monopolistic bottleneck facility are fulfilled, first, if a facility is essential in order to reach customers—if there is no second or third such facility, in other words if no active substitute is available. This is the case if, due to bundling advantages, there is a natural monopoly situation, meaning that one supplier can make the facility available more cost-efficiently than several suppliers; and secondly, if at the same time the facility cannot be duplicated on reasonable economic terms—if there is no potential substitute available. This is the case if the facility's costs are irreversible and if, as a result, there is no functioning second-hand market for these facilities.

The criterion for the localization of the remaining sector-specific need for regulation within network infrastructures is always the question of whether access to these facilities is indispensable for offering a complementary service at an upstream or downstream production level. It is therefore necessary to ensure nondiscriminatory access to the bottleneck through tailor-made bottleneck regulation. In all other network areas, however, the situation is completely different because there is active and potential competition.

The bottleneck theory was not developed specifically for a single-network sector. Whereas there are no monopolistic bottlenecks at the level of network services and infrastructure management, monopolistic bottlenecks do exist on the infrastructure level. Examples are airports, railway infrastructure, electricity transmission, and distribution networks. Nevertheless, not every network infrastructure possesses the characteristics of a natural monopoly in combination with irreversible costs. For example, supraregional high-pressure gas pipeline transmission in Germany is not a monopolistic bottleneck due to the broad competition potential created by pipelines operated by project companies, through ownership in undivided shares and through access options to competing backbone pipelines (Knieps 2002). Long-distance telecommunications networks are characterized by the existence of alternative network providers, and the remaining bottleneck problem is limited to the local loop (Knieps 1997, Laffont and Tirole 2000). Compared to other European countries (e.g., Switzerland, Great Britain) developments of interactive cable TV networks in Germany are still at an early stage. A major reason for this slow development can be found in the institutional separation of the vertical industry structure, in particular, the separation between the local access points and subsequent in-house provisions (Distelkamp 2000).

Competitive network infrastructures do not create regulatory problems. Due to network alternatives, the problem of avoiding discriminatory access disappears; incentives do exist for the efficient allocation of network capacities; excessive profits cannot be expected; and the subsidy problem disappears.

Regulating those parts of network infrastructures characterized as monopolistic bottlenecks remains an important task even after full market opening. Where network sectors have monopolistic bottleneck areas, they need specific regulation to discipline remaining market power. This requires, above all, symmetric access to the monopolistic bottleneck areas for all active and potential providers of network services to allow (active and potential) competition to fully develop. Moreover, price cap regulation should be applied, limited to the monopolistic bottleneck areas.

There are still network infrastructures where access charges do not allow cost covering. The provision of infrastructure investments in streets, canals, airports, and rails has traditionally been considered a typical task of the state. As long as the use of the infrastructure is so low that there is no rivalry, market prices do not make sense, and the state plays a significant role in guaranteeing financing. The introduction of time- and capacity-dependent landing fees or railroad access charges significantly improves the financing of the infrastructure costs. Nevertheless, it seems important that public subsidies to guarantee cost cover requirements of infrastructures with low demand (*Infrastrukturvorhaltefunktion*) should be granted only as a result of a transparent political process.

7.4 Conclusions

When the debate on the possibilities of privatization and liberalization started in the late 1970s and early 1980s, the primary focus was on network service level. Therefore, this reform process has been strongly related to the EC policy of liberalizing European service markets. Nevertheless, the reform process of liberalizing network services was strongly path dependent. After all, the process took nearly two decades.

The gradual opening of network service markets has had a positive impact on the performance of markets for network services. Significant price reductions due to tariff flexibility have been observed in German inland navigation, whereas entry has always been free. Large price reductions due to tariff liberalization could be observed in truck transport. After entry, deregulation prices decreased, service quality increased, and industry efficiency improved. Increasing competition promoted innovation and encouraged firms to improve their services and develop a wide range of specialized transport services. As a consequence of airline deregulation in Germany, product differentiation increased, a large number of different tariffs were established, and the application of yield management was increased. The price level for long-distance voice telephony decreased substantially during the first years of global entry deregulation. After the initial period of strong price decline during 1998–1999, price levels began to stabilize.

The more the aim of liberalizing network services succeeded (e.g. entry deregulation, price deregulation), the more did the focus of EC directives as well as the national sector-specific laws shift to the problems of infrastructure management and access to network infrastructure, and in particular to the future role of sector-specific regulation of the remaining network-specific market power. Therefore, it seems useful to differentiate network services, infrastructure management, and the (noncompetitive) monopolistic bottleneck areas of the network infrastructure.

Since the complete entry deregulation of the telecommunications market in 1998, massive private investments in alternative long-distance infrastructures have been undertaken, and in this area there is now both active and potential competition. In contrast, airports and railway infrastructures are monopolistic bottlenecks and need adequate access regulation. In the meantime, there is an intense debate on introducing a market for slots, focusing on nondiscriminatory and efficient allocation of airport capacities. Ex ante regulation of nondiscriminatory access to railway infrastructures should lead to improved competition in markets for railway traffic. The shift toward market power regulation of rail access that has been initiated by EU Directive 2001/14[28] of the railroad infrastructure package of February 2001 introduces several regulatory obligations for the provider of track access and requires a regulatory body to be set up in each member state. Negotiations concerning the level of infrastructure charges will in the future only be permitted if they are carried out under the supervision of the regulatory body (Art. 30). In the meantime, a new infrastructure utilization regulation has been passed in Germany.[29] Based on the new

EU directives, a set of detailed requirements has been specified in order to improve the transparency of the principles and criteria for the allocation of track capacities as well as the principles of access tariffs. In addition, the current reform proposals by the European Commission are focusing on the harmonization and integration of infrastructure management in order to overcome the strong national orientation of the infrastructure management. These efforts are also intended to contribute to increased efficiency on the European transportation markets.

Electricity transmission networks are also monopolistic bottlenecks, without active and potential competition on the level of infrastructure. The deregulation of the electricity market focused strongly on the role of retail competition but ignored the role of access regulation to ensure this competition. The comparison of retail prices of incumbent firms and market entrants as well as the market exit of the new competitors has been a result of this shortfall. Currently, with the installation of a regulatory authority, public attention shifts to the future role of access regulation of electricity networks.

Notes

I thank R. Soltwedel, C. Mallin, and anonymous referees for constructive comments on earlier versions of this chapter.

1. The agency that has been in charge of privatization is the Treuhandanstalt. In East Germany, 4,223 of 12,036 key sector enterprises were totally privatized between October 3, 1990, and July 31, 1992; moreover, 3,981 parts of enterprises were privatized with a minority participation of the Treuhandanstalt (Bös 1993).

2. In this chapter, the term *privatization* is used in its most common sense as sale of publicly owned assets (Kay and Thompson 1986), in contrast to *deregulation*.

3. For a detailed explanation of this case, see Schulte-Braucks (1986).

4. In addition, the commission pleaded for a liberalization of the procurement policy of the national telecommunications administration as well as for an introduction of European-wide telecommunications standards.

5. Only the margins of the physical networks (mobile radio and low-speed satellite communication) were opened for competition.

6. Tarifaufhebungsgesetz vom 13, August 1993.

7. Gesetz zur Neustrukturierung des Post- und Fernmeldewesens und der Deutschen Bundespost (Poststrukturgesetz) vom 8. Juni 1989, Bundesgesetzblatt Teil I vom 14. Juni 1989, pp. 1026–1051.

8. Such golden shares, called "kiwi shares", were introduced during the privatization process in New Zealand (Ergas 1996).

9. Commission Directive 96/19/EC of March 13, 1996, amending Directive 90/388/EEC with regard to the implementation of full competition in the telecommunications markets, OJ L 74, 22. 3. 1996, p. 13 (the "Full Competition Directive").

10. Private shareholders (including institutional shareholders like insurance companies) hold 67 percent of the shares, and municipals hold 33 percent of the shares of RWE AG (RWE 2003).

11. Details on the German electricity sector can be found in Brunekreeft and Keller (2000) and Brunekreeft (2003).

12. Energiewirtschaftsgesetz (EnWG) vom 7. Juli 2005, Bundesgesetzblatt Jahrgang 2005, Teil I, Nr. 42, ausgegeben zu Bonn am 12. Juli 2005, 1970–2018.

13. The bulk of international routes outside Europe is still governed by restrictive bilateral air service agreements (ASAs) (Gönenç and Nicoletti 2001).

14. The problem of nondiscriminatory access to airport slots will be considered in section 7.2.

15. Bundeskartellamt, 9. Beschlusskammer, B9–144/01, February 18, 2002. In this context, the role of reallocation of scarce airport slots and the subsequent challenge of grandfathering could be observed (Bundeskartellamt, 9. Beschlusskammer, B9–62100–Z–75/02, August 7, 2002) (see section 7.2).

16. Voice telephony, which accounts for about 85 percent of total returns, as well as network infrastructure, remained monopolized until January 1998.

17. The required nondiscriminatory access to the complementary local networks, including number portability, has been granted by sector-specific regulation.

18. See Statistisches Bundesamt, Verbraucherpreisindex für Telekommunikationsdienstleistungen, Mitteilung Nr. 41 vom January 31, 2001.

19. At that time, no preselection and call-by-call were available for local calls.

20. For detailed analysis, see Brunekreeft and Keller (2000) and Brunekreeft (2003).

21. CC Docket No. 96-45, In the Matter of Federal-State Joint Board on Universal Service, May 8, 1997, in particular pp. 227, 318; April 10, 1998.

22. Universal Service Contribution Factor, CC Docket No. 96-45, September 5, 2003.

23. Network-specific market power due to the absence of significant sunk cost cannot be expected (see the next section).

24. For the experience of coordination in the electricity pool of England and Wales, see Brunekreeft (1997).

25. Telekommunikationsgesetz (TKG) vom 22. Juni 2004, Bundesgesetzblatt Jahrgang 2004, Teil I, Nr. 29, ausgegeben zu Bonn am 25. Juni 2004, 1190–1243.

26. Energiewirtschaftsgesetz (EnWG) vom 7. Juli 2005, Bundesgesetzblatt Jahrgang 2005, Teil I, Nr. 42, ausgegeben zu Bonn am 12. Juli 2005, 1970–2018.

27. The share of private capital in Düsseldorf is 50 percent, in Frankfurt 28.97 percent, in Hamburg 36 percent, and in Hannover 30 percent (Gerber 2002).

28. Commission Directive 2001/14/EC of February 26, 2001, on the allocation of railway infrastructure capacity and the levying of charges for the use of railway infrastructure and safety certification, OJ L 75, 15. 3. 2001, pp. 29–46.

29. Verordnung zum Erlass und zur Änderung eisenbahnrechtlicher Vorschriften vom 3. Juni 2005, Bundesgesetzblatt Jahrgang 2005, Teil I Nr. 32, ausgegeben zu Bonn am 13. Juni 2005, pp. 1566–1577.

References

Aberle, G., and Eisenkopf, A. 2002. *Schienenweg und Netzzugang-Regulierungsprobleme bei der Öffnung des Schienennetzes und wettbewerbspolitische Empfehlungen zur Gestaltung des Netzzugangs.* Hamburg: Deutscher Verkehrs-Verlag.

Blankart, Ch. B., and Knieps, G. 1989. "What Can We Learn from Comparative Institutional Analysis? The Case of Telecommunications." *Kyklos* 42, 579–598.

Bös, D. 1993. "Privatization in Europe: A Comparison of Approaches." *Oxford Review of Economic Policy* 9(1), 95–111.

Boss, A., Laaser, C.-F., Schatz, K.-W., et al. 1996. *Deregulierung in Deutschland—Eine empirische Analyse.* Tübingen: J. C. B. Mohr (Paul Siebeck).

Boyfield, K. 2003. "Who Owns Airport Slots? A Market Solution to a Deepening Dilemma." In K. Boyfield, ed., *A Market in Airport Slots.* London: Institute of Economic Affairs.

Boylaud, O., and Nicoletti, G. 2001. "Regulatory Reform in Road Freight." *OECD Economic Studies* 32, 229–251.

Brunekreeft, G. 1997. *Co-ordination and Competition in the Electricity Pool of England and Wales.* Baden-Baden: Nomos Verlag.

Brunekreeft, G. 2003. *Regulation and Competition Policy in the Electricity Market—Economic Analysis and German Experience.* Baden-Baden: Nomos Verlag.

Brunekreeft, G., and Groß, W. 2000. "Prices for Long-Distance Voice Telephony in Germany." *Telecommunications Policy* 24, 929–945.

Brunekreeft, G., and Keller, K. 2000. "The Electricity Supply Industry in Germany: Market Power or Power of the Market?" *Utilities Policy* 9, 15–29.

Brunekreeft, G., and Neuscheler, T. 2003. "Preisregulierung von Flughäfen." In G. Knieps and G. Brunekreeft, eds., *Zwischen Regulierung und Wettbewerb—Netzsektoren in Deutschland,* 2nd ed. Heidelberg: Physica-Verlag.

Deutsche Flugsicherung. 2003. *Geschäftsbericht 2002.* Langen.

Distelkamp, M. 2000. "Wettbewerbspotenziale der deutschen Kabel-TV-Infrastruktur." Discussion paper no. 203, Bad Honnef, Wissenschaftliches Institut für Kommunikationsdienste.

Ergas, H. 1996. *Telecommunications across the Tasman: A Comparison of Regulatory Approaches and Economic Outcomes in Australia and New Zealand.* University of Auckland, May 15.

Eurocontrol. 2002. *Performance Review Report: An Assessment of Air Traffic Management in Europe during the Calendar Year 2001.* Brussels.

European Commission. 1987. Green Paper on the Development of the Common Market for Telecommunications Services and Equipment. KOM (87) 290 fin. Brussels.

European Commission. 1994. Green Paper on the Liberalisation of Telecommunications Infrastructure and Cable Television Networks. KOM (94) 440 fin. Brussels.

European Commission. 2002. *A Single European Sky: Broadening Horizons for Air Travel.* Brussels.

Ewers, H.-J. 1994. "Privatisierung und Deregulierung bei den Eisenbahnen—Das Beispiel der Deutschen Bundesbahn und der Deutschen Reichsbahn." *Jahrbuch für Neue Politische Ökonomie* 13, 178–208.

Gabelmann, A., and Groß, W. 2003. "Telekommunikation: Wettbewerb in einem dynamischen Markt." In G. Knieps and G. Brunekreeft, eds., *Zwischen Regulierung und Wettbewerb—Netzsektoren in Deutschland*, 2nd ed. Heidelberg: Physica-Verlag.

Gerber, P. 2002. "Success Factors for the Privatisation of Airports—An Airline Perspective." *Journal of Air Transport Management* 8, 29–36.

Gönenç, R., and Nicoletti, G. 2001. "Regulation, Market Structure and Performance in Air Passenger Transportation." *OECD Economic Studies* 32, 183–227.

Horn, M., Knieps, G., and Müller, J. 1988. *Die gesamtwirtschaftliche Bedeutung von Deregulierungsmaßnahmen in den USA: Schlussfolgerungen für die Bundesrepublik Deutschland.* Baden-Baden: Nomos-Verlag.

Immenga, U., Kirchner, C., Knieps, G., and Kruse, J. 2001. *Telekommunikation im Wettbewerb—Eine ordnungspolitische Konzeption nach erfolgreicher Marktöffnung.* Munich: Verlag C. H. Beck.

Kay, J. A., and Thompson, D. J. 1986. "Privatisation: A Policy in Search of a Rationale." *Economic Journal* 96, 18–32.

Klophaus, R. 2003. "Vielfliegerprogramme für Low-Cost Airlines." *Zeitschrift für Verkehrswissenschaft* 74(2), 115–128.

Knieps, G. 1989. "Telecommunications Policy—Assessing Recent Experience in the US, Japan and Europe and Its Implications for the Completion of the Common Market." In H. Giersch, ed., *Services in World Economy.* Tübingen: J. C. B. Mohr (Paul Siebeck).

Knieps, G. 1995. "Standardization: The Evolution of Institutions versus Government Intervention." In L. Gerken, ed., *Competition among Institutions.* London: Macmillan.

Knieps, G. 1996. *Wettbewerb in Netzen—Reformpotentiale in den Sektoren Eisenbahn und Luftverkehr.* Tübingen: J. C. B. Mohr (Paul Siebeck).

Knieps, G. 1997. "Phasing out Sector-Specific Regulation in Competitive Telecommunications." *Kyklos* 50(3), 325–339.

Knieps, G. 2002. "Wettbewerb auf den Ferntransportnetzen der deutschen Gaswirtschaft—Eine netzökonomische Analyse." *Zeitschrift für Energiewirtschaft* 26(3), 171–180.

Laffont, J.-J., and Tirole, J. 2000. *Competition in Telecommunications.* Cambridge, Mass.: MIT Press.

Monopolkommission. 2001. *Wettbewerbsentwicklung bei Telekommunikation und Post 2001: Unsicherheit und Stillstand.* Sondergutachten, Bonn.

Müller, J., and Vogelsang, I. 1979. *Staatliche Regulierung—Regulated Industries in den USA und Gemeinwohlbindung in wettbewerblichen Ausnahmebereichen in der Bundesrepublik Deutschland.* Baden-Baden: Nomos-Verlag.

RWE. 2003. Facts and Figures. ⟨www.rwe.com⟩.

Schleusener, M. 2003. "Low Cost Airlines: Focus on Pricing." Präsentationsfolien von Simon, Kucher & Partners, Cologne, January 20. ⟨http://www.wiso.uni-koeln.de/marketing/Vortrag_schleusener.pdf⟩.

Schulte-Braucks, R. 1986. "Das 'British Telecom'-Urteil: Eckstein für ein europäisches Fernmelderecht?" *Wirtschaft und Wettbewerb* 3, 202–215.

Sinn, G., and Sinn, H.-W. 1991. *Kaltstart: Volkwirtschaftliche Aspekte der deutschen Vereinigung.* Tübingen: J. C. B. Mohr (Paul Siebeck).

Stumpf, U., and Schwarz-Schilling, C. 1999. "Wettbewerb auf Telekommunikationsmärkten." Discussion paper no. 197, Bad Honnef, Wissenschaftliches Institut für Kommunikationsdienste.

Vogelsang, I. 1988. "Deregulation and Privatization in Germany." *Journal of Public Policy* 8, 195–212.

Windisch, R., ed. 1987. *Privatisierung natürlicher Monopole im Bereich von Bahn, Post und Telekommunikation.* Tübingen: J. C. B. Mohr (Paul Siebeck).

Wissenschaftlicher Beirat beim Bundesministerium für Verkehr. 1997. Bahnstrukturreform in Deutschland—Empfehlungen zur weiteren Entwicklung. Stellungnahme vom November 1997, *Internationales Verkehrswesen* 49, 626–633.

Zimmer, C. 2004. Knappe Interkonnektorkapazitäten—Wie löst man die "Stauprobleme" im europäischen Höchstspannungsnetz? In Schriftenreihe der Deutschen Verkehrswissenschaftlichen Gesellschaft: *Versteigerungen und Ausschreibungen in Verkehrs- und Versorgungsnetzen—Praxiserfahrungen und Zukunftsperspektiven,* Reihe B, B 272, Berlin.

8 Privatization in Italy, 1993–2003: Goals, Institutions, Outcomes, and Outstanding Issues

Andrea Goldstein

In 1992, when a large-scale privatization program was launched in the midst of a dramatic political, economic, and financial crisis, the Italian public enterprise sector was larger than in other major OECD countries. Although state-owned enterprises (SOEs) may have made a significant contribution to growth in the 1950s and early 1960s (Barca and Trento 1997), over time they became the source of production inefficiencies and misallocation of resources. Noneconomic goals were imposed on public managers, effective incentive systems and monitoring devices were lacking, and the response to changes in market and technological developments was slow due to the lack of competitive pressures in the sheltered markets where most of these enterprises were operating.

A complex legal framework, capped at least temporarily by the 1994 privatization law, allowed successive governments to complete large selloffs, increasing both stock market capitalization and the number of shareholders and contributing substantially to the reduction of public debt and therefore to the convergence toward the Maastricht criteria. Quantitative results have been nothing short of outstanding: Italy topped the OECD privatization ranking each year from 1995 to 1999 (from number 9 in 1992) before falling to the second place in 2000. Annual proceeds averaged some US$12 billion from 1992 to 2000 (OECD 2002), equivalent to 1.1 percent of 2000 GDP. Albeit only partial, the 1999 privatization of ENEL, the electricity utility, was the world's largest initial public offering (IPO) ever at that time. IRI, the state-owned industrial holding created in the 1930s that played such an important role not only in the country's postwar catch-up but was also a model for policymakers in many late-industrializing countries, was liquidated; control over ENI, the oil and gas group, was transferred to the private sector; the state exited almost completely from a wide range of manufacturing sectors; and in telecommunications, not only was the historical operator sold off, but control over Telecom Italia (TI) has changed hands twice since privatization—an occurrence that is un-heard of in the world history of utilities privatization. Finally, there are good reasons to believe that on account of credibility gains and improvements in the size and efficiency of financial markets, privatiza-tion contributed to fiscal consolidation through positive effects on net debt service.

This chapter reviews the motives, methods, and results of Italian pri-vatizations. It describes the role of the public enterprise sector in the Italian economy and the main problems hindering SOEs. The policy, legal, and operational framework in which privatizations were imple-mented are analyzed, along with a short history of state sell-offs. The chapter also analyzes the performance of privatized companies using a variety of indicators, such as profitability, technical efficiency, invest-ment, employment, and productivity. Finally, it reviews the success in increasing the size, depth, and sophistication of financial markets but also the limits in liberalization and regulatory reform and the remain-ing uncertainties in the restructuring of the main assets still under pub-lic control.

8.1   The Public Enterprise Sector in the Early 1990s

In terms of both scale and scope, the Italian public enterprise sector ranked high among OECD countries in the early 1990s.[1] Shares of employment, value added, and gross fixed capital formation of public enterprises generally exceeded those of other founding members of the EU. The three main conglomerates (IRI, ENI, and EFIM) controlled nu-merous firms, operating in a wide and heterogeneous range of sectors, and employed over half a million people altogether in 1992. Of the largest Italian nonfinancial firms (ranked according to net sales), the state in 1991 owned twelve out of the top twenty and over one-third of the largest fifty. At the same time, the vast majority of financial intermediation—about 90 percent of total financial investment and 80 percent of total deposits in 1991—was ensured by public credit institutions.

The pervasiveness of state ownership in the Italian business sector was compounded by a control and management structure that was ex-tremely complex, opaque, and prone to political interference. A large number of Italian public enterprises were still operating under public law in 1992. Moreover, Italian public groups suffered from the overlap of several layers of control: the political decision level, dispersed over a large number of entities; their own boards of directors, often inflated with a large number of representatives designated by political parties; and the management of the controlled subsidiaries. Management independence was further limited by the inclusion of the conglomerates in the planning legislation. As a result, especially during economic downturns, noneconomic goals were put above corporate policy considerations: public enterprises were used to preserve jobs, sustain investment levels, and rescue ailing private firms, while tariff and pricing policies aimed at damping inflation.

Public nonfinancial enterprises were constantly less profitable than their private counterparts over the 1974–1991 period. Even allowing for the higher leverage ratios of public enterprises, which boosted financial charges, especially in periods of sustained inflation and rising interest rates, their operating surpluses were, on average, much lower than in the private sector. The comparison with private businesses is particularly telling when comparing the performance of firms engaged in the same activity in competitive markets. According to sectoral 1991 data on profits, labor income, and labor productivity, private firms outperformed public firms in virtually all competitive sectors. Public services were, on the whole, produced less efficiently and had a lower quality than in comparable countries. The gap between Italy and other OECD countries was particularly large in cost and tariff levels. Since technologies, ownership, and market structures are similar in most other European countries, this gap is largely attributable to regulatory failure.

Despite some consolidation in the 1980s, the financial position of public conglomerates deteriorated dramatically toward the end of the decade. Apart from sporadic sales of public enterprises, the share of public enterprises in economic activity (as measured by the average of the value added, gross fixed capital formation and employment shares) remained broadly constant during the 1980s. With government transfers dropping dramatically in the 1987–1990 period and virtually ending more recently, the situation became critical for EFIM and the nonfinancial section of IRI. The deterioration of the financial situation of the oil and gas conglomerate, ENI, and of the electricity concern, ENEL, was less serious.

8.2   The Institutional Setup

In 1992 the Italian government presented a framework document on privatization to parliament, in which four general goals were indicated: (1) improve corporate efficiency, (2) increase the degree of market competition, (3) widen the financial market and promote the internationalization of the industrial system, and finally, and residually, (4) increase fiscal revenues and reduce public debt. The main legislative actions concerning privatization (Goldstein 2003) can be categorized under different, albeit obviously intertwined, headings.

Corporatization—the application of the rules of the civil code to SOEs—entrusted their single shareholder, the treasury, and their managers with the same responsibilities and obligations faced by the owner of a private firm.[2] This virtually eliminated activities run by administrative bodies, drastically reducing the number of legally autonomous activities run under public law and simplifying the control structure.[3] In addition, the so-called golden share granted the treasury special powers in public enterprises operating in the areas of defense, transportation, telecommunications, and energy.

In theory the law imposed a cumbersome, seven-step *procedure*, augmented to nine if the privatization was complete (Cassese 1996). De facto the treasury—and, in particular, its privatization division—has kept most of the powers, providing technical support to the interministerial committee on privatization and liaising with the management of the public enterprises. The privatization process was also made more flexible than in other EU countries by the wide latitude given to the management of IRI and ENI over the day-to-day conduct of the restructuring process of their subholdings and subsidiaries. Finally, a special commission (Comitato permanente di consulenza globale e di garanzia), composed of the treasury director and four independent experts, was set up in June 1993.[4]

Beyond and above the intention stated by the government of making the greatest effort to achieve the Maastricht convergence criteria and ensure Italy's participation as a founding member of the Economic and Monetary Union, *external pressures* to privatize took the form of two binding commitments with the European Commission. This stance was partly the result of pressures by the European Commission for policies consistent with Article 90 of the Treaty of Rome and the EU-wide restructuring of the steel industry.[5]

Concerning *methods*, Law 474 made explicit the preference for public offers. In order to dilute ownership concentration and ensure a better representation of small shareholders, statutes were changed to put limits on the number of shares owned by single investors and introduce proportional representation for the election of the boards of directors. The resort to mixed techniques, involving direct sale to long-term investors, was legalized in 1995.

Finally, the privatization law made the sale of public utilities conditional on the institution of *independent regulatory authorities* (IRAs) to fix tariffs and oversee compliance with quality standards.

8.3   Italian Privatization, 1993–2003: A Synthesis

Although companies to be sold were identified as early as December 1992, privatization properly started only in late 1993, when a precise timetable was established and the first private sales took place. This long period of gestation reflected the need to establish the legal and policy framework as much as the persistence of diverging views among political parties supporting the government on the aims and scope of state divestitures. In the seven months to June 1994, three major banks and INA, Italy's second-largest insurance company, were sold through public offers (table 8.1). ENI pruned noncore activities through plant closures and widespread asset sales. EFIM received 439 million euros from the sale of its core assets (e.g., aluminum, glass) and transferred its subsidiaries in defense, aerospace, and rail equipment to Finmeccanica. IRI was liquidated on June 28, 2000, and the treasury mandated the Comitato dei Liquidatori to finalize the sale of remaining assets by the end of 2003 (Bianchi 2002a). Its shareholdings in Alitalia (53 percent) and RAI (99.5 percent) were transferred to the treasury.

Sales can be categorized according to different classifications. In terms of timing (table 8.2), activity peaked in 1997–1999 at roughly two-thirds (65.11 percent) of the 1992–2000 total. In 1997, in particular, privatization accounted for 45.9 percent of the total capital raised on the Milan Stock Exchange. The decline in activity in 2001 was due in part to unfavorable equity market conditions leading to postponement of planned transactions such as the sale of further stakes in ENEL. The only significant activity recorded in 2002 was the sale of the residual 3.5 percent treasury stake in TI. In July 2003, a consortium led by British American Tobacco bought ETI, the tobacco monopoly, for 2.3 billion

Table 8.1
Major privatizations in Italy since 1993

	Corporation (Group)	Method of sale	Percent-age sold	Gross proceeds (millions of euros)
1993	Italgel	Private agreement	62.12	223
	Cirio-Bertolli-DeRica	Private agreement	62.12	160
	Credito Italiano (IRI)	Public offering	58.09	930
	SIV (EFIM)	Auction	100.00	108
	Total for year			2,630
1994	IMI—first tranche	Public offering	32.89	927
	COMIT (IRI)	Public offering	54.35	1,493
	Nuovo Pignone (ENI)	Auction	69.33	361
	INA—first tranche	Public offering	47.25	2,340
	Acciai Speciali Terni	Private agreement	100.00	322
	SME—first tranche	Private agreement	32.00	373
	Total for year			7,590
1995	Italtel	Auction	40.00	516
	Ilva Laminati Piani	Private agreement	100.00	1,298
	Enichem Augusta (ENI)	Auction	70.00	155
	IMI—second tranche	Private agreement	19.03	472
	SME—second tranche	Accept takeover bid	14.91	176
	INA—second tranche	Private agreement	18.37	871
	ENI—first tranche	Public offering	15.00	3,253
	ISE	Auction	73.96	191
	Total for year			8,440
1996	Dalmine	Auction	84.08	156
	Nuova Tirrena	Auction	91.14	283
	SME—second tranche	Accept takeover bid	15.21	62
	INA—third tranche	Converted bond issue	31.08	2,169
	IMI—third tranche	Public offering	6.94	259
	ENI—second tranche	Public offering	15.82	4,582
	Total for year			7,742
1997	ENI—third tranche	Public offering	17.60	6,833
	Aeroporti di Roma	Public offering	45.00	307
	Telecom Italia	Core investors plus public offering	39.54	11,818
	SEAT editoria	Core investors plus public offering	61.27	854
	Banca di Roma	Public offering plus bond issue	36.50	980
	Total for year			20,940
1998	SAIPEM (ENI)	Public offering	18.75	589
	ENI—fourth tranche	Public offering	14.83	6,711
	BNL	Public offering	67.85	3,464
	Total for year			10,764

Table 8.1
(continued)

	Corporation (Group)	Method of sale	Percent-age sold	Gross proceeds (millions of euros)
1999	ENEL	Public offering	31.70	16,550
	Autostrade	Auction plus public offering	82.40	6,722
	Mediocredito Centrale	Auction	100.00	2,037
	Total for year			25,382
2000	Aeroporti di Roma	Direct sale	51.2	1,327
	Finmeccanica	Secondary public offer	43.7	5,505
	COFIRI	Direct sale	100.0	504
	Banco di Napoli	Tender share to takeover bid	16.2	493
	Total for year			7,933
2001	ENI—fifth tranche	Accelerated block building	5.0	2,721
	Total for year			2,907
2002	Telecom Italia	Placement with institutions	3.5	1,400
	Total for year			1,498
2003	ETI	Auction	100.0	2,325
	ENEL	Bought deal	6.6	2,170
	Total for year			4,556
	Total, 1993–2003			**100,382**

Sources: Ministero del Tesoro, Bilancio e Programmazione Economica (2000), *Italy's Report on Economic Reform* and other sources.

euros. In October 2003 a 6.6 stake in ENEL was sold to a bank in a bought deal.

In terms of sequencing, as more than 80 percent of credit was state controlled, it was paramount to privatize public banks first. This reflected both the danger that banks acquire shares of state-owned enterprises or convert debt of private nonfinancial enterprises into equity, and the fact that the so-called banks of national interest owned by IRI were among the most profitable and attractive state enterprises. Concerning manufacturing enterprises, the initial emphasis was on the food and heavy industries (steel and glass in particular). In fall 1993, in the face of mounting debt that was on the verge of wiping out net capital, IRI's subholding for iron and steel (Ilva) was liquidated, its industrial activities were transferred to two new companies that were

Table 8.2
Privatization classified by sector, in percentages 1992–2003

	Steel	Food and tobacco	Capital goods	Services	Chemicals	Mining and NFM	Glass, aluminium, and cement	Banking	Insurance	Textile	Oil and energy	Transport	Telecoms and media	Local utilities	Public works
1992	36.7	8.8	2.6	13.1	3.0	1.4	34.4	0.0	0.0	0.0	0.0	0.0	0.0	0.0	0.0
1993	0.0	21.1	26.0	0.0	2.8	0.7	4.8	41.5	0.0	0.5	2.5	0.0	0.0	0.0	0.0
1994	4.8	5.7	3.4	0.0	3.3	1.6	0.0	41.8	35.9	1.5	2.0	0.0	0.0	0.0	0.0
1995	16.4	2.3	2.7	0.0	6.1	1.9	0.0	17.7	0.0	0.0	45.3	0.9	6.8	0.0	0.0
1996	2.9	0.8	3.2	1.5	1.2	0.6	3.2	3.2	24.3	1.2	56.6	0.0	0.0	1.3	0.0
1997	0.1	0.0	0.9	0.4	0.0	0.0	0.1	8.4	0.0	0.0	33.0	0.0	55.5	1.5	0.0
1998	0.0	0.0	11.1	0.6	0.0	0.0	0.0	26.5	0.0	0.0	44.6	3.0	9.0	5.1	0.1
1999	0.1	0.0	4.2	0.1	0.1	0.0	0.0	17.1	0.0	0.0	59.7	14.9	0.0	3.6	0.1
2000	0.0	0.0	61.8	0.0	0.0	0.0	0.0	0.2	0.0	0.0	0.0	24.9	0.0	13.1	0.0
2001	0.0	0.0	0.0	0.0	0.0	0.0	0.0	6.4	0.0	0.0	93.6	0.0	0.0	0.0	0.0
2002	0.0	0.0	0.0	0.0	0.0	0.0	0.0	6.6	0.0	0.0	0.0	0.0	93.4	0.0	0.0
2003	0.0	51.0	0.0	0.0	0.0	0.0	0.0	1.4	0.0	0.0	47.6	0.0	0.0	0.0	0.0

Source: Own elaboration on table 8.1.

privatized, and the giant Bagnoli plant was closed down. Not surprisingly, in peak years, oil and utilities companies (including local ones) accounted for the largest share of receipts by far. Finally, the weight of the transport sector is minimal, as railways, the ferry operator, and the airline remain under state control.

The choice of the sale technique has an obvious impact on the desired structure of property rights in privatized firms, and ambiguity about sale procedures indeed reflected conflicts within the government over what kind of private ownership structure was to be encouraged. Partisans of *noyaux durs* and people's capitalism, using the French and the British experiences as showcases, entered into a heated cabinet dispute that risked derailing the process. Although a number of nonfinancial enterprises were initially sold to strategic investors through trade deals, by 1994 the government decisively showed its preference for public offers. Such placements proved especially successful in the late 1990s when companies such as TI, ENI, and ENEL were put on the stock market (table 8.3). Mixed techniques, associating public offers and trade deals, have been used in a few cases, notably TI and Autostrade. On the other hand, management buyouts (MBOs) have been rare, the major instance being Esaote, a global leader in research, production, and marketing of medical diagnostic equipment and related services.

Table 8.3
Privatization classified by sale technique, in percentages 1992–2003

	Stock market offers	To strategic investors	To institutional investors	Management buyouts	Other techniques
1992	0.0	100.0	0.0	0.0	0.0
1993	49.6	48.6	1.8	0.0	0.0
1994	80.5	17.7	1.4	0.4	0.0
1995	44.7	43.8	0.0	0.0	11.5
1996	59.1	16.9	3.2	0.0	20.8
1997	83.7	16.3	0.0	0.0	0.0
1998	84.6	15.2	0.0	0.2	0.0
1999	91.8	8.0	0.0	0.0	0.2
2000	53.5	38.0	8.5	0.0	0.0
2001	0.0	6.4	93.6	0.0	0.0
2002	0.0	6.6	93.4	0.0	0.0
2003	0.0	52.4	47.6	0.0	0.0

Source: Own elaboration on table 8.1.

Concerning fiscal treatment, a special public debt redemption fund was created in 1993 in order to draw a clear line between transitory proceeds from asset sales and the deficit-reducing effects of other budgetary measures. This stands in contrast to the attitude of both the British government, which used proceeds to reduce the PSBR by almost 1 percent of GDP on average over the 1984–1988 period, and the French government, which used proceeds to reduce the state sector deficit by three-quarters of a percentage point in both 1993 and 1994. In any case, even if all public enterprises were to be sold, with all privatization proceeds used to redeem public debt, the impact would be limited, since their estimated value amounts to only 15 percent of public debt.[6]

Given the wide variety of techniques used, it is not easy to classify buyers in a clear and comprehensive manner. Suffice for our purposes to analyze public offers. Domestic retail investors have always represented the largest category of public offering investors (with percentages ranging between 33 and 79) and accounted for 47.3 percent of the unweighted average (table 8.4).[7] International capital markets have also been very receptive, absorbing on (unweighted) average a third of the offers.[8] The relatively smaller role played by Italian in-

Table 8.4
Privatization on the stock exchange by investors category, in percentages

	Retail in Italy	Institu- tions in Italy	Institutions abroad		
			Continental Europe	UK and Ireland	North America
IMI 1	42.9	11.4	29.7		16.0
INA 1	68.3	9.5	15.3		6.9
ENI 1	33.4	29.6	15.0		22.0
ENI 2	40.3	14.0	16.4	15.6	13.7
IMI 2	0.0	42.6	20.2	27.9	9.3
INA 3	0.0	50.0	50.0		
ENI 3	52.3	11.9	10.7	10.3	14.8
Telecom Italia	75.0	5.8	8.1	2.9	8.2
ENI 4	76.4	8.0	2.8	6.8	6.0
BNL	62.9	10.5	21.6		5.0
ENEL 1	36.6	25.7	37.7		
ENI 5					
Autostrade	79.1	10.7	10.2		
Finmeccanica					
Unweighted average	47.3	19.1	33.6		

Source: Own elaboration on Ministero del Tesoro (2001).

stitutions is not surprising in view of the infancy of the country's pension funds.

While absolute figures are impressive by international standards, the picture is more controversial when considering only sell-offs that have led to control change. Out of total 1993–2001 proceedings of 121.3 billion euros, the amount corresponding to a control transfer is considerably lower (50.4 billion euros). Considering then that *Fondazioni*—charitable foundations controlled by local authorities—have acquired assets of 13.4 billion euros, "pure" privatization receipts have been as low as 37 billion euros (De Nardis 2000).

8.4 The Effects of Selling Nonfinancial Enterprises

Although many summaries of different countries' privatization programs have been written, they are mostly qualitative in nature. Exceptions include papers covering countries with the longest-running experimentation with privatization such as Chile (Fischer, Gutierrez, and Serra 2002), Mexico (La Porta and López de Silanes 1999), and the United Kingdom (Cragg and Dyck 1997). Other quantitative cross-country studies include two influential contributions by Galal et al. (1994) and Megginson and Natter (2001). As in the cross-sectional studies of public-private ownership, the evidence from longitudinal studies about the efficiency impact of privatization is not totally conclusive (Villalonga 2001).

In the Italian case, quantitative analyses are few and far between. Mediobanca (2000) concludes that the treasury has gained from the appreciation of its stockholdings in listed companies such as ENI and ENEL. Although industrial concentration has increased, this may have been necessary in order to enhance production and technology efficiency.[9] Erbetta (2001) analyzes the dynamics of performance in the years before privatization, finding a significant growth in productivity levels in the four years preceding the shift from public to private ownership, attributable mainly to employment cuts. Munari (2002) examines the consequences on corporate innovation activities, finding that privatization led to a reduction in both the number of research personnel and the overall budget, although also to an increase in patenting propensity (at least in low-innovation sectors).

In the spirit of the benchmark approach of Megginson, Nash, and van Randenborgh (1994), this section seeks to provide an ex post performance analysis of privatization based on a sample of nonfinancial enterprises. Privatizations undertaken in the financial sector are excluded as they involved specific issues that would require a specific analysis. The sample comprises twenty-five companies that operate in the following industries: food and retail distribution (Gs, Autogrill, Cirio Bertolli De Rica, PAI), steel (Dalmine, Tubi Ghisa), aluminium (Alumix, Comital, Euroallumina), cement and glass (Cementir, SIV), chemicals and fibers (Montefibre, Enichem Augusta, Inca International, Alcantara), electronics, machinery and equipment (Nuovo Pignone, Savio Macchine Tessili, Esaote, DEA), construction (Società Italiana per Condotte d'Acqua, Italstrade), telecommunications (Telecom Italia), energy (ISE), and media (Editrice Il Giorno, Nuova Same). Data come from Mediobanca (a), an annual publication on the financial statements of Italy's largest enterprises, and cover eight variables: net sales, operating income, net assets, investment, fixed investment, number of employees, debt, and an index of liquidity. Each firm is compared to itself (a few years earlier) using simple sales and income data (that produce results in simple percentages). Indexes have been constructed to analyze profitability (operating income to sales; operating income to PPE [property plants, and equipment], net income to sales, return on assets, and return on equity); operating efficiency (sales to PPE and operating costs to sales); investment and assets [log(PPE), investment-to-sales, investment to PPE]; output [log(sales)]; finance (long-term debt to equity and current ratio);[10] and taxes (net taxes to sales). To circumvent the fact that changes in performance could reflect cyclical movements of the economy rather than privatization, data on private companies in the same industry are used for control (Mediobanca b). The performance of privatized companies was adjusted by taking the difference between the indicator for the privatized enterprise and the average for the control group (excluding the enterprise itself). The Wilcoxon rank sum test (with its Z-statistic) was employed as the test of significance for the change in median value.

Results are somewhat tentative (tables 8.5 to 8.6). Most indexes show an improvement in average profitability indicators, with the exception of net income to equity, although no change is statistically significant. Adjusting from same-industry development, in particular, operating income to PPE rose from −25 percent to 7 percent. Operating efficiency indicators, albeit again with no statistical significance, point to a very minor effect of the control change—in particular, the average ratio of operating costs to sales moved barely from 85.59 percent to 85.22 percent. However, investment indicators show a marked and

Table 8.5
Performance changes in privatized companies

	Number	Mean before, median before[a]	Mean after, median after[a]	T-statistic for change in mean	Z-statistic for change in median
Profitability					
Operating income/sales	25	0.031, 0.058	0.052, 0.035	−0.931	−0.568
Operating income/PPE	25	−0.083, 0.151	0.198, 0.156	−1.257	−0.893
Net income/sales		−0.029, 0.010	0.011, 0.015	−1.630	−1.248
Net income/total assets	25	−0.021, 0.012	0.008, 0.015	−1.055	−0.755
Net income/equity	25	−0.045, 0.090	0.033, 0.06	−0.847	−0.834
Operating efficiency					
Log (sales/PPE)	25	0.515, 0.479	0.518, 0.653	−0.062	−0.000
Operating costs/sales	25	0.856, 0.925	0.852, 0.955	0.169	−0.331
Investment and assets					
Log (PPE)	25	4.977, 5.184	5.026, 5.176	−0.746	−0.256
Investment/sales	25	−0.009, −0.002	0.055, 0.022	−2.420396**	−1.92132*
Investment/PPE	25	−0.130, −0.012	0.136, 0.049	−2.093582**	−2.02618**
Output					
Log (sales)	25	5.492, 5.426	5.544, 5.426	−1.768036*	−0.332
Finance					
Current	25	1.173, 0.999	1.275, 1.077	−0.875	−0.674
LTD/equity	25	0.618, 0.555	1.389, 0.677	−2.049611*	−2.04806**
Net Taxes					
Net taxes/sales	25	0.023, 0.007	0.008, 0.005	0.891	1.017

[a] The first number given is the mean, and the second is the median.
* significant at 10% level. ** significant at 5% level. *** significant at 1% level.

Table 8.6
Performance changes in privatized companies (adjusted)

	Number	Mean before, median before[a]	Mean after, median after[a]	T-statistic for change in mean	Z-statistic for change in median
Profitability					
Operating income/sales	20	−0.021, 0.003	0.005, −0.00589	−1.147	−0.615
Operating income/PPE	20	−0.251, 0.029	0.072, 0.037	−1.377	−0.812
Net income/sales		−0.025, 0.00994	−0.012, −0.00889	−0.478	−0.341
Net income/total assets	20	−0.021, 0.013	−0.010, −0.007	−0.355	−0.226
Net income/equity	20	0.373, 0.124	−0.013, −0.010	1.565	1.616
Operating efficiency					
Log (sales/PPE)	20	0.187, 0.28257	0.172, 0.18873	0.235	0.150
Operating costs/sales	20	−0.172, −0.07	−0.169, −0.047	0.394	−0.029
Investment and assets					
Log (PPE)	20	−1.661, −1.553	−1.661, −1.732	−0.065	−0.021
Investment/sales	20	−0.048, −0.025	0.042, 0.001	−2.492775**	−2.02208**
Investment/PPE	20	−0.233, −0.038	0.099, 0.018	−2.075066*	−2.15551**
Output					
Log (sales)	20	−1.479, −1.471	−1.489, −1.577	0.320	0.043
Finance					
Current	20	0.157, 0.05871	0.221, 0.05726	−0.425	−0.363
LTD/equity	20	5.328, 0.153	0.920, 0.268	1.786276*	1.77759*
Net taxes					
Net taxes/sales	20	0.004, −0.006	−0.015, −0.003	0.933	1.115

[a]The first number given is the mean, and the second is the median.
* significant at 10% level; ** significant at 5% level; *** significant at 1% level.

significant improvement in both specifications, moving from negative to positive values. This seems consistent with the hypothesis that SOEs were investment constrained under the weight of the early 1990s fiscal crisis. Sales also increased significantly in privatized companies, although the change is not significant against the control group.

A clearer picture emerges with the indicators of financial management. There was a nonsignificant increase in the current ratio, both in absolute terms and in comparison with the private firms. With respect to long-term debt to equity (LTD to equity), privatization has a positive and significant impact in absolute terms. However, when compared with the performance of private sector firms, a different picture emerges, as the coefficients become negative. These results are similar to those reported for Brazil and Mexico and suggest that once their credit status is no longer guaranteed by the government, former SOEs are forced to adjust by decreasing their LTD to equity and increasing the current ratios.

Although these results provide an addition to the literature on the results of privatization in Italy and indirectly support those of Erbetta, a word of caution is in order. Among the problems in using accounting data in measuring performance changes are determining the correct measure of operating performance, selecting an appropriate benchmark with which to compare performance, and determining the appropriate statistical tests to use (Megginson and Netter 2001). Also, due to severe data limitations, the Italian data set is unfortunately much smaller (in terms of number of both firms and years) than in La Porta and López de Silanes (1999) on Mexico, Fischer, Gutierrez, and Serra (2002) on Chile, and Anuatti-Neto et al. (2002) on Brazil. A further problem is the use of those very years that are best excluded in such exercises because of the potential presale accounts cleansing effect and of the ongoing reorganization process that, begun prior to sale, may continue immediately afterward.

8.5   Privatization, Financial Markets, and Corporate Governance

Privatization and deregulation of price and entry restrictions affect the governance structures of firms in two ways (Lehn 2002). First, granting managers a clear profit-maximization objective, as well as more authority to establish prices and enter new markets, increases the importance of their function; second, deregulation injects uncertainty and instability into the business environment and may thus increase the costs of monitoring managerial performance. On both accounts, the method of privatization has important consequences on the nature of agency relationship. Against the background of the discussion concerning the relative costs and benefits of bank- and market-based financial systems in addressing such issues (Levine 2002), two privatization models influential in Western Europe have been the French one of forming *noyaux durs* of core investors and the British one of people's capitalism.

In Italy, much more than in other European countries, deciding how to sell state assets and to whom has been a central issue in the early debate on privatization. Although the ratio of financial instruments to GDP in the early 1990s was similar to that prevailing in other large OECD countries, the structure of financial markets was rather atypical. In 1991, the number of companies listed on the Milan stock exchange was less than a third of those listed in Paris, with trading and the ratio of market capitalization to GDP being the lowest among the major six OECD countries.[11] On the other hand, government securities listed in the Milan Stock Exchange exceeded 85 percent of GDP. The composition of financial savings by households was also remarkably different: in 1988, shares directly held by Italian households amounted to less than 15 percent of GDP, compared to holdings of around 70 percent in both France and the United States and 40 percent in the United Kingdom. Indirect investment in shares through mutual funds was also relatively small.

The limited size of the stock exchange was accompanied by the opaque nature of corporate ownership and control. The Italian corporate sector is dominated by a small core of pyramidal groups mutually protected by cross-ownership of shares, interlocking boards, and informal ties. These groups have extensively tapped into the stock market, while often proving scornful of the rights of minority shareholders. Through the chain of equity holdings linking the top of the pyramid to lower levels, control over all firms belonging to the group is exercised with a minimum amount of capital invested. Intergroup cross-shareholdings facilitate strategic alliances, potentially leading to collusive behavior. Severe restrictions have also limited ownership linkages between banks and industry, depriving the system of the kind of monitoring provided by *hausbanken* in Germany. Only Mediobanca acquired large and stable shareholdings in all major industrial and insurance groups, usually participating in their controlling coalitions and acting as a sort of main bank for a tight and exclusive northern financial and industrial elite.[12]

Boards of directors are dominated by insiders or represent the interests of the controlling shareholders. Insufficient application of directors' fiduciary duties, inadequate safeguards for minority shareholders, and the dominant role of a single investment bank combined to thwart the emergence of a well-functioning market for corporate control, keeping the number of mergers and acquisitions at low levels relative to other European countries. Private benefits of control on the Milan Stock Exchange were enormous and could easily be worth more than 60 percent of the value of nonvoting equity (Zingales 1994).

With the privatization plan of 1992 foreseeing the near tripling in future years of the amount of fresh capital raised on the Milan Stock Exchange in 1992, doubts about the ability of a small market to absorb such a large number of shares were justified. Many observers warned that widening share ownership was impossible to achieve without major tax incentives, huge underpricing, increases in households' saving propensities (already high by international standards), or a reallocation of households' portfolios away from public debt and bank deposits. And yet privatizations through the stock market were highly successful, with public offers largely oversubscribed and underpricing on average lower than in other EU countries over the same period (Macchiati 1999). This outcome was the result of a combination of factors. The government's success in lowering interest rates more rapidly than in other European countries made stocks relatively more attractive than government securities to hold. An effective advertising campaign and investors' feeling that subscribing to the offers was a way to participate in a historical event were other factors.[13] In addition, a significant number of shares were sold to foreign investors, which benefited from the weakness of the lira (table 8.7).

Privatization has prompted the adoption of new legislative measures providing better safeguards to shareholders through greater transparency, a restrictive regulation of shareholder agreements, and a more effective representation in governing bodies (Goldstein 2003, table 1). The need to extend such reforms to all quoted companies led to the 1998 so-called Draghi bill. According to the stock market regulator, the bill has been effective in increasing transparency, informational symmetry, and price significance on Italian financial markets (Consob 2001). While this is not due solely to privatization, an example of a direct link is provided by the reinforced transparency obligations that followed foreign listing of privatized companies. When Pirelli took over Olivetti, for instance, Security Exchange Commission regulations

Table 8.7
Ownership composition of listed companies (percentage)

	1995	1996	1997	1998	1999	2000	2001: First half
Foreign	**11.6**	**15.0**	**18.6**	**19.6**	**16.3**	**15.7**	**15.5**
Domestic	**88.4**	**85.0**	**81.4**	**80.4**	**83.7**	**84.3**	**84.5**
Institutional investors	13.4	13.5	15.7	15.5	12.3	13.2	13.7
Insurance	4.3	4.4	4.9	3.9	2.5	3.1	3.9
Pension funds	0.9	0.9	0.9	0.7	0.6	0.6	0.8
Asset managers	2.6	3.0	3.4	2.8	2.8	2.7	2.6
Mutual funds	5.7	5.3	6.5	8.1	6.4	6.8	6.5
Banks	5.8	4.0	5.7	10.0	5.5	6.3	4.8
Fondazioni	3.1	3.5	2.8	4.7	4.3	4.8	4.8
Holding companies	18.7	12.8	22.0	17.8	24.2	23.7	22.8
Households	21.2	18.7	23.1	23.4	26.2	26.4	29.3
Public sector	26.1	32.5	12.0	8.9	11.2	9.9	9.1

Source: Filippa and Franzosi (2001, table 1).

obliged it to release information on TI's shareholders' agreement since the latter has a dual listing in Milan and New York. In Italy, Consob required only their partial publication (Bortolotti and Siniscalco 2001). The five privatized Italian companies that belong to the EURO STOXX 50 index perform remarkably well in corporate governance terms, with an average score of 7.43 versus 6.86 for the whole sample (DWS 2002). Other indicators suggest that changes have not been dramatic. A 2000 Consob survey showed that of 242 listed companies, only 5 had reduced the capital threshold for calling an extraordinary shareholders' meeting, 4 had increased the minimum quorum for deliberations, and 7 had introduced mail voting. Moreover, only once has the minority exerted its right to call a shareholders' meeting, and never have the powers to file a lawsuit against directors and to solicit proxies been used.

More fundamentally, privatization has not seen the surge of public companies, whose shares are widely held and which are subject to the discipline of the market for corporate control. Ownership control separation through pyramidal structures persists. In 2001 the largest shareholder owned on average 42 percent of a quoted company, while the share corresponding to the market (including all investors holding less that 2 percent each) was less than 50 percent, a threshold surpassed only in 1997 and 1998 (Spaventa 2002). In the attempt to prevent the acquisition of control in privatized companies by small groups of shareholders, the government limited the number of shares to be owned by single investors. However, these limits have proved largely ineffective and, paradoxically, in the future, they will also make it more difficult for possible riders to take over control.[14] Even at TI, where such rules did not exist and control has changed hands not once but twice, the rights of minority shareholders have not been respected (see Goldstein 2003, box 1).[15]

More fundamentally, market-friendly legal norms did not automatically translate into their more efficient application by the judiciary. Bortolotti and Siniscalco (2002) calculate that the Draghi reform resulted in a three-notch increase in the La Porta et al. (2000) investors' protection index, and yet the consequent increase in stock market capitalization has been far lower than expected. Analyzing Milanese (and by extension, Italian) corporate law judges, Enriques (2002) highlights egregious cases of deference to corporate insiders, especially with regard to parent-subsidiary relationships. It appears to be rare for the court to take the substantive reasons for the dispute into any account, and judges do not seem to care about whether their decisions provide the right incentives for directors and shareholders.

8.6   Privatization and Regulatory Reform

In 1991, up to two-thirds of IRI's workforce and up to 30 percent of ENI's employees produced goods and services in markets sheltered by legal monopolies, exclusive state concessions, or dominant state demand. Exclusive state concessions were generally granted to state-controlled enterprises, and the regulatory regime, based on direct management of public utilities or indirect control through IRI and ENI, blurred the relationship between the regulator and the producer, allowing a high degree of monopoly power. Moreover, the authority over concession, monitoring, and regulation of public services was extremely fragmented among several ministries, local authorities, public companies, and national committees. Tariff setting was the responsibility of a single government committee, the CIP (Comitato Interministeriale Prezzi), whose decisions were often subordinated to macroeconomic or social policy objectives, such as inflation control or equity considerations.[16]

International experiences show how a combination of privatization, liberalization, and better regulatory design holds the promise of

Table 8.8
International comparison of public service prices (2001 data)
(Italy = 100)

	France	Germany	Italy	Sweden	UK
Telecommunications					
Monthly spending (private)	83	74	100	60	79
Monthly spending (business)	79	78	100	52	97
Mobile services	78	74	100	76	79
Electricity					
Annual consumption of 600 kWh	177	255	100	266	221
Annual consumption of 7,500 kWh	59	77	100	54	54

Sources: Own elaboration on AEGG data (*Il Sole-24 Ore*, December 5, 2002), Oftel (2002), *International benchmarking study of mobile services,* and Wissenschaftliches Institut für Kommunikationsdienste (2002), *Situation of the Swiss Telecommunications Market in an International Comparison.*

large efficiency gains. Moreover, insofar as belated liberalization may amount to a breach of commitments taken with shareholders, it is easier to open markets before rather than after privatization—although conditioning divestiture on liberalization may play into the hands of antireform groups (Giavazzi 1996). Unfortunately, measured with respect to its impact on competition, Italy's regulatory environment was in 1998 (the most recent year for which comparative cross-country data for product market regulations are available) much stricter than in the average European country or the United States (Nicoletti 2002). Although average telecom tariffs have significantly declined for both fixed and mobile calls (Cavaliere 2001), a variety of utility indicators shows that Italy is generally less competitive than other major EU countries, especially for business users (table 8.8).

8.6.1 Structure Regulation

Structural regulation involves the breakup of public utilities, functional separation of competitive and noncompetitive activities, and access liberalization to networks. The public telecom operators were reorganized in view of their privatization, with the unification of various IRI subsidiaries[17] into a new holding, TI, the world's sixth largest telecom operator. This decision was hardly optimal in view of the desirable liberalization of telephone services. A better alternative would have been to privatize the subsidiaries separately, thereby injecting elements of competition in the system. Given that financial markets usually discount closed-end financial holdings relative to the cumulated value of their subsidiaries, selling Stet's operational companies separately could have also maximized revenue for the government. In 1994, a second mobile telephone services license was awarded, and between 1991 and 1995, the markets for telecommunications equipment, access to the public switched network, and telecommunication services, except voice telephony, were liberalized.[18]

For the electricity supply industry, several proposals were advanced to open production and maintain an exclusive concession for grid operation in order to ensure coordination and safety of electricity supplies. Opinions diverged on whether to unbundle ENEL prior to sale, whether to liberalize electricity supply to large customers, and the extent and the features of price regulation.[19] However, unbundling proposals met fierce opposition within the government, which sought to avoid further delays and maximize proceeds from the sell-off, and from the managers and trade unions of the state company. In addition, disagreements at the EU level on the completion of the single market for energy have further weakened the momentum for reforms.

According to a timetable laid out in the so-called Bersani decree in 1999, by 2003 no utility can produce or import more than half of total consumption. To reduce its market share to around 40 percent, ENEL spun off three separate and independent generating companies, totaling 15,000 megawatts (MW) of generation capacity, and put them on sale by public auction. No company was allowed to acquire or hold stakes in more than one of the three companies, and no buyer can be more than 30 percent government held.[20] Elettrogen—the second largest, based in Rome and Piacenza—was sold to Endesa of Spain (with Brescia's ASM local utility) for 2.63 billion euros in the summer of 2001.[21] Eurogen—the largest company, based in Rome and Milan— was put up for sale in September 2001 and finally purchased by the Edipower consortium of utilities and financial institutions.[22] The terms of the sale included a 3.05 billion euros equity price and required Edipower to reimburse Eurogen's 750 million euros debt to ENEL. A consortium including Belgium's Electrabel and Rome's utility ACEA paid 551 million euros for the smallest company, Interpower, based in Naples and Rome, and took on an additional 323 million euros in company debt. ENEL must also shed market share in power distribution to comply with the requirement of a unique distributor in each municipality. It has proved arduous for ENEL and the municipalities to agree on prices, and only in August 2002 did ENEL transfer network capacity and clients to the Milan and Verona utilities. The transport and dispatch functions have been transferred to a new company (Gestore Rete Trasmissione Nazionale, GRTN) 50 percent owned by the treasury. The grid remains 90 percent owned by Terna, which is 36 percent owned by the state.

In the natural gas market, Italy has exceeded the obligations set in the June 1998 EU Directive. In May 2000, the government directed that no single company could supply more than 50 percent of the natural gas sold to final users by 2003 and send more than 70 percent of natural gas put into the transmission system beginning in 2002 (reduced to 61 percent by 2009). The legislation also requires corporate separation of natural gas storage and transport activities, exceeding the EU obligation of accounting separation. SNAM retains control of the 30,000 kilometer grid, but SNAM had to set up a new pipeline company (SNAM Rete Gas) separate from commercial and sales activities. SNAM was subsequently taken over by ENI. In late November 2001, 35 percent of SNAM Rete Gas Italia, the new company controlling the gas grid, was sold through an IPO, which was heavily oversubscribed.

8.6.2 Conduct Regulation

Limited progress in structure regulation has put an additional burden on conduct regulation to determine the permitted patterns of behavior of regulated firms in the public interest. Conduct regulation can include both (product and access) price regulation and regulation of nonprice behavior, such as service and product quality, quantity, investment, and environmental impact.

In the case of telecommunications, recent decisions by the AGC (Autorità per le garanzie nelle comunicazioni) have introduced flat rate Internet access call origination (FRIACO), leveled access conditions for other licensed operators (OLO) and Internet service providers, and regulated shared access, subloop unbundling, leased wholesale lines, and wide bandwidth (DSL, CVP) (AGC 2002). Following a two-year investigation, the AGC also imposed TI stricter cost accountancy obligations so to prevent the incumbent from using information provided by competitors as anticompetitive tools. Although the incumbent owns nearly all fixed access lines, it is not difficult to receive a fixed-line license as proved by the existence of 253 operators (AGC 2003).[23] There are four GSM operators and five third-generation licenses were also awarded in October 2000. New regional operators have begun forming but are still in the initial network buildout phases and will not be capable of offering alternative infrastructure to TI for several years. Unbundling is becoming an option for more operators now that TI has made 939 exchanges available (of 1,040 whose opening was required by competitors), which cover approximately half the total subscriber lines (AGC 2002). Some 35,000 lines have also been disaggregated, a level surpassed only by Germany in Europe. Carrier preselection began in January 2000, and by the end of August 2001, about 2 million subscribers used it.[24] Number portability was available in 2001 for fixed users and almost two years later for mobile subscribers.[25] The license fee was increased in 2001 and tariff rebalancing completed in 2002. TI's share of the fixed telephony market has been decreasing progressively; it stood at about 70.8 percent at the end of 2002, compared with 77 percent a year earlier. The mobile sector is the largest in Europe in terms of revenue and the highest in Europe (except for Luxembourg) in terms of penetration rate. This is reflected by the fact that mobile and fixed telephony services have equal shares of the total telecommunications market. In 2003, for the first time, TIM's market share fell below 50 percent.

ENEL enjoys a dominant position in the upstream market for electricity generation. This is shown by its share of the gross installed capacity (approximately 53 percent in 2000) and of the actual electricity produced in Italy (approximately 77 percent, excluding self-generation, in 2000), as well as by the type of power plants at its disposal (base load, midmerit, and peak load) AEEG (2002). Moreover, ENEL is dominant in the downstream, partly liberalized Italian electricity supply market (37 percent in the first nine months of 2001), also because of its position in the upstream market where ENEL is vertically integrated. Price regulation is designed to impose a uniform tariff across Italy, thereby reducing the possible beneficial effect on consumers of the limited liberalization of electricity generation. Meanwhile, red tape has held up applications to build new generating plants that might compete with ENEL. In February 2002 the Ministry for Productive Activities intervened to speed things up by instituting a single, 180-day, one-stop centralized authorization system for plants with capacity greater than 300 MW. By early 2004 the ministry had authorized projects for 9,000 MW extra capacity.[26]

Competition for delivery and sale to actual and potential "eligible customers" (that is consuming less than 0.1 GWh per year) is still limited. The electrical power exchange (Borsa Elettrica) that, according to the Bersani decree was to be operative in January 2001, was launched only on April 1, 2004. The advantages of having an exchange include transparency (given that strategic behaviors would be detected) and the possibility of exerting pressure on the dominant supplier through the aggregation of dispersed users. Successive late deadlines could not be met due to unsolved issues such as the treatment of imports and subsidized production (so-called Cip6). Falling short of limiting ENEL's freedom of maneuver (and knowing that new generation capacity will not be fully operative before long), what is needed is the development of derivative instruments and mechanisms to "contractualize" generation capacity, such as those introduced in France on the Powernext market (Checchi, Saraceno, and Vaciago 2002). The resistance has come from both large users, which currently benefit from cross-subsidies (Gallo and Checchi 2002), and the government's insistence on inserting a clause to give the ministry the power to correct prices in case of "excessive" volatility.

An outline of a draft law, Reform and Reorganization of the Energy Sector, was presented in July 2002. The intent seemed more to control ENEL than to reduce its size and market power (Scarpa 2002). Although the framework text has not been turned into law, specific decrees have phased out the fees paid to ENEL for the "hydroelectric rent"[27] and compensation stranded costs for past investments. All nondomestic clients were also eligible as of July 2004.

The Antitrust Authority (AGCM, Autorità garante della concorrenza e del mercato) has emerged as an effective competition advocate in the regulatory arena. After complaints from several alternative fixed-line providers and the Italian Association of Internet Service Providers, the AGCM launched an investigation into TI's provision of access and found that the incumbent had taken advantage of its ownership of the PSTN (public switched telephone network) access network by refusing requests from alternative operators for wholesale DSL services, while at the same time offering its own DSL retail service. TI was fined 59 million euros for abusing its position as a carrier with significant market power. In the SNAM/Edison case the competition authority has dealt with refusal of access. In March 2002, the AGCM launched a full investigation into ENEL, alleging infringement of Article 82 in the liberalized market for supply of electricity to eligible clients, and unannounced investigations have been carried out at ENEL's premises throughout Italy.

8.6.3 Regulatory Governance

Key issues in regulation include the designation of independent regulatory authorities (IRAs), their de jure independence, the definition of their powers, their accountability, and the role of the existing antitrust authority in monitoring access to networks and competition in the liberalized service markets. The 1994 law made the creation of IRAs a prerequisite for the privatization of public utilities. A much-delayed bill creating separate IRAs for electricity and gas (AEEG) and for telecommunications and media (AGC) was approved by parliament in 1995 after no fewer than 180 hours of debates. IRAs regulate access to the market, ensure the universality and quality of services, supervise the operating companies' balance sheets, set service tariffs, investigate possible misbehavior of licensees (either independently or on reports of customers), and rule the repeal of licenses or pecuniary sanctions pending judiciary appeal by faulty companies.

Law 249 gave the AGC two overriding objectives: to introduce liberalization, also on the basis of EU-wide choices, and guarantee cultural, political, and social pluralism in the media sector. In a country where the private TV industry, the largest publishing house, and various newspapers are controlled by the head of the largest political party and his associates, the creation of a single IRA for both telecom and media, while partly justified by technological convergence, was dictated by clear political considerations (Petretto 2000).[28] These found its reflection in the power granted to parliament of appointing the regulators, in the lack of specific eligibility criteria, and in the excessive frequency of parliamentary hearings (Pontarollo and Oglietti 2000). Concerns have also emerged regarding the slowness of the decision-making process and its opacity: there are no public hearings, and the AGC does not prepare position papers to guide the regulatory game. On the other hand, and despite the heavier burden brought about by the relative lack of progress in structural deregulation, the AEEG— which has fewer members (three rather than nine) appointed by government and sits in Milan (while other IRAs are in Rome)—has been more successful in gaining credibility.

It is not straightforward to identify some independent variables that explain such differences.[29] That TI is fully private (bar the golden share, of course) while ENEL is still government controlled has not made any significant difference on their approach to the regulatory game, which has been confrontational in both cases. Enforcement appears to be hampered by lengthy and cumbersome procedure, but also by the incumbents' practice of appealing systematically against the IRA decisions. While due process is a fundamental legal principle, IRAs need to put in place disincentives for excessive delaying measures (Nicoletti 2002).[30] Although hard to test, it is intuitively clear that even in collegiate bodies such as the Italian IRAs, the personal qualities of the AEEG's president have played an important role, confirming that "persons appointed to these positions must have personal qualities to resist improper pressures and inducements [and] must exercise their authority with skill to win the respect of key stakeholders, enhance the legitimacy of their role and decisions, and build a constituency for their independence" (Smith 1997).

The 1990s saw a general proliferation of delegation to nonrepresentative institutions around Europe (Thatcher 2002), and Italy was no exception. One may indeed argue that the traditional weakness of ministerial bureaucracy strengthened the process even more than in other EU members. There is a perception that IRAs have on some occasions filled the void left by executive inactions and converted themselves in law-making bodies (De Nicola 2001). For this reason, the ongoing debate on IRAs is legitimate, provided of course that the principle of safeguarding investors and consumers against the risk of undue interference remains overriding. The bicameral commission for constitutional reform debated the opportunity of giving selected IRAs a constitutional ranking. The current majority has acknowledged the need to preserve independence and autonomy, but argued that "political organs must proceed in fine-tuning the instruments that are necessary to carry out the functions that should remain under their control, especially as concerns the IRAs' decisions of highest social and economic impact" (Camera dei Deputati 2002). The instrument to implement this function is identified in the Documento di programmazione economica e finanziaria, hence making parliament responsible for ensuring the fulfillment of the government's guidelines. An early majority proposal called for merging the AEEG and AGC into a single regulator, an issue on which the international debate is far from settled, and suggests that its members should be appointed by the government, hence reducing their independence and credibility.

Finally, brief mention should be made of the consequences of the 2001 reform of the Constitution (Title V of the Second Part). This includes at Article 117 the decentralization of the authority over transport and cabotage networks, the organization of the telecommunications and media sectors, as well as energy generation, transport, and domestic distribution. In accordance with the subsidiarity principle, regions and local authorities already have broad competencies in the energy domain. Insofar as this is a sector where benefits (and interdependencies) are national, whereas negative externalities are often local, cooperation among different levels of government is required (Galbiati and Vaciago 2002). Early evidence, unfortunately, shows that the governance game is characterized by strong animosity. Regions have challenged the 2002 decree to speed up new generation projects, claiming that grid ownership should be allocated among local governments by voltage. The AEEG has also expressed concern for Sicily's decision to delay to 2010 the liberalization of the gas retail market that at the national level is foreseen for 2003.[31] A further problem is that the text of the July 2002 draft law is vague as to what principles are fundamental and henceforth reserved to the state.

8.7   The Future of State Ownership

8.7.1   *Industrial Policy and the Scope for Further State Retrenchment*

Other EU countries have accompanied state retrenchment from manufacturing with various industrial policy measures. In France, the 1986 privatization law put a 20 percent limit on nonresidents' investment in privatized enterprises, which was relaxed in 1993 to apply only to non-EU citizens (Goldstein 1996). Moreover, in both the late 1980s and the mid-1990s, the government selected core groups of mainly domestic investors (*noyaux durs*, later renamed *groupes d'actionnaires stables*) and retained special voting rights (*action spécifique*). A complex "industrial Meccano" has also been played to create sorts of national champions in different segments of the aerospace and defense industry (Goldstein 2001).

In Italy, the 1992 framework plan left the scope for state retrenchment largely undefined. Moreover, special powers would be retained in areas defined as "strategic," with the strategic nature of an activity loosely defined as "the ability to influence outcomes in several other sectors."[32] Although the 1994 privatization law circumscribed strategic areas to defense, transportation, telecommunications, energy, and "other public services," the plan still outlined a future industrial structure in which the government would continue to have significant, albeit generally minority, shareholdings in a long list of activities, including many competitive markets. Shareholdings and supervisory functions were concentrated in the treasury (now economy) ministry (table 8.9). This was deemed to serve the public interest in the event that the state were to maintain a significant presence in some sectors at the end of the privatization process.[33]

The implications of privatization for the structure of Italian industry have been the source of harsh political conflicts. Reinforcing economic democracy through the emergence of new business actors was a peculiar aim made in the 1992 plan, which made explicit reference to an increase in the number of large-sized groups from six (IRI and ENI, plus IFI-Fiat, Ferfin-Montedison, CIR-Olivetti, and Fininvest) to ten or twelve. It is a moot point whether this goal, sometimes loosely rationalized as a means to increase competition in the Italian economy, had any economic content. In any case, the strategy has met limited success in nurturing new large-sized actors. A simple analysis of the "boundaries" of the twenty largest domestic business groups shows that the assets bought during privatization account for a sizable share of 2000 consolidated turnover in three cases only: Olivetti (96 percent), Edizione Holding (59.6 percent),[34] and Riva (74.7 percent). On the other hand, the IFI-Fiat group, in cooperation with different allies, has played an active role in financial privatization.

In the 1990s most industries saw a consolidation at the European global level. Italian business was left largely aside from this process, as very few firms had the organizational capabilities and financial resources to take over foreign competitors or merge with them on an equal footing (Bianchi 2002b). Size remains a problem for Italian business, and this finds its manifestation in a trade structure that puts it in competition with low-wage emerging economies. Above and beyond ideological a prioris, however, the criticism that state retrenchment has not supported industrial restructuring is not accurate.[35] Suffice it to briefly cite the cases of STMicroelectronics (STM) and Finmeccanica, as well as the ultimately failed attempt to merge Alitalia with KLM in what was then a path-breaking agreement in European air transport.

8.7.2   *The Governance of* Fondazioni

Corporate governance problems linked to the residual, if not dominating, role of public institutions appear to be particularly severe in the banking sector, where they may indeed pose severe obstacles on the way toward a more competitive and efficient industry structure. At

Table 8.9
Share stakes held by the Ministero dell'Economia

Name	Sector	Stake (percent)	Market value, October 31, 2003 (millions of euros)	Sales, 2002 (millions of euros)	Employees, 2002
ENEL	Energy	61	19,983	29,336	71,204
ENI	Energy	30	16,379	47,922	80,655
Finmeccanica	Defense and aerospace	32	1,651	7,775	44,963
Alitalia	Transport	62	670	4,737	22,536
Poste Italiane	Postal services	100	NA	7,712	161,403
Ferrovie dello Stato	Transport	100	NA	5,085	102,607
Rai	Media	100	NA	2,764	11,443
Gestore Rete Trasmissione Nazionale	Energy	100	NA	6,137	702
Consap	Insurance	100	NA	NA	NA
Consip—Concessionaria Servizi Informativi Pubblici	Services (diversified)	100	NA	NA	NA
ENAV	Transport	100	NA	NA	NA
IRI	Holding	100	NA	NA	NA
Italia Lavoro	Social development	100	NA	NA	NA
Sogesid—Società per la Gestione degli Impianti Idrici	Water	100	NA	NA	NA
SOGIN—Società Gestione Impianti Nucleari	Energy	100	NA	NA	NA
Sviluppo Italia	Regional development	100	NA	NA	NA
EUR	Services (diversified)	90	NA	NA	NA
Coopercredito	Banking	14	NA	NA	NA

Sources: Sales and employment from Mediobanca. Market value OECD elaboration based on Borsa Italiana and Direzione Generale del Tesoro–Ministero dell'Economia.

the end of 1999, Fondazioni held at a minimum a relative majority in each of Italy's five largest banking group and in six of the top nine (De Nardis 2000), and the four largest groups are also intertwined throughout a web of mutual shareholdings. Assets under their control amount to 35 billion euros.

In its original formulation, the 1992 Amato law created individual charitable Fondazioni as spin-offs of public sector banks and forbade them from controlling any other bank. Parliament, however, added the obligation of safeguarding public control over such assets.[36] Proposals and laws in the 1990s aimed at turning the Fondazioni into private sector players, attentive to science and culture promotion on a local basis but mainly focused on managing the return on the investment rather than the assets themselves. The 1999 Ciampi Law, in particular, streamlined governance structures, introduced tax incentives to push Fondazioni to exit banks by 2005, and forbade them to control companies that are not instrumental to social objectives.[37] The law's weak point is the definition of control that still allows them to team up with other investors, most often other Fondazioni, to form a voting syndicate.[38] Furthermore, the requirement for their board members not to be directors of the banks that are each foundation's main asset is not enforced adequately.

The 2002 budget law has pushed back by one year the term for privatization; granted local government bodies the authority to appoint a majority of directors;[39] transferred to the treasury the power to fix the range of permissible investment; imposed that 10 percent of nonbanking assets be invested in Infrastrutture spa, a new state corporation funding public works, and that banking participations be placed with assets management funds (Società di Gestione del Risparmio) that for all practical purposes are simply subject to the treasury's moral suasion (Giavazzi 2001). Equally troublesome, the text does not clarify the criteria to identify (now outlawed) joint control over banks. In sum, the debate on the ultimate function of such institutions—to make grants to finance project, directly supply social services, or gather funds to be used in combination with own endowment to serve the community— is still far from solved.

8.7.3 The Case of Local Utilities

Italy counts 1,300 local utilities, providing services such as local transport, water and sanitation, and gas and electricity distribution, with a total turnover of 19 billion euros and profits of more than 1 billion euros in 2001. The first round of reforms, introduced in the early 1990s, was designed to cut costs and reduce deficits.[40] Later in the decade, a second round of reforms introduced incentives to corporatize local utilities, and the number of corporations indeed rose to 640 in July 2003.

Owing to the great influence of vested interests at the local level, however, the regulatory reform process has proved especially problematic (OECD 2002). In 1999, the D'Alema government issued a *decreto legislativo* to introduce liberalization in local transport and gas in accordance with EU laws. The reform aims at safeguarding services universality, but obliges local authorities to verify whether the market can supply them better than public-owned utilities can.[41] Parliament, however, failed to convert the proposal into a law. The 2002 budgetary law introduced the obligation to split network ownership and services provision (that remains public) and to rely on competitive tendering to grant operating licenses. Municipalities have the option to reduce their stakes in utilities below 51 percent, but after fixed assets (plants, grid) have been transferred to a public-owned company.

It is doubtful that these changes go in the direction of introducing more liberalization (Pera 2001, Massarutto 2002). These are simple general guidelines, at any rate, and implementing regulations (*regolamenti attuativi*) have not been issued yet, although they were expected by the end of 2002. Regions, moreover, have appealed to the Supreme Court on the grounds that the principles of federalism introduced in the Constitution (heading V) give them the powers to regulate territorial public services. Some local utilities are medium sized and in some cases provide multiple services, but most of them are far too small to survive in a liberalized environment. Normative uncertainty has hindered the industry consolidation and slowed listing plans on the stock exchange (Goldstein 2003, table 12). The 2003 budgetary law also contains specific provisions that run counter to the logic of liberalization.

8.8 Conclusions, or the Political Economy of Italian Privatization

This chapter has summarized the often momentous vicissitudes of Western Europe's largest privatization program in the 1990s and provided evidence on the effects on productivity, quality, and prices. No ex post analysis can forget how deep and widespread the skepticism was surrounding its quantitative and qualitative goals at launch. In this sense, the pace and the extent of privatizations in the midst of the worst political and economic crisis in postwar Italy have been nothing short of surprising. Successful solutions were found in a number of areas, including the sequencing of sales, the use of privatization proceeds, and the creation of a wide audience of investors attracted by state divestitures. Domestic financial markets proved far more adequate than previously expected in absorbing large numbers of new shares. Partly due to the simultaneous reduction of yields on government bonds, oversubscription has been generally larger than elsewhere in the EU, even with lower underpricing. And Italy has shown a higher degree of transparency in the conduct of private sales than France in the 1980s, as well as making sparse use of special powers (such as special voting rights) to prevent foreign acquisitions of privatized firms.

However, the policy drive also suffered from several unsettled issues, which limited its beneficial effects. First, a sizable share of privatization activity has concerned noncontrolling stakes in SOEs. This means that capital market discipline through both monitoring by private agents and the threat of takeover cannot function properly. Second, despite the spreading out of shareholdings and attempts at limiting single equity stakes, public companies have not emerged, and the stock market does not allocate corporate control. Such a market for corporate control will remain quiescent as long as the respect of minority shareholders' rights is lax, the application of existing laws (such as those concerning takeover bids and insider trading) is feeble, and the role of institutional investors is subdued. Third, in public utilities, opportunities have been lost to use divestiture as a Trojan horse to introduce more competition, in particular throughout the vertical separation of hitherto public sector monopolists and more audacious forms of asymmetric regulation. This problem is particularly severe in electricity and (to a lesser degree) natural gas. Fourth, uncertainties abound concerning the conditions for privatizing the post office and the transport companies, as well as many smaller energy and water utilities owned by local authorities. And finally, public sector bodies maintain control over companies that operate in competitive sectors.

If the potential economic benefits from state divestitures have not been fully realized, it has been partly for the inherent weakness of the coalition governments that have run the country for most of this ten-year period. The Italian system is clearly different from the ideal type for fast and effective market reforms in which a strong executive is capable of assuming long-term commitments, with relatively few counterchecks and a reduced number of veto players. Divergences among political parties over key issues such as the very extent of the divestiture program, the nature (if not the identity) of private investors, the speed of market liberalization, and the powers and independence of regulators have slowed progress on many occasions. It is not surprising that an opinion poll conducted before the 2001 polls ranked privatization as the lowest among twelve policy priority alternatives. Having said that, this was the policy area on which the government recorded the second-lowest score of very negative opinion. Moreover, roughly 60 percent of respondents thought that electricity, gas, water, and transport should be fully liberalized.[42]

This, however, is only part of the story. Despite widespread technical and intellectual agreement on the correct forms of privatization, the literature on the political economy of reforms has long highlighted the importance of the "three I's"—institutions, interests, and ideas—and shown that "politicians' preferences shape the specific institutions that will be used to implement those policies introducing a 'political bias,' which is contingent on the privatizing government" (Murillo 2002, p. 463). The significant deceleration of privatization since 2001 finds its origin in the lack of a clear vision on the limits to the process of state retrenchment and the hesitancy that policymakers have shown between the free-market doctrines of Margaret Thatcher and the centralized power policies of Jean-Baptiste Colbert. On the one hand, the current government exposed during the 2001 electoral campaigns strong views against state intervention and argued that the *entire* country should be managed like the private sector. On the other hand, economy minister Tremonti repeatedly stated that the government can be a good shareholder and that a proactive industrial policy to correct market failures is preferable to "a dogmatic interpretation of anti-trust principles" (Tremonti 2002). Tommaso Padoa-Schioppa of the European Central Bank's executive board recently said that "to be Thatcher one needs the courage to take unpopular choices and see them through to the end, and that's missing. To be Colbert, one needs a state that works, and that's missing, too."[43]

Notes

This is an abridged version of Goldstein (2003). I thank Norberto Pignatti for careful research assistance and Patrizio Bianchi, Bernardo Bortolotti, Franco Debenedetti, Reiner Fehn, Cino Molajoni, Flavio Padrini, Pippo Ranci, Carlo Scarpa, Hans-Werner Sinn,

Ferdinando Targetti, John Whalley, and an anonymous referee, as well as participants at the two CESifo conferences "Privatization Experiences in the EU" in Munich (January 2003) and Cadenabbia (November 2003) and seminars at the University of Trento and the European University Institute, for comments and suggestions on earlier drafts. The usual caveats apply: in particular, the opinions expressed and arguments employed are my sole responsibility and do not necessarily reflect those of the Organisation for Economic Co-operation and Development (OECD) and its members.

1. This section is based on Goldstein and Nicoletti (1996).

2. An important precedent was the corporatization of banks in the early 1990s.

3. Bertero and Rondi (2000) study the budget regime for a panel of manufacturing SOEs over the period 1977 to 1993. They identify a switch from a soft to a hard budget constraint regime in 1987, associated with reining in excessive managerial discretion and an important change in their investment decisions.

4. In contrast with the French Commission de la privatisation, in Italy the commission's decisions over pricing and other issues are not binding for the government and are not legally enforceable.

5. The Treaty of Rome defines as "incompatible" state aid to either public or private enterprises, except in specified cases.

6. A more sizable contribution to rapid public debt reduction could come from the sale of public real estate, whose value is estimated at around 50 percent of public debt. Real estate sales have been planned since 1987, when an ad hoc government commission produced a report on this subject, but to date, few sales have been completed. The most significant has been the partial privatization of railway stations (Grandi Stazioni), which has led to a 7,500 percent increase in net assets value.

7. The exceptions are IMI 2 and INA 3, which were reserved to institutional investors.

8. Foreign direct privatization investment has included General Electric in Nuovo Pignone, RWE in Enichem, Wartsila in Fincantieri, Pilkington in SIV, and Krupp in AST.

9. The analysis of the performance impact of privatization included in the report is at the level of each firm and thus does not allow broader generalizations.

10. Current assets over current liabilities.

11. At the end of 1992, the state controlled over 18 percent of the number of listed enterprises, accounting for over 25 percent of total market capitalization: candidates for privatization had a share of 18.5 percent of the total (Consob 1993).

12. In 1987, stakes of Mediobanca in other major groups accounted for 40 percent of the market value of total intergroup shareholdings (Brioschi et al. 1990). In turn, virtually all major private groups (with the exception of Fininvest), as well as Credito Italiano, Banca Commerciale, and Banca di Roma, had shareholdings and a seat on the bank's board.

13. The promotional leaflet distributed by the government in late 1993 stated that "privatization is a policy that indirectly concerns all citizens as [it aims at] creating a sounder economic democracy free from political abuses."

14. Shortly after the sale of Banca Commerciale and Credito Italiano, Mediobanca molded controlling coalitions in the two banks, undermining attempts by the government to turn them into public companies.

15. Another company that has seen control change is GS, a supermarket chain, sold to France's Promodés. Leonardo Holding, a consortium that holds the majority shareholding in Aeroporti di Roma, sold a 44.7 percent stake to a technical operator, Australia's Macquarie Airports Group.

16. The committee was dissolved in 1993.

17. Stet's subsidiaries for domestic, international, and satellite services (Iritel, Sip, Italcable and Telespazio Stet, a listed financial holding in which IRI owned 65 percent of shares) held a 60 percent stake in TI.

18. Liberalization was the result of the belated adoption by the Italian parliament of a series of EU directives concerning telephone equipment (301/88), access to public networks (387/90), and telecommunication services (388/90). Several rulings by competition authorities were instrumental in accelerating liberalization of terminal equipment and network access regimes. The opening up of the mobile telephone market spurred a dispute with the European Commission, which began legal proceedings against Italy in October 1995. In the exploitation agreement, the new entrant was asked to pay the government a fee in return for the GSM license, while the incumbent operator was granted it for free. The commission deemed this arrangement unfair and asked the government to find adequate compensation for the new entrant.

19. In principle, vertical unbundling is the only way to ensure competition in electricity generation and supply, as well as free access to the network. At the same time, horizontal unbundling—the sale of production plants and distribution networks to several private (possibly regional) companies—could allow "yardstick" regulation based on the comparative performance of independent companies.

20. This last requirement was to prevent Electricité de France (EdF) from acquiring these companies. Previously, EdF had already acquired a 20 percent share of Montedison, parent company of Edison (Italy's largest IPP). EdF and Fiat formed a consortium called Italenergia that received permission from the EU antitrust authority to take over Montedison in August 2001.

21. In September 2001, ENEL purchased Nueva Viesgo from Endesa, making it the fifth largest generator in Spain.

22. Edipower comprises Edison, AEM, AEM Torino, Aar e Ticino SA di Elettricità (Atel), Unicredito, Interbanca, and MRBS Capital Partners.

23. Awards for fixed-wireless access licenses are still planned.

24. In Germany call-by-call carrier selection was introduced in December 2002.

25. In France mobile number portability has been operational since July 2003.

26. Other projects for which authorization is currently pending would add an additional 39,000 MW capacity.

27. The temporary charge on hydrogenerated electricity is meant to compensate for the windfall gain produced by the transition from an administered price regime, which only in the case of thermal generation included a reimbursement for fuel costs, to a free market where the price is unique regardless of fuel.

28. In the 1997 Green Paper, the EC put forward as one proposition for a future regulatory model the creation of a new horizontal regulatory model to cover the whole range of existing and new services in the communications sector. Nevertheless, not many

institutional changes have been made to take into account convergence between telecommunications and broadcasting. Along with the political difficulty of integrating separate regulatory institutions, the special role played by media and content policy in some countries makes it delicate to merge broadcasting and telecommunications regulatory institutions. In the Besley and Pratt (2001) model, in particular, media ownership patterns may generate capture through a channel that is industry specific and demands media-specific regulation.

29. An obvious one would be the degree of statutory independence. Gilardi (2002) builds aggregate independence scores that have rather similar values for both IRAs. Individual variables, however, show that the AEEG is more independent insofar as the statuses of the agency head and board members and the relationship with political bodies are concerned, although less so in terms of financial rules.

30. An interesting parallel can be made with New Zealand, where the absence of a regulator provided the incumbent operator, Telecom New Zealand, with the competitive weapon of most use to an incumbent: the ability to delay. Instead of being obliged to interconnect on specific terms by law, Telecom New Zealand was able to convert disputes into full-blown litigation, with numerous appeal stages throughout the legal system.

31. Pippo Ranci, personal communication to the author, October 30, 2002.

32. The plan identified nine sectors in which the government intended to keep significant (although generally minority) stakes: electricity, energy and chemicals, banking, insurance, airline transportation, high-tech manufacturing, distribution and catering, plant engineering and installation, and telecommunications. The European Commission ruled in June 2001 that capital flows may not be restricted merely because of varying degrees of liberalization. The initial privatization sale may be restricted, but such restrictions can be in place for only a limited period, after which the privatized companies can be resold to state-owned companies.

33. Ministers in the current executive, however, have suggested that the Ministry for Productive Activities should also have a voice.

34. In this case, the holding firm of the Benetton family, the share is potentially underestimated as the company also holds important, albeit not absolute majority, participations in Autostrade and Aeroporti di Roma. In November 2002 investors led by the Benettons bought full control of Autostrade in a takeover bid costing up to 8 billion euros (Italy's second largest ever after the second TI one).

35. A case in point is Clô (2002), who argues that trimming ENEL's size to the benefit of foreign competitors will generate long-term inefficiency for the country.

36. Translating the term *Fondazioni d'origine bancaria* is not easy; the closest is "bank-derived foundations" or "foundations having their origin in banking assets."

37. The law was presented in early 1997, approved by parliament in late 1998, and finally issued by the Council of Ministers in May 1999.

38. Insofar as the participation to voting syndicates is taken into account only when an individual Fondazione exercises a dominating role, in the Ciampi law, the definition of control is looser than in the 1994 banking law (Testo unico bancario) and in the Draghi bill. Exploiting this legal loophole, in many cases the Fondazioni have built a web of interlocking shareholdings, further decreasing control contestability (Messori 2000).

39. The 2002 *Finanziaria* introduces the principle of "prevailing territorial representation" in place of that of of balancing the powers of local authorities and "civil society" (Article 11). This provision was declared unconstitutional by the Supreme Court.

40. In the case of water and sanitation, the 1994 Galli law aimed at improving supply service through gradual privatization and consolidation (in 1999 Italy counted more than 8,100 different suppliers, and even Acquedotto Pugliese, the largest one, is one-twentieth in size compared to major European competitors). Investment needs over the next twenty years are estimated to amount to 45 billion euros, far in excess of public sector's available resources.

41. Exclusive management (*gestione in esclusiva*) is deemed necessary in both sectors— in the case of transport in order to ensure financial sustainability, for gas distribution to reflect its peculiar techno-economic characteristics.

42. See *Sondaggio CONFCOMMERCIO-Cirm sui temi di politica economica* at ⟨http://www.confcommercio.it/Iniziative/Cernobbio/popolazione.pdf⟩.

43. "Italy 'gambling away credibility'—de Benedetti," *Financial Times*, September 17, 2002.

References

Abate, Antonio, and Clô, Alberto. 2000. "La regolazione elettrica in Italia, alcune prime valutazioni." *L'Industria* 21(4).

Anuatti-Neto, Francisco, Barossi-Filho, Milton, Gledson De Carvalho, A., and Macedo, Roberto. 2002. "Benefits and Costs of Privatization: Evidence from Brazil." Working Paper, no. R-455, Inter-American Development Bank.

Autorità per l'energia elettrica e il gas (AEEG). Various years. *Relazione annuale sullo stato dei servizi e sull'attività svolta.*

Autorità per le garanzie nelle comunicazioni (AGC). Various years. *Relazione annuale sull'attività svolta e sui programmi del lavoro.*

Barca, Fabrizio, and Trento, Sandro. 1997. "La parabola delle partecipazioni statali." In F. Barca, ed., *Storia del capitalismo italiano dal dopoguerra a oggi*. Rome: Donzelli.

Bertero, Elisabetta, and Rondi, Laura. 2000. "Financial Pressure and the Behaviour of Public Enterprises under Soft and Hard Budget Constraints: Evidence from Italian Panel Data." *Journal of Public Economics* 75(1), 73–98.

Besley, Timothy, and Prat, Andrea. 2001. "Handcuffs for the Grabbing Hand? Media Capture and Government Accountability." Mimeo., London School of Economics and Political Science.

Bianchi, Patrizio. 2002a. "La chiusura dell'IRI. Considerazioni al mergine di un evento storico." *L'Industria* 23(1).

Bianchi, Patrizio. 2002b. "Grandi imprese, privatizzazioni e riorganizzazioni produttive." In Giampaolo Galli and Luigi Paganetto, eds., *La competitività dell'Italia*. Milan: Il Sole 24 Ore.

Bortolotti, Bernardo, and Siniscalco, Domenico. 2002. "Importare la Corporate Governance?"

Brioschi, Francesco, Buzzacchi, Luigi, and Colombo, M. G. 1990. *Gruppi di imprese e mercato finanziario*. Florence: La Nuova Italia Scientifica.

Camera dei Deputati. 2002. *Indagine conoscitiva sulla situazione e le prospettive del settore energetico*. X Commissione Attività Produttive.

Cassese, Sabino. 1996. "Le privatizzazioni in Italia." *Stato e mercato* 47, 323–349.

Cavaliere, Alberto. 2001. "I servizi pubblici: privatizzazioni e liberalizzazioni in corso." In Luigi Bernardi and Alberto Zanardi, eds., *La finanza pubblica—Rapporto 2001*. Bologna: Il Mulino.

Cecchi, Claudia, Saraceno, Pia, and Vaciago, Giacomo. 2002. "Subito la Borsa elettrica." *Il Sole 24 Ore*, June 14.

Clô, Alberto. 2002. "I grandi gruppi energetici in Italia tra passato, presente e . . . futuro?" *L'Industria*, 23(1).

Clô, Alberto, Goldoni, Giovanni, and Pastorino, Davide. 2002. "Di male in peggio." *Energia*, no. 3.

Consob. Various years. *Relazione annuale*. Rome.

Cragg, Michael, and Alexander Dyck, I. J. 1997. "Management Control and Privatization in the UK." *Rand Journal of Economics* 30, 475–497.

De Nardis, Sergio. 2000. "Privatizzazioni, liberalizzazioni, sviluppo: introduzione e sintesi." In Sergio De Nardis, ed., *Le privatizzazioni italiane*, Bologna: Il Mulino.

De Nicola, Alessandro. 2001. "Autorità di garanzia, separiamo i poteri." *Il Sole 24 Ore*, December 19.

DWS. 2002. *Corporate Governance Survey of EURO STOXX 50 Companies*.

Enriques, Luca. 2002. "Off the Books, But on the Record: Some Evidence from Italy on the Relevance of Judges to the Quality of Corporate Law." Paper presented at the conference Global Markets, Domestic Institutions: Corporate Law and Governance in a New Era of Cross-Border Deals, Columbia Law School, New York, April.

Erbetta, Fabrizio. 2001. "Does the Run-Up of Privatization Work as an Effective Incentive Mechanism? Preliminary Findings from a Sample of Italian Firms." Working paper no. 11, Ceris-Cnr.

European Commission. 2001. *Seventh Report on the Implementation of the Telecommunications Regulatory Package*.

Filippa, Luca, and Franzosi, Alessandra. 2001. "Capitalizzazione di Borsa, settori istituzionali e portafoglio *retail*." *Bit Notes* no. 2, Borsa Italiana.

Fischer, Ronald, Gutierrez, R., and Serra, Pablo. 2002. "The Effects of Privatization on Firms and on Social Welfare." University of de Chile.

Galal, Ahmed, Jones, Leroy, Tandon, Pankaj, and Vogelsang, Ingo. 1994. *Welfare Consequences of Selling Public Enterprises*. Washington: The World Bank.

Gallo, Nicola, and Cecchi, Claudia. 2002. "La Borsa elettrica boicottata dalle imprese sussidiate." *Corriere della Sera*, July 8.

Giavazzi, Francesco. 1996. "Privatizzazioni, liberalizzazione dei mercati e assetto proprietario delle imprese: alcuni falsi dilemmi." *Stato e mercato* 47, 351–360.

Giavazzi, Franceso. 2001. "I gattopardi del credito." *Corriere della Sera*, December 7.

Gilardi, Fabrizio. 2002. "Policy Credibility and Delegation to Independent Regulatory Agencies: A Comparative Empirical Analysis." *Journal of European Public Policy* 9.

Goldstein, Andrea. 1996. "Privatizations and Corporate Governance in France." *BNL Quarterly Review* 196, 455–488.

Goldstein, Andrea. 2001. "Stato, mercato ed Europa nel capitalismo francese: il caso dell'industria della difesa." *Stato e Mercato* 61, 161–196.

Goldstein, Andrea. 2003. "Privatization in Italy 1993–2003: Goals, Institutions, Outcomes, and Outstanding Issues." Working paper no. 912, CESifo.

Goldstein, Andrea, and Nicoletti, Giuseppe. 1996. "Italian Privatization in International Perspective." *Cuadernos di Economía* 33(100), 425–451.

La Porta, Rafael, and Lopez de Silanes, Florencio. 1999. "The Benefits of Privatization: Evidence from Mexico." *Quarterly Journal of Economics* 114(4), 1193–1242.

La Porta, Rafael, López-de-Silanes, Florencio, Shleifer, Andrei, and Vishny, Robert. 2000. "Investor Protection and Corporate Governance." *Journal of Financial Economics* 58(1–2), 3–27.

Lehn, Kenneth. 2002. "Corporate Governance in the Deregulated Telecommunications Industry: Lessons from the Airline Industry." *Telecommunications Policy* 26, 225–242.

Levine, Ross E. 2002. "Bank-Based or Market-Based Financial Systems: Which Is Better?" Working paper no. 9138, National Bureau of Economic Research.

Macchiati, Alfredo. 1999. "Breve storia delle privatizzazioni in Italia." *Mercato concorrenza regole* 1(3).

Massarutto, Antonio. 2002. "La riforma dei servizi pubblic locali. Liberalizzazione, privatizzazione o gattopardismo." *Mercato concorrenza regole* 4(1).

Mediobanca (a). Various years. *Le principali società italiane*. Milan.

Mediobanca (b). Various years. *Dati cumulativi di 1760 società italiane*. Milan.

Mediobanca. 2000. *Le privatizzazioni in Italia dal 1992*. Milan: R&S (Ricerche e Studi).

Megginson, William L., and Netter, Jeffry M. 2001. "From State to Market: A Survey of Empirical Studies on Privatization." *Journal of Economic Literature* 39(2), 321–389.

Megginson, William L., Nash, Robert C., and van Randenborgh, Matthias. 1994. "The Financial and Operating Performance of Newly Privatized Firms: An International Empirical Analysis." *Journal of Finance* 49(3), 403–452.

Messori, Marcello. 1999. "Gli assetti proprietari delle maggiori banche italiane." In Luigi Paganetto, ed., *Banche e concorrenza in Europa*. Bologna: Il Mulino.

Messori, Marcello. 2000. "Fondazioni e assetti proprietari del sistema bancario." In L. Filippini, ed., *Economia delle fondazioni*. Bologna: Il Mulino.

Messori, Marcello. 2002. "Fondazioni bancarie indietro tutta." *La Repubblica*, April 22.

Ministero del Tesoro, del Bilancio e della Programmazione Economica. 2001. *Libro bianco sulle privatizzazioni*.

Munari, Federico. 2002. *Privatizzazioni e innovazione. Nuovi assetti proprietari e investimenti in ricerca e sviluppo.* Rome: Carocci.

Murillo, María Victoria. 2002. "Political Bias in Policy Convergence." *World Politics* 54(4).

Nicoletti, Giuseppe. 2002. "Institutions, Economic Structure and Performance: Is Italy Doomed?" In ISAE, *Annual Report on Monitoring Italy.*

OECD. Various years. *Economic Survey of Italy.* Paris.

Pera, Alberto. 2002. "Concorrenza tradita." *Il Sole 24 Ore,* December 18.

Pontarollo, Enzo, and Oglietti, Andrea. 2000. "La performance dell'Autorità per le Garanzie nelle Comunicazioni: un primo esame." *L'Industria* 21(4).

Scarpa, Carlo. 2002. "Energia: dal pubblico al privato. E ritorno." *Energia* 23(4).

Smith, Warrick. 1997. "Utility Regulators—The Independence Debate." In The World Bank, *Viewpoint,* no. 127.

Spaventa, Luigi. 2002. "Indagine conoscitiva sul Testo Unico della Finanza. Audizione alla VI Commissione Finanza della Camera." March 20.

Thatcher, Mark. 2002. "Regulation after Delegation: Independent Regulatory Agencies in Europe." *Journal of European Public Policy* 9(6), 954–972.

Tremonti, Giulio. 2002. "Il mio new deal." Interview, *La Stampa,* November 16.

Villalonga, Belén. 2000. "Privatization and Efficiency: Differentiating Ownership Effects from Political, Organizational and Dynamic Effects." *Journal of Economic Behaviour and Organization* 42(1), 43–74.

Zingales, Luigi. 1994. "The Value of the Voting Right: A Study of the Milan Stock Exchange Experience." *Review of Financial Studies* 7(1), 125–148.

9   Privatization in Ireland

Sean D. Barrett

The Irish economy since 1990 has experienced unprecedented economic growth while employment in state commercial enterprises has fallen. The causes of the economic growth of the 1990s include investment in education; deregulation and openness to foreign trade and investment; the 1993 devaluation of the Irish pound; large foreign investment flows, especially from the United States; subsidies from the EU; order in the public finances, leading to tax cuts for both individuals and corporations in a so-called process of expansionary fiscal contraction with high economic growth; and a declining public sector share of GNP (Barry 1999).

Table 9.1 shows the decline in state commercial enterprise employment since 1980 from 90,000 to 48,000, a fall of 47 percent, and the rapid rise in total national employment since 1990 by 64 percent from 1.1 million at work to 1.8 million. The share of commercial state enterprise (CSE) in total national employment thus fell from 7.8 to 2.7 percent. About two-thirds of this decline is accounted for by the massive rise in total national employment, and one-third is due to the reduced numbers employed in state commercial enterprises. The decline in state enterprise employment is due to both privatizations and reduced employment in the companies that remained in state ownership, such as transport and energy companies. The Irish labor market since 1990 has been dominated by a massive increase in overall employment achieved in the era of the Celtic Tiger of 0.7 million and the reduction of unemployment from 17 percent in the 1980s to 4.5 percent currently. The reduction in state commercial employment by 24,000 has been a little over 3 percent of the overall employment gain in the economy. In the words of Wolff (2003), it is a time when "entrepreneurs and managers seem to have fallen in love with Ireland (1)." The parameters of Ireland's recent economic growth experiences have moved

Table 9.1
Employment in commercial state enterprise (CSE) and total national employment, 1980–2002

	CSE employment	National employment (000)	CSE share (%)
1980	90,375	1,163	7.8
1990	71,913	1,100	6.5
2002	47,700	1,761	2.7

Sources: Chubb (1970); *Irish Statistical Bulletin* (March 2003); *Department of Finance Annual Review and Outlook.*

policymakers away from state commercial enterprises as engines of growth in the economy. The emphasis has changed to the private sector and export-led growth.

9.1   Origins of State Ownership and Interventionism

The Republic of Ireland, then known as the Irish Free State, gained independence from Britain in 1922. The independence movement was strongly interventionist in its economics. The belief in interventionism was founded on a perceived failure of British economic policies in particular during the famine of the 1840s and the decades of emigration that followed; the belief that a period of legislative independence between 1782 and 1800 brought economic growth stimulated by the Irish Parliament; successful rent seeking by Irish politicians at the Westminster Parliament, where they from time to time held the balance of power; a belief among British governments that they could "kill home rule with kindness" by placing moderate Irish nationalists on public boards; and finally a lack of empathy between Irish nationalists and the business community. The last were mainly based in the northeast and relied on foreign trade in particular with the British Empire and saw little future in serving just the Irish home market.

Daly (1981) states that "the belief that the Act of Union (1800) brought industrial decline and that Home Rule would mean prosperity was an important dimension in Irish nationalism" (79). Arthur Griffith, the founder of Sinn Fein, the independence movement, cited the infant industry argument of German economist, Frederich List, to justify protection of industry (Daly 1992). Daly (1992) also states that "the apparent coincidence between industrial decline and loss of an Irish parliament encouraged an exaggerated belief in the power of politics to determine economic well-being, an interpretation given greater credence because the interventionist policies of the late eighteenth century coincide with a period of prosperity" (4).

A delayed consequence of the Act of Union between Britain and Ireland was the abolition of the Irish currency in 1826. Ireland had a monetary union with Britain from 1826 until 1979, when it joined the European Monetary System. The lack of an independent exchange rate as an instrument of economic policy increased the emphasis in Irish economic policy after independence on direct state intervention to respond to economic problems such as unemployment and deficits in the balance of payments.

Under "killing home rule with kindness," the independence movement was given more state boards on which constitutional nationalists sat. This rewarded rent seeking and replaced normal economic activity by lobbying for, and sitting on, the boards. Sir Robert Peel, chief secretary for Ireland (1812–1818) stated that "everybody in Ireland, instead of setting about improvement as people elsewhere so, pester government about boards and public aid. Why cannot people in Ireland fish without a board (for fishing) if fishing be so profitable?" (Guiomard 1995, 201–202) Guiomard also found that "by 1914 there were forty government departments in Ireland. Although eleven were Irish branches of British Departments, twenty-nine had no British equivalents" (207). Ireland thus arrived at independence with a strong belief in intervention by the state and an inherited tradition of setting up state boards. This would dominate economic policy for six decades. Ownership of enterprises by the state was a dominant goal in economic policy, and the enterprises were seen as symbols of the new state. Little thought was given to either regulation of the enterprises or how they would compete in the marketplace. Having the enterprises in public ownership became an end in itself, and the motivation was founded on nationalism rather than Marxism.

9.2   The Era of State Commercial Enterprises, 1927–1984

The first Irish tariffs were imposed in 1924. "By 1929 the government claimed that 60% of non-agricultural jobs were subject to tariffs creating an extra 15,000 jobs" (Daly 1992, 41). The first state commercial enterprises were established in 1927. These were the Dairy Disposal Company to acquire bankrupt creameries and rationalize the sector and the Electricity Supply Board to acquire 160 electricity undertakings in the state and the Agricultural Credit Corporation to provide credit for that sector.

Economic nationalism increased after the change of government in 1932. A trade dispute with Britain, known as the economic war, escalated from a disagreement over land annuities from the British government to tenant farmers to buy out agricultural landlords during the last forty years before independence. Since 95 percent of Ireland's trade was with Britain in the 1920s (O'Leary and Leddin 1995), a trade war strengthened interest on state enterprises serving the home market. Firms with large markets in Britain served the market from bases there, such as Ford, which opened at Dagenham; Guinness, which opened at Park Royal, London; and Jacobs, which expanded its Liverpool factory to serve a British market previously served from Ford's Cork depot and the Guinness and Jacob plants in Dublin. In addition, the move away from free trade reduced the availability of inputs for industries such as Jacobs and the Irish whiskey companies. O'Maitiu (2001, 81) states that "in one fell swoop, the huge export trade so painstakingly built up by the Jacob family in Dublin and supplied by Dublin workers over the decades was lost by the city." O'Maitiu states also that restriction on ingredients "was a large contributory factor to the success of Scotch in the post-war years in America, to the detriment of Irish whiskey" (81). The casualness with which Ireland discarded export markets in the protectionist era contrasts with the current appetite for free trade in an economy that has, after Luxembourg, the highest ratio of foreign trade to GNP in the EU and the lowest unemployment.

In the 1930s, new state enterprises were established in areas such as industrial credit, sugar manufacture, chemicals, shipping, insurance, steel, and aviation. The list of state companies lacks any pattern. There is no stated reason that some sectors were chosen for state enterprise participation and others were not. The government minister most associated with state enterprise and later prime minister (Taoiseach), Sean Lemass, espoused pragmatism as his philosophy. According to Chubb (1970) the growth of public enterprises in Ireland "owed little to socialist theory. After the eclipse of the left wing of the labour movement during the latter part of the First World War, there were few socialists in Ireland, no socialist movement worth the name and no developing body of socialist doctrine" (274).

Before examining the case studies of the era of state commercial enterprise in Ireland, it is appropriate to review the wider macroeconomic impacts:

• *A rent-seeking or dependency culture in the Irish private sector.*   With exporting severely curtailed, major exporters located in Northern Ireland and others relocating to England, Irish industry became protectionist and dependent on tariffs, quotas, state purchasing, and other forms of state aid. As Daly (1992) states, "One major legacy of the thirties was the institutionalisation of an Irish dependence on the state, and on politicians, for economic benefits" (178).

• *The growth of political clientalism.*   Keogh (1994) noted that in 1992 there were some 2,200 appointments to state boards compared to 1,500 locally elected public representatives. Lee (1989) identified the patronage of appointments to state boards with the prime minister in the 1930s, Eamon de Valera: "He encouraged the gradual growth of an insidious, if initially discreet spoils system in the army, the judiciary, and the state sponsored bodies" (322). With political loyalty rather than commercial ability influencing board appointments, the system of political patronage undermined the quality of board members, reduced the independence of the state commercial enterprises, and lowered their public standing.

• *The growth of a trade union veto in state commercial enterprises.*   Lemass was close to the trade union movement. State companies were quickly heavily unionized in contrast with minimal unionization among the 700,000 extra at work in the 1990s. With weak management and politically appointed boards, the commercial state enterprises were captured by public sector trade unions. This persists to the present day. In 2003 there were work stoppages against the minister for transport's proposals to introduce competition between the three state airports and to liberalize the bus market.

• *The growth of regulatory capture of regulatory bodies by state companies.*   Since state enterprises were seen as an end in themselves, there was no provision to regulate them in the public interest or ensure that the state enterprises competed in the marketplace. The state companies achieved regulatory capture over their supervising government department, which already faced the conflicting roles of owning the company and regulating the market. The study and practice of economics in Ireland was weak throughout this period. It was not until 1950 that economists were employed in the civil service, and in the initial stages they were confined to the Department of Finance (Fanning 1985).

• *Emergence of a state managerial class.*   In an economy characterized by lack of opportunity elsewhere, Lee (1989) states that "not until the state sponsored bodies began to develop did some openings arise for managers who had lacked the foresight to be born into the right families" (393).

9.3   Rationale for Commercial State Enterprise: Some Illustrations

Irish nationalism and ignorance of market economics are the recurring themes in the establishment of state commercial enterprises. For example, in 1928 in the parliamentary debate on the Creamery Act establishing the Dairy Disposal Company, concern was expressed that control of 112 creameries would pass into the hands of Lovell and Christmas, "the biggest grocers in the world" (PDDE, vol. 25, 233). Rather than a market opportunity to gain access to the shelves of the biggest grocers in the world, this was seen as a threat and a case for nationalization.

In 1933 the state sugar company was established. According to its official historian, its objects included "a national wish to be independent of foreign supplies of basic needs" (Foy 1976, 23). The relative cost of cane and beet sugar was not apparently a factor in deciding to establish the company.

The nationalist dimension was extended to the services sector in 1936 when the minister proposing the insurance bill stated that "we are taking steps to promote the extension of native insurance by prohibiting the entry of any further insurance companies into the Saorstat [Irish Free State]" (PDDE, vol. 63, 2650).

The official history of Aer Lingus records the evolution of protectionism in the aviation sector for over fifty years. The Air Navigation (International Lines) Order of 1935 gave the minister for industry and commerce control over air services "with a view to the limitation or regulation of competition as may be considered necessary in the public interest" (Share 1988, 3). In 1935 Crilly Airways, seeking to operate air services between Ireland and Britain, was informed that "the Minister was unable to entertain his proposals. The reason given was the government's intention to set up a national airline at the earliest possible date" (Share 1988, 3). In 1949 a proposal for service from Cork to Britain was refused "on the grounds that air transport policy did not contemplate that airlines other than Aer Lingus would operate a scheduled service between the two countries" (Share 1988, 69). In 1950 a proposal from a British airline for service from Liverpool to Dublin was refused because Aer Lingus "was considering the opening of a similar service on the route" (Share 1988, 69).

The recurring theme of economic nationalism is reflected in the official airline history's reference to the opening of the New York route by Aer Lingus in 1960: "You saw for the first time an Irish plane with a shamrock. There was a great deal of emotional pride in the thing" (Share 1988, 95).

The alternative interpretation was that Irish aviation policy represented an extreme case of regulatory capture. The Department of Transport was referred to informally as "the downtown office of Aer Lingus." The airline held out for protectionism because Irish routes, not the airline, were inherently uneconomical. The chief executive of the airline wrote in 1998 that "the traditional Aer Lingus view was that the short-haul and seasonal nature of our European network was inherently not economic, or at least only marginally so, and would have to be supported by a profitable Atlantic operation" (Kennedy 1988, 174).

The OECD (2001) stated that airline deregulation "provided a clear demonstration of the potential benefits of competition to all consumers in Ireland, having a significant effect on public opinion." The Irish airline deregulation in 1986 led to an immediate reduction in fares of 54 percent on the Dublin-London route and an increase of 92 percent in passenger numbers in August 1987 over the preregulation levels in August 1985. The average Ryanair fare in 2002 was 38 euros per single journey compared to the 500 euros, which is the 2002 value of the 208 pounds Irish return fare charged before deregulation in 1986. The number of tourists, which had been 2 million for some twenty years, increased to 6 million in the years after deregulation. Tourism employs 140,000, and its employment growth has exceeded the strong employment growth of the economy as a whole. The airline facilitated most by deregulation, Ryanair, will have 35 million passengers in 2005 compared to 7 million by Aer Lingus. The short-haul routes have been highly profitable, and the capitalization of Ryanair at some 5 billion euros in 2003 was the highest of any European airline. Since 2001 Aer Lingus has adopted the low-fare, low-cost model and is a candidate for privatization. The policy before 1986 failed to consider the wider economic impacts of the European airline cartels on the economy of an outer offshore island. The policy was changed because of a revolt in the parliament against legislation designed to prevent rather than promote competition.

In 1965 the state nationalized the B and I Line, a shipping company operating on the Irish Sea. The minister stated in parliament that "a

272 Sean D. Barrett

greater measure of Irish participation in the cross channel trade for a long time has been an important objective of government policy" (PDDE, vol. 214, 974). The acquisition was warmly supported by the opposition parties. "It is a good thing that the B and I Line is now in Irish hands.... There are far too many foreigners buying land and public firms in this country" (PDDE, vol. 214, 974). The nationalized shipping company continued to participate in a cartel with the British Rail shipping subsidiary and became heavily loss making until privatized in 1992.

9.4 Ex Post Analysis of State Enterprise

In 1961 Garret FitzGerald, a future prime minister, published the first major volume on Irish state companies. He noted that they "had not hitherto received the attention they merit by virtue of their importance in the life of the country" (3). He attributed the dearth of analysis to "their relative novelty as an instrument of government." In his analysis of state trading enterprises, FitzGerald gave two main reasons for their establishment: "a desire to maintain in existence a bankrupt, or virtually bankrupt, undertaking, whose preservation is believed to be in the national interest," and "a desire to initiate an economic activity deemed necessary in the national interest—but one which for one reason or another private enterprise has failed to inaugurate or to operate on a sufficiently extensive scale" (15). In his first category— nationalization to preserve bankrupt companies—FitzGerald included the state transport company, CIE, and Irish Steel. In his second category, state commercial enterprise where the private sector did not exist, he included the state companies in air transport, shipping, capital for industrial development, and peat.

The policy of nationalization to rescue private sector firms from bankruptcy runs the risk that the necessary reforms of the company will be made more difficult by nationalization because the nationalized company does not face a bankruptcy constraint. In the CIE case, its nationalization was accompanied by the payment of large subsidies and investment grants and a rigid licensing regime to severely restrict new market entry and competition. The Department of Transport owns CIE, awards it operating subsidies and investment grants, and protects it from competition. The contradictions in banning new entrant transport companies, eliminating some 1,561 independent transport operations from the market by legislation in 1932 and 1933, and then subsidizing the monopolist because its services were deemed essential are not examined by FitzGerald. The other example in the category of preserving bankrupt companies cited by FitzGerald, the Irish Steel Company, was uneconomical in both the public and private sectors and closed in 2001.

The sectors that became state commercial enterprises because the private sector did not exist, FitzGerald's second category, might be said not to have stood the test of time.

We have seen that far from filling a void left by the private sector, Aer Lingus successfully lobbied governments to keep other airlines out of the market. There proved to be no need for state bodies either to run shipping or provide industrial financing. The privatized shipping company competes rather than colludes, and the state banks have been privatized and compete with a large and active financial services sector. In summary, the FitzGerald theoretical attribution of state enterprises to either failure in the market by the private sector or private sector failure to enter markets is seen to be doubtful as both a theoretical explanation for Irish public enterprise and a correct historical record.

9.5   Disillusionment with State Commercial Enterprise in the 1970s and 1980s

State commercial enterprises in Ireland became identified over time not as development corporations as intended by Lemass, but with producer dominance, high costs, indifference to consumers, regulatory capture, and subsidy seeking. Lee (1989, 536) notes that in the early 1980s the Labour party proposal for a national development corporation failed to generate enthusiasm because "the public had so lost confidence in the capacity of any state organisation to serve any purpose except its own self-interest that the proposal generated more scepticism than enthusiasm. A series of poor returns on several enterprises and the apparent casualness with which public sector trade unions resorted to the tactic of inflicting suffering on the public, the same public they claimed to serve in their more esoteric flights of rhetorical fancy, in order to intimidate the government into concessions left public opinion increasingly dubious about the likely results of direct state intervention."

The case studies of public enterprises as inefficient included a report by the National Prices Commission (1972), which found that bus and train fares in the public sector were substantially above those charged by the small, rural, unsubsidized independent bus companies. In 1979 the Dargan Report found that the state telephone company was over-staffed by a factor of three compared to Britain, four compared to the United States, and almost eight compared to Switzerland. The Report of the Enquiry into Electricity Prices in 1984, chaired by E. G. Jakobsen, managing director of ELSAM Denmark, found staffing levels double those in Scotland, three times those in Denmark, and six times those in Vermont (1984). The report also found that the level of overstaffing in Ireland's electricity sector was higher in newer plant than in older plant when contrasted with plant of similar size and age elsewhere.

The 1980s was also a decade of reassessment in Irish national economic policies. Between 1982 and 1987, both national debt and un-employment doubled. In 1987 the debt-to-GNP ratio was 1.3, and un-employment was almost 17 percent, with heavy emigration. Marginal tax rates were as high as 73 percent for persons on the average indus-trial wage. The Public Capital Programmes for 1983 and 1984 noted that Ireland's high ratio of investment to GNP, one of highest in the OECD, had not resulted in either output or employment growth.

9.6   New Economic Policy and Privatization

Emphasis in Irish macroeconomic policy changed in 1987 under the above influences away from the closed economy to a small, open econ-omy model with an emphasis on competitiveness within the EU and a wider global economy. State spending became seen not as an engine of economic growth but as a possible negative impact on national com-petitiveness. The new emphasis from the 1987 crisis on was expansion-ary fiscal contraction—a proposition that the more public expenditure contracted, the more the economy would expand (McAleese, 1990). The years since 1987 have seen reductions in personal and corporate taxation and rapid increases in economic growth and employment.

Table 9.1 indicates that commercial state enterprise played little part in the Celtic Tiger economy after 1987. Employment in commercial state enterprises declined in both absolute terms and as a proportion of total employment. FitzGerald (1961) noted two important character-istics of state enterprise: capital intensity and high wages. State compa-nies accounted for 30 percent of total gross fixed investment in 1960 and "earnings per head in this sector appear to be about 40% above the national average for employees" (2). By the late 1980s, these were seen as causes for concern, reflecting both inefficiency in the public capital program and regulatory capture.

The first state company, the Dairy Disposal Company, was also the first to be privatized. Founded in 1927 to rationalize the creamery sector with the aim of protecting farmers from ruin as creameries in both the private and cooperative sectors began to fail, the company was sold in 1974 to the infant Kerry Group for £1.15 million. The success of Kerry following its stock exchange flotation in 1986 indicated to the investment community that the company might be a model for future privatizations. The share price rose from 52 pence at launch to 200 pence in 1991. In October 2000 Kerry's market capitalization was £2.5 billion, making it the fourth largest company on the Irish Stock Exchange. It employed 14,000, and only a quarter of its turnover was generated in Ireland (Kennelly 2001).

In 1984 the government for the first time liquidated a state company. The Irish Shipping Company had assets of £23 million and liabilities of £117 million. The minister for communications estimated that the cost of keeping the company in operation for the period 1984–1989 would be £144.45 million, after which it would have a debt of £59 million. He told the parliament that "charter agreements were entered into on behalf of Irish Shipping without the knowledge or consent of the then Minister for Transport or the Minister for Finance and have led to the destruction of what was, up to then, a viable and successful state enterprise."

The liquidation of Irish Shipping was a signal to the state commercial sector that taxpayers could not be taken for granted in the future. The case illustrated the weaknesses in the ministerial, administrative, and parliamentary controls over the state commercial sector. The company engaged in unsuccessful speculation in international charter rates without referral to government ministers, the supervising department, or Parliament. Guiomard (1995) pointed out that "in the public sector, it is unheard of for senior managers of public companies, no matter how loss-making, to be called to account. None of the senior executives responsible for managing companies like Irish Steel, Aer Lingus or Team [the maintenance section of Aer Lingus] which went on to make huge losses, were even called before a Dail [parliament] Committee to explain themselves" (193). Weak financial controls became unacceptable in the new economic climate from 1987. The foundation of the Progressive Democrats in 1985 introduced privatization to the Irish political agenda. The large and immediate impact of airline deregulation in 1986 undermined the long-standing arguments in favor of protected state enterprises in aviation and in the view of the OECD "provided a clear demonstration of the potential benefits of competition to all consumers in Ireland, having a significant effect on public opinion" (29).

The wave of privatizations in the United Kingdom after 1979 evoked much interest in Ireland. In view of Ireland's problems with access by air under airline cartels, there was particular interest in the transformation of British Airways from a loss-making airline with 54,000 staff in the early 1980s to almost £200 million profits and 36,000 staff in the mid-1980s (Vickers and Yarrow 1989). The legal and financial experience in preparing British firms for privatization and the popularity of the policy in Britain also influenced Irish politicians.

A further milestone in the evolution of public opinion on the issue of privatization was the May 1989 conference at University College, Dublin, on the topic and the publication of the proceedings in 1990 (Convery and McDowell 1990). The Irish Economics Association was founded in 1986 at the Kenmare Conference on Economic Policy, and the privatization conference brought to privatization the focus of a more organized economics profession. Convery and McDowell emphasized the imminent single European market, the importance of property rights transfers caused by privatization, the resulting benefits of a market in corporate control and a bankruptcy constraint, and the problems of monitoring nationalized industries in Ireland.

In regard to the single European market, it was pointed out that there were massive market opportunities opening up for Ireland and that the emphasis should therefore switch from protecting state enterprises to improving competitiveness in order to avail itself of the new market opportunities. It was also pointed out that the Irish government could not continue to both own companies and regulate sectors in the interests of these companies as heretofore.

In regard to property rights, it was stated that shareholders in private companies held a negotiable asset. Through the market in shares, a market in corporate control is created, and company efficiency is monitored. By contrast, taxpayers are involuntary holders of equity in state companies and are powerless to influence the efficiency of these companies. Parliamentary control is weak, and the state companies have achieved regulatory capture over their supervising departments. State companies are therefore controlled by their management and staff and are not amenable to outside parliamentary, bureaucratic, or public scrutiny and control. Wolff (2003) describes privatization in Ireland as a series of transfers of property rights:

1. Transfer of control of enterprises from politicians, management, and trade unions to management

2. Transfer of profits from the state to shareholders

3. Transfer of liability from the state to shareholders

4. The sale of property rights from politicians and management to shareholders (tables 9.1 and 9.2).

The voluntary holding of equity in a privatized company with the consequent incentives to secure enhanced efficiency thus replaces the involuntary captive holding of equity in state companies with no incentives to secure enhanced efficiency. The allocation of benefits and liability to a decision maker is a prerequisite of efficient allocation of resources; in addition, privatization in Ireland saw political clientalism, rent seeking, and regulatory capture replaced by market forces.

9.7   Privatizations 1990–2003

Table 9.2 indicates the flow of privatization receipts to the exchequer over the years 1990 to 2003. The table indicates the exit of the state from food, telecommunications, shipping and fertilizer, oil refining, steel, and banking sectors.

The Irish Sugar Company sale was completed between 1991 and 1993. Sugar growing in Ireland was part of the policy of the independence movement from 1908. In 1926 the state began subsidizing the Lippens Company, a Belgian concern, at the rate of £400,000 a year for one sugar refinery. In 1933 the Irish Sugar Company was established when the state incorporated the Lippens operation. Three other refineries were established in order to develop alternative products and markets for farmers whose exports collapsed during the economic war with Britain. In the 1980s the Irish Sugar Company was in financial difficulty. Losses peaked at £50.7 million in 1982. During the 1980s, 1,800 jobs—half of the employment in the company—were shed. Twenty-three subsidiaries and two sugar refineries were closed or sold. Turnover declined from £384 million in 1980 to £199 million in 1987 when the company returned its first profits in the decade, £10.4 million. The holding company, Greencore, was formed in February 1991 and was

Table 9.2
Privatization receipts, 1990–2003 (millions of pounds Irish)

	Receipts	
1990		None
1991	63.0	Greencore
	270.4	Irish Life
1992	33.0	Greencore
	8.5	B and I Line
1993	69.9	Greencore
	104.5	Irish Life
1994		None
1995	99.2	Irish Life
	2.3	Interim Milk Board
1996	7.1	Interim Milk Board
1997		None
1998		None
1999	3,677.4	Telecom
2000	1,138.1	Telecom
2001	8.8	Telecom
	321.6	TSB Bank
	253.8	ICC Bank
2002	154.6	ACC Bank
	24.0	INPC oil refinery
2003		None

Sources: Finance accounts; annual budget statements.
Note: £1 Irish was designated as 1.27 on the establishment of the currency.

offered for sale in April at a market capitalization of £192.5 million. The purpose of the privatization was to ensure that "the development of Irish Sugar will no longer be constrained by the fact that it has a single ordinary shareholder which, for policy reasons, may not be in a position to provide funding in the future" (Greencore 1991, 7). The company was sold in three stages, as shown in table 9.2. Staff members were given 109 shares each, and staff and sugar beet suppliers were given preference in the purchase of shares. Nine new directors were appointed in 1991, and the size of the board was reduced from twelve to ten by the removal of the trade union representative and the worker directors. By 1996 market capitalization was £589 million and pretax profits increased from £21 million in 1990 to £54 million in 1996. In 2004 turnover was €797 million, profits were €109 million and there were 9,000 employees. Davy Research states that the group is redefining itself as a food manufacturer and not as an agriprocessor (2002). In 2004, through its acquisition of Hazlewood, it has become a leader in the sandwich sector in the United Kingdom.

The Irish Life Assurance Company was offered for sale in 1991, 1993, and 1995. In the offer document, it was stated that "the Minister has decided to reduce his shareholdings in order to realise part of his investment and to facilitate the future development of the Group and its products" (Irish Life 1991, 4). Of the five members of the executive board in 1991, one remained in 1995.

In 1992 the Irish Continental Group bought the B and I Line shipping company from the government. The B and I Line had accumulated losses of £128.5 million and a capital deficiency of £26.5 million. The fleet in 1989 had only two ships. Between 1985 and 1989, turnover fell by 45 percent in real terms, and staff numbers fell by half to 897. No director of the B and I Company was retained when Irish Continental bought the company in 1992. In 1990 the profits of Irish Continental Group were £2.3 million and the losses at B and I Line were £3.4 million. The Irish Continental Group was acquired from the liquidator of the Irish Shipping Company by a number of institutional investors in 1987 and in 1987–1988 had profits of £0.869 million on a turnover of £34.1 million. The profits of the amalgamated group of two former state shipping companies, now known as Irish Ferries, in 1995 were £11.0 million and were in 2002 26.4 million euros on sales of 272 million euros.

The largest privatization in table 9.2 is the Telecom sale. The privatization and deregulation of the sector has changed it from a high-cost system with political lobbying for phones to a competitive system. The Culleton Report (1992) noted that "telecom revenue in Ireland—at 2.7% of GDP—was by far the highest of any EC country in 1989, with most other Member States having revenue in the range of 1.3 to 1.8% of GDP. International charges are higher than in competitor countries and this will not alter with the proposed 1992 tariff rebalancing which Telecom has announced" (47). The OECD (2001) wrote that while "Ireland had relatively high international collection charges which were above the OECD average in the past," reductions through indirect competition and a government decision to end an earlier derogation from EU liberalization in 1998 resulted in the OECD finding in August 2000 that "Ireland's international charges are less than half of the OECD average both for business and residential calls in USD/PPP" (83). Ireland thus improved from above-average charges to half of the OECD average. The Comreg index of telecoms prices in Ireland (2002) indicates a fall from an index of 100 in November 1996, to 95 in January 1998, to 75 in January 2002.

As investor confidence in the telecoms sector declined, share prices of all telecoms companies fell, including Eircom's, although the fall in Eircom's share price was in fact less than the industry average. However, the company did not tackle its long-standing productivity problems, and investors lost an estimated 30 percent on the flotation price. The company was taken over and removed from the stock exchange by Valentia, a U.S. venture capital group, in November 2001. Thus, the shareholders exited, and the mobile phone business was sold to Videophone. The company lost 104 million euros in 2001–2002 compared with a profit of 104 million euros in the previous year. Sales declined from 2.2 billion euros to 1.8 billion in 2001–2002, and the company's share of the voice market declined to 38 percent. Mobile phones had 52 percent market share and other fixed-line operators the remaining 10 percent. The company returned to the stock exchange in March 2004 with strong institutional investor interest. The operating profit in the year to March 2005 was €246 million on turnover of €1.6 billion.

The three remaining privatizations in table 9.2 were trade sales. The state sold its oil refinery to Tosco. The state banks were sold to Bank of Scotland in the case of the Industrial Credit Corporation, Rabobank in the case of the Agricultural Credit Corporation, and Irish Permanent Building Society in the case of TSB Bank. Dublin had become a major financial services center by the 1990s. The factors that influenced the establishment of state banks to serve industry and agriculture were not perceived to be significant almost eighty years later.

9.8   Privatization: The Irish Template

The change in ownership in Irish privatizations has transferred control of the companies from their managers and staff to the new owners. Ownership of state companies by taxpayers was a theoretical rather than negotiable property right. Taxpayers have gained relatively small receipts from privatization receipts but support transfer to the private sector in order to improve efficiency. Market forces operate in the case of all the companies privatized, as shown in table 9.2.

The sectors privatized and shown in table 9.2 operate in contestable markets. The state comes under less pressure to intervene to weaken competitive forces when it no longer owns one or more of the companies in the market, and overall efficiency is improved. The state has not privatized public monopolies such as electricity, gas, railways, and water. Regulatory bodies to deal with public sector monopolies are relatively new in Ireland. Previously, public monopolies were subject to ministerial order to control prices and provide services. Given these ministerial powers, further independent regulation of the company was not regarded as important until recently. Since 1999, however, regulatory bodies have been established in such sectors as energy, telecoms, airports, and health insurance, but only in the telecoms sector has there been privatization. In contrast with companies trading in contested markets, there has been a political unwillingness to privatize what might be called strategic network activities, such as electricity networks, gas pipelines, water, and seaports. This policy was expressed by the minister for communications and natural resources in an address to the Oireachtas (parliament) committee supervising his department in March 2004. The minister stated that "infrastructure such as wires and pipes are critical national assets and should remain in Statre ownership." The minister also stated that privatization of the ESB's generating business was unlikely in the short or medium term: "I am opposed to any privatisation which would result in a private monopoly in the power generation sector." The minister admitted that the separation of the distribution grid from the ESB had not been accomplished but admitted that returning the grid to the ESB would "send a negative signal to the market." (Oireachtas Joint Committee Minutes, March 10, 2004.)

The perceived problems in Britain in privatization of railways, water, and electricity have probably influenced Irish politicians away from areas that generated controversy in Britain.

There are no formal performance measures for Irish privatized enterprises, but in general, the lower prices from airline deregulation and the limited bus competition would be seen as price reducing. The Megginson and Netter (2001) finding, based on some 227 studies of privatization throughout the world, that "privately owned firms are more efficient and more profitable than otherwise-comparable state-owned firms" (380), corresponds to the Irish experience also.

Ownership is important in the Irish privatization studies. State ownership was associated in the public mind with heavy subsidization, requests for free capital, poor service, and regulatory capture. The special feature of the Irish case has been the replacement of Irish nationalism and protectionism by support for the EU single market and global free trade.

The perception about privatization in Ireland is pragmatic, with a high degree of support for lower air fares since deregulation in 1986.

Public sector trade unions are hostile to privatization in sectors such as airports, public transport, and waste collection.

The ability of policymakers to ban or restrict new entrants from a sector appears since the High Court deregulation of taxis in 2000 to be in doubt. The taxi deregulation decision was based on the rights of persons to enter a sector for which they had the training and skills and the rights of the public to the services of such persons. The judgment also referred to EU law on competition. Since the majority of the insiders in the Irish taxi market were Irish citizens, the protectionist policy invited challenge because of the virtual exclusion of other EU citizens from the Irish taxi sector (Murphy 2000). The Competition Authority (2001) ponders the extension of taxi deregulation by the courts to the bus sector: "In the light of a recent High Court decision, it may actually be questionable whether quantitative restrictions on licensing such as those provided for by the practice of the Minister under the 1932 Act are constitutional or compatible with EC Treaty Rules" (6).

The receipts from privatization in 2001 were equal to 2.6 percent of that year's government expenditure. Fears that governments would "sell the family silver" for short-term gains have not been realized. Receipts in the early 1990s were used to retire national debt, while the later receipts were used to fund future state pension liabilities through a designated fund.

The lessons for other countries from Irish privatizations, deregulations, and a general movement to free trade and away from protectionism are positive. In particular, Ireland may offer a role model for the new, smaller economies about to join the EU. The market opportunities created by the EU and global moves toward freer trade have transformed the Irish economy.

The changes in regulation in Ireland, in addition to greater market forces, include the establishment of regulators for the energy, telecom, broadcasting, airport, and health insurance sectors. Two privatized companies failed under both public and private ownership: Irish Steel closed in 2001 and Irish Fertiliser in 2002. There were no adverse impacts in the product markets for either steel or fertilizer.

9.9   The Future of Privatization

Table 9.3 shows the exchequer shareholding in state-sponsored bodies at the end of 2001. The list is a useful starting point for assessing likely candidates for future privatizations.

Table 9.3
Exchequer share capital in state-sponsored bodies, 2001

Body	Sector	Shareholding (£ million)
Aer Rianta	Airports	146.7
Aer Lingus	Airline	239.8
An Post	Post	44.4
BNM	Peat	61.9
Coillte	Forestry	626.2
IAA	Air traffic control	17.9
National Stud	Horse breeding	9.8
Shannon Development	Regional body	144.4
Seaports		
Dublin		5.9
Drogheda		5.6
DunLaoghaire		11.5
Galway		6.9
Cork		13.3
Waterford		8.4
NewRoss		3.7
Shannon-Foynes		3.0

Source: Finance Accounts, 2002.
Note: £1 = 1.27 euros.

Aer Rianta is the state airport company at Dublin, Cork, and Shannon, with a 98 percent market share of passenger traffic in the Republic of Ireland. It was widely seen as a candidate for privatization in the 1990s with an estimated flotation value of £700 million (Business and Finance 1998). The establishment of the Commission for Aviation Regulation has brought to the company a stricter regulatory regime than the previous supervision by the government department. The company has appealed to the Supreme Court against the High Court judicial review verdict in its dispute with the regulator's controls over its prices and investment plans. Regulation in the interest of efficiency has replaced privatization as the policy priority in the sector. The government in May 2005 rejected proposals for competing independent terminals at Dublin. The decision to have separate boards for three competing airports was opposed by both management and trade unions. In addition Aer Rianta has stakes at the Birmingham, Hamburg, and Düsseldorf airports and operates duty-free shops in Europe, North America, and the Middle East.

Aer Rianta owns the Great Southern Hotel group of nine hotels. In 2001 the hotel group had profits of 4.7 million euros on revenues of 42.5 million euros and 738 employees. The airport group wishes to sell the hotels, but the trade unions have successfully opposed the sale. In September 2004 the government announced the break-up of Aer Rianta and separate airport authorities at Dublin, Cork and Shannon.

Aer Lingus restructured following difficulties in 2001. Reducing employment from 6,000 to 4,000 while increasing passenger numbers above 6 million, accompanied by board and management changes, have turned the airline's European operations into a low-cost carrier. A free trade agreement in aviation between the EU and the United States would allow the company to expand its North Atlantic operations. The 2000 estimate of the value of the airline was 950 million euros. The operating margin of Aer Lingus in 2004 was 11.8 percent. In May 2005 the government announced its decision to privatize the airline.

An Post is in financial difficulties. The An Post board was charged in 2001 with bringing in a strategic partner to take up to 35 percent of the equity, but this now appears unlikely. BNM already has commercialization experience in fuel and horticulture and has a large land bank, as has Coillte. Air traffic control has a strong cash flow from overflights due to Ireland's strategic location as well as the Irish traffic. The National Stud is an inheritance from cavalry training for the British army and has income from horse breeding and tourism. Seaports have been a highly successful privatization in Britain. The port of Larne, in Northern Ireland, is privately owned. Widely regarded as the most efficient port on the island, it draws traffic from large areas of the Republic.

Privatizations in public transport depend on the level of subsidy for socially desirable services since Irish Rail, Irish Bus, and Dublin Bus are all subsidized. The contract to operate the Dublin light rail service has been awarded to Connex, a French company. The lengthy Nestor Bus case, concerning a private bus operator, in the High Court in 2001 resulted in the award of extra licenses to Nestor, and the state paid all costs. There is likely to be more private participation in the bus sector such as Nestor and Citylink on the Dublin-Galway route and Aircoach between Dublin city and Cork and Belfast and between Dublin suburbs and the airport.

In the energy sector, in addition to BNM, the state owns the Electricity Supply Board and the Irish Gas Board. The electricity board dominates the market with revenues of 2 billion euros and profits of 314 million euros in 2001. The market was liberalized in February 2005, two years ahead of the EU deadline of 2007. The sector is regulated by the Commission for Energy Regulation, established in 1999 for electricity and extended to cover gas in 2002. The results to date have been disappointing. The National Competitiveness Council (2003) found that in 2002, industrial electricity prices per 10 GWh at 7.42 euros in Ireland were the second highest of eight countries surveyed. Italy was the most expensive at 9.53 euros and Sweden the cheapest at 2.83 euros. The council stated that "an important issue here is the level of cross-subsidisation of domestic users by industry. Unfortunately, there is insufficient data to properly analyse the situation and so further study is merited to clarify this issue" (p. 14). Given the weakness of deregulation to date, it may be necessary to split the company's generation and distribution sections into independent companies and to split its generating stations into several competing groups in order to achieve competitive efficiency. The council noted in its 2005 report that "the price of electricity is around 51 percent higher in Ireland than in the UK" (p. 45).

The state-owned Voluntary Health Insurance Company has enrolled almost 40 percent of the population and is seven times larger than its only competitor, BUPA. Under risk equalization rules, BUPA will be required to compensate VHI for taking a younger age profile of customers. BUPA believes that its lower premiums are due to a genuine lower cost base and has referred the risk equalization scheme to the European Court. The regulatory body for the sector, the Health Insurance Agency, established in 2001, recommended in March 2005 that the risk equalization scheme should be activated because the estimated risk difference between the two companies exceeded 10 percent. The Minister for Health declined the recommendation in order to promote competition.

The state television and radio company, RTE, has about a 50 percent market share in each case. Independent radio stations, licensed since 1989, have taken more than half the listenership, while the main competition for RTE television is from U.K. channels. There is also a considerable privatization of activities rather than organizations such as the school bus service, railhead deliveries from rail stations, privatized rubbish collection, and vehicle testing, urban car parking control, clamping, and removal.

9.10 Conclusion

Irish commercial public enterprise has declined rapidly as a proportion of total employment. This is due to the rapid rise in market sector

Table 9.4
A transformed economy: Ireland in 1986 and 2000

	1986	2000	Index (1986 = 100)
Employment (million)	1.1	1.7	155
Unemployment rate (%)	17.4	4.7	27
GNP per head/EU average (%)	60	100	167[a]
Government spending/GDP (%)	52.7	33.3	63
Corporate tax rate (%)	50	12.5	25
Personal income tax rates (%)	35–60	22–44	63–73
Tourist numbers (million)	2	6	300
Public debt/GDP (%)	131	33	25
Exports/GDP (%)	56	80	143

Sources: Department of Finance Annual Review and Outlook, Annual Budget Statements, Revenue Commissioners Annual Reports. Economic and Social Research Institute, Medium Term Review, 2003–2010.
[a] GDP per head in Ireland exceeded GNP per head by 24 percent in 2004 due to large net factor payments.

employment and a decline in commercial state employment due to a combination of privatizations and employment reductions in the remaining enterprises. The success of the Irish economy since 1987 has been based on reducing the government share of GDP from 53 to 33 percent, reducing personal and corporate taxation, promoting inward investment especially from the United States, and having the highest ratio of foreign trade to GDP in the EU after Luxembourg. In 2001, unemployment was 3.7 percent, down from 18 percent in the 1980s and a little over a third of the core euro countries of Germany, France, and Italy. The increase in employment by 64 percent from 1.1 million in 1987 to 1.8 million in 2003 is the largest percentage increase of any OECD member state. Table 9.4 contrasts the changed economic policy in Ireland in 2000 compared to the 1980s. The economy as a whole was privatized, liberalized, and opened to foreign markets. State commercial enterprises were no longer seen as major drivers of economic growth.

Nationalized commercial enterprises were at the core of Irish economic nationalism and have faded as Ireland became part of the single European market and world free trade. The Irish state enterprise model by contrast was based on economic nationalism, reinforced in the aftermath of the 1929 depression, universal protectionism in the 1930s, and difficult trading conditions for a neutral state in World War II. In past and present periods of free trade, the Irish economy has achieved its best performances. Geary and Stark (2002) estimate that

Ireland's economic performance was good enough to locate the economy among the richest in the world in the 1870s and on the eve of the Great War. Cullen (1972) pointed out that by the end of the nineteenth century, "its large foreign trade, its export-oriented industries, its highly developed infrastructure of banking, commerce and railways, and its foreign investment yielding a sizeable income made Ireland comparable in some respects to a handful of highly developed nations" (p. 170). The basic tenet of Irish economic nationalism—that state enterprises were required because market forces had failed, or would in the future fail, to develop the Irish economy—was historically inaccurate. Since participating in the single European market, Ireland has again enjoyed success in free trade and returned to the relative economic position it occupied in the world ninety years ago. The assumption that Ireland would fail in the market economy had no foundation in the past or in the 1990s. It is no surprise that the return of state enterprises to the market economy has happened without controversy in a wider context of deregulation, reducing the economic role of the state and globalization.

References

Chubb, B. 1970. *The Government and Politics of Ireland*. London: Longmans.

Commission for Energy Regulation. 2004. *Customer Information*. March.

Competition Authority. 2001. *Report on the Bus and Rail Passenger Sector*. Dublin.

Comreg. 2002. *Quarterly Review of Telecoms Prices in Ireland*. December 31.

Convery, F., and McDowell, M. 1990. *Privatisation*. Dublin: Gill and Macmillan.

Cullen, L. M. 1972. *An Economic History of Ireland since 1660*. Dublin: Gill and Macmillan.

Culleton Report. 1992. *Report of the Industrial Policy Review Group*. Dublin.

Daly, M. E. 1981. *Social and Economic History of Ireland since 1800*. Dublin: Gill and Macmillan.

Daly, M. E. 1992. *Industrial Development and Irish National Identity 1922–1939*. Dublin: Gill and Macmillan.

Davy Equity Research. 1991–2003. *Reports on Irish Life: Greencore, Kerry Group, and Irish Continental Group*.

Fanning, R. 1985. "Economists and Governments." In A. E. Murphy, ed., *Economists and the Irish Economy*. Dublin: Irish Academic Press.

FitzGerald, G. 1961. *State Sponsored Bodies*. Dublin: Institute of Public Administration.

Foy, M. 1976. *The Sugar Industry in Ireland*. Dublin: Irish Sugar Company.

Geary, F., and Stark, T. 2002. "Ireland's Post-Famine Economic Growth." *Economic Journal*, October, 919–935.

Greencore, PLC. 1991. *Offer for Sale*.

Guiomard, C. 1995. *The Irish Disease*. Dublin: Oaktree.

Irish Life PLC. 1991. *Offer for Sale*.

Jakobsen, E. 1984. *Report of the Enquiry into Electricity Prices*. Dublin.

Kennedy, D. 1988. "Aer Lingus." In R. Nelson and D. Clutterbuck, eds., *Turnaround: How Twenty Well-Known Companies Came Back from the Brink*. London: Mercury Books.

Kennelly, J. 2001. *The Kerry Way*. Dublin: Oak Tree.

Keogh, D. 1994. *Twentieth Century Ireland: Nation and State*. Dublin: Gill and Macmillan.

Lee, J. J. 1989. *Ireland, 1912–1985*. Cambridge: Cambridge University Press.

McAleese, D. 1990. "Ireland's Economic Recovery." *Irish Banking Review*, Summer, 18–32.

Megginson, W., and Netter, J. 2001. "From State to Market: A Survey of Empirical Studies on Privatisation." *Journal of Economic Literature* 39, 321–389.

Murphy, J. 2000. *Humphrey and others v The Minister for the Environment and Local Government, Ireland, the Attorney General and Others*. Dublin: High Court.

National Competitiveness Council. 2003. *Annual Competitiveness Reports 2002 and 2005*.

National Prices Commission. 1972. "CIE Rates and Fares." Occasional paper 4.

OECD. 2001. *Regulatory Reform in Ireland*. Paris: OECD.

Oireachtas Joint Committee on Communications, Marine, and Natural Resources. 2004. Minutes of meeting, March 10.

O'Maitiu, S. 2001. *W and R Jacob*. Dublin: Woodfield.

PDDE. 1928. *Parliamentary Debates Dail Eireann* (Parliament of Ireland). vol. 25, 233; 1965, vol. 214, 974.

Share, B. 1988. *The Flight of the Iolar: The Aer Lingus Experience, 1936–1986*. Dublin: Gill and Macmillan.

Vickers, J. 1997. "Privatisation, Regulation and Competition: Some Implications for Ireland." In A. Grey, ed., *International Perspectives on the Irish Economy*. Dublin: Indecon.

Vickers, J., and Yarrow, G. 1988. *Privatization: An Economic Analysis*. Cambridge, Mass.: MIT Press.

Wolff, B. 2003. "Privatisation in Ireland—A Comment." CES/ifo Seminar. Munich, January.

10

Pragmatic Privatization: The Netherlands, 1982–2002

Eric van Damme

In its May 2002 survey of the Dutch economy, under the heading "The Rule of Common Sense," the Economist wrote: "In the spirit of their pragmatic traditions, the Dutch have understood and accepted two things that many other Europeans find doctrinally objectionable. One is that it does not matter who delivers public services, so long as the job is well done; the other is that competition, in some form, can help to make that more likely."

When confronted with the question about how to divide responsibilities between the state and the private sector in reaching public policy goals, the Dutch indeed have always taken, and still take, a pragmatic attitude. The most recent (December 2003) parliamentary discussion on state participations provides a nice illustration: after the representatives of the major political parties had stated their overall party positions, the responsible minister, Gerrit Zalm, responded: "I like the fact that one can have such nice ideological discussions about this topic, however, we have to try to bring these back to practical proportions" (Kamerstukken 2003–2004a, 10).

The Dutch pragmatic attitude may be explained by the fact that in the Netherlands, it has always been necessary to form coalition governments. Pragmatic policy, of course, runs the danger of being ad hoc. Although the Dutch have run into this trap to some extent, Dutch pragmatism has been disciplined by the view, held by the majority (the Christian Democrats and the Liberals), that the primary role of the state is to help citizens and firms go about their own business; the state should intervene only when there is market failure, and in these cases, private interests should be mobilized for the public cause as much as possible. Traditionally, religious groups have had their own social organizations and institutions; they want to maintain their identity and independence and prefer to keep government interference low. Of course, they also seek political power to get the state to cofinance their activities. Being aware of this political reality, in the 1930s, the Labour party, under the influence of Jan Tinbergen, explicitly expressed a preference for planning economic activities above nationalization of industries. As a consequence, there is relatively little involvement of the state in the supply side of the economy, and there is a preference to reach public policy goals by using instruments such as subsidization, contracting, or regulation. The Dutch state is small in terms of the activities it performs, but large in terms of the financial claims it lays on society. The state acts more as a financier than as a producer.

The Dutch preference for private provision of public services, subject to government regulation and subsidization, can probably best be illustrated by the important case of education. In the Netherlands, only about 30 percent of all pupils attend public schools, and 70 percent of the schools are privately owned. Parents are free to decide to which school to send their children and schools are paid on the basis of the number of pupils that they have; hence, there is competition among schools. The system resulted from religious groups' arguing that they should not be forced to pay for their own private schools and subsidize public ones. They insisted on equal treatment of public and private schools, which they achieved in 1920. Article 23 of the Dutch Constitution states: "Education shall be the constant concern of the Government. All persons shall be free to provide education, without prejudice to the authorities' right of supervision.... Private primary schools that satisfy the conditions laid down by Act of Parliament shall be financed from public funds according to the same standards as public authority schools."

The principle expressed here has also been applied in relation to other public services, such as health care, welfare work, housing, and the media. The first question to be addressed always is: Is there a need for the government to step in, or can groups in society take care of the problem? Given the political preferences stated above, the answer will frequently be no. Second, even if there is a public interest, hence, a need for the state to intervene, whether there is room for the private sector will be investigated. As a result, although the share of government expenditures in GDP is large (government expenditures being 46.4 percent in 2001), the public sector is not large in terms of employment or output, with several core public goods being provided by private parties, usually nonprofits. For example, 75 percent of the hospitals are private nonprofits, and of the stock of social housing, only 1.5 percent is rented out by government agencies. As a consequence, the Dutch economy has a large nonprofit sector (about 13 percent of all nonagricultural jobs and 10 percent of GDP), which is financed to a large extent (59 percent) by the state, and provides service on a competitive basis (SCP 2001).

This policy principle has important consequences for terminology. If one defines *privatization* as transferring ownership of assets from the state to the private sector, the Netherlands has seen relatively little of it, since very few government assets could be privatized. In fact, although asset sales have taken place, this was not labeled privatization since just transferring ownership is believed not to affect the outcome: government firms are assumed to be operating as ordinary profit-maximizing enterprises. In line with the above principle, in the Netherlands, *privatization* is defined more broadly as "making more use of private actors and the market mechanism to achieve public goals" (Boorsma 1984, WRR 2000). Defined in this way, privatization naturally links up with attempts to introduce more competition in the provision of public services, and as such it was a hot topic of general and political discussion during the last two decades in the twentieth century, under the governments of Ruud Lubbers (1982–1994) and Wim Kok (1994–2002). In this chapter, I will describe and discuss the Dutch experiences during this period.

In 1982, when the first Lubbers cabinet came into office as a result of the oil crises and "Dutch disease," the Dutch welfare state had gotten out of hand: more than 70 percent of income was spent collectively, the government budget deficit was 11 percent of GDP, and unemployment kept increasing. To get the economy back on track, this "no-nonsense" coalition of Christian Democrats and Liberals adopted the motto, "More market less government," and it outlined five "large operations," including privatization and deregulation programs, with the aim of reducing government expenditures, to make the public sector smaller and more flexible and create more room for private initiative, thereby fostering economic growth. The second Lubbers cabinet (1986–1989) intensified this course; in its 1986 government declaration, it boldly stated, "All services that do not necessarily have to be performed by the government are candidates for privatization." Around that time, the finance minister, Onno Ruding, formulated frameworks for deciding which services should preferably be performed by the state and, with minor modifications, these continue to guide policy. In section 10.1, I discuss these principles, how they were applied, and what the results have been.

In 1989, Lubbers's Christian Democratic party formed a coalition government with Labor, and privatization became less prominent, with the interdepartmental committee on privatization being abolished in 1992. In 1994, after a national debate on the challenges the Dutch economy faced in a globalizing world, it was concluded that large-scale deregulation of the economy was necessary, and the first purple cabinet (a coalition of Labor with two liberal parties), headed by Wim Kok, revived the liberalization and deregulation programs. Rather than focusing on privatization, the microeconomic policies of this government stressed regulatory reform; *marktwerking* (making use of market forces) became a key term in policy discussions. What was lacking, however, was a clear view of what benefits competition could achieve and what government actions were needed to achieve more intense competition. At least initially, policy seemed to be based on the naive ideas that competition would automatically take care of all the public interests at stake and that government policy could be limited to opening up and fully deregulating markets (Van Damme 2001). While this policy worked reasonably well for the "easy" projects handled under Kok I (1994–1998), when the focus was mainly on increasing competition in the business sector, it became more problematic during Kok II (1998–2002), when the emphasis shifted to making use of market forces within the public sector and to the liberalization of network industries. Around 1999, when it was clear that the results were not always satisfactory, high advisory councils started to criticize the government for not having formulated a consistent vision about how to proceed and for not having been thoughtful enough in the liberalization, deregulation, and privatization processes. In response, the government formulated principles to guide policymaking on liberalization and privatization of network industries. These are discussed in section 10.2.

In sections 10.3 to 10.5, I illustrate these principles by describing the developments and experiences in specific network sectors: post and telecommunications, electricity and gas, and public transport. We will see that although policy documents consistently advocated privatizing when possible, practice proved more stubborn, and restructuring frequently involved both nationalization and privatization. The 1990s can best be described as a period of muddling through, with privatization and deregulation not always being successful and the public becoming increasingly skeptical about their benefits. The experiences have, however, led to the debate about proper institutional arrangements in network industries to be more informed about what the practical constraints are, what is feasible, and more realistic expectations. There is now a better sense of the risks involved in privatization and policy now proceeds in a more cautious, pragmatic way. As a result, the words *privatization* and *use of market forces* now no longer seem to have the same negative connotation as they had around the year 2002.

10.1 Privatization

When the first Lubbers government came into office in 1982, it announced large-scale programs of privatization and deregulation, aimed at pushing back the role of the state.[1] As the involvement of the state in the production of market goods was already limited (in the 1970s, government-controlled enterprises were responsible for only 3.6 percent of GDP, compared to about 10 percent in France, Germany, and the United Kingdom; see Short 1984), the focus of the privatization program was on the reorganization of government. The aim was threefold: to achieve budgetary savings and improve public finances, reduce the size of the public sector and increase its efficiency, and strengthen the private sector. It is important to note that selling shares in state-owned enterprises (SOEs) was formally not part of the privatization program, but fell under a different policy line—that on state participations (see Kamerstukken 1985–1986). The motivation was that since SOEs were already operating in competitive markets, they were disciplined by market forces, so that a change in ownership would not lead to changes in behavior or efficiency. As such asset sales fall under the international definition of *privatization*, we will also consider them here. First, however, we discuss those projects that fell under the formal Dutch program.

10.1.1 *Privatization* à la Hollandaise

The 1983 implementation plan of the Ministry of Finance (Kamerstukken 1982–1983) adopted a broad definition of privatization and distinguished between outsourcing of government services, corporatization (a government unit is put at arm's length and becomes a separate legal entity, so that it can operate in a more businesslike fashion, less burdened by bureaucratic control), and real privatization (transfer of asset ownership to private parties).[2] The plan expressed a preference for contracting out and real privatization, and viewed corporatization as being second best, since this involved the government's giving up control rights without a corresponding reduction in financial risks. While corporatization was viewed as a first step toward "real privatization," it would turn out that most "privatizations" would not make it beyond this step, with all the associated consequences.

The 1983 implementation plan already contained a list of fourteen candidates for privatization, and when a first evaluation was made in 1988, eight projects (of which five were real privatizations) were finished, while forty projects (of which eleven were real privatisations) were scheduled to be finished before the end of the Lubbers II cabinet period in 1990 (see Kamerstukken 1987–1988). In total, slightly fewer than 120,000 employees were involved in these operations, but almost all of them (115,000) were in corporatization projects. Indeed the largest projects involved nothing more than transforming state enterprises (state firms that fall under public law) into SOEs—firms that fall under private law but are wholly owned by the state. Two of these, PTT in 1989 and Postbank in 1986, were responsible for 85 percent of the jobs involved. Both incorporation activities were a first step toward real privatization, which would occur in the 1990s. One other smaller state enterprise, the State Port Authority of IJmuiden, followed a similar track; the other two state enterprises were corporatized (the State Printing Office in 1988, the State Mint in 1994), but they are still 100 percent government owned.

The smaller projects on the 1988 list form a mixed bag, including agencies with certification or standardization tasks or occupying monopoly positions. The organization supplying pilotage services, which are very important for bringing large ships safely into the harbor of Rotterdam, had been privatized in 1983, without accompanying price regulation. The government soon suffered the consequences. The pilots were well aware of their bargaining power, and they quickly seized the opportunity to demand higher salaries; before privatization, the service was making a surplus of some 10 million euros a year; after privatization, the government had to pay a similar amount on a yearly basis. This privatization was heavily criticized by the Court of Auditors (Algemene Rekenkamer 1989). The important distinction between privatization in a competitive market context and privatization in a monopoly environment would be made only later, during the Lubbers

II cabinet, when it was argued that monopolies could not be privatized. It seems that the possibility of using regulation to discipline private monopolies was considered only around 1995.[3]

Although the official privatization program was stopped around 1990, after the Labor party had entered the government, with the interdepartmental committee on privatization being abolished in 1992, the process of giving more autonomy to government organizations has continued. The government report *Verantwoord Verzelfstandigen* (Kamerstukken 1994–1995a) contains recommendations about when and how government agencies could be "hived off" (given a certain form of independence) and what legal form would be most appropriate, but that report is noneconomic in nature and does not take into account the warnings issued at the start of the privatization program. In many of these cases of "privatization *à la Hollandaise*," the second step of "real" privatization did not follow: the process remained stuck halfway, after having created organizations, quangos, that frequently face neither market discipline nor effective administrative control. Not surprisingly, these organizations did not always function efficiently or in the public interest, although evidence of that would frequently become available only much later. All this may explain why "privatization" was not always successful and has gotten a bad name. The netherworld of "quangoland" is not very transparent, but thanks to the efforts of the Netherlands Court of Audit, the situation has improved a great deal (see the reports on "independent organisations with public tasks," most recently Kamerstukken 2003–2004b). In June 2004, the *Financieel Dagblad* reported that a government committee had concluded that it would be better to bring all quangos back within the government (Financieel Dagblad 2004).

10.1.2　Real Privatization

In international comparison, asset sales in the Netherlands have not been negligible. As far as the population is concerned, the Netherlands is about one-fifth the size of Germany and one-fourth of the size of France, Italy, and the United Kingdom, and Dutch GDP is 1.7 percent of the OECD total. Over the period 1990–2001, privatization proceeds in the Netherlands were $14.5 billion, which is 58 percent of the proceeds in Germany over the same period, 19 percent of those in France, 13 percent of those in Italy, 34 percent of those of the United Kingdom, and 2.2 percent of those in the OECD member countries. In 1994, 1995, and 2001, the Dutch share was above average: respectively, 6.7 percent and 7.3 percent, and 4 percent of those in the OECD (OECD 2002).

It is worthwhile to briefly describe the major privatizations since 1982. Before 1989, the state had sold part of its shares in KLM and Hoogovens (a steelmaker now part of Corus) and divested some smaller companies, but with less than 250 million euros, proceeds were limited. Revenues were considerably higher in 1989, when the state reduced its stake in DSM (Dutch State Mines) to 31 percent by selling shares to the public for 1.3 billion euros. In 1996, the remaining shares were sold for slightly less than 0.8 billion euros. In 1990 Postbank was sold to ING Bank for 0.6 billion euros in cash and a stake in ING, a stake that was successively reduced to zero by selling shares on the market in 1993, 1997, and 2002, total revenue being something like 0.75 billion euros of which 80 percent was received in 1993. PTT was privatized in 1994, with the initial public offering (IPO) yielding 3 billion euros. One year later, a second batch of shares was sold with revenue in the same order of magnitude. In 1998, the company was split in a telecommunications company, KPN, and a postal company, TPG, which are both listed on the stock market. In 2001, the state reduced its stake in TPG to 35 percent (revenue 0.9 billion euros) and, in October 2002, it reduced its share in KPN from 31.3 to 19.3 percent. By means of a share sale in 1997 that yielded 0.75 billion euros, the stake in KLM was reduced from 38 to 14 percent, and in 2004 KLM merged with Air France. Worth mentioning also are, in 1998, the partial sale of the government computer center, now PinkRoccade, yielding 0.4 billion euros, and the partial sale in NIB Capital Bank in 1999, yielding almost 1 billion euros.

In the Netherlands, asset sales fall under the policy with respect to state participations, which that can be summarized by "privatize when possible and financially sensible." This line was formulated first in the 1985 report "Selling State Participations" (Kamerstukken 1985–1986), prepared under the responsibility of the minister of finance, Onno Ruding, and was strongly influenced by the bad experience with active industrial policy in the Dutch shipbuilding industry during the 1960s and 1970s.[4] Accordingly, this 1985 report takes as its starting point that state participation in a business firm requires special justification, and it proposes that the state portfolio be regularly evaluated. For each participation, the following questions should be addressed: Why was the participation taken? Has the aim been achieved? Are the original reasons still valid? Is participation still the best instrument to reach the goals? The report proposes that if the goals can also be achieved by divesting the participation, such divestiture should be seriously considered and should be implemented when market conditions allow it. Only two specific instances are described where divestiture might not be a good idea: when the firm has a monopoly position, or when the state is (by far) the largest buyer of the firm. In short, the 1985 memo states that state participation should be divested unless there are decisive reasons for not doing so.

When the policy framework was revisited in 1997 (Kamerstukken 1996–1997c), it was concluded that the general principles formulated in 1985 still formed an excellent basis for future policy. In fact, the 1997 memo argues that the two exceptions to privatization explicitly discussed in 1985 are no longer relevant. It states that monopolies, such as KPN, can be privatized: monopoly power can be countered by stimulating entry, or, in the case of insurmountable entry barriers, regulating the firm. In case the state is the sole buyer, such as with the Royal State Mint, the relation with the firm can be a purely contractual one, and privatization is possible as well. Interestingly, when, in the parliamentary discussion, various MPs asked about the consistency of this policy with that on privatization more generally, and that with respect to hiving off (corporatization) in particular, the answer was that these were two different policy domains and that different rules might apply. It was the Ministry of Economic Affairs that was responsible for that other policy, and at the time the Ministry of Finance was advocating "unconditional" privatization, that ministry seemed to move in the direction of "liberalize first, then privatize."

Policy with respect to state participation was most recently revisited in a memo from 2001 (Kamerstukken 2001–2002a), which was discussed in parliament in December 2003 (Kamerstukken 2003–2004a). That memo proposes to make a clear distinction between the state as shareholder and the state as guardian of the public interest, with the Ministry of Finance responsible for the first role, and a second-line ministry for the second. The memo, written under the responsibility of the Ministry of Finance, focuses mainly on the shareholder role of the state, and in this domain, there are few things to which one can object, although one can question the remark of the minister of finance that participation should yield the state a return on investment of some 3 percent above that on government bonds (Zalm 2003). The memo argues that the policies with respect to state participation, corporatization, and the liberalization of network industries are consistent with each other, and it succinctly summarizes the overall policy line. The cabinet continues its course: state participations are temporary and "participations are divested if this is possible taking into account the public interests and the business interests of the state" (Kamerstukken 2001–2002a, 17).

What is new, compared to the earlier memos from 1985 and 1997, is the explicit reference to the public interest. The explanation why the term appears is that around 1999, two high advisory councils had criticized the government for not having taken the public interest sufficiently into account in its privatization policies. What is not new is the preference for guarding the public interest by means of regulations and contracts rather than by government ownership. This immediately raises a question: Why doesn't the government show more faith in public enterprises and in ownership as an instrument to safeguard the public interest? The 2001 memo contains a small section that addresses this issue, but we defer a discussion of it to section 10.2. For now, we note that the consistency in policy also throws up a puzzle: given that privatization (possibly subject to regulation) is to be preferred, shouldn't we have seen more privatizations? Why, during the past twenty-five years, has the Dutch state always participated in some forty firms, with many of these participations lasting for such a long time? A glance at the 2001 list of state participants (see the appendix), shows that next to companies (such as the publicly traded companies) that are on the divestiture path, the financial institutions and regional development companies (which serve as instruments to facilitate business and to attract investments and whose presence is in line with the general preference of the Dutch State to finance), and a mixed bag of firms associated with various forms of alleged market failure are in network sectors.[5] The conclusion that we can draw is that in network industries, the public interest may have prevented selling state participation.

10.2   Liberalization and Privatization in Network Industries

The "purple cabinet," consisting of Labor (red) with two liberal parties (green and blue), chaired by Wim Kok, which was formed after the 1994 elections, stated in its government declaration that it wanted to modernize Dutch society; one of the ways was by engaging in processes of deregulation and liberalization. It stated three priorities for its microeconomic policy: regulatory reform (among others through the MDW program; Kamerstukken 1994–2004) that aimed at increasing competition throughout the economy; liberalization of network industries; and modernization of the competition law, bringing it in line with the EU prohibition system (Before, cartels were allowed if they were in the public interest; now they were prohibited by the equivalent of Article 81 of the EU Treaty.) The third track was completed in 1998 when the new competition law came into effect and when the competition authority (NMa) started operations. The two other tracks are related in that both aim at increasing competition, either from a situation where competition is not very intense or where it is absent. Both of these tracks would be continued under the second purple cabinet, Kok II (1994–1998), but with a shift in emphasis. During Kok I, the focus was on deregulation in the business sector; in Kok II, the emphasis was more on the introduction of market mechanisms in the public sector and on liberalization of network industries. This section describes the policy framework during the two purple cabinet periods and the policies pursued, with emphasis on network industries.

10.2.1   Regulatory Reform without Design

The regulatory reform projects pursued under the purple cabinets seem to have been based, at least initially, on a somewhat naive view of the market process (Van Damme 1996, 2001). Policy proposals were based on the twin ideas that competition would automatically take care of the public interests involved and that opening up and deregulating markets would be sufficient to create a competitive market. In short, the view was that more competition was better and that "more competition" was equivalent to "fewer rules"; hence, there was little attention for market design issues and for managing the transition process. Under Kok I, the resulting policy led to some successful projects, such as the liberalization of shop opening hours; others, such as the reform of the taxi market, were outright failures or were too ambitious and never made it to the implementation phase. Of course, in network industries, establishing competition is even more difficult, and market design and transition management become even more important. For the latter, it is essential to have sector-specific rules and a powerful independent regulator. Unfortunately, in line with the "fewer rules means more competition" view and Dutch political tradition, there has been a reluctance to impose such rules and set up such regulators.

In the Dutch administrative tradition, setting up regulators is seen as expansion of the government, with the independent agency not falling under full political control. It is accepted to have supervisors who check whether businesses play according to the rules; however, the traditional view of administration argues that regulation is part of law making and, hence, has to pass through parliament (Kamerstukken 1994–1995b). Supervisors cannot make rules themselves; they cannot be regulators. For example, the law establishing the telecommunications regulator OPTA (Kamerstukken 1996–1997a) clearly states that the ministry is responsible for rule making, while OPTA has the power to apply the rules in specific cases. It is quite remarkable that it took until March 1999 before the government formulated its general "vision on supervision," consisting of three main lines: aloofness with respect to sector-specific competition rules, caution with respect to sector-specific regulators, and good coordination between different supervisors (Kamerstukken 1998–1999a). From an economic point of view, one can question at least the first two principles. Indeed, OPTA has frequently complained that as a result of the government's not having delegated real regulatory powers to OPTA and the general rules being vague, it does not have enough power to optimally serve the public interest, and it is not able to do its job properly.

Given all this, it should not come as a surprise that during the Kok II government, the liberalization and reform projects met with difficulty. In essence, the low-hanging fruit had been picked during the early years; now the more complicated problems had to be tackled. The government slowly learned that it had weak instruments but more work to do. On top of that, ideological differences between the coalition parties started to show up, first in relation to a proposal for a new law on water supply (Kamerstukken 1997–1998a, no. 3). The first government proposal (Kamerstukken 1997–1998a, no. 1) argued at a rather general level that more competition was desirable because it would improve efficiency, but it did not advocate changes in ownership. With the exception of VVD (Liberals), all other political parties approved a motion that pointed out that the sector was delivering high-quality water at a very reasonable price, that the sector objected strongly to the new plans, and that it advised the government to drop its plans for introducing competition. Confronted with such opposition, the Kok II government backed out further. It stated that privatization would give rise to cumbersome regulation and was undesirable, and it abandoned its plans for legal separation between infrastructure and service provision:

water would remain in public hands, but with the local public utilities being benchmarked against each other. Since then, the situation in the water sector has remained unchanged. In the summer of 1999, the conflict would come out in the open with two cabinet ministers taking diametrically opposite positions on the privatization issue in two articles that appeared, on July 14, on the same page in the same newspaper, NRC. After the summer, during the general discussions at the opening of the new parliamentary year, Prime Minister Kok was forced to explain what the policy line of his cabinet was. As it turned out, he was forced in the defense by the advice of the Raad van State (the highest advisory council of the government) on the government's plans for the year 2000.

In this advice (and later again in its annual report on the year 1999), the Raad van State called attention to the fact that the desire to reach the government's goals by means of market instruments and privatization had not always yielded the results hoped for; it raised the question of the proper intellectual framework for thinking about these issues; and it asked to proceed on the path of introducing competition only after careful analysis. Furthermore, the council pointed to the drawbacks of privatizing monopolies in network industries, such as high regulatory burdens associated with protecting consumer interests, and it praised the government for its decision not to privatize the water companies (Kamerstukken 1999–2000a), Raad van State (2000). Obviously, it is quite remarkable that the call for reflection and careful analysis was made after the policy had been in place for about twenty years. Remarkably, the Raad van State was not alone in making this plea. Half a year later, the Wetenschappelijke Raad voor het Regeringsbeleid (WRR), the highest scientific advisory board of the government, went even further: it concluded that the decision to privatize had sometimes been made without due consideration, and it called the entire policy in question (WRR 2000). What is perhaps most remarkable is that the WRR report on how to guard the public interest, while making strong claims, did not refer to the relevant international economic literature, although that literature was highly relevant.

Motivated by these critical reports and taking into account public dissatisfaction with the results achieved thus far, as well as negative news from the United Kingdom (the October 5 train accident outside Paddington station killing thirty-one people), the Labor party changed its view on privatization from the official "yes, subject to conditions" to "no, unless." Because the other two coalition parties did not change their position, the overall government standpoint on privatization was maintained at "yes, provided that certain conditions are satisfied." The ideological conflict within the cabinet in effect led to policymaking under Kok II coming to a standstill, increasing the dissatisfaction of the voters, and this paved the way for the populist Pim Fortuyn party to win 25 percent of the votes in the 2002 elections.

10.2.2 The Policy Framework

As a result of the critical comments of the Raad van State during the general political considerations in 1999, both chambers of parliament asked the government for an integral view on the policy of liberalization and privatization. The government complied by providing two memos: one on guarding the public interests (Kamerstukken 2000–2001a) and the other on liberalization and privatization in network industries (Kamerstukken 1999–2000b). In this section, I discuss the latter memo and show how it relates to the most recent memo on selling state participation (Kamerstukken 2001–2002ab).

The government memo "Liberalization and Privatization in Network Industries," written under the responsibility of the Ministry of Economic Affairs, expresses a preference to guard the public interest by means of contracting and regulation with appropriate monitoring, but it formulates policy in somewhat cautious terms. It proposes a pragmatic five-step procedure:

1. Identify the public interests (e.g., universal service, security of supply) that have to be protected and for which government intervention may be necessary.

2. Translate these public interests into hard, verifiable constraints that have to be satisfied by the firms in the industry.

3. Set up an appropriate independent supervisory arrangement for checking whether contractual conditions and the public interests are met.

4. Investigate whether competition can help in reaching the public goals, and implement the appropriate market structure.

5. Investigate whether privatization is possible.

It is worthwhile to comment briefly on these steps. First, the memo notes that several of these steps will be required (steps 1 and 2) or will add value (steps 3 and 4) in the case of public ownership and public provision. We see that with respect to guarding the public interest, again little faith is displayed in public ownership. In line with the "the fewer rules, the more competition" doctrine, the memo stresses that restraint should be exercised in the creation of sector-specific competition rules, and it expresses a preference for monitoring (ex post) ex ante supervision. Relatedly, there is a preference to concentrate all regulatory powers with the NMa, the Dutch Competition Authority. With respect to competition, the memo rightly notes that the design has to be tailor-made, and it distinguishes between infrastructure competition, service competition over one infrastructure, competition for the market, and yardstick competition, where the first mentioned are the most preferred. With respect to the ownership issue, the overall conclusion is that in a competitive market, provided there is adequate supervision, privatization can take place, while in markets in which there is not yet sufficient competition, privatization is an option but imposes more demands on the supervisory arrangements. In referring to Newbery (1997), the memo states that the first priority is to have an adequate market structure; the privatization question can be answered only after that.

Note that this conclusion is consistent with that of the most recent memo on state participations. One difference between these memos is that the one on networks devotes more attention to the limits involved in contractual and supervisory arrangements, while the one on participation stresses the drawbacks of ownership. Nevertheless, the memo on networks also derives the preference for contractual relations and privatization from the consideration that the alternative instrument of (partial) public ownership has drawbacks: having a firm in the hands of the government offers no automatic guarantee that the public interest will be met, and it requires special contractual arrangements as well, especially since direct government influence on state participations will frequently be limited.

The memo on state participation contains a small section that explains that the limited direct influence of the government on state participation is mainly the result of the Dutch legal regime for business firms. Consistent with the general preference to separate policymaking from service provision and to induce efficient production, if the government provides market services itself, it will usually choose the organizational form of a limited liability company (NV). For NVs, at least if they are of sufficient size, Dutch corporate law, the so-called *Structuur-regime*, limits the influence of shareholders severely. In essence, the structural regime invests all power with the supervisory board of the company (the RVC), of which existing members decide which new members will replace those that leave the board, and that is supposed to act in the interests of the firm, not those of any stakeholder in particular. Consequently, even if the government wanted to influence the management of a government NV (which is not clear, as this might jeopardize the efficiency goal), it will have limited direct influence. In other words, if additional goals are to be pursued, then these should be imposed on the firm through statute or regulatory or contractual obligations.

More generally, in the choice between full privatization and public provision by an SOE that has the legal form of an NV, the government has to gauge the strengths of the various instruments that are its disposal. Broadly speaking, the state can influence state participation through four different channels: by means of regulation, by writing specific duties in the firm's corporate charter, by appointing members to the Supervisory Board, or by exercising its rights as a shareholder.

The first instrument is also available when dealing with private firms; hence, this is no argument for public provision. The second instrument is a weak one: statutory obligations cannot be written in great detail; the goals of the company will be described in general terms and cannot be easily adjusted to changing circumstances. Interestingly, the government has eliminated the possibility of using the third instrument. While in the past the state had the power to appoint certain members in the Supervisory Board, that policy has been discontinued, as it did not prove a very workable solution and the state did not want to have special privileges for itself (Kamerstukken 2000–2001b). Finally, if the *Structuurregime* applies, an ordinary shareholder has only limited powers to influence the company. Of course, the state might want to reserve a golden share for itself, giving it the right to veto important decisions or fundamental changes in the charter. The Dutch State has done this in the case of TPG (post) and KPN (telecommunications). The European Commission and the European Court of Justice have, however, argued that these golden shares limit capital mobility in Europe, hence, should be withdrawn (European Court of Justice 2003). In response, the state has indicated that it is willing to withdraw its golden share in KPN but not in TPG. In the latter case, government ownership is said to be necessary to guarantee that TPG will keep out of financial trouble and always be able to offer universal postal services. The strength of this argument remains to be tested, but it would seem wise for the state to take into account the contingency that in the near future, this instrument could no longer be used.

It follows that in the Netherlands, an SOE is not a very attractive instrument to pursue the public interest. Nevertheless, this does not imply that it cannot be the best instrument, and in this respect, the 2001 memo on state participations is not convincing: while it describes the drawbacks involved in the state influencing SOEs, it does not discuss the limits of contractual arrangements with private firms. As a result, the trade-offs are not made visible. As we will see, the concern is that contractual relationships would not be sufficiently powerful to protect the public interest, and this has led to reluctance to fully privatise SOEs and participations of lower levels of government. In some sectors, such as electricity, privatization has been blocked, since the government was not sure that the conditions for regulation and monitoring were adequate, that is, that the government had sufficiently powerful regulatory instruments to allow privatization to take place.

10.3   Post and Telecommunications

In August 1997, OPTA, the Dutch regulator for post and telecommunications, started operations. OPTA states as its mission to stimulate effective competition in the markets for electronic communication and postal services and to protect consumers whenever these do not have sufficient choice. OPTA, however, has only weak instruments to realize its mission. It is not a regulator; its formal tasks are limited to monitoring whether players keep to the rules of the game and to resolve conflicts between market players. The ministry is responsible for rule making, which OPTA has to apply in specific cases. Because the rules are vague, parties have ample opportunity to appeal to OPTA's decisions on formal procedural grounds, on the argument that OPTA has overstepped its powers or has misinterpreted the rules. While these court cases have delayed competition, we will see that, thanks to high level of expertise at the office, OPTA has helped make the markets that it supervises more competitive.

10.3.1   Telecommunications

Dutch liberalization policy has followed the steps of the EU directives, but implementation has been slow. The original European ONP framework, aiming at fully liberalizing telecommunications markets by

January 1998 and at making the transition to a competitive market, was implemented by means of the Telecommunicatiewet (Kamerstukken 1996–1997b), which came into effect at the end of 1998. The new EU telecommunications package (the set of directives that the European Parliament and the Council agreed on February 14, 2002) should have been implemented by the summer of 2003, but the new law (Kamerstukken 2003–2004c) came into effect only on May 19, 2004. Although law making is slow, competition has developed in most market segments.

The national PTT was incorporated in 1989 and privatized in 1993. In 1998, PTT was split into a telecommunications company, KPN, and a postal company, TPG, which are both listed on the stock exchange. Already at the time of incorporation, that part of the company that had regulatory functions had become a separate unit within the Ministry. The separation between rule making and market supervision was made in 1997 when OPTA was established, with full market liberalization taking place shortly after. Privatization thus took place well before the market was liberalized. The government has sold the majority of its shares in KPN. In October 2003, the state share was reduced from 31.3 to 19.3 percent and the state has been willing to sell more when the time is right. It still has a golden share, but it has indicated that it is willing to give this up. Now that the telecommunications market is considered sufficiently mature, the state views KPN as an ordinary investment; there are no special strategic interests involved. In response to the question why the state did not sell in better times, such as in 1999, the minister of finance has always answered that there was never a moment in which he did not have inside information; hence, that stock market regulations have prevented the state from selling earlier.

In fact, there is no evidence that as of 1993, the state viewed the company any differently from an ordinary investment; in any case, it has not prevented the company from getting into trouble. It allowed KPN to realize its ambitions to become a European player by, among others, taking over E-plus in Germany, taking a share in Hutchinson's "3" in the United Kingdom, and participating in UMTS auctions in the Netherlands, Germany, and Belgium. After the 2000 telecoms crash, however, when KPN needed new money to write off these investments and pay its debts, the state participated in KPN's new share issue and thus played an important role in preventing KPN from going bankrupt. The state, however, claims that in this respect, it did not behave differently from what any other large shareholder would have done.

It is important to note that KPN has been privatized with the fixed network included. Clearly, the fixed network is an important asset on KPN's balance sheet, and as company data (available at ⟨www.KPN.com⟩) show, the company receives a steady stream of income from its fixed telephony business, although that revenue has started to decline recently. Since 2000, a discussion has taken place about whether privatizing KPN as an integrated company, that is, including the fixed network, was a wise decision. Two drawbacks have been mentioned: privatizing KPN as an integrated company might have jeopardized the public interest of uninterrupted telephony service and it may have delayed competition in some market segments.

The first point was discussed for the a first time when KPNQwest, a participation of KPN active in the broadband backbone market, went bankrupt in 2002. Although Internet traffic was uninterrupted, the question about what would happen with voice telephony if KPN itself went under arose. According to OPTA, there could be severe problems, as the bankruptcy administrator would have to take into account only the interests of the debt holders and could choose to neglect the public interest. The government always took the view that things were not so serious, but on March 12, 2004, it announced that it had decided to arrange for a special fund that the administrator could draw on in case of calamity, so as to guarantee uninterrupted service. We can infer that the risks involved in privatization of firms possessing essential assets in the past may have been underestimated.

Moving to the second drawback, in some market segments, such as fixed voice telephony, privatizing KPN as an integrated company probably delayed competition somewhat. The local loop of the network is traditionally considered an essential facility that cannot be economically duplicated by entrants; hence, KPN should give entrants access on nondiscriminatory terms. Clearly, the fact that KPN is both service provider and network owner gives it an incentive to raise rivals' costs, and this creates difficulties for the regulator, OPTA. Since several key terms in the law and OPTA's powers have been unclear, there have been many legal disputes in this area. Nevertheless, OPTA has taken a tough stance, for example, by imposing price squeeze tests on KPN that force the company to leave some margin between its retail and wholesale tariffs and that allow CPS operators (carrier select) to compete. (See Bouckaert and Verboven 2004 for a description and economic analysis of price squeeze tests.) As a result, competition has developed in this market also. At the time of writing, about a third of

Table 10.1
International comparison of the cost of fixed telephony for a ten-minute call (in euros)

	Local	National	To the United States	To a neighboring country
The Netherlands	0.33	0.49	0.85	0.85
Sweden	0.30	0.30	1.12	0.59
Germany	0.42	1.22	1.23	1.23
Spain	0.28	0.88	1.53	1.53
Italy	0.25	1.22	2.12	2.12
France	0.39	0.96	2.34	2.34
United Kingdom	0.64	1.29	3.37	4.06

Source: OPTA (2004).

the users of the fixed network are using CPS services, and a typical consumer has the possibility of cost savings of 15 percent when switching to a CPS provider. As OPTA (2004) shows, in most market segments, KPN's market share is now smaller than that of incumbents in other EU countries, with the share in international traffic (45 to 50 percent) being low in particular. In international perspective, fixed voice telephony in the Netherlands is cheap, as Table 10.1 shows. It should be noted, however, that since 2001, KPN's prices have increased by 9 percent and that over 2002, prices of CPS providers increased by 7 percent.

The Dutch government has always stressed that full infrastructure competition is preferable to service competition over one network. Fortunately, in important market segments such as broadband Internet access, infrastructure competition is possible since 98 percent of Dutch houses are connected to both the telephony and the cable TV network. To make such competition possible, KPN was forced to sell its (considerable) interests in cable early on. At the same time, municipalities, the traditional owners of other cable networks, did not have the expertise, money, or interest to upgrade their networks. In the 1990s, in a situation with eager buyers, they were interested in selling, and the government did not oppose privatization in this domain. As a result, UPC (a daughter company of UGC Europe) was able to buy many networks, and it is now the largest cable operator in the Netherlands. The big three cable operators (UPC; Casema, which is currently owned by the investment companies Carlyle and Providence from the UK; and Essent, a Dutch multi-utility) together have 85 percent of all connections. While privatization of cable has not been without problems

Table 10.2
International comparison of mobile telephony tariffs: Annual expenditures (2000–2003) of a residential client in US$ against purchasing power parity

	2000	2001	2002	2003
Finland	140	159	157	146
The Netherlands	252	291	252	229
Sweden	165	204	213	255
Germany	329	338	309	323
Italy	303	367	356	343
United Kingdom	309	337	319	355
United States	396	343	409	409
Australia	369	285	293	419
France	382	420	395	468

Source: OPTA (2004).

(several firms have been accused of abusing their dominant position in the TV market), the competing infrastructure has proved beneficial for broadband Internet access. OPTA, in forcing KPN to unbundle its local loop, which resulted in the Netherlands having (together with Denmark and Sweden) the largest percentage of unbundled lines in the hands of entrants, provided an additional boost to competition. As a result, there is strong competition between various xDSL providers and between xDSL and cable, with prices decreasing rapidly. (Many Internet Service Providers halved prices and doubled speed in 2003.) In May 2004, OPTA reported there were 1.1 million xDSL connections (and 1 million broadband cable connections, resulting in a large European penetration). At the same time, KPN reported that it had over 0.9 million connections; hence, KPN's share in the xDSL market is around 80 percent, while it is 42 percent in the overall broadband market.

As far as mobile telephony is concerned, since the 1998 DCS 1800 auction, the Dutch market has had five license holders with full networks, and since then, several additional service providers (virtual operators) have become active as well. While the fact that there were already five operators led to relatively low revenue for the government in the 2000 UMTS auction, there is an important benefit of the Dutch mobile market's probably being one of the more competitive in Europe. Table 10.2 shows that in the Netherlands, mobile telephony is cheap indeed. Not surprisingly, then, the penetration rate is above 80 percent of the population, with more than 13 million active connections (table 10.2).

This is not to say that there are no problems in the mobile market. Just as in other countries with the CPP (calling party pays) system, there is the issue of high mobile-terminating tariffs—an operator needs to pay a high price to a competitor for terminating a call on the latter's network. This translates into higher retail tariffs, with fixed-to-mobile calls being particularly expensive. Indeed, and perhaps caused precisely by the intensive competition on the mobile market, terminating tariffs have been especially high in the Netherlands. In 2003, they were 22 eurocents per minute, only slightly less than those in Portugal, the most expensive European country. OPTA has been worried about this for a long time, and together with NMa, it has threatened to intervene on the basis of the competition law, claiming prices to be excessive. As a result, in 2003, mobile operators agreed to halve their terminating rates in two years. In April 2004, the terminating rate was reduced to 16 c/m (eurocents per minute), it was further reduced to 14 c/m by the end of 2004 and stands of 12 c/m in December 2005, which is the lowest rate that is currently available in Europe.

All in all, consumers are satisfied with the way the Dutch telecommunications market works. There is active competition and convergence between infrastructures. The outlook is that broadband penetration will increase further and that there will be a shift from fixed voice telephony to mobile. As the fixed telephony tariffs have been rebalanced since the end of the 1990s, the fixed subscription rate is relatively high, and for almost 20 percent of the fixed callers, it is now more than 75 percent of the bill. As a result and since subscription fees for mobile are much lower, 7 percent of consumers have terminated their fixed-line subscription, and it is predicted that another 20 percent of consumers will do that before long. The result will be higher subscription fees for the remaining callers on the fixed network, inducing some more of them to leave, which raises concerns for the future. In any case, OPTA (2004) concludes that there is healthy infrastructure competition and that the local loop of the fixed network no longer seems to be essential.

10.3.2 The Postal Sector

In January 2004, the minister of economic affairs published his most recent "vision on the postal market" (Kamerstukken 2003–2004e) in which he outlined his plans up to 2007. Taking this memo as our starting point, this section briefly describes the current state of affairs in the postal market.

Traditionally, the main consideration underlying the legislation of this market is that universal service must be guaranteed: letters and some other items have to be collected and delivered everywhere within the country six days a week at a geographically uniform tariff, with a certain percentage being delivered overnight; in addition, a certain number of post offices have to be operated. TPG, the postal arm of the former PTT that was split off from KPN in 1998 and is listed on the stock market, with the Dutch government holding 34.7 percent of the shares, carries the universal service obligation. To allow the company to fulfill its obligations, it has been given a monopoly on the transport of letters up to 100 grams costing no more than three times the base rate (3×0.39 euros), as well as on some other services. European liberalization of the postal sector consists in gradual reduction of the reserved sector: from 100 grams since January 2003 to 50 grams from January 2006, with the intention being to fully liberalize the market as of 2009 (Postal Directive 2002/39/EC). In the Netherlands, direct mail (nonpersonalised advertisement letters) does not fall in the reserved segment, so that the monopoly is smaller than in neighboring countries and narrower than what Directive 2002/39/EC allows. Of all letter mail, only 48 percent is reserved, which compares to 59 percent in the United Kingdom, 68 percent in Germany, and 82 percent in France. The "vision" document proposes to stay ahead of the European average, but in the interest of TPG and its workers and to maintain a level playing field with Germany and the United Kingdom, it is proposed to fully liberalize the market in 2007. The government is trading off multiple goals here: one would expect a faster pace to be better for (large) consumers.

Even if a relatively large part of the market is already open to competition and the incumbents from neighboring countries (Deutsche Post, La Poste, Consignia), as well as several small players, are active on the Dutch market, TPG still has a dominant position on most market segments. Experience in countries such as Finland and Sweden that are further down the liberalization path has shown that competition will develop only slowly, if at all. The question is whether, in accomplishing the transition to a more competitive market, entrants should be given the right to make use of TPG's facilities at regulated terms and, if so, to which facilities or services and at what price. OPTA has argued that TPG should offer "an access menu" and that, at least temporarily, access to TPG's sorting facilities and distribution network should be mandatory at regulated rates. On the basis of several studies (SEO 2003; De Bijl, van Damme, & Larouche 2003), the minister has concluded that although the market has some natural monopoly segments, negotiated access should be sufficient. Competitors to TPG, such as Sandd, are now successfully rolling out their own networks; hence, full infrastructure competition seems to be developing. Since such competition is to be preferred above service competition, the government's hands-off approach may well be justified.

Another important issue on which OPTA has come to a different conclusion from the ministry concerns tariff regulation. In the past, the price of a stamp was allowed to rise with the general rise in the wage level; there was price cap regulation with no adjustment for efficiencies. OPTA has argued that while this system has given TPG strong incentives to cut cost and improve efficiency, consumers have benefited insufficiently. While, in international comparison, sending a letter of up to 20 grams is cheap in the Netherlands, heavier mail is relatively expensive (see OPTA 2004, figure 6). OPTA argues that after correcting for population density, Dutch tariffs are not low and that TPG is making excess profits on the reserved segment; it has proposed reducing the price by some 25 percent (OPTA 2002). The minister has refused to reduce the price; he has decided, as a sort of compromise, that the price of a stamp will remain fixed at 0.39 euros until 2005, and in the "vision document," he proposed extending this period until 2007. This proposal not only makes OPTA unhappy; TPG has argued that since the postal volume is decreasing (with some 20 percent up to 2040) and there are economies of scale, unit costs are rising, and the company should be allowed to increase its prices. TPG appealed the decision and won: the minister was forced to withdraw its decision. Nevertheless, in June 2004, TPG announced that it would not increase base prices until 2007. Note that OPTA has no regulatory powers here.

In its vision document, the government argues that the public interest requires that universal service be maintained and that a fully liberalized market will deliver a level of service that falls short of what is desired: single item mail (small-volume mail that is put in mailboxes, a segment that is less than 10 percent of the market) is not very attractive for competitors, so that a duty to carry such mail should be assigned to TPG. As TPG falls under the Dutch structuurregime, direct influence of the state on TPG is limited, and to protect its interests, the state has a golden share in TPG that gives it a veto right concerning certain key decisions. The government has argued that at least for the moment, it needs to maintain this golden share in order to ensure universal service and that this instrument is proportional for this purpose, but there is discussion with the EC about the issue. The Dutch government argues that in a liberalized postal market without the golden share, TPG might get into financial trouble, jeopardizing universal service. It remains to be seen how strong this argument is.

In international comparison, the Dutch postal market is functioning efficiently: TPG, which in effect has operated as a regulated private profit-maximizing firm for the past decade, is an efficient firm that is making healthy profits; quality of service is high; prices are reasonable and declining in real terms; competition is developing in certain market segments; and overall satisfaction with how the market operates is good. What explains the success is probably the fact that this market is relatively simple: there are only artificial and strategic barriers to competition, no natural ones; the government has been willing to open the market more than in most other European countries, and it has not intervened in TPG's policymaking.

10.4   Energy

DTe, the Dutch "regulator" for energy markets, was established through the Electricity Law 1998 (Kamerstukken 1997–1998b) that implemented Directive 96/92EC. Noteworthy is that the explanatory memorandum to this law expresses regret at yet another "independent supervisor"; it should therefore not be too surprising that DTe is set up as a chamber of the NMa, the Dutch competition authority. At first, DTe had responsibilities only for supervising the electricity market, but after the Gas Law came into effect in 2001 (Kamerstukken 1998–2000), DTe received formal powers in that domain also. In spring 2004, parliament discussed the implementation law (Kamerstukken 2003–2004d) for the second EU Electricity Directive (2003/54/EC) and the second EU Gas Directive (2003/55/EC). As of this writing, the new law has passed both chambers of parliament and has been put into effect. As a result of this new law, the independence of network management is strengthened, there is a clear separation between policymaking (the responsibility of the ministry) and supervision (the task of DTe), and there will be regulated access to gas networks. In this section, we discuss liberalization of and privatization in the Dutch energy markets.

10.4.1   Electricity

The electricity sector has been restructured in line with the two EU directives, but as was the case with post, Dutch policy has been ahead of the European average. The government memo *Stroomlijnen*, published in 1996, anticipated the EU electricity market liberalization, Directive 96/92/EC, and outlined the essentials of the Electricity Law 1998. At the time that document was published, municipalities and provinces, directly or indirectly, owned all players in the Dutch electricity sector. There were four large-scale producers (responsible for some 80 percent of supply) and twenty-three local distribution companies. Large-scale generation was centrally coordinated by SEP, a cooperative joint venture of these producers. In addition to imports, domestic production involved small-scale self-generation by industrial units and distribution companies. In line with Directive 96/92/EC, the Electricity Law proposed gradual liberalization of demand and stressed the importance of nondiscriminatory access to the transport and distribution networks. We describe the developments in the various market segments (production, transport, distribution and supply) since the 1998 law was passed.

With respect to generation, the (draft) 1998 law was based on the idea of creating a national champion by merging the four large-scale producers and with the government facilitating the merger by providing subsidies for stranded assets. In the spring of 1998, however, the producers could not agree on how to share the remaining costs, and the merger plans were abolished. Subsequently, during 1999, foreign energy companies (Electrabel, E.On, and Reliant) bought three of these generation companies, while the fourth generator remained in the hands of Essent, a vertically integrated energy company. In the generation segment, the law did not impose any sector-specific restrictions on asset sales; if anything, privatization was encouraged, the only constraints being that buyers had to commit to honor the obligations with respect to stranded assets and not to exert any influence on the national grid company TenneT. Indeed, based on the idea that efficient scale in generation is relatively small and that the wholesale market would be competitive, the production sector has been left unregulated since 1999; hence, only the general competition and environmental laws apply.

Since 2001, after the expiration of a transition period needed to unwind the cooperative SEP agreement that blocked competition between domestic generators, generators have competed for the liberalized market segment. Because domestic competition is gas based, there is room for cheap imports, and indeed 15 percent of total supply is imported. Various marketplaces facilitate competition. In addition to the somewhat informal OTC market, the APX has offered a daily spot market since May 1999. At the borders with Belgium and Germany, the import capacity is auctioned so as to ensure efficient use of this capacity. As a result of these organized markets, the Dutch electricity market is reasonably transparent. In retrospect, the possibilities for exerting market power on the wholesale market might have been underestimated at the time the law was drafted, and there might have been insufficient awareness of the potential pitfalls involved. After the California crisis, it has been discussed whether, to guarantee the public interest, some type of licensing of generation would be desirable. In any case, the wholesale market is monitored closely: the DTe has set up a Market Surveillance Committee, on which several academics are active.

In 2003, after having been active on the generation market for less than four years, Reliant has left the country again; Nuon, a large, integrated energy company, bought its assets. With this merger creating a market structure with two large vertically integrated energy companies and wholesale markets that are not very liquid, the NMa was concerned that this is another step on the road to a tight oligopoly with three or four integrated players. It decided that the concentration can be allowed provided that 900 MW of capacity is divested by means of a VPP auction (NMa 2003), a decision that Nuon has appealed. The NMa decision is noteworthy; it stresses that in delineating the relevant market, the time dimension is important: when the market is tight, players (even those with small market shares) may have substantial market power.

The requirements of nondiscrimination and accounting separation imposed by Directive 96/92/EC were implemented by insisting on legal unbundling between production, network services, and supply, as well as by certain other procedural safeguards. Consequently, the 1998 Dutch Electricity Law goes much further than what the First Directive demands; in fact, most of the requirements of the second Electricity Directive (2003/54/EC) are already met by that law. The 1998 law forces the economic owners of the networks to appoint independent network managers, with the appointment to be approved by the minister. In what is probably best seen as an attempt to block network investments that could be used to expand imports, and hence, increase competition,

SEP, the joint venture of the generating companies that owned the transport grid, at first refused to delegate important investment decisions to the national transport grid manager, TenneT. As a result, it took until 2000 before the minister could approve the appointment of TenneT. When the government was dealing with this issue, the question came up as to whether government ownership would be necessary to ensure nondiscriminatory access to the transmission grid. The original law was based on the idea that to guarantee independence of the network company, it would be sufficient for the state to temporarily acquire the majority (50 percent plus 1) of the shares: after the transition period, full privatization could take place. However, during the summer of 1999, the Christian Democrats changed their position on the privatization issue and concluded that all essential grids, including the national transport grid, should be owned by the state. Over time, other parties, with the exception of the Liberal party, also came to adopt this position. In October 2001, the state fully acquired TenneT as well as Saranne BV, the legal owner of the grid, with the state paying slightly over 1 billion euros. Interestingly, the 2001 government memo on state participation expresses some regret that parliament forced the cabinet to make this acquisition; the Ministry of Finance was clearly reluctant to take the ownership role, or maybe it just regretted having had to pay 1 billion euros. With the Christian Democrats in government at the moment, it is unlikely that the state will soon sell any of its shares in the national grid or in the systems operator, TenneT.

Since then, there have been further interesting developments with respect to the national grid manager and system operator, TenneT. In 2003, TenneT bought a lower-voltage grid that also has a transport function. In May 2001, TenneT bought the power exchange APX, the day-ahead spot market on which approximately 15 percent of all energy consumed in the Netherlands is traded. In turn, in 2003, the APX bought APX (UK), a U.K. spot market for electricity. In June 2004, TenneT bought an auction house on which long-term energy contracts are traded (2.3 TWh in 2003). While it does make sense for TenneT to operate the APX (in its capacity of system operator, it also operates a balancing market, which can be used for last-minute adjustment), it is less clear what the driving force is behind the other acquisitions, in particular the foreign expansion. The DTe has published a consultation document on how TenneT should be regulated.

The demand side of the market is liberalized in four steps, and liberalization proceeds at a faster pace than the Second Electricity Directive

(2003/54/EC) requires. Large users, representing about one-third of demand, were given freedom of supplier in 1999 and the middle group, again representing about one-third of demand, in January 2002. Immediately after liberalization, some 30 percent of the middle segment switched suppliers, and it turned out that the sector was not well prepared for this. In July 2001, the market for green electricity was opened for all consumers, and the entire market will be open as of July 2004, when supply will be unregulated. As a result of relatively generous subsidies, a large number of small consumers (about one in three at the moment) are consuming green energy, where one also sees that there are a large number of suppliers of such energy, that the market is transparent, and that there is still considerable price dispersion. (For further discussion on the green market, see Van Damme and Zwart 2003, who argue that the subsidies have largely been ineffective.) It was predicted that full liberalization as of July 1, 2004, would not lead to much switching; and, indeed, in the first year only about 5 percent of the consumers switched suppliers. Consequently, one may expect that, just as in the United Kingdom (Waddams Price 2004), retail competition will probably not be very effective.

DTe regulates distribution rates and, in setting the network charges, it is making use of yardstick competition; hence, network charges of different distribution companies are compared to each other, and inefficient companies are forced to reduce their charges more than others. While in the first regulation period (2001–2003) there was regulation only on price, in the second period (2004–2006), network quality will be regulated as well. DTe claims that as a result of regulation, in the period 2001–2006, network tariffs decreased by 17 percent on average, leading to cost savings of some 1.9 billion euros in total (NMa 2004).

Article 93 of the 1998 Electricity Law states that privatization of distribution companies is possible, subject to ministerial approval. Since 1999, there has been heated political discussion on the conditions under which such privatization could take place, while at the same time, a few distribution companies have been sold to German utilities. Each time this happened, the responsible minister (Jorritsma, Liberals) applauded the developments, but parliament objected. When it tried to block the sale but failed to do so, the minister was forced to impose stricter rules on privatization. As a result, the cabinet has proposed guidelines (Staatscourant 2001) and a draft law, Privatisation of Energy Distribution Companies (Kamerstukken 2001–2002c), that would allow privatization, provided it was guaranteed that the network manager could and would operate in a way "sufficiently independent" from the rest of the company. Both of these were very complex and did not meet with any enthusiasm. When in 2002, before the privatization law could be discussed, another distribution company was bought by RWE, parliament was so upset with the fact that it could not block this privatization that it forced the minister to withdraw both the guidelines and the draft law. After the 2002 elections, the new minister withdrew both, while announcing that he would not allow any further privatizations until the market could be fully liberalized. Since that time, the deadline has been shifted further in the future.

At issue in this discussion is, first, the question of what can be privatized: the vertically integrated company, or the distribution network, or just the supply business? The current owners of the companies (local municipalities and provinces) are in favor of full privatization: they argue that government regulation is sufficient to guard the public interest, that they have no real power to influence the decisions of the distribution companies in any case (this again as a consequence of the Structuurregime), and that they have good use for the money that privatization would bring. At the same time, it has been argued that there are several risks involved in full privatization and that regulation might not be sufficiently powerful to deal with these. The main concern is that an integrated (private) company would have an incentive to discriminate against competing supply companies, hence, that it would frustrate supply competition. Other concerns are that it could use revenues from the network business to cross-subsidize its supply business (again leading to "unfair competition"), and it might underinvest in the network, with the state not having powerful legal means to intervene in case of mismanagement.

One way of dealing with these concerns is to insist on unbundling supply and distribution and indeed, to guarantee nondiscriminatory access to the grids, the 1998 law already forces distribution companies to legally unbundle their distribution networks from their supply business. In other words, the 1998 law already implements an important requirement that, at the EU level, is imposed only by the second Electricity Directive (2003/54/EC). Although the law contains some other safeguards that are supposed to guarantee that the network manager operates in a way sufficiently independent from the rest of the company, there has been some concern that network companies have not been able to do this. For example, when one pure supply company, Energy XS, went bankrupt in 2003, each network company switched the consumers of Energy XS to its sister supply company. The 2004 law implementing the second EU directive therefore imposes even stronger independence requirements, such as that the network company should be the owner of the grid.

Recently the minister has argued that even these additional measures might not be going far enough; hence, he has argued that full privatization of the integrated company poses great risks and that legal unbundling between distribution and supply is insufficient to deal with the concerns. The current proposal (Ministry of Economic Affairs 2004) hence entails full (ownership) unbundling of the distribution company from supply and generation; it is thus proposed to fully separate the competitive parts of the value chain from the monopolistic elements. Such unbundling would have to take effect before 2007, where the nonnetwork part of the company is allowed to be privatized immediately after the unbundling has taken place. The minister argues that this plan offers the best of all worlds: generation and supply can remain together, allowing companies economies of scale and scope, while separation will effectively deal with the anticompetitive concerns. He also argues that full structural separation does not destroy any value, so current owners should be happy as well. The vast majority of parliament supports these plans, but current owners have not yet been convinced. In part, this is because the minister has not yet made up his mind on the privatization of the network companies; it is clear that in the future, they cannot be sold to firms that are also active in supply or generation (line of business restrictions will remain in place), but it is not clear whether they can be sold at all. We thus see a major change in policy: whereas five years ago privatization of distribution companies was considered to be unproblematic, it is now judged to be impossible.

10.4.2   Natural Gas

In 1997, the government published the white paper *Gasstromen* that anticipated EU Directive 98/30/EC and outlined the essentials of a new gas law. With this gas law (Kamerstukken 1998–2000), which was approved by parliament in 2000, rules for transport and supply of gas were introduced in the Netherlands; up to that time, the rules related only to production. The law formulates uninterrupted supply of natural gas and optimal exploitation of Dutch natural gas resources as the public interests involved. The latter is the main difference with any of the other network sectors discussed in this chapter: in a public-private partnership with ExxonMobil and Shell, the Dutch state is an important producer of natural gas, and Gasunie, the "national monopolist," is the largest player on the European gas market, with a market share of 17 percent in 2000. Given that natural gas is an important source of revenue for the Dutch state (during the past decade, annual revenue from gas was 1.2 percent of GDP on average), it is not surprising that the Explanatory Memorandum to the Law explicitly refers to industrial policy and states that Gasunie should be well positioned in Europe. To put this in comparison, while in the period 1990–2001, Dutch privatization proceeds were $14.5 billion, gas revenue was over 47 billion euros. According to estimates of the National Audit Office, as a result of liberalization, state revenue might decrease considerably, with up to 1 billion euros a year (Kamerstukken 1999–2000d). It should therefore not be too surprising that Dutch liberalization policy in gas is somewhat different from and less ambitious than that in electricity. What is perhaps more surprising is that the Netherlands is not dragging its feet more. Indeed, the most recent change in law by means of which the second EU Gas Directive (2003/55/EC) is implemented insists on regulated access to the gas network; hence, it does away with the asymmetry that existed between gas and electricity (see Kamerstukken 2003–2004d).

Gasunie is the central player in the Dutch gas building: it coordinates production and sales and is responsible for purchasing, storage, transport, and sales. It is a public-private partnership in which the state participates at 50 percent and ExxonMobil and Shell each at 25 percent. It was set up around 1960 to allow optimal exploitation of the gigantic Slochteren gas field which was discovered by NAM, a joint venture of Exxon (50 percent) and Shell (50 percent). At that time, NAM was the only party licensed to search for oil and gas in the Netherlands, and its license stipulated that it had to sell to the state, at a reasonable price, all gas that was found. The state, for its part, operated a transport network, among others to transport coke oven gas from Germany to several Dutch cities. Upon discovering the large volume of natural gas, the parties joined forces. For gas production and the management of the Slochteren field, they set up the Maatschap Groningen, a joint venture of the state (40 percent) and NAM (60 percent). For transport and trade, Gasunie was set up. It was given a (regulated) double monopoly position on the input market (with respect to NAM and the Maatschap

Groningen) and the domestic output market, and it was assigned the task of developing the gas market in the Netherlands. The minister of economic affairs was given power to intervene: approving tariffs, monitoring supply, and possibly assigning special privileges to certain industrial sectors (e.g., greenhouses). During the 1960s, an extensive network was rolled out quickly, and by the end of that decade, 99 percent of Dutch households were connected to the "public" network.

Dutch natural gas policy has always been based on the assumption that natural gas is scarce as well as on the idea that taxing at the production stage maximizes government revenue. Specifically, policy has consisted of providing incentives to exploit smaller fields first and to maintain the Slochteren field as much as possible—the "small fields policy." To make exploration and exploitation attractive, Gasunie has been forced to pay all producers of Dutch gas a reasonable price, related to the "market value" of gas, the latter being the opportunity cost of the final gas consumer. If a small field producer sells its gas to Gasunie, it receives a price related to the (average) retail price over the previous calendar year. Consequently, Gasunie makes little profit itself; the profits are transferred to the producers, which are then heavily taxed. In essence, producers pay a profit tax to the state, the rate being somewhere between 50 and 99 percent, with the state getting some 70 percent of the profit on average, and 70 to 90 percent on the Slochteren field. Is not obvious that the small fields policy is consistent with maximizing government revenue: as Slochteren has much lower production costs than other fields (0.5 eurocents versus 2–3 eurocents; see Correlje and Odell 2000), that field yields the highest revenues. In defense, the government points to the balancing function of the Slochteren field; in essence, production costs of the small fields are lower as long as the large field is filled sufficiently.

The first EU Gas Directive 98/30/EC proposes gradual liberalization of the gas market, with nondiscriminatory access to the grids being an important requisite for competition to develop. The directive is satisfied with accounting unbundling of integrated gas companies and negotiated third-party access, with an independent authority resolving conflicts. In line with the directive, the Gas Law imposes on Gasunie accounting separation between storage, transport, and supply activities. Like the directive, the Gas Law is satisfied with negotiated access to the grids, and it appointed DTe as the agency to deal with conflicts. After the law was passed in 2000, the 200 largest consumers (those with an annual demand more than 10^7 cubic meters of gas, which represents 46 percent of total demand) were free to choose supplier, and on liberalization, Gasunie lost 37 percent of this market. The middle segment (annual consumption more than 10^4 cubic meters of gas) was liberalized in 2002 and the market was fully liberalized as of July 1, 2004. The market share of Gasunie has gradually decreased: 100 percent in 1999, 82 percent in 2000, 79 percent in 2001, 77 percent in 2002, and 74 percent in 2003 (see ECN 2004). We note that while the sales of Gasunie in the Dutch market have gradually decreased from around 44 billion cubic meters until 1997 to 34 billion cubic meters in 2003, exports have remained roughly constant around 43 billion cubic meters per year.

In 2001, the minister of economic affairs argued that the existing structure and agreements in the gas sector would increasingly lead to tensions with European policy and announced his intention to come to a complete restructuring of the "gas building" (Kamerstukken 2001–2002c, no. 1). Not surprisingly, given the financial interests of the state, the letter stresses that the operation should be budgetary neutral for the state and that there should be no changes in production. Interestingly, the letter also states that privatization is possible "if the public interest can be taken care of by means of regulation, and if production, transport and trade can be adequately separated." As with electricity, policy would move in the opposite direction. In the next letter on the topic (Kamerstukken 2001–2002d, no. 2), the minister proposed ownership unbundling—that Gasunie be split into three independent companies: one for transport and system operation (owned by the state) and two competing trade companies (one owned by ExxonMobil, the other by Shell). In effect, a similar structure as the one that exists for electricity was proposed. Valuation of the different parts of Gasunie proved difficult, however, and in October 2003, after three years of negotiation, the parties concluded that they could not agree on unbundling the firm (Kamerstukken 2001–2002d, no. 5). In the draft law for implementing Directive 2003/55/EC, the minister wrote that it still was his intention to come to a full unbundling. Note, however, that the directive is satisfied with legal unbundling—that since 1999 Gasunie has been split in two divisions (Gastransport Services, GTS, and Gasunie Trade and Supply), hence, legal unbundling can be easily achieved. If the experience from electricity is anything to go by, going further and nationalizing GTS could be costly for the state.

10.5   Public Transport

On January 1, 2004, the transport chamber of the NMa, the organization supervising the public transport sector, officially started its operations. In this section, we describe the relevant laws (two for train transport and one for bus transport) and the current situation in this sector.

10.5.1   Train Services

In 2003, Dutch parliament adopted two new laws that implement the second package of measures to revitalize the railways that were adopted by the European Commission on January 23, 2002. The first of these laws, the Spoorwegwet (Kamerstukken 2000–2001b), establishes full unbundling of infrastructure and service provision, with the first being the responsibility of the SOE Prorail. The second law, the Concessiewet personenvervoer per trein (Kamerstukken 1999–2000b, no. 27216), arranges that passenger traffic will be governed by a competitive (exclusive) licensing system; hence, there will be (limited) competition for the rails. Specifically, until 2015, the concession for the core network will be granted to NS, a state-owned enterprise, while smaller lines will be contracted out on a competitive basis, and the high-speed connection between Amsterdam and Brussels (which will start running in 2007) has been tendered to a joint venture of KLM and NS until 2022. We briefly describe how this structure came about.

In the 1980s, when the position of both passenger and freight traffic deteriorated, the Dutch government set up the Wijffels Committee to come up with recommendations for increasing the share of rail transport in the total transport market. In its 1992 report, that committee recommended loosening the relation between NS (the Dutch railroads) and the state by giving NS room to transform itself into a "normal" business and making the state responsible for rail infrastructure. The government accepted the recommendations, and the process of reducing the direct government influence on the company was started. In June 1995, NS and the Dutch state signed the agreement "Over de wissel," which also aimed at implementing EU Directive 91/440/EC, which required accounting separation between infrastructure and train service provision. The agreement stated that in return for the government's no longer providing subsidies for passenger transport, NS was given more freedom to determine the time schedules and tariffs.

Since 1995, the price of train tickets has roughly increased with the rate of inflation. Subsidies, which amounted to some 200 million euros in 1992 (of which more than 60 percent were exploitation subsidies), were reduced considerably, with operational subsidies not being given as of 1998; instead, as of 1996, NS started to pay for using the infrastructure, the tariff being 84 million euros in 2003. While the subsidies were reduced, the cost recovery ratio increased from 50 percent in 1992 to 100 percent at the end of the 1990s, with NS making profits (of around 4 percent of turnover, yielding a return on investment around 1 percent) since 1995. From 1995 until 2000, the passenger transport division also made small annual profits, but since 2001, that division has been slightly in the red, mainly as a result of international transport being unprofitable, this as a consequence of cheap international flights. For example, in 2003, on total turnover of 2.7 billion euros, NS made a profit of 81 million euros, with the passenger transport division making a loss of 37 million on a turnover of 1.6 billion euros (58 percent of the NS total) (see the annual report over 2003, available at ⟨www.ns.nl⟩). From a financial perspective, the 1995 "hiving-off" of the NS can thus be classified as a remarkable success. No doubt, the government plan, announced in the 1998 policy document "De derde eeuw spoor" (Third century of rail), of privatizing NS, contributed to the company's improving its operating efficiency considerably.

As far as quality of service is concerned, the record has not been so good. With the company aiming for at least 87 percent of the trains to arrive on time (that is, with a delay of less than three minutes), that goal has not been achieved since 1996. In fact, the quality level has been around 83 percent, with 2001 setting a record low at 79.9 percent. Clearly, passengers were very dissatisfied with this performance. In 2003, consumer organizers blocked a tariff increase of 4.15 percent that NS had planned. The company agreed that it would increase tariffs only after quality had improved. It would increase price by 2.075 percent only after quality had been above 84.4 percent for twelve consecutive months and, counting from that point in time, increase with a further 2.075 percent only after quality had been above 86.6 percent for another twelve consecutive months. NS reported that in the first quarter of 2004, 85.3 percent of the trains had a delay of less than three minutes; hence, it was allowed to increase its prices. Note, however, that the quality is still below the standard that the company has set for itself. Dissatisfaction with performance has led to the conclusion that privatization of NS is not an option at the moment: the political consensus is that this could only make matters worse.

The 1995 contract made the state responsible for general policy concerning infrastructure investment and track use, but it delegated the associated operational tasks (maintenance, capacity allocation, and traffic management) to NS. In effect, NS was made into a hybrid company, consisting of a public arm and a market organization. The public arm consisted of three "task organizations" that were responsible for building and maintaining the infrastructure (Railinfrabeheer NV), entry to the tracks, capacity allocation and safety (Railned BV), and operational traffic management (Verkeersleiding BV). While these task organizations are structured according to private law, NS annual reports refer to them as being nonprofit oriented and financed by and working on behalf of the government. The market organization of NS, NS Groep, originally consisted of divisions for passengers, freight, stations, real estate, and supporting services, but in 1999, NS Cargo, the freight division, was sold to Deutsche Bahn. (The freight market, which has been fully liberalized since 1995 and in which there is competition on the tracks, will not be considered here.) The private arm of NS has always pointed to the public, infrastructure, branch of the company for being partly responsible for the low quality of service and for low consumer satisfaction. In 1999, a report of the General Audit Chamber (Kamerstukken 1998–1999c) put part of the blame for the low quality on the government and the three task organizations. It concluded that the Ministry of Transport had not adequately supervised the public task organizations of NS and that there were coordination problems among these three organizations.

While the 1995 agreement stated that the intention was to have competition on the tracks, it is clear that the hybrid structure that was chosen was not conducive for such competition to develop. Indeed, the report of the general audit chamber also concluded that the task organizations were not always operating independently of the rest of the company; in fact, on several occasions, the NS board had directly influenced them without the ministry's intervening. One new player entered by exploiting a line that had been abandoned by NS; when it was not allocated more capacity, it quickly left the market. A review of the political discussion (Kamerstukken 1995–1996, 18986, no. 18) makes it clear that the importance of the true independence of the task organizations for competition to develop was probably underestimated. For passenger transport, the idea of competition *on* the tracks has meanwhile been given up as well; the choice now is for competition *for* the tracks.

As a result of general public dissatisfaction with the quality of train transport services, a second step of unbundling has since taken place. In 2000, the process started of lifting the three task organizations out of NS and bundling them into a separate 100 percent state-owned limited liability company, ProRail, that falls directly under the control of the Transport Ministry. In the meantime, the government has also changed its views on competition: it has concluded that competition on the tracks is not feasible and has settled for competition for the tracks on the basis of a concession system. While it was intended to have a new structure in place by 2000, the transition will be completed only after 2005. The General Audit Office has criticized the ministry for not having a clear vision of the appropriate structure and for having caused this delay.

It is the system sketched above that is formalized in the new Spoorwegwet (Kamerstukken 2000–2001c). This law formally establishes the SOE ProRail, which will be fully independent as of January 2005, and it implements full separation between infrastructure services, to be provided by ProRail, and transport services, which fall under the responsibility of the state-owned company NS. The Concessiewet that deals with traffic services distinguishes among three submarkets: the high-speed connection Amsterdam-Brussels-Paris, the core rail network in the Netherlands, and the regional lines. For each of these three, concessions will be, or are, given out, but details differ somewhat. For the high-speed services, a competitive tender has been organized, with the winner being a consortium of NS and KLM. For the core network, a contract, with duration until 2015 and performance clauses, has been negotiated with NS. The plan for the regional lines is to shift authority to the regions themselves so that better integration with other forms of regional transport can be established. These regional authorities can give subsidies if they consider this to be necessary. In this domain, relatively little progress has been made.

10.5.2 Public Bus Transport

On January 1, 2001, a new law on public bus transport (the Wet Personenvervoer 2000, Kamerstukken 1998–1999b) came into effect designed to increase the quality of public bus transport, increase the share of that transport in the total mobility market, and increase cost coverage to at least 50 percent. The idea underlying the law is that more competition within the public bus market will make bus transport more competitive. In this section, we describe the market structure in this sector.

The regional public bus transport industry started with competition between bus companies, but these merged one after the other. In 1937, NS bought up a number of the regional transport companies and transformed them into VSN. In 1969 the state took over the shares in VSN, which at the time had a monopoly on regional public bus transport. In the mid-1990s, when the sector was in severe trouble (ticket receipts covered only about 30 percent of cost, direct labor costs were about 7 percent higher than in other countries, and indirect labor costs might have been even 40 percent higher), the government installed the committee Brokx to advise on how to restructure the sector. After two tender experiments had been successfully conducted in 1995, this committee recommended splitting the Netherlands into several regions and tendering local monopoly licenses in each of these.

The Law Passenger Transport 2000 implements the proposals of the Brokx committee. It created thirty-five regional public transport authorities, RTAs (twelve provinces, seven areas, and sixteen cities), which are made responsible for public transport in eighty-one different areas. The law introduced a two-year learning period, in which the RTAs could experiment with tendering, and it specified a target level of 35 percent of the relevant market having been awarded through competitive tendering by the end of 2002. If this target is not met, the minister can force the RTAs to tender at least 35 percent of the contract value from 2003 on, and the law's premise is that by 2006 (2007 for cities), all licenses will be tendered competitively. We note that the licenses have a maximum duration of six years and that until 2010, the winner of a tender is forced to take on board all bus drivers and other direct personnel of the company that was carrying out the transport in that area. Obviously, as labor costs are around 70 percent of total costs, this requirement can be major handicap for new entrants.

At present, total turnover in the Dutch market for public transport is 3.1 billion euros; the submarket for local and regional public transport (including tram and metro) has a value of 1.7 billion euros, of which 1.2 billion euros is public bus transport (Ecorys 2004). This latter market can be separated into bus transport in the major cities (0.3 billion euros) and bus transport in other cities and regions (0.9 billion euros), with only the latter market being contestable at the moment. In eight of the larger cities (Amsterdam, Rotterdam, Den Haag, Utrecht, Groningen, Dordrecht, Nijmegen, and Maastricht), local bus transport in the mid-1990s was carried out by a municipal organization. To prevent any conflict of interest resulting from such a city being active on both sides of a tender, these cities have been given until 2006 to corporatize or privatize their local bus companies and open their markets. In fact, the law forces the cities to corporatize at least their bus companies. Article 48 of the law states that a bus company that is under the control of an RTA is not allowed to participate in the tender organized by that RTA; Article 109 is a fair competition clause stating that as long as its own local market has not been opened up sufficiently, a municipal bus company cannot participate in any tender. A similar reciprocity clause applies to foreign firms: if these are from countries that have not opened up their markets, they can be banned from the Dutch tenders. The city bus companies, however, found a loophole: they simply formed a joint venture, SVN, that was not caught by the latter clause. Three of the larger city bus companies—GVB (Amsterdam), RET (Rotterdam), and GVU (Utrecht)—are still municipal units, and they have asked for the 2007 deadline to be shifted. The other local bus companies that existed in 1996 have been privatized.

Privatization is thus viewed as a necessary step to allow competition to develop. Of course, the fact that the market is contestable does not imply that competition will come about. There are only a few (about fifteen) parties active on the Dutch market, most of these only on their home markets, and the reciprocity clause clearly does not help in increasing the number of bidders. Around 1998, the 100 percent state-owned VSN (now Connexxion) had about 90 percent of the market. As owner of VSN and as guardian of the public interest, the state thus had a double position. To make competition possible, in 1999, under the threat of banning the company from the tenders, it forced Connexxion to divest its business in the North, and this was bought by Arriva plc, a U.K. company. In 2001, in the south, BBA, a company in which Connexxion held 47 percent of the shares (the rest being held by several municipalities and a province) was privatized and sold to CGEA, the largest private bus company in Europe, a subsidiary of Vivendi. As a result, the share of Connexxion in the regional bus market has shrunk to 52 percent (74 percent in the contestable part). In the contestable part of the market, Arriva has 15 percent, while BBA/Connex has 11 percent.

It will be clear that in such a concentrated market, conditions for competition to develop are not the most favorable ones imaginable. To help competition develop, the law gives the minister the power to refuse to give a license to a winner of a tender that has too high a market share on the relevant market. In the Explanatory Memorandum to the Law, percentages of 50 percent (for the regional market) and 35 percent (for the market including cities) are mentioned, but the relevant markets have not yet been identified and the clause, which would effectively have excluded Connexxion, has not yet been applied. Note that Article 9 of the most recent (amended), February 21, 2002, version of the proposal of the European Commission for a regulation on awarding public service contracts in transport specifies an even lower threshold: a tendering authority can decide not to award a contract to a company that would thereby get more than 25 percent of the relevant market (European Commission, 2002).

RTAs have been free to organize the tenders as they saw fit. They have been slow, however, and the goal of tendering 35 percent before 2003 was not achieved. Nevertheless, thus far the minister has not forced the RTAs to tender more. One reason for lack of speed is that the RTAs had to learn how to play the game and how to deal with strategic behavior. For example, in the early tenders, there was not a level playing field, as incumbents refused to reveal essential information about their labor force, and the courts had to step in. Until the summer of 2003, some fourteen tenders had taken place (good for in total less than 10 percent of the market). It should not come as surprise that the number of active bidders has been limited: in three tenders, there were four competitors; in six, there were three bidders; in two, there were two; and in the remaining three, only the incumbent bid. The incumbent won the tender in all but four cases. In its annual report over 2002 (2003), Connexxion stated that it participated, as incumbent, in five (six) tenders, of which it lost two (none); in 2003, the company also participated once as entrant, but it lost that tender. The company states that it views the market as being very competitive and that in 2003 and 2004, approximately 40 to 50 percent of its turnover in the public bus market (680 million euros) will be involved in tender procedures. As the data show, however, most incumbents have been successful in defending their home markets.

Detailed information about the improvements (in price and quality) achieved as a result of the tenders is not publicly available, although KPMG (2002) presents some details on three tenders and suggests that

cost savings or quality improvements have been obtained. It is probably still too early to do a serious evaluation, but the minister has committed to do a first evaluation of the tenders that have taken place
before the end of 2004.

10.6   Conclusion

In the Netherlands, privatization is defined differently from the international convention: it is the process of transferring activities from the
government to the private sector, including the nonprofit sector. As in
the Netherlands, there has always been a consensus that the primary
role of the government is to create the right conditions to allow individuals and firms to go about their own business and to correct market
failures; there is a long and strong tradition of such privatization. But
in the Netherlands, selling shares of state participation traditionally
was not classified as privatization since these SOEs have always
largely been run as ordinary business firms; hence, pure transfer of
ownership was not considered to influence the outcome.

As a result of the need to form coalition governments, privatization
policy has always been pragmatic. Remarkably, in the Netherlands,
this pragmatism has not led to privatization policy with a strong empirical basis. At the beginning of the 1980s, observers noted that remarkably few data were available about the effects of privatization
and increasing competition (Boorsma 1984). When preparing this
chapter, I came to the same conclusion: very little information is in the
public domain. While in the general discussion in the Netherlands, reference has been made to economic surveys such as Megginson and
Netter (2001) and Winston (1993) that document the efficiency gains
that can be obtained from privatization and deregulation, public debate in the Netherlands has not been much informed by local data. In
this respect, I can only join in the chorus of the earlier writers and
hope that there will be more empirical research in the future. As shown
in this chapter, the practical experiences of the past two decades have
shown that both pure contractual arrangements and government ownership have drawbacks; hence, pragmatic policy should be well informed about the trade-offs involved.

During the period covered, and especially in the period 1994 to 1998,
Dutch policymakers showed a strong belief in market forces, leading to
the idea that market liberalization would be sufficient to establish a
competitive market and take care of the public interests, and a corre-

sponding neglect for issues of market design and the transition from monopoly to market. While the Ministry of Finance defended the standard position that regulation of private business was the preferred alternative and may have neglected the limits of contracting, the Ministry of Economics seems to have been drifting, and it was not always able to manage the transition process in various network sectors adequately. In the implementation of EU directives, there has frequently been lack of vision; policy was not in line with the recommendations that were contained in the economic literature at the time; in fact, economists did not seem to have much influence on microeconomic policy in this domain. Policy moved with the tide of the time, and as we have seen, the compromise solution that was reached frequently conflicted with official policy. In retrospect, not all decisions taken during that period have proved to be wise ones.

The government has learned from its mistakes and responded by setting up initiatives such as "the knowledge center on network industries" that aim at sharing knowledge within the administration. At the same time, the lack of success with some privatizations has shown Dutch economists that their services might be useful here. Although the number of Dutch economists working in the area of industrial organization and regulatory economics is still small, thanks to specific government subsidies, such as those to the ENCORE network, the number is increasing and we may expect that in the future, Dutch microeconomic policy, while remaining pragmatic, will be better informed about economic insights than it was in the last decade of the twentieth century.

Appendix: State Participations Between January 1, 1997, and November 1, 2001

A first group consists of publicly traded companies in which the state still holds a minority share, either for political reasons (KLM is an example) or since the time has not yet been ripe to sell the remaining shares. These companies are on the divestiture path, and some have been divested in the meantime. This group simply illustrates practical difficulties; it does not contradict the general policy line. Second, there are financial institutions and regional development companies that serve as instruments to facilitate business and attract investments. The companies on the list are in line with the general preference of the Dutch state to finance. Note that although the Dutch Central Bank

Table 10.A1

Participation	Estab-lished	Legal form	Share, 1997 (%)	Share, 2001 (%)
Listed on stock exchange				
TNT Post Groep NV	1997	NV	—	34.90
Koninklijke KPN NV	1989	NV	44.30	34.69
PinkRoccade NV	1990	NV	100.00	28.40
Koninklijke Luchtvaart Maatschappij NV	1920	NV	25.00	14.10
Koninklijke Hoogovens NV	1918	NV	11.50	—
Internationale Nederlanden Groep NV	1991	NV	0.90	—
Alpinvest Holding NV	1991	NV	30.30	—
Financial institutions				
De Nederlandsche Bank NV	1864	NV	100.00	100.00
NV Bank Nederlandse Gemeenten	1914	NV	50.00	50.00
NV Nederlandse Waterschapsbank	1954	NV	17.20	17.20
Financierings-Mij.Ontwikkelingslanden NV	1970	NV	51.00	51.00
CF Kantoor voor Staatsobligaties BV	1973	BV	100.00	100.00
MTS Amsterdam NV	1999	NV	—	5.00
NIB Capital Bank NV	1945	NV	50.20	14.66
Regional development companies				
NV Brabantse Ontwikkelingsmaatschappijj	1983	NV	64.50	64.50
NV Gelderse Ontwikkelingsmaatschappij	1979	NV	66.60	66.60
NV Industriebank LIOF	1935	NV	94.30	94.30
NV Noordelijke Ontwikkelingsmaatschappij	1974	NV	99.97	99.97
NV Overijsselse Ontwikkelingsmaatschappij	1975	NV	74.30	74.30
Energy				
Energie Beheer Nederland BV	1973	BV	100.00	100.00
NV Nederlandse Gasunie	1963	NV	10.00	10.00
Ultra Centrifuge Nederland NV	1969	NV	98.90	98.90
Nl. Onderneming voor Energie en Milieu	1976	BV	100.00	100.00
BV Nederlandse Pijpleiding Maatschappij	1966	BV	50.00	50.00
Tennet BV	1998	BV	—	100.00
Saranne BV	2001	BV	—	100.00
Transport and infrastructure				
NV Nederlandse Spoorwegen	1937	NV	100.00	100.00
VSN NV (Connexxion)	1994	NV	—	100.00
NV Luchthaven Schiphol	1958	NV	75.80	75.80
NV Luchthaven Maastricht	1956	NV	34.80	34.80
Groningen Airport Eelde NV	1956	NV	80.00	80.00
NV Luchtvaartterrein Texel	1956	NV	65.30	65.30
Haven van Vlissingen NV	1934	NV	35.50	—
NV Westerscheldetunnel	1998	NV	—	95.40
Other				
Koninklijke Nederlandse Munt NV	1994	NV	100.00	100.00
NV Nederlands Inkoop Centrum	1990	NV	100.00	100.00
Arbo Management Groep BV	1997	BV	48.00	—
NV SDU	1988	NV	100.00	100.00
Thales Nederland BV	1989	BV	1.00	1.00
Eurometaal Holding NV	1993	NV	33.33	13.20

Table 10.A1
(continued)

Participation	Estab-lished	Legal form	Share, 1997 (%)	Share, 2001 (%)
Centrale Organisatie voor Radio-actief Afval	1982	NV	10.00	10.00
Vuil Afvoer Maatschappij NV	1929	NV	99.97	—
AVR Chemie BV	1984	BV	30.00	30.00
DLV Groep NV	1993	NV	—	82.50
Twinning Holding BV	1998	BV	—	100.00
NOB Holding NV	1999	NV	—	100.00
NederlandseOmroepzendermaatschappij NV	1935	NV	59.00	59.00
Holland Weer Services BV	1999	BV	—	100.00
Holland Metrology NV	1995	NV	100.00	—

(DNB) has public responsibilities, it has been set up as a private limited liability company. Third, there are companies in the energy sector, including those dealing with exploration and transportation of gas, and TenneT, the TSO for the electricity market that is also responsible for the high-voltage electricity grid. Fourth, there are companies in the transport sector, besides the airports, a harbor, and a public private partnership for constructing and exploiting a tunnel; there are also the Dutch railroads (NS) and a bus company (Connexxion). The fifth category is somewhat of a mixed bag, containing the former state firms that have been transformed into participations (DNM, SDU), some public broadcasting companies, waste disposal companies, and Twinning, an incubator for "new economy" companies that the state set up since the market did not do this.

Notes

Thanks to Joyce Sylvester, Rob Aalbers, and Arjen Gielen for their contributions to an earlier version of this chapter.

1. Some other papers on this topic, all focusing on privatization efforts of the Lubbers cabinets, are Andeweg (1994), Boorsma (1984), De Ru and Van Aalst (1987), Haffner and Berden (1998), Hulsink and Schenk (1998) and Van de Ven (1994). De Ru (1981) gives a very readable overview of the history of privatization in the Netherlands up to 1982.

2. The term is from Andeweg (1994).

3. On June 22, 2004, the Ministry of Public Works announced that the monopoly would remain until 2019, but that there would be supervision by the competition authority, NMa.

4. In the 1960s, the government had stepped in by providing subsidies to assist the ship-building sector in rationalizing and creating a national champion; the resulting company,

RSV, however, was not viable and in 1983 finally collapsed. A parliamentary investigation revealed that more than $1 billion had been wasted and concluded that industrial policy should not be conducted in this way.

5. Note that the participation of lower-level government is not included in this table. Municipalities and provinces own important assets such as the electricity distribution grids, and possible privatization of these has been hotly debated.

References

Algemene Rekenkamer. 1989. *Verzelfstandiging van de Loodsdienst.* August 22.

Andeweg, R. B. 1994. "Privatization in the Netherlands: The Results of a Decade." In V. Wright, ed., *Privatization in Western Europe: Pressures, Problems and Paradoxes.* London: Pinter Publishers.

Bouckaert, J., and Verboven, F. 2004. "Price Squeezes in Regulatory Environment." Discussion paper, University of Antwerp.

Boorsma, P. 1984. "Privatisering." *Openbare Uitgaven* 16, 282–303.

Correlje, A., and Odell, P. 2000. "Four Decades of Groningen Production and Pricing Policies and a View to the Future." *Energy Policy* 28, 19–27.

De Bijl, P., van Damme, E., and Larouche, P. 2003. "Towards a Liberalized Postal Market." TILEC research institute, Tilburg University.

De Ru, H. J. 1981. "Staatsbedrijven en staatsdeelnemingen, juridische aspecten en de gevolgen daarvan voor het economisch beleid." Ph.D.-dissertation, Stichting Ars Aequi.

De Ru, H. J., and Van Aalst, H. J. 1987. *Privatisering in de praktijk: juridische aspecten.* Zwolle: Tjeenk Willink.

ECN. 2004. "Referentieraming Energie en CO2 2001 tot 2010." ⟨www.ECN.NL⟩.

Economist. 2002. "Model Makers: A Survey of the Netherlands." May 4–10.

Ecorys. 2004. "Concurrentieverhoudingen en marktmacht in het OV." February. ⟨http://www.minvenw.nl/cend/bsg/brieven/data/1062424700.doc⟩.

European Commission. 2002. "Amended Proposal for a Regulation of the European Parliament and of the Council on Action by Member States Concerning Public Service Requirements and the Award of Public Service Contracts in Passenger Transport by Rail, Road and Waterway." *COM.* 107 final, 2002/0212(COD).

European Court of Justice. 2003. "Commission vs Spain." C-463/00, and "Commission vs UK and Northern Ireland." C-98/01.

Financieel Dagblad. 2004. "Coalitie wil greep op zbo's." June 25.

Haffner, R., and Berden, K. 1998. *Reforming Public Enterprises—Case Studies: The Netherlands.* Paris: OECD.

Hulsink, W., and Schenk, H. 1998. "Privatisation and Deregulation in the Netherlands." In D. Parker, ed., *Privatisation in the European Union: Theory and Policy Perspectives.* London: Routledge.

Kamerstukken. 1982–1983. "Privatisering" (Privatization). 17938, no. 1.

Kamerstukken. 1985–1986. "Heroverweginsrapport Verkoop Staatsdeelnemingen" (Reconsideration of Selling State Participations). 16625, no. 73.

Kamerstukken. 1987–1988. "Privatisering" (Privatization). 17938, no. 42.

Kamerstukken. 1994–1995a. "Verantwoord Verzelfstandigen" (Careful Corporatization). 21042, no. 15.

Kamerstukken. 1994–1995b. "Herstel van het primaat van de politiek bij de aansturing van zelfstandige bestuursorganen" (Political Influence on Quango's). 24130, no. 5.

Kamerstukken. 1994–2004. "Marktwerking, Deregulering en Wetgevingskwaliteit" (Competition, Deregulation and the Quality of Law). 24036, various numbers.

Kamerstukken. 1995–1996. "Verhonding Rijksoverheid—NS" (Relation between the Government and the Railroads). 18986, no. 18.

Kamerstukken. 1996–1997a. "Wet onafhankelijke post- en telecommunicatieautoriteit" (Law Concerning Regulations for Post and Telecommunications). 25128, various numbers.

Kamerstukken. 1996–1997b. "Telecommunicatiewet" (Telecommunications Law). 25533 (Staatsblad 1998, 610).

Kamerstukken. 1996–1997c. "Beleid inzake staatsdeelnemingen" (Policy with respect to state participations). 25178, no. 2.

Kamerstukken. 1997–1998a. "Herziening Waterleidingwet" (Discussion on revision of water law). 25869.

Kamerstukken. 1997–1998b. "Electricity Law." 25621.

Kamerstukken. 1998–1999a. "Zicht op toezicht" (Vision on Supervision). 24036, no. 127.

Kamerstukken. 1998–1999b. "Wet Personenvervoer 2000" (Law on Public Transport). 26456.

Kamerstukken. 1998–1999c. "Rapport Rekenkamer" (National Chamber of Auditors). 26456.

Kamerstukken. 1998–1999d. "Toezicht op het spoor" (Supervision of public train transport). 26615.

Kamerstukken. 1998–2000. "Gas Law." 26463.

Kamerstukken. 1999–2000a. "Advies Raad van State over de toestand van's-Rijks Financiën" (Advice on the Government's Budget). 27018, no. 1.

Kamerstukken. 1999–2000b. "Liberalisering en privatisering in netwerksectoren" (Liberalization and privatization of network industries). 27018, no. 1.

Kamerstukken. 1999–2000c. "Concessiewet personenvervoer per trein" (Train Passenger Transport). 27216.

Kamerstukken. 1999–2000d. "Aardgasbaten" (Revenue from Natural Gas). 26811, no. 2.

Kamerstukken. 2000–2001a. "Borging van publieke belangen" (Guarding the Public Interests). 27771, no. 1.

Kamerstukken. 2000–2001b. "Commissarissen van Overheidswege" (Government Representatives on the Supervisory Board). 22064, no. 5.

Kamerstukken. 2000–2001c. "Spoorwegwet." 27482, no. 1–2.

Kamerstukken. 2001–2002a. "Selling State Participations." 28165, no. 2.

Kamerstukken. 2001–2002b. "Wijziging van de Elektriciteitswet 1998 en de Gaswet (nadere regels voor netbeheerders en voor privatisering en enkele voorzieningen ingeval van wanbeheer van een net)" (Revised Electricity Law). 28190.

Kamerstukken. 2001–2002c. "Herstructurering Gasgebouw" (Restructuring the Gas Sector). 28109, no. 1, 2, 5.

Kamerstukken. 2003–2004a. "Nota deelnemingenbeleid" (State Participations). 28165, no. 13.

Kamerstukken. 2003–2004b. "Verantwoording en toezicht bij rechtspersonen met een wettelijke taak" (Supervising Agencies with Legal Tasks). 29450, no. 2.

Kamerstukken. 2003–2004c. "Wijziging van de Telecommunicatiewet i.v.m. implementatie Europese regelgeving" (New Telecommunication Law Implementing the New EU Framework). 28851.

Kamerstukken. 2003–2004d. "Wijziging Elektriciteitswet 1998 en Gaswet in verband met implementatie en aanscherping toezicht netbeheer" (Revision of Electricity Act and Gas Act). 29372.

Kamerstukken. 2003–2004e. "Toekomstige ontwikkeling van de Nederlandse Postsector. Notitie Post" (Vision on the Postal Market). 29502, no. 1.

KPMG. 2002. "Openbaar busvervoer op de goede weg? Resultaten van marktwerking in het openbaar busvervoer" (Competition in Bus Transport). Report to Ministry of Economic Affairs, December.

Megginson, W., and Netter, J. 2001. "From State to Market: A Survey of Empirical Studies on Privatization." *Journal of Economic Literature* 39(2), 321–389.

Ministry of Economic Affairs. 2004. "*Visie op de toekomstige structuur van de energiemarkt*" (Vision on the future structure of the energy market). Letter to Parliament, March 31.

Newbery, D. 1977. "Privatisation and Liberalisation of Network Utilities." *European Economic Review* 41, 357–383.

NMa. 2003. "NMa Approves Take-Over over Reliànt Netherlands by Nuon." Decision of August 12. ⟨www.nmanet.nl⟩.

NMa. 2004. *Annual Report*. 2003.

OECD. 2002. "Recent Privatisation Trends in OECD Countries." Paris: OECD.

OPTA. 2002. *Vision on the Market and Annual Report 2001*. ⟨www.opta.nl⟩.

OPTA. 2004. *Vision on the Market and Annual Report 2003*. ⟨www.opta.nl⟩.

Raad van State. 2000. *Jaarverslag 1999*. The Hague.

SCP. 2001. "The Non-Profit Sector in the Netherlands." Working document 75, Sociaal en Cultureel Planbureau, April. ⟨www.scp.nl⟩.

SEO. 2003. *Tante Pos krijgt concurrentie; effecten van liberalisering van de postmarkt.* Amsterdam, September.

Short, R. P. 1984. "The Role of Public Enterprises: An International Statistical Comparison." In R. H. Floyd, C. S. Gray, and R. P. Short, eds., *Public Enterprise in Mixed Economies.* Washington, D.C.: International Monetary Fund.

Staatscourant. 2001. "Beleidsregels privatisering energiedistributiemaatschappijnen." July 11, no. 132.

Van Damme, E. 1996. "Marktwerking en herregulering." In R. van Gestel and Ph. Eijlander, eds., *Markt en Wet.* Zwolle: W.E.J. Tjeenk Willink.

Van Damme, E. 2001. "Marktwerking vereist Maatwerk." *Maandschrift Economie* 65(3), 185–207.

Van Damme, E., and Zwart, G. 2003. "The Liberalized Dutch Green Electricity Market: Lessons from a Policy Experiment." *De Economist* 151(4), 389–413.

Van de Ven, A. T. M. L. 1994. "The Changing Role of Government in Public Enterprises: Dutch Experiences." *International Review of Administrative Sciences* 60(3), 371–383.

Waddams Price, C. 2004. "Spoilt for Choice? The Costs and Benefits of Opening UK Residential Energy Markets." CSEM working paper.

Winston, Clifford. 1993. "Economic Deregulation: Days of Reckoning for Microeconomists." *Journal of Economic Literature* 31, 1263–1289.

WRR. 2000. *Het borgen van het publiek belang.* The Hague: SDU Publishers.

Zalm, G. 2003. "De staat als uw aandeelhouder" (The state as shareholder). Speech to managers of state-owned enterprises, September 10. ⟨www.minfin.nl⟩.

11 Privatization Policy in Spain: Stuck between Liberalization and the Protection of Nationals' Interests

Pablo Arocena

The privatization of public firms started to be significant in Spain from the mid 1980s and has been conducted under two different administrations: the Socialist administration (1982–1996) and the Conservative administration (1996–2004). Privatization was especially intense between 1996 and 2000, when the large utilities and industrial groups, which rank at the top of the largest Spanish firms, were totally privatized. As a result, the participation of the public enterprise sector in the GDP was reduced from 3 percent in 1995 to 1 percent in 2002. According to OECD (2002) data, Spain's privatization program raised 38,401 US$ million between 1990 and 2001, which ranks Spain fourth among European privatizing countries.

This chapter provides an overview of the recent history of privatization in Spain. It analyzes the economic, financial, and political objectives that the successive Spanish governments pursued. It also reviews the still scant empirical evidence on the economic consequences of privatization on firms' and markets' performance, with emphasis on the analysis of privatization and liberalization in the utilities sectors.

11.1 Privatization under the Socialist Administration, 1983–1996

In Spain, the international economic recession of the 1970s coincided with the start of the transition toward democracy after Franco's death in 1975. Hence, the government's intervention in the public enterprise sector (PES) between 1977 and 1982 was marked by industrial crisis and social instability.

The combination of economic and political turmoil led the successive governments of the democratic transition to use the National Institute of Industry (INI), created during Franco's dictatorship in 1941, as an instrument to support the level of employment and income distribution.

As García-Fernández (1990) argues, it was a time of political solutions for the business crisis. The nationalization of a large number of loss-making companies led to the creation of a huge, unprofitable PES suffering from overcapacity, overstaffing, and chronic financial needs. The INI was configured to help firms in crisis—as a sort of "hospital of firms".

The victory of the Socialist Workers party (PSOE) in the general elections of 1982 initiated a period of successive Social-Democratic governments presided over by Felipe González. The first socialist cabinet implemented a set of global reform policies and intense sectoral adjustments. The stated aim of the government's industrial adjustment policy was to adapt Spanish industry to the changing economic environment that would lead to the integration of Spain in the European Community in 1986. The possibility of joining was a formidable challenge for the Spanish PES, which was virtually bankrupt. First, it had to deal with adapting to the European competition policy, which required eliminating subsidies and dismantling various public monopolies. Second, it implied the opening of the industrial sector to a more competitive environment.

11.1.1   The Rationalization and Reorganization of the PES

The first measure toward reforming the PES consisted of introducing profitability criteria and control mechanisms in the management of public holdings. Simultaneously, the state-owned sector was fully re-organized through a strategy of concentration of business lines around strong companies. This was part of the cabinet's effort to build a set of national champions, capable of reaching leading positions in the world market. Up to then, the Spanish public industrial sector mostly consisted of small and medium-sized companies by world standards. They were too small to compete internationally with other European players and to access new markets and technologies, thereby leading the way for other Spanish businesses.

Therefore, this was the time of the creation and strengthening of large Spanish industrial public groups. Thus, the dominant position of the power generator Endesa in the electricity market was reinforced by the ascription of all the state-owned electrical companies. The iron and steel, aluminum, and electronic sectors were organized around CSI-Aceralia, Inespal, and Inisel, respectively, through several mergers and share exchanges. The oil and gas companies that formed the National

Institute of Hydrocarbons were consolidated into a single company, Repsol, which became the largest Spanish industrial company. And all state banks were merged into Argentaria to form the third largest banking group.

Parallel with this strategy of concentration, the investment in public companies increased dramatically between 1985 and 1991. The investment effort concentrated on the telecommunications, transport, and energy sectors. At the same time, the utilities sectors—and consequently the three state-owned bigs Repsol, Endesa, and Telefonica—were protected from foreign and domestic competitors well after the incorporation of Spain to the European Community. In this respect, the regulation of the energy sectors was clearly pro-industry biased, allowing the companies to keep all the productivity gains and cost reductions and thereby increase their profitability (Arocena, Contín, and Huerta 2002). The PSOE tried to be clear from the outset that it had no aim of nationalizing any of these industrial groups and that they would contribute dividends to the public purse.

11.1.2 Privatization

The PSOE had no privatization program that defined objectives, criteria, sectors, companies selected, methods, guarantees for the process, or general time line. As Bel and Costas (2001) argue, privatization was part of the strategy of rationalization of the PES and later of reducing the budget deficit. Initially, socialist politicians were even reluctant to use the term *privatization* and instead used other words such as *disinvestment* or *denationalization*. As Claudio Aranzadi (1989), minister of industry and energy from 1988 to 1993 and chair of the INI from 1982 to 1988, declared, "The decisions of disinvestment of the INI do not respond to political or ideological reasons, but to criteria of industrial and financial rationality."

The first firms that were privatized shared some (or several) of the following features:

• Small and medium-sized companies that had been nationalized during the transition toward democracy for social or political reasons. This reprivatization of these companies was the logical consequence of INI's relinquished role as hospital of firms.

• Companies operating in competitive environments of little relevance in their respective sector.

• Companies that could no longer be competitive as PEs because of their small size, technological backwardness, or insufficient distribution networks.

The restructuring of these firms would have involved major investment. Instead, they were sold to foreign groups that would provide technology improvements, synergies, and economies of scale. Such were the cases of the carmaker SEAT and the truck maker Enasa, which were sold to Volkswagen and Iveco, respectively. Table 11.1 lists all firms privatized during this period.

The bulk of companies were sold directly each to a single buyer after financial restructuring involving outright grants under the context of the Plan of Restructuring and Reindustralization, led by Royal Decree-Law 8/1983 of November 30 and Law 27/1984 of July 26. Under this plan, the state administered monetary subsidies and compensation to laid-off workers and supported labor relocation or early retirement programs. Comín (1995) estimates that over the period 1985–1994, the INI raised 1,833 million euros by the sale of publicly owned companies but had previously devoted 2,290 million euros to restructuring. It also liquidated some companies with substantial losses because it could not find a buyer.

Finally, as shown in Table 11.2, between 1986 and 1990, the government also sold blocks of shares of profitable PEs in the stock market, but with the firm remaining under the state's control. The goal of these partial sales was to obtain cash to finance the capital needs of these firms, and thus avoiding resorting to the national budget (Aranzadi 1989, De la Dehesa 1993).

In February 1992, the Treaty on European Union was signed at Maastricht. The Program of Convergence of Spain was presented in March 1992 with the objective of ensuring that Spain gain admittance to the third phase of the European Monetary Union. Additionally, the slowdown of the economic activity in 1992 forced the government to adopt a series of urgent budgetary measures through Royal Decree Law 5/1992 of July 21. The need to fulfill the convergence criteria and the economic recession required reducing the budget's deficit and the debt, which to a great extent marked the entrusted objectives to the public sector. Hence, from 1992, the sales of packets of shares of very profitable firms were significant (see table 11.2). In fact, the income collected from these sequential IPOS accounted for 80 percent of the total income collected from privatizations under the socialist administration.

The Program of Convergence also meant an important instrument to encourage the liberalization of some economic sectors. Thus, it assigned the antitrust authority (Tribunal de Defensa de la Competencia) the task of elaborating reports on deregulation intended to increase the liberalization of the Spanish economy. This impulse led to the approval of deregulating measures in service and transport sectors and laying the foundation of the liberalization of the energy and telecom sectors. Also, the approval of the Electricity Act in 1994 established the first independent electricity regulator (the National Electricity Commission) and opened the way for liberalizing the electricity market.

The government had advocated maintaining a controlling share in privatized companies. Besides, the socialist administration used the privatization program to create groups of stable shareholders, the so-called *núcleos duros*, with the aim of keeping control of the privatized firms in Spanish hands. This policy was intended to avoid losing national sovereignty in sectors considered of strategic interest. To that effect, the Ministry of Industry issued guidelines to encourage the participation of the Spanish financial and industrial groups in the institutional tranches of the initial public offerings (IPOs). This policy reinforced the power that financial oligarchy had traditionally in the Spanish economy (Lancaster 1989, Rodríguez 2000). Further, this strategy succeeded in preventing any of these firms from being taken over by any major international player in these sectors, which arguably restricted capital market pressures to be efficient.

In 1995, the government passed Law 5/1995 of March 23, described as the "legal framework for disposal of publicly owned holdings in certain companies." The law provided the government a tool to prevent eventual takeovers in leading privatized companies: the golden share. The conservative government used this veto power later to frustrate an attempted acquisition of Telefónica by the Dutch company KPN in 1999. Golden shares are still in force in Telefónica, Endesa, Repsol, Indra, and Iberia.

Finally, some months later, Royal Decree Law 5/1995 of June 16 dissolved the INI and divided the state holdings into two groups: the State Industrial Agency (AIE) and the State Corporation for Industrial Participations (SEPI). AIE grouped a set of chronically unprofitable companies located in mature sectors subject to plans of industrial restructuring—mining, iron and steel, shipbuilding and military constructions—whereas SEPI was created as the shareholder of the most profitable public firms.

Table 11.1
Total privatizations under the PSOE administration, 1985–1996

Year	Company name	Industry	Method	Buyer	% share sold	Gross proceeds (millions of euros)
1985	Textil Tarazona	Textiles	DS	Entrecanales	69.6	1
	Ingenasa	Biotechnology	DS	ERT	67.6	NA
	Igfisa	Food	DS	Pleamar	100	NA
	Cesquisa	Chemical	DS	Cepsa	45.4	NA
	Secoinsa	Electronics	DS	Fujitsu	69.1	18.63
	SKF Española	Automobile bearings	DS	Aktiebogalet SKF	98.8	7.81
	Viajes Marsans	Tourism	DS	Trapsatur	100	NA
	Grossypium	Textiles	DS	Textil Guadiana	100	NA
1986	Entursa	Tourism	DS	Ciga	100	31.17
	Frigsa	Food	DS	Saprogal	100	4.8
	Gypisa	Food	DS	Norteños	100	NA
	La Luz	Food	DS	Prevert	100	NA
	Inisa	Engineering	DS	Accionistas privados de Inisa	60	NA
	Remetal	Aluminum	DS	Socios fundadores de Remetal	66.6	NA
	Issa	Aluminum	DS	Aluperfil	100	NA
	Aluflet	Aluminum	DS	Accionistas privados de Aluflet	40	NA
	Motores MBD	Shipbuilding	DS	Klockner Humboldt Deutz AG	60	NA
	Pamesa	Paper	DS	Torras Hostench	100	6.8
	Fovisa	Iron and steel	DS	Gekanor	100	NA
	Indugasa	Car industry	DS	Grupo GKN	50	NA
	Seat	Car maker	DS	Voskswagen	100	NA
	Telesincro	Electronics	DS	Bull	100	NA
	Amper	Electronics	PO	Many	68	26.3

Year	Company	Sector	Type	Buyer	%	Value
1987	Dessa	Shipbuilding	DS	Forestal del Atlántico	80	NA
	Evatsa	Aluminum	DS	Cebal	100	NA
	Litofan	Aluminum	DS	Baumgartner Ibérica	100	NA
	Alumalsa	Aluminum	DS	Montupet	44	NA
	Purolator	Car industry	DS	Knecht Filterwerke	97.4	NA
	Victorio Luzuriaga	Car industry	DS	Eisenwerk Bruhl	33.3	NA
	Dirsa	Food	DS	Promodes/BBV	50	NA
	Miel Española	Food	DS	Agrolimen	51	NA
	Miraflores	Food	DS	Queserías Miraflores	NA	NA
	Acesa	Highways	PO	Many	58	131.6
1988	—	—	—	—	—	—
1989	Astican	Shipbuilding	DS	Italmar	90.7	3.97
	MTM-Ateinsa	Capital goods	DS	GEC Alsthom	100	21.52
	Enfersa	Fertilizers	DS	Ercros	100	44.7
	Oesa	Food	DS	Ferruzzi	100	14.72
	Pesa	Electronics	DS	Amper	97.4	0
	Ancoal	Aluminum	DS	Omnium Industrie	75.2	NA
	Intelhorce	Textiles	DS	Benorbe	100	12
1990	Adaro Indonesia	Engineering	DS	Indonesia Coal and others	80	NA
	Hytasa	Textiles	DS	Textil Guadiana	100	0.6
	Imepiel	Shoes	DS	DFG Grupo Cusi	100	0.6
	Dirsa	Wholesaler	DS	Promodes/BBV	75.1	72.7
	Salinas Torrevieja	Salt	DS	Solvay	38.5	0.6
	Coifer	Food	DS	BBV	50	NA
1991	Coisa	Food	DS	Rústicas	100	NA
	Enasa	Truck maker	DS	Iveco	100	12
	Fridarago	Food	DS	Rústicas	100	NA
	Grupo Alvarez	Porcelain	DS	Estudesa	100	0.6
	Jobac	Wholesaler	DS	Erosmer/Eroski	100	NA
	TSD	Electronics	DS	Telepublicaciones	100	NA

Table 11.1
(continued)

Year	Company name	Industry	Method	Buyer	% share sold	Gross proceeds (millions of euros)
1992	Icuatro	Health	DS	Grupo Alegre	90	NA
1993	Automoción 2000	Car industry	DS	Inversores Reo	100	NA
	Fábrica San Carlos	Capital goods	DS	Grupo Navacel and others	100	NA
	Ineco	Engineering	DS	Varios	66	NA
	Palco	Aluminum	DS	Alcan Deutschland	100	NA
1994	Artespaña	Craftsmanship	DS	Medino, S.L.	100	0.3
	ASDL	Aerospace	DS	Quadrant Group	87	NA
	Caivsa	Gas	DS	Gas Natural	100	16.61
	Cia. Transatlántica	Shipping	DS	Naviera Odiel/Mar. Valenciana	100	NA
	Enagas	Gas	DS	Gas Natural	91	306.5
	Royal Brands	Food	DS	RJR Nabisco	50	103.7
1995	Lesa	Food	DS	Leyma/Iparlat	100	15
	Refinalsa	Aluminum	DS	Remetal	50	2.7
	Sidenor	Iron and steel	DS	Digeco/Olarra/Rodac	50	12
1996	Sagane	Gas	DS	Enagas	91	30

Sources: Own elaboration on data from economic press and Cuervo (1997).
Note: DS = direct sale; PO = public offering.

Table 11.2
Partial sales under the PSOE administration, 1985–March 1996

Year	Company name	Industry	Method	Buyer	% share sold	Gross proceeds (millions of euros)
1985	—	—	—	—	—	—
1986	Gesa	Energy	PO		39	54
1987	Telefónica I	Telecommunications	PO		6	282.5
1988	Ence I	Paper	PO		39.3	106.9
	Endesa I	Energy	PO		20.4	480.8
1989	Repsol I	Energy	PO	(BBV 4%)	30.6	939
1990	Repsol II	Energy	DS	Pemex	5	191.8
1991	—	—	—	—	—	—
1992	Repsol III	Energy	PO		10	420.7
1993	Argentaria I	Banking	PO		25	661.1
	Argentaria II	Banking	PO		23	1,081.8
	Repsol IV	Energy	PO		13	661.1
1994	Endesa II	Energy	PO		8.7	1,081.8
1995	Ence II	Paper	PO		19	70.3
	Repsol V	Energy	PO		19	1,206.8
	Telefónica II	Telecommunications	PO		11	1,172
1996	Argentaria III	Banking	PO		25	1,021.7
	Repsol VI	Energy	PO		11	781.3

Sources: SEPI (2003), Gámir (1999).
Note: DS = direct sale; PO = public offering.

11.2   Privatization under the Conservative Administration, 1996–2004

11.2.1   The Program for the Modernization of the Public Enterprise Sector

The model of privatization changed radically in 1996 following the victory of the right-wing People's party (PP) in the March elections. Under the new conservative administration, Spain moved quickly toward privatization out of conviction and because it was a ready means for curbing the budget deficit. Thus, the first step of the new cabinet was to approve the Program for the Modernization of the Public Enterprise Sector, which set up the foundation of the government's privatization strategy.

The program of privatization created the Consultative Council on Privatizations (CCP) along with a new state holding company, the State Corporation for Property Participations (SEPPA), to hold the share packages controlled by the Department of Government Property. This new body, along with the SEPI and the AIE, came to be called "managing agents of the privatization process." The main function of the CCP consists of reporting on all privatization issues brought forth by the managing agents. It must judge whether each process and proposal of sale complies with the publicity, transparency, and open competition principles. It also is obliged to answer questions raised by the government or the managing agents during the process of privatization.

The program of privatization classified state-owned companies into four groups according to a time line for privatization. It set out to sell most profitable companies immediately and to sell the others after they had become profitable. In cases of extreme deficit, any action to be taken was postponed.

11.2.2   Full Privatization: The "Crown Jewels" On Sale

Privatizations carried out since 1996 have been channeled through direct sale and public offerings and have included the largest and most profitable state-owned enterprises. Included here were such "crown jewels" (a term widely used by the Spanish economic press) as Repsol, Endesa, Telefónica, and Tabacalera. These operations accounted for an enormous amount of funds obtained from privatization in comparison to that of the previous administration, as shown in table 11.3. Hence, according to SEPI (2003) the state raised 13,222.27 million euros between 1982 and 1996. Between June 1996 and December 2003, SEPI privatized forty-eight companies and disposed of minority stakes in another five companies. These operations generated an income of 29,400 million euros, which were devoted to reducing national debt. According to estimates by Vergés (1998), up to 75 percent of proceeds served to reduce current fiscal deficit.

This massive placement of the shares of state companies contributed to the strengthening of the Spanish financial markets. The capitalization of the stock exchange increased from 189,794 million euros in 1996 to 419,451 million euros in 2002. While the state share in the market's total capitalization declined from 16.64 percent in 1992 (10.87 percent in 1996) to 0.21 percent in 2001, the number of shares of listed Spanish companies held by households as a percentage of market capitalization increased from 24.44 percent in 1992 (23.59 percent in 1996) to 27.96 percent in 2001.

Although privatization extended share ownership to many people who had never owned shares before, the culture of a new "popular capitalism" is far from being fully supported by the Spanish people. Nonfinancial assets—mostly real estate—still account for 80 percent of the total assets held by Spanish families in 2002. Indeed, the proportion of financial assets was reduced from 26.13 percent in 1996 to 20.30 percent in 2002.

The president of SEPI was clear in November 2000 when announcing in the Spanish parliament that SEPI was expected to be completely privatized by 2003. However, the current privatization agenda does not include the coal mining group HUNOSA, the shipbuilding group IZAR, the Radio and Television Broadcasting RTVE, and the National Railways RENFE, which together account for more than 90 percent of total state subsidies.

11.2.3 Liberalization, Competition, and the Role of the European Directives

The PP administration passed a number of important legislative reforms according to the liberalizing principles of the European directives. Thus, the approval of the Electricity Act at the end of 1997 placed the Spanish power market among the most liberalized in Europe, well above the minimum required in European Directive 96/92EC (see

Table 11.3
Privatization under the PP administration, March 1996–2003

Year	Company name	Industry	Method	Buyer	% share sold	Gross proceeds (millions of euros)
1996	Gas Natural	Energy	PO	Many	4	216.7
	Sefanitro	Fertilizers	DS	Fertiberia	52.6	3.3
1997	Aceralia	Steel	DS	Arbed/Aristrain/Gestamp	47.2	268.6
	Aceralia	Steel	PO	Many	52.8	794.3
	Aldeasa	Duty-free shops	PO	Many	80	273.7
	Almagrera	Mining	DS	Navan Resources	100	2.65
	Auxini	Construction	DS	OCP Construcciones	100	35.76
	Elcano	Sea transport	DS	Grupo Marítimo Ibérico	100	34.7
	Ferroperfil	Aluminum	DS	Executives (MBO)	100	1.2
	Infoleasing	Leasing	DS	Liscat	100	18.6
	Hijos J. Barreras	Shipbuilding	DS	Grupo Barreras	100	4.5
	Iongraf	Aluminum	DS	Executives (MBO)	100	1
	Repsol VII	Energy	PO	Many	10	1,012
	Retevisión I	Telecommunications	DS	Endesa-Stet and others	70	1,087.8
	Surgiclinic Plus	Medical products	DS	Hambros	50	0
	Sodical	Regional development	DS	Many	51	4.6
	Enagas	Energy	DS	Gas Natural Group	9	84.1
	Endesa III	Energy	PO	Many	27.5	4,029.2
	Tisa	Telecommunications	DS	Telefónica	23.8	763.3
1998	Argentaria IV	Banking	PO	Many	29.2	2,276.3
	Productos Tubulares	Steel	DS	Tubos Reunidos	100	0
	Tabacalera	Food/Tobacco	PO	Many	52.4	1,722.1
	Endesa IV	Electricity	PO	Many	29.5	6,323.2
	Inima	Environment	DS	Grupo OHL	100	3.75

Year	Company	Industry	Method	Buyer	%	Value
	Comee	Energy	A	Diverse	100	9
	Serausa	Highways	A	Areas, S.A.	100	14.8
	Potasas	Mining	DS	DSW/La Seda/Tolsa	100	103.4
	Inespal	Aluminum	DS	Alcoa	100	375.6
	Telefónica III	Telecommunications	PO	Many	21.16	3,786.4
	Retevisión II	Telecommunications	A	Shareholders and others	30	739.2
1999	INDRA	High technology	PO	Many	66.1	393.3
	Red Eléctrica	Electricity	PO	Many	31.5	341
	ICSA-AYA	Aerospace	DS	Mecanizaciones Aeronáuticas	100	0.72
	Astander	Shipbuilding	DS	Italmar	100	1.8
	LM Composites Toledo	Engineering	DS	LM Glasfiber	50	5.2
	Enatcar	Road transport	DS	Alianza Bus	100	157.4
	Iberia I	Airlines	DS	Diverse	40	1,093.8
2000	—	—	—	—	—	—
2001	Conversion Aluminio	Aluminum	DS	Alucoil, S.A.	100	0.7
	Santa Barbara	Armament	DS	General Dynamics Corporation	100	5
	Iberia II	Airlines	PO	Many	48	524
	EXPASA I	Agriculture	A	Diverse		31.6
	ENCE I	Paper	PO	Many	26	99.3
	ENCE II	Paper	DS	CaixaGalicia, Bankinter, Zaragozano	25	130.5
	Interinvest	Airlines	DS	Air Comet	99.2	0
2002	Coosur/Olcesa	Olive/Sunflower oil	DS	Consorcio Jaén Oliva	89.4/100	7
	Química del Estroncio	Mining	DS	Fertiberia	51	10.4
	EXPASA II	Agriculture	A	Diverse		45.4
	Transmediterránea	Sea transport	DS	Acciona and others	95.24	259
2003	Grupo ENA	Highways	DS	Sacyr, Banco Santander & others	100	1,586.3
	Mussini	Insurance	DS	Mapfre Caja Madrid Holding	100	297
	Turbo2000	Engines/Turbines	DS	Sener	100	66

Sources: Own elaboration on data from economic press, SEPI (2003), and Gámir (1999).

Note: DS = direct sale; PO = public offering; A = auction.

Table 11.4
Implementation of the European energy directives in Spain

	Electricity	Gas
Declared market opening by 2003	100%	100%
Unbundling: transmission system operator-owner	Ownership	Ownership
Unbundling: Distribution system operator	Legal	Legal[a]
Regulation of network tariffs	Ex ante	Ex ante
Overall network tarriffs	Average	Normal
Number of transmission companies	1	1
Regulatory body	Yes (National Energy Commission)	Yes (National Energy Commission)
Competence on regulating access conditions	Ministry	Ministry
Competence on dispute settlement	Regulator	Regulator
Balancing conditions and charges set by	Market	Regulator
Balancing period	60 minutes	Daily
Power exchange	Yes	
Intraday market possible	Yes	
Transmission tariff structure		Postalized
Storage available for TPA		Yes

Source: EC (2002).
[a] Gas Natural retains a 40 percent share and is the largest shareholder in the transmission system operator, Enagas.

table 11.4). The same applies to the approval of the Hydrocarbons Law (1998) and the Royal Decree Law of Urgent Measures of Deregulation and Increase of Competition (1999). The pace of market liberalization introduced by these reforms was faster than the European Directive 98/30/EC concerning the common rules for the internal market of natural gas. The Hydrocarbons Law also created the National Energy Commission as an independent regulator overseeing all energy industries.

In the telecommunications sector, full liberalization occurred in 1998 through the approval of Law 12/1997 and Law 11/1998, which are the transposition of the successive amendments of Directive 90/388/EEC with regard to the implementation of full competition in telecommunications markets. Similarly, the approval of the Law 24/1998, the legal transposition of the Postal Directive 97/67/EC, established the gradual liberalization of the postal services. Although privatization has not occurred in this sector, since 2002 two private newcomers, Via Postal and Unipost, have been competing with the state-owned incumbent, Correos y Telégrafos S.A., in the liberalized segments of the market: urban mail, intercity mail up to 350 grams, and direct advertising.

However, liberalizing laws were undertaken together with decisions aimed at managing and protecting the interest of national incumbents. Thus, some reforms were biased by previous agreements between the government and the companies, as in the electricity sector (Arocena, Khün, and Regibeau 1999). Further, following the privatization of utilities, the state retained direct control over firms' strategic decisions through golden shares, while persons close to the government were appointed as chairmen of privatized firms. Telefónica and Endesa were well known examples of these practices. Even as a number of independent regulatory bodies were created, the ministry always retained the authority to intervene and make decisions in key operations like mergers, ignoring the recommendations of the regulators.

In December 1999 the government passed a controversial law intended to prevent hostile takeovers of Spanish energy companies by foreign companies. Budget Law 14/2000 included a provision that allowed the Spanish government to limit the voting rights in a Spanish energy utility of any shareholder being a state-controlled foreign company. This policy was shaped by the government's goal of preserving the Spanish ownership in strategic sectors (e.g., telecommunications and energy) (Expansion, May 4, 2000; El Mundo, December 19, 1999). The government resorted to this law to restrain the takeover bid of Electricité de France for the electric utility Hidroeléctrica del Cantábrico.

Finally, the policy of creating stable Spanish shareholders in privatized firms contributed to expanding the complex network of cross-participation between financial and industrial groups characteristic of the Spanish economy. This has resulted in an enormous concentration of power in a few hands (Lasheras 1999). As Arocena (2003) argues, the extensive cross-ownership among these firms generated a web of common interests, raising concerns about their ability to distort entry and competition.

In this respect, Vergés (1999, 2000) argues that privatization has not been used in Spain to increase competition by eliminating the former public monopolies, rather, monopoly positions still exist but under private ownership. Table 11.5 shows the Herfindahl-Hirschman Index (HHI) and two-firm concentration ratios (CR2) as indicators of the likely competitive potential in four industries affected by privatization and liberalization in the mid-1990s. By any standard, concentration is massive. A high degree of concentration persists years after liberalization and reflects the slow progress of competition in these

Table 11.5
Concentration in liberalized industries

	1994	1998	2002
Electricity			
Generation			
HHI	2127	3550	3150
CR2	59.5	78	74
Distribution			
HHI	2086	3534	3210
CR2	53	81	77
Natural Gas			
HHI	8125	8200	5200
CR2	97.8	95.5	78
Telecommunications			
Fixed telephony			
HHI	10000	9570	6940
CR2	100	99.7	88.8
Mobile			
HHI	10000	5896	4060
CR2	100	100	82.1
Oil fuels			
HHI	3616	3310	2540
CR2	79	75	66

Sources: Own elaboration from CMT (2002), CNE (2001), and companies' annual reports.
Note: CR2 = two-firm concentration ratios. Figures show the market shares of the two biggest firms in an industry, $0 < CR2 \leq 100$. HHI = Herfindahl-Hirschman Index. Figures show the sum of the squares of the market-shares of all firms in an industry, $0 < HHI \leq 10,000$.

sectors. This is very discouraging since economic theory suggests that competition rather than ownership leads to performance gains.

11.3   Results and Consequences of the Privatization Process

There have been a number of studies on the performance differences between private and state-owned enterprises in Spain. They are basically based on an analysis of economic and financial ratios and systematically show superior performance by private firms (Cuervo 1989; Argimón, Artola, and González-Páramo 1999). This is not surprising given that the Spanish PES has acquired a large number of private companies to avoid their bankruptcy and liquidation.

By contrast, empirical research about the effects of privatization on former state-owned companies is scant. This scarcity is certainly due to the difficulty of obtaining reliable data on Spanish privatized firms, particularly on the earliest privatizations, which occurred between 1985 and 1996, and because privatization is an ongoing process.

11.3.1   The Impact of Privatization on Firms' Performance

The first attempt to test the effects of privatization on firm's efficiency was offered by Sanchís (1996). He used a sample of seventeen Spanish public firms that were privatized between 1985 and 1990. His results suggest that both competition and restructuring had a positive impact on productivity growth and that the effect of privatization was relatively weak. Nevertheless, these conclusions should be taken with caution because only five of the seventeen companies included in this study were fully transferred to the private companies and he included data for only one year after their privatization.

Melle (1999) studied the magnitude of various performance indicators of ten firms before and after their privatization. She examined changes resulting from privatization in the same set of economic variables analyzed by Megginson, Nash, and Van Randenborgh (1994): profitability, operating efficiency, capital investment, output, employment level, leverage, and payout. Her sample included only the major firms privatized through public share offerings between 1990 and 1999. She did not reach conclusive results on the improvement of performance induced by the change of property. She also observed that her results might be biased because the firms in her sample operated in sectors with different degrees of market competition. This limitation was surmounted by Villalonga (2000). She used a sample of twenty-four Spanish firms that were operating in competitive environments at the time of privatization (1985–1993), so that no (de)regulation or liberalization interfered with the estimation of strict privatization effects. She found no statistical support of the hypothesis that privatization increases a firm's efficiency, measured by return on assets. She further claimed that privatization involves more than pure ownership effects and looked for other political and organizational factors that influenced the observed effect of privatization on efficiency. Her results show that selling off the firm in a period of economic growth (recession), the foreign (national) nature of the buyer, large (small) firm size, and high (low) firm capital intensity are factors that significantly reinforce (counteract) the effect of firm's privatization on efficiency.

Cabrera and Gómez (2003) represent the latest and most comprehensive attempt to test the effect of privatization on performance. Like

Melle (1999), these authors compared the mean and median values of various firms' profitability and efficiency indicators in the three years before and after privatization. Interestingly, unlike previous studies, their results show a statistically significant improvement following privatization on both profitability and operating efficiency. These conclusions are of special relevance because the authors analyze the most extensive sample of privatized firms that anyone could construct in Spain. They examined fifty-two nonfinancial enterprises, which accounts for more than 45 percent of the total number of firms privatized in Spain—by either public offerings or direct sales—and more than 95 percent of the total gross proceeds raised by privatization between 1985 and 2000.

However, the positive relationship between privatization and firm performance is not statistically significant for the group of firms sold by public offerings, which includes the largest public utilities. This is particularly noteworthy, since its privatization happened with the liberalization of their respective sectors.

11.3.2   The Effect of Privatization and Liberalization in the Utilities Sectors

A common weakness of the cited studies is that they do not compare the evolution of performance of privatized firms with that followed by their competitors that did not experience any change in ownership. We carry out such a comparison for the main privatized utilities—Endesa, Repsol, Telefónica, and Enagas—which together roughly accounted for 60 percent of total gross proceeds raised from privatization in Spain. In particular, we compare the performance level of formerly public utilities before and after their privatization with that achieved by private rivals that simultaneously faced the same change in the environment in the same time period: market liberalization, technical change, or demand growth for the whole sector, but not privatization. Table 11.6 summarizes the average of four key performance indicators for each utility and time period, as well as their average growth rates relative to the corresponding sector.

Figures clearly show that the four companies substantially improved their labor productivity and operating efficiency (value added per employee and sales per employee) after privatization and liberalization. For example, the first row in table 11.6 shows that Repsol annually generated on average 92,000 euros per employee before privatization

Table 11.6
Performance of utilities before and after privatization

	Repsol		Endesa		Telefónica		Enagas	
	Preprivatization, 1988–1994	Postprivatization, 1996–2002	Preprivatization, 1994–1997	Postprivatization, 1999–2002	Preprivatization, 1994–1997	Postprivatization, 1999–2002	Preprivatization, 1989–1993	Postprivatization, 1995–1999
VAE								
Mean[a]	92	130	130	197	89	103	120	287
Annual ΔVAE	18.6	1.4	23.2	15	-6.6	-20.7	-3.1	-15.4
SE								
Mean[a]	487	653	222	483	113	179	643	1210
Annual ΔSE	11.7	-2.9	24	24.8	-0.5	-17.2	2.4	-37.7
RoS								
Mean (%)	7.8	9.6	28.5	20.2	26.2	17.7	5.4	11.9
Annual ΔRoS (%)	-1.3	1.6	-0.8	7.2	0.8	-6.3	-16.6	-1.8
RoE								
Mean (%)	26.6	22.1	23.4	25.5	26.2	18.0	5.6	12.3
Annual ΔRoE (%)	0.8	-2.4	-1.1	20.3	11.4	-15.2	-7.1	-16.8

Source: Companies' annual reports.
Note: VAE = value added/employees (value added = wages + depreciation + profit before interest and tax). SE = sales/employees. RoE = profit before interest and tax/equity. RoS = profit before interest and tax/sales:

$$\Delta X = (\Delta X_{firm} - \Delta X_{sector}) = \left(\frac{X_{firm}^{t+1}}{X_{firm}^{t}}\right) - \left(\frac{X_{sector}^{t+1}}{X_{sector}^{t}}\right).$$

[a] Thousands of euros at constant 1990 prices.

and 130,000 afterward, both at constant 1990 prices. However, regarding the average annual changes, our results show that postliberalization performance in labor productivity and operating efficiency for the group of privatized utilities was actually poorer than that achieved by their private counterparts. For example, the second row in column 2 shows that Repsol's annual increased sales per employee were 11.7 percent higher than those of its competitors over the preliberalization period but 2.9 points lower following privatization.

With regard to profitability, the picture is somewhat different. Endesa and Telefónica show substantial reductions in their return on sales ratios after liberalization, which indicates lower prices and tighter profit margins. The opposite applies to Repsol and Enagas, which suggests that competitive pressure or price regulation was weaker in these sectors.

11.3.3   Prices and Quality of Service in the Utilities Sectors

The postprivatization period witnessed substantial price reductions in utilities together with an increase in the range of services and bill paying options. Relating price and service changes to privatization is complicated by technological progress and, in the case of gas and electricity, variations in fuel input prices. Thus, in most countries, telecom prices fell under state ownership in the 1990s as well as under private ownership. Similarly, lower oil prices in the 1990s drove down gas and electricity prices in Europe, again regardless of ownership.

As shown in table 11.7 the cumulative reduction of average prices of telecommunications services in Spain has been remarkable since market liberalization. According to the telecommunications market regulator (CMT 2002), prices for fixed telephone services fell about 50 percent

Table 11.7
Evolution of utilities average prices and consumer price index in Spain, 1997–2002

	Telecommu- nications	Electricity	Natural Gas	CPI
1997	100	100	100	100
1998	95	96	96	101.4
1999	88	91	94	104.3
2000	62	87	106	108.5
2001	52	85	108	111.4
2002	45	86	125	115.8

Source: Own elaboration on data from CNE (2001) and CMT (2002).

on average between 1998 and 2002. The sharpest price reduction is observed for long-distance calls, which fell around 58 percent in the same period. Prices of mobile telephone services also declined by 30 percent.

Nevertheless, the price of telephone services, and particularly Telefónica's, is still relatively high in Spain. The Spanish Association of Consumers and Users (OCU 2001) compared Telefonica's prices adjusted by power purchase parities (PPP) with those of the dominant players in seventeen countries (fourteen European countries plus Australia, Canada, and the US). The study ranked Telefónica as the third most expensive company behind Portugal Telecom and Telekom Austria. This means a relative worsening of the Telefonica's fifth position in 2000 ranking (OCU 2000).

In the electricity sector, the energy regulator (CNE 2002) compares the evolution of electricity prices in sixteen European countries between 1997 and 2002—since the liberalization of the Spanish power market. Household tariffs decreased by 13 percent in monetary terms during that period, which ranks Spain at the top of the list of price cutting in Europe. Likewise, industrial electricity prices fell between 1997 and 2002. For the smallest industrial consumers, the reduction was relatively moderate (about 5 percent in monetary terms) in comparison with that registered in the rest of Europe. By contrast, price reductions for the largest industrial users were among the highest in Europe (between 10 percent and 21 percent depending on consumer type). However, as in the case of telecommunications, the international comparisons of average prices (before taxes and converted at PPPs) show that Spanish domestic and industrial tariffs are the third and the fifth most expensive in Europe, respectively.

Natural gas prices for the industrial sector were mostly stable during the 1990s. However, in May 1999, prices started to rise rapidly, and by the beginning of 2003, industrial prices were about 40 percent higher than in 1994 (CNE 2003). Households' gas prices continued to rise over the decade, and by 2003, average domestic tariff was 30 percent higher than in 1994. According to the International Energy Agency (CNE 2001), average natural gas prices in Spain are the highest in Europe, in both the domestic and industrial sectors.

Table 11.8 reports consumers' satisfaction on six criteria for eight services of general interest in Spain as well as in the fifteen member states of the European Union. The criterion that provokes the greatest dissatisfaction is that of price. For example, the first row in column 2

Table 11.8

Consumers' satisfaction on services in Spain and the European Union, December 2002 (in percentages)

	Access	Prices	Quality of service	Information	Contract terms	Customer service
Mobile telephone services	81 (75)	32 (44)	81 (84)	60 (67)	46 (59)	68 (72)
Fixed telephone services	92 (89)	36 (51)	87 (90)	68 (75)	48 (64)	69 (77)
Electricity supply services	91 (88)	49 (55)	89 (91)	67 (73)	54 (68)	68 (77)
Gas supply services	86 (67)	53 (55)	89 (86)	67 (69)	57 (65)	68 (67)
Water supply services	93 (86)	60 (56)	91 (89)	69 (72)	60 (66)	69 (74)
Postal services	92 (87)	68 (68)	82 (82)	68 (78)	54 (70)	64 (74)
Transport services within towns and cities (bus, tram, subway, etc.)	82 (69)	56 (47)	74 (66)	72 (68)	51 (57)	61 (59)
Rail services between towns and cities	71 (61)	50 (38)	71 (59)	67 (62)	51 (51)	60 (54)
Mean	86 (78)	51 (52)	83 (81)	67 (71)	53 (63)	66 (69)

Source: EORG (2002).

Notes: Figures report percentages of satisfied consumers in Spain and, in parentheses, those corresponding to European Union (15 countries). These percentages of "satisfaction" result from harmonizing responses to questions Q2, Q3, Q4, Q5, Q6, and Q8 included in the questionnaire of the Eurobarometer no. 58 into two types of reply ("satisfied" or "not satisfied") in the following way:

Q2. In general, would you say that **access** to **** services is easy (= "satisfied") or difficult (= "not satisfied") for you?

Q3. In general, would you say that the **price** you pay for the **** services you use is fair (= "satisfied") or unfair (= "not satisfied")?

Q4. In general, what do you think of the **quality** of the **** services you use? Would you say it is very good, fairly good, fairly bad, or very bad? ("very good" + "fairly good" responses = "satisfied"; "fairly bad" + "very bad" responses = "not satisfied")

Q5. In general, would you say that the **information** (bills, contracts, advertising, tickets, leaflets, etc.) you get from your **** provider is clear ("satisfied") or unclear ("not satisfied")?

Q6. In general, would you say that the terms and conditions of the **contract** with your **** provider are fair ("satisfied") or unfair (not satisfied)

Q7. In general, would you say that the **customer service** provided by your **** service provider is very good, fairly good, fairly bad, or very bad? ("very good" + "fairly good" responses = "satisfied"; "fairly bad" + "very bad" responses = "not satisfied") shows that only 32 percent of Spanish consumers believe that prices for mobile telephone services are fair. Prices for telephone, electricity, and gas supply services are perceived as excessive by a majority of Spanish consumers. The level of satisfaction on this point is below the overall European mean. By contrast, prices for water, post, transport, and rail services, which are supplied by state-owned enterprises and municipalities, show percentages of satisfaction above those registered in the European Union.

Table 11.8 also informs about satisfaction regarding access and quality of service. The satisfaction rate of Spanish consumers concerning access is high. Four services out of the eight studied are easy to access for more than 90 percent of Spanish consumers. Rail services between towns and cities are accessible only for 71 percent of Spanish consumers, which is still above the overall European mean of 61 percent.

Further, a high percentage of Spanish consumers also regard themselves as satisfied with the quality of their services. On average, 83 percent of Spanish users declared themselves satisfied concerning the quality of services. Five services received higher satisfaction rates than the overall European average.

However, the percentage of satisfaction is rather low concerning clarity of information, fairness of contract terms, and quality of customer service provided by service suppliers. On average, two-thirds of Spanish consumers are not satisfied with the information and customer service they receive from their suppliers, and only 53 percent feels satisfied with the contracts made with service providers. In comparative terms, Spanish consumers are less satisfied on these criteria than EU consumers except for city transport and rail services.

11.4 Conclusion

My purpose here is to summarize in which sectors privatization has failed or was successful. The consideration of failure and successful is often ambiguous and subject to qualitative judgments in particular cases. First, early sales of public small-sized companies were used to return previously nationalized firms to the private sector. The state had rescued many firms in bankruptcy during the politically unsettled period of democratic transition. The economic and financial measures applied to these firms before reprivatization should be judged as a success of management under public ownership, since it allowed most of them to survive.

In terms of the impact of privatization on firms' efficiency, the evidence is not conclusive. Rather, it suggests that other factors are more important than pure ownership change: competition, buyer type, and the firm's size and capital intensity. In these cases, privatization always plays a complementary and reinforcing role (Villalonga 2000). The cases of SEAT and ENASA in the automobile industry are representative.

The role of the public sector and the subsequent privatization of state-owned companies in Spain reflect a story of socialization of losses and privatization of profits. Thus, the enormous financial effort made by the state in creating strong leading industrial groups following dramatic sectoral restructuring ended in their selling off once they turned into competitive and profitable companies. This has been the case in the iron and steel sector (CSI-Aceralia), aluminum (INESPAL), and electronics (INDRA), which continue to be competitive as private firms in their respective sectors.

The same applies to the utilities sectors, where high household prices for telephone, electricity, gas, and oil products served to strengthen companies like Repsol, Endesa, Gas Natural, and Telefónica under public ownership. Their huge cash flows financed their Latin American expansion throughout the 1990s without incurring state capital subsidies. In contrast, the traditional loss-making companies remain in public hands: coal mining, radio and television broadcasting, railways, and shipbuilding.

The government's liberalizing effort resulted in a number of major legislative and regulatory reforms in many industries, sometimes even bringing forward or accelerating the timing established by the EU directives. However, the government's goal to obtain as large a financial contribution from privatization to the budget as possible was achieved at the expense of market restructuring and consequently of faster and more effective market competition in newly liberalized sectors: oil, gas, electricity, and telecommunications. In other words, while the privatization policy carried out by the government suited the goal of raising cash to reduce the state budget, it was intrinsically incompatible with that of market liberalization and increased of competition. The Spanish process of privatization reflects and has been marked by the conflict between the advocacy of market liberalization and the protection of the interests of entrenched Spanish economic groups. Thus, the formation of national champions led to an increase in the level of vertical and horizontal concentration in the utilities sectors and a corresponding reduction of domestic rivalry. As the former president of the Competition Body and chair of the National Energy Commission (1995–2000), Fernández-Ordóñez (2000) argues, the anxiety in creating leading Spanish industrial and financial groups able to compete with foreign multinationals explains the inconsistency between Spanish industrial policy and pro-competitive policies. This contradiction has been shared by the different Spanish administrations over the past twenty years, regardless of their ideological divergences.

References

Aranzadi, C. 1989. "La política de desinversiones del INI." *Papeles de Economía Española* 38, 258–261.

Argimón, I., Artola, C., and González–Páramo, J. M. 1999. "Empresa pública y empresa privada, Titularidad y eficiencia." *Moneda y Crédito* 209, 45–93.

Arocena, P. 2003. "The reform of the utilities sector in Spain." In C. Ugaz and C. Waddams–Price, eds., *Utility Privatization and Regulation, A Fair Deal for Consumers?* Cheltenham: Edward Elgar Publishing.

Arocena, P., Contín, I., and Huerta, E. 2002. "Price Regulation in the Spanish Energy Sectors: Who Benefits." *Energy Policy* 30, 885–895.

Arocena, P., Khün, K. U., and Regibeau, P. 1999. "Regulatory Reform in the Spanish Electricity Industry: A Missed Opportunity for Competition." *Energy Policy* 27, 387–399.

Bel, G. and Costas, A. 2001. "La privatización y sus motivaciones en España, de instrumento a política." *Revista de Historia Industrial* 19/20, 39–65.

Cabrera, L. and Gómez, S. 2003. "Un estudio de la eficiencia económica del proceso de privatizaciones español." Paper presented at the Thirteenth Conference of the Asociación Científica de Economía y Dirección de la Empresa. Salamanca, Spain, September.

CMT. 2002. *Informe anual 2002.* Madrid, Comisión del Mercado de las Telecomunicaciones.

CNE. 2001. *Información básica de los sectores de la energía.* Madrid: Comisión Nacional de la Energía.

CNE. 2002. *Precios de la electricidad en el entorno europeo en el año 2002.* Madrid: Comisión Nacional de la Energía.

CNE. 2003. *Boletín mensual de estadísticas de gas natural.* Madrid: Comisión Nacional de la Energía.

Comín, F. 1995. La España pública en la España contemporánea: formas históricas de organización y gestión 1770–1995. Working paper 9505, Historia Económica. Fundación Empresa Pública, Madrid.

Cuervo, A. 1989. "La empresa pública: Estructura financiera, rentabilidad y costes financieros." *Papeles de Economía Española* 38, 177–198.

Cuervo, A. 1997. *La privatización de la empresa pública*. Madrid: Encuentro.

De la Dehesa, G. 1993. "Las privatizaciones en España." *Moneda y Crédito* 196, 131–141.

EC. 2002. *Second Benchmarking Report on the Implementation of the Internal Electricity and Gas Market*. Brussels: European Commission.

EORG. 2002. *Consumers' Opinions on Services of General Interest*. Eurobarometer 58—Special Edition. European Opinion Research Group.

Fernández-Ordóñez, M. A. 2000. *La competencia*. Madrid: Alianza.

Gámir, L. 1999. *Las privatizaciones en España*. Madrid: Pirámide.

García-Fernández, J. 1990. "Política empresarial pública 1973–1988." In P. Aceña and F. Comín, eds., *Empresa pública e industrialización en España*. Madrid: Alianza Editorial.

Lancaster, T. D. 1989. *Policy Stability and Democratic Change, Energy in Spain's Transition*. University Park: Pennsylvania State University Press.

Lasheras, M. A. 1999. *La regulación económica de los servicios públicos*. Barcelona: Ariel.

Megginson, W. L., Nash, R. C., and Van Randenborgh, M. 1994. "The Financial and Operating Performance of Newly Privatized Firms: An International Empirical Analysis." *Journal of Finance* 49(2), 403–452.

Melle, M. 1999. "Algunos resultados efectivos de las privatizaciones en España, una primera aproximación." *Economía Industrial* 330, 141–158.

OCU. 2000. *Compra Maestra 236*. Organización de Consumidores y Usuarios.

OCU. 2001. *Compra Maestra 253*. Organización de Consumidores y Usuarios.

OCU. 2002. *Compra Maestra 265*. Organización de Consumidores y Usuarios.

OECD. 2002. "Recent Privatization Trends in OECD Countries." *Financial Market Trends* 82, 43–55.

Rodríguez, J. A. 2000. "El círculo del poder, La estructura social del poder económico en la España de los noventa." *Sistema* 158, 53–89.

Sanchís, J. A. 1996. "Privatización y eficiencia en el sector público español." *Revista de Economía Aplicada* 10, 65–92.

SEPI. 2003. *Privatizaciones*. Sociedad Estatal de Participaciones Industriales. http://www.sepionline.com.

Vergés, J. 1998. "Efectos de las privatizaciones españolas sobre los presupuestos generales del Estado." *Hacienda Pública Española* 147, 215–231.

Vergés, J. 1999. "Balance de las políticas de privatización de empresas públicas en España 1985–1999." *Economía Industrial* 330, 121–139.

Vergés, J. 2000. "Privatizations in Spain, Process, Policies and Goals." *European Journal of Law and Economics* 9(3), 255–280.

Villalonga, B. 2000. "Privatization and Efficiency, Differentiating Ownership Effects from Political, Organizational and Dynamic Effects." *Journal of Economic Behavior and Organization* 42, 43–74.

12

The United Kingdom's Privatization Experiment: The Passage of Time Permits a Sober Assessment

David Parker

The British Labour government of 1974–1979 arranged the sale of some of the state's shareholding in the petroleum company BP. However, this sale was dictated by budgetary pressures and did not reflect a belief within government that state industries should be privatized. Indeed, the same Labour government took into state ownership two major industries: aerospace and shipbuilding. Only with the election of a Conservative government in 1979, led by Margaret Thatcher, did a sea change in attitude occur within government toward the role of the state in the economy. Although it is often pointed out that the Conservative party election manifesto in 1979 paid little attention to what became known as privatization, referring in the main simply to restoring to the private sector the two industries recently nationalized by labor, there can be no doubt that Thatcher developed a personal crusade against state ownership during the 1980s. As she later wrote in her memoirs:

Privatization...was fundamental to improving Britain's economic performance. But for me it was also far more than that: it was one of the central means of reversing the corrosive and corrupting effects of socialism....Just as nationalization was at the heart of the collectivist programme by which Labour Governments sought to remodel British society, so privatization is at the centre of any programme of reclaiming territory for freedom. (Thatcher 1993, p. 676)

Table 12.1 provides a summary of the major privatizations during the 1980s and 1990s and table 12.2 a summary of the amounts raised through state asset sales in the same period.[1] Privatization receipts peaked in the United Kingdom in the early 1990s. In 1997 a new Labour government was elected, but despite promises when in opposition to reverse at least some of the privatizations, this government has continued its own, though much smaller-scale, privatizations, especially

Table 12.1
Major privatizations

	Date of sale[a]
British Petroleum	October 1979
	September 1983
	November 1987
British Aerospace	February 1981
	May 1985
Cable & Wireless	October 1981
	December 1983
	December 1985
Amersham International	February 1982
National Freight Corporation	February 1982
Britoil	November 1982
	August 1985
Associated British Port Holdings	February 1983
	April 1984
Enterprise Oil	July 1984
Jaguar	August 1984
British Telecommunications	December 1984
	December 1991
	July 1993
British Shipbuilders and Naval Dockyards	1985 onward
British Gas	December 1986
British Airways	February 1987
Rolls-Royce	May 1987
BAA (British Airports Authority)	July 1987
British Steel	December 1988
Anglian Water	December 1989
Northumbrian Water	December 1989
North West Water	December 1989
Severn Trent	December 1989
Southern Water	December 1989
South West Water	December 1989
Thames Water	December 1989
Welsh Water	December 1989
Wessex Water	December 1989
Yorkshire Water	December 1989
Eastern Electricity	December 1990
East Midlands Electricity	December 1990
London Electricity	December 1990
Manweb	December 1990
Midlands Electricity	December 1990
Northern Electric	December 1990
NORWEB	December 1990
SEEBOARD	December 1990
Southern Electric	December 1990
South Wales Electricity	December 1990
South Western Electricity	December 1990
Yorkshire Electricity	December 1990

Table 12.1
(continued)

	Date of sale[a]
National Power	March 1991
PowerGen	March 1991
Scottish Hydro-Electric	June 1991
Scottish Power	June 1991
Trust Ports	1992–1997 (various dates)
Northern Ireland Electricity	June 1993
British Coal	December 1994
Railtrack	May 1996
British Energy	July 1996
AEA Technology	September 1996
Train Operating Companies	Various dates in 1996–1997
National Air Traffic Services	July 2001

Note: Where more than one date is given, the shares were sold in tranches.

Table 12.2
U.K. privatization receipts, 1979–2000 (£ billion)

1977–1978	0.5
1978–1979	0.0
1979–1980	0.4
1980–1991	0.2
1981–1982	0.5
1982–1983	0.5
1983–1984	1.1
1984–1985	2.1
1985–1986	2.7
1986–1987	4.5
1987–1988	5.1
1988–1989	7.1
1989–1990	4.2
1990–1991	5.3
1991–1992	7.9
1992–1993	8.2
1993–1994	5.4
1994–1995	6.4
1995–1996	3.0
1996–1997	4.4
1997–1998	1.8
1998–1999	0.1

Sources: HM Treasury. *The Financial Statement and Budget Report* (various years).
Note: Figures exclude council housing receipts and receipts of subsidiaries retained by the parent. The figures after 1998–1999 are negligible.

in the form of what it calls "public-private partnerships" (Parker and Hartley 2003).

The passage of time since the commencement of the U.K. privatization program in the early 1980s now permits a sober assessment of the results, looking at the longer-term evidence. We start the discussion of the privatization experiment by considering its main characteristics. We then examine its results in terms of its effects on economic performance. A number of studies have been undertaken on the results of privatizations in the United Kingdom, and I provide a summary of key studies (a number of which I wrote). As we shall see, the results confirm what we might expect from economic theory: changes in ownership lead to performance improvements where there are appropriate changes in the competitive or regulatory environments. The chapter concludes by considering the wider lessons for economic policy of the privatization experiment within the United Kingdom.

12.1   Privatization in the United Kingdom

As the details in tables 12.1 and 12.2 confirm, the privatization experiment began cautiously in the United Kingdom. Unlike in a number of other countries, no privatization plan was published by government setting out a timetable for future privatizations. Rather, the policy evolved, with each seemingly successful sale—defined in terms of the government's ability to sell the enterprise—triggering the planning of a further sale. Some privatizations were postponed for a number of years, for example, British Airways from 1980 to 1987, in the face of difficult economic conditions for the airline, while others seem to have been sold quickly and opportunistically, such as Jaguar cars in 1984. Although government denied that the privatizations were determined by the need to raise annual revenues for government to support tax cuts and public expenditure plans, and in relation to tax and spending levels privatization receipts were always small, it does not seem that generating government funds was an irrelevant consideration in the timing of privatizations throughout the 1980s. The Thatcher government set about introducing a lower tax regime from 1980 but lacked the ability or willpower to cut public expenditure dramatically (Burton and Parker 1991). Annual privatization revenues helped fund some of the gap. At the same time, a fully articulated rationale for privatization was never formally provided by government. With some justification,

Kay and Thompson titled their early study of the United Kingdom's experience in the *Economic Journal* in 1986, "Privatisation: A Policy in Search of a Rationale." More recently, the various studies in Parker and Saal (2003) illustrate the great diversity in rationales for privatization that still exist worldwide.

The first major privatizations in the United Kingdom occurred in the early 1980s and involved reversing the Labour government's nationalizations of the 1970s. British Aerospace, formed under state ownership from three private sector aerospace companies in 1977, was privatized in 1981 through an initial public offering (IPO) of 51.6 percent of the shares. The state enterprise that controlled the shipbuilding industry, British Shipbuilders, by contrast, was split up and sold off piecemeal in later years. Another high-focus sell-off involved the state's road-freight and storage business, the National Freight Corporation, which had almost gone bankrupt in the mid-1970s. This sale in 1982, unusually for a large privatization, involved a management and worker buyout. Other early privatizations involving IPOs included state enterprises that the public in general were almost certainly unaware of. Good examples were Amersham International and Enterprise Oil, which specialized in science-based products and North Sea oil production, respectively. The Thatcher government also began an ambitious sale of the state's stock of housing (council housing), although other areas of the welfare state were little affected by privatization. Privatization of welfare services, especially health and education, was seen as a far too political step. In the face of public concern that the Conservatives might dismantle the National Health Service (NHS), Thatcher repeatedly confirmed that "the NHS is safe with us"—to the undoubted disappointment of some of her supporters (Berry 2002, 2).

Sell-offs took a number of forms, including IPOs (mainly through offers for sale but some through sales by tender),[2] trade sales (e.g., the sale of Rover cars, formerly British Leyland, to British Aerospace in 1988), private placements in favor of institutional investors, and, on occasion, management and worker buyouts (e.g., National Freight, some shipyards, and a few coal mines). The early industry state sell-offs involved businesses that were in competitive markets. Aerospace and shipbuilding, for example, faced intense international competition for orders; indeed, in the face of such competition, the U.K. shipbuilding industry was in terminal decline, something privatization failed to reverse. The National Freight Corporation faced competition from numerous smaller domestic private freight companies, and although it was state owned, it never held more than 10 percent of the U.K. market for freight and storage services.

By contrast, a number of the major privatizations from the mid-1980s involved state enterprises that operated in monopoly markets. These firms are often referred to as public utilities or network industries, reflecting their economies of scale and scope; they include telecommunications, gas, water and sewerage, electricity, and rail transport. Previously they had been seen as "natural monopolies" and therefore unsuitable for private ownership. Official policy on the ownership of the public utilities began to change in 1982–1983. Telecommunications experienced fast technological change that reduced its earlier natural monopoly characteristics, such as fiber-optic cables, new switching gear, and wireless-based technologies. At the same time, technological change necessitated large-scale investment to meet the expected demands for telecommunications services, especially data transmission and cellular phones, which the U.K. government with its budgetary problems felt unable to meet. In 1980 British Telecom (BT) had been separated from the Post Office into a new "public corporation" owned by government. In 1983 the decision was taken to privatize BT. The 1984 Telecommunications Act led to the flotation of 50.2 percent of BT's shares in the stock market in November of that year;[3] the remainder of the shares were sold by government in two further tranches, in December 1991 and July 1993. In 1982 BT had an entire monopoly of telecommunications services and equipment supplies within the United Kingdom. The provision of equipment was first opened to competition, in spite of protests from BT, and in 1984 a new fixed-line operator was licensed, Mercury Communications (later fully owned by Cable and Wireless the U.K.-based international telecommunications company, itself privatized between 1981 and 1985).

To protect consumers from monopoly abuse until competition developed, a new telecommunications regulator, the Office of Telecommunications (Oftel), was hastily created. Initially, during the planning of BT's privatization, it seems that government considered regulating BT using normal competition law. But in the face of concerns about the workload that might be placed on the Office of Fair Trading (the government's competition department) and a need to build up specialist telecommunications regulation expertise, the decision was taken to include in the Telecommunications Bill provision to establish Oftel.

The BT privatization was a success in the sense that the IPO was greatly oversubscribed. Concerned that the London stock market might not absorb what was then the largest single flotation in the market's history, the government had mounted a campaign, including TV and press advertising, to attract small investors. The result was an outstanding success. Instead of the expected widespread public opposition to the privatization of BT—in a sense the public already "owned" BT as a state enterprise and therefore might have been expected to object to being asked to buy shares in the company—the public backed the sale through share buying. The outcome was a landmark in the United Kingdom's privatization experiment, for a number of reasons.

First, the sale of BT established the principle that public utilities could be sold off in spite of their size; second, Oftel became the regulatory model for later sector regulatory offices for gas (Ofgas), water and sewerage (Ofwat), electricity (Offer), and the railways (ORR).[4] Third, the sale proved that small investors could be attracted if the shares were sold at a discount.[5] This helped to meet the Conservatives' objective of creating a share-owning democracy as a bulwark against socialism; a number of later privatizations included provisions that favored small shareholders. In 1986 British Gas was privatized, followed in 1989 by the water industry, and in 1990–1991 by the electricity power industry (excluding nuclear generation, which was partially privatized later, in 1996, as British Energy).[6] In all cases incentives were created for small investors to buy shares, including loyalty share bonuses and discounts on utility bills. The percentage of adults holding shares consequently rose during the 1980s, from around 7 percent to 25 percent. However, small investors held only very small percentages of the total stock of each enterprise, and the long-run trend toward increased institutional share ownership in the United Kingdom continued (Buckland 1987). The share of the stock market accounted for by private investors fell from 28 percent in 1989 to under 17 percent by 1997. Moreover, arguably, effective corporate governance is better achieved by creating blocks of large shareholdings, and therefore investors with a large individual stake in the future of the business, rather than small shareholdings (for a review of the relevant literature on share ownership and corporate governance, see Filatotchev 2003). It was therefore by no means self-evident that promoting small shareholders through privatization was consistent with the objective of raising economic efficiency in the enterprises sold. As events unfolded, however, many small shareholders sold their holdings to make a quick, and effortless, capital gain. For example, of the 2.2 million initial shareholders in BT, some 500,000 left the share register within six months (Ernst and Young 1994).

In 1980 interurban coach services were opened up to competition with some resulting success in terms of lower fares and improved services. However, National Express, originally state owned, maintained dominance in the sector assisted by its entrenched position operating out of Victoria coach station in London. In 1992 National Express was floated in the stock market. In 1985 local bus transport was also liberalized (except for services in London), and tenders for routes were organized.[7] The overall results were less positive. A number of towns faced a concentration of services on the profitable routes; some saw unruly competitive practices such as cutting in front of competitor buses to reach passengers first and experienced other practices aimed at driving out rival operators. During the late 1980s, many local bus services were privatized, and while total costs per passenger journey fell, fares rose and the long-term trend of a decline in bus passengers continued outside London (Fawkner 2003). The industry quickly consolidated,[8] and the U.K. competition authorities on a number of occasions investigated anticompetitive practices in the industry, especially the suspected use of predatory pricing. In 1993 the decision was taken to extend privatization to the railways. This occurred between 1995 and 1997 and has proven especially controversial. We return to rail privatization later in the chapter.

Across the EU, European Commission directives have played a part in stimulating privatization. Directives have required, in particular, the opening up of telecommunications (European Commission 1996/19) and electricity power (European Commission 1996/92) to competition. There have also been measures liberalizing the provision of services in posts, gas, and rail transport. However, because the United Kingdom has been a leader in privatization (except in postal services), the EU directives have not been the same stimulus for privatization in the United Kingdom as they have been in some other parts of Europe (Parker 1998; Clifton, Comín, and Fuentes 2003). The EU directives have had an impact in the United Kingdom in terms of harmonization of regulatory rules across Europe rather than in terms of triggering state asset disposals (Dassler and Parker 2003). At the same time, the United Kingdom's privatization and deregulation experience has had an impact on EU policy in areas such as telecommunications, power, and transport (Parker 1998).

12.2 The Results for Economic Performance

There have been a number of empirical studies of the impact of U.K. privatizations on economic performance, adopting a range of performance measures to assess changes in allocative and productive efficiency and distributional effects. But most commonly, studies have concentrated on productive efficiency, measuring changes in profitability, productivity, and costs of production. Whereas profit is a useful measure of productive efficiency in competitive markets, its use in imperfectly competitive conditions is problematic because profits may reflect higher prices rather than more efficient production practices. For this reason, productivity and cost calculations are usually preferred when assessing productive efficiency in the (monopoly) public utilities. However, productivity measures that involve all inputs—measuring total factor productivity with productivity gains shown as a residual—face reliability problems. This is because the capital input is usually difficult to measure accurately. At the same time, the alternative of measuring labor productivity trends may produce biased results due to capital for labor substitution and, where output rather than value added is used as the numerator, contracting out of labor-intensive services. At the same time, calculating efficient costs of production involves specification of a cost function. To overcome problems in specifying the appropriate functional form, some studies adopt mathematical modeling techniques, including nonparametric frontier estimation using data envelopment analysis (DEA), which capitalizes on Farrell's (1957) earlier exposition of the "efficiency frontier."[9] But DEA as a technique is sensitive to outliers in the data, and it assumes that all of the unexplained data variance results from inefficiency. Recently, an alternative parametric approach involving stochastic cost frontiers (SCF) has attracted interest, but the properties of SCF are not well understood, and so far the method has been little used to assess the performance of privatizations in the United Kingdom.

12.2.1 Economic Efficiency

Table 12.3 provides a summary of key studies of the impact of privatization on economic efficiency in the United Kingdom, detailing the author, the industry, the performance measures used, and the main findings. Most of the studies in the table have been concerned with productive efficiency, although some have attempted to assess wider

Table 12.3
U.K. privatization: Performance studies

Author	Industry	Main performance measures used	Findings
Hutchinson (1991)	17 U.K. firms in several industrial groupings	Labor productivity, profitability, and technology mix	Privately owned firms outperformed comparable state-owned firms in the 1970s and 1980s in terms of profitability only. Less certain whether privatization had improved performance.
Bishop and Thompson (1992)	9 privatized enterprises across a range of U.K. industries, including BT, British Gas, and electricity supply	Labor productivity and TFP, 1970–1980, compared with 1980–1990	There was higher growth in labor productivity in BT, but the growth in total factor productivity (TFP) fell in the 1980s. In British Gas labor productivity grew at the same rate in the 1970s as the 1980s, while the growth of TFP declined. Electricity supply saw a fall in both labor productivity and TFP growth.
Haskel and Szymanski (1993)	12 privatized firms between 1972 and 1988, including BT, British Gas, electricity supply, and water	Estimates of productivity growth (output per employee)	In the main, productivity grew faster in the 1980s. Competition is the significant causal factor.
Burns and Weyman-Jones (1994)	Electricity distribution	Multiple input, multiple output model of before and after privatization using mathematical programming techniques	The 12 electricity distribution companies have been more efficient since privatization, but this continues a long-term historical trend. There is also a greater diversity of performance among the 12 since privatization.

Parker (1994)	British Telecom (BT), 1979–1980 to 1993–1994	Productivity and employment costs in total costs. R&D expenditures	Labor productivity has grown faster since privatization, but the record for TFP is much less impressive. Employment costs have declined as a percentage of all costs, continuing a trend that dates back to before privatization. R&D expenditures as a percentage of turnover have fallen, but this result is difficult to interpret because it may reflect a more efficient use of resources.
Bishop and Green (1995)	6 privatized enterprises including British Gas and BT	TFP and financial data, 1989–1994	Competition rather than ownership is important. Growth in TFP in BT was in part due to technical change.
Waddams Price and Weyman-Jones (1996)	Gas industry, 1977–1978 to 1991	Malmquist indexes of productivity growth	Postprivatization productivity growth was around 5–6 percent per annum compared with 3 percent a year before privatization in 1986. However, differences remain in technical efficiency among British Gas's regions.
Newbery and Pollitt (1997)	Electricity generation	Various	Labor productivity has more than doubled since 1990, mainly due to shedding labor. Real unit costs have declined.
Shaoul (1997)	Water industry	Cost and output data	Greater efficiency gains, meaning lower costs relative to output, occurred prior to privatization.
Saundry and Turnbull (1997)	Ports	Traffic and financial data including capital expenditure, mainly for the 1980s	The privatized ports did not perform better than trust ports and municipally owned docks. Service improvements have came mainly from employment deregulation (the abolition of the so-called Dock Labour Scheme).
Martin and Parker (1997)	11 privatized organisations studied, including British Gas and BT. Years before and after privatization included.	Labor productivity, TFP, various financial ratios, and data envelopment analysis (DEA)	Mixed results with labor productivity growth evident but TFP growth lagging behind.

Table 12.3
(continued)

Author	Industry	Main performance measures used	Findings
O'Mahony (1998)	Sectors of U.K. economy including electricity, gas, and water	Labor productivity and TFP in the U.K. relative to U.S., France, Germany, and Japan	Productivity gap declined in 1995 compared to 1989; but evidence of a closing gap from the 1970s except relative to France.
Parker and Wu (1998)	U.K. steel industry compared to steel producers in 6 other countries	DEA analysis of relative input-output efficiency and productivity figures	A large improvement in relative performance occurred in the British steel industry before the privatization. Privatization was followed by a decline in relative performance.
Parker (1999b)	British Airports Authority—largest airport operator in the U.K. privatized in July 1987	DEA analysis of the relative performance of BAA pre- and postprivatization and the relative performance of its individual airports compared with other airports in the U.K. privately and publicly owned	No evidence that privatization had a significant effect on performance. Performance improvements were a continuation of a longer-term trend.
Harris, Parker and Cox (1998); Cox, Harris and Parker (1999)	Procurement practices in 28 privatized companies	Questionnaire and case studies	Evidence of improvements in procurement efficiency after privatization, but some firms progressing faster than others and few close to achieving best practice.
Saal and Parker (2000, 2001)	Water and sewerage industry in England and Wales	Labor and total factor productivity and cost function	Privatization led to no obvious rise in productivity or lowered costs of production. Higher productivity and lower unit costs came when the regulatory price caps were tightened in 1995.

Pollitt and Domah (2001)	Regional electricity companies in England and Wales	Social cost-benefit analysis using a counterfactual	Privatization did yield significant net social benefits, but these were unevenly distributed across time and groups in society. Government gained £56 million in sales proceeds and taxes, but consumers did not begin to gain until 2000. Producers benefited from large increase in after-tax profits.
Pollitt and Smith (2002)	Britain's railways	Social cost-benefit analysis using a counterfactual	Major efficiencies have been achieved and consumers have benefited from lower prices. Increased government subsidy has been largely recouped through privatization proceeds. Output quality is not lower.
Florio (2002)	Social cost-benefit analysis of U.K. privatizations in aggregate	Labor and total factor productivity, employment, prices, and abnormal returns to investors. Econometric analyses of structural breaks in GDP growth and changes in welfare	Privatization has had no noticeable effects in terms of trends in productivity, employment, and price levels at the firm or sector levels after allowing for changes in technology and input prices, or on GDP growth and productivity at the national level. Overall household expenditure on utility services including coal and transport remained remarkably stable at around 8 percent of the total value of consumers' expenditure: "Our overall result . . . [is] . . . that taxpayers suffered a loss of £14 billion, but this was cancelled out by the equivalent transfer to shareholders, workers' welfare was probably slightly negatively affected, but overall this impact was negligible, consumers enjoyed a perpetual discount in prices worth less that £1,000 for each British citizen. . . . Apparently, far from being a 'revolution', the great divestiture was a reshuffling

Table 12.3
(continued)

Author	Industry	Main performance measures used	Findings
			of relative positions of various agents, probably a regressive one, with a rather modest impact on aggregate economic efficiency" (41).
Shaoul (2003)	National Air Traffic Services (NATS)	Financial analysis	The resulting PPP is not financially viable given revenues, costs, and investment needs.
Florio (2003)	BT's long-term performance over 40 years	Output, prices, revenues, costs, employment, productivity, profits, and investment	The rate of growth of output was higher before privatization. Prices fell, with business users and international calls the biggest gainers. There was evidence of capital for labor substitution, while R&D expenditures fell as a percentage of turnover. Operating profits were stable before and after privatization, and privatization had little discernible effect on productivity trends before 1991, when the introduction of more competition and new regulatory pressures led to large gains.

social welfare impacts. Investigation of the price-cost wedge, required in allocative efficiency studies, is complex and requires information on a firm's efficient costs of production and price-cost margins elsewhere in the economy (to address the "second-best" problem; Lipsey and Lancaster 1956). Where markets become more competitive after privatization, it might be expected that prices would move closer to marginal costs, implying higher allocative efficiency. However, this depends on the pricing strategy followed under state ownership. Under state ownership and constant cost production, a break-even objective will lead to prices equaling marginal costs, and a profit-maximizing, unregulated monopolist produces a lower output than a state enterprise with a break-even strategy. Also, in empirical studies, it often proves difficult to separate out the effects of ownership, competition, regulation, and technological change on efficiency. Therefore it is often unclear how far privatization rather than other factors is responsible for any economic efficiency gains achieved.

Principal agent theory and its implications for effective corporate governance suggest that in privately owned enterprises, management faces superior incentives to drive out waste and maximize productivity (De Alessi 1980, Bös 1991, Boycko, Shleifer, and Vishny 1996).[10] Public choice theory maintains that within government, as elsewhere in the economy, self-interest is the dominant motive, with the result that state ownership is associated with empire building, goldplating of public investments, overmanning, and, in general, economic waste (Niskanen 1971, Tullock 1976, Mitchell 1988). Together, principal-agent theory and public choice theory provide a powerful theoretical rationale for privatization (Boycko, Shleifer, and Vishny 1996). However, it is uncertain how much politicians in the 1980s were knowledgeable about the two theories, although they may have been made aware of their general conclusions through the actions of organizations such as the Institute of Economic Affairs and Adam Smith Institute in London. Nor, indeed, is it obvious that economic theory played the dominant part in the form and timing of privatizations in Europe (Parker 1998). Also, a fuller economic appraisal of privatisation (Kay and Thompson 1986, Vickers and Yarrow 1988, Martin and Parker 1997) demonstrates that if ownership change is to have reliable efficiency results, then the roles of competition and regulation may be crucial.

Turning to the studies in table 12.3, a number were unable to reject the null hypothesis that ownership change has had no effect on economic performance. And there is no evidence that later privatizations outperformed earlier privatizations in terms of raising performance, which would have been consistent with learning effects within government. In a number of cases, the improvements in productive efficiency recorded simply reflected long-run growth trends that predated privatization. The most comprehensive study of U.K. privatization (Martin and Parker 1997) found no consistent relationship between ownership and performance. For example, labor productivity growth in BT and British Gas fell after privatization and recovered sharply only after both telecommunications and gas supplies were opened up to more competition. In telecommunications this occurred in the early 1990s and in gas during the 1990s. In both industries, at first the regulatory pressures (including the price caps imposed by the regulatory offices) seem to have provided generous scope to raise profits without major cost cutting. In the face of tightening regulation and more competition in the 1990s, productivity responded. The average annual rise in labor productivity was around 15 percent in BT and 6 percent in British Gas in the early to the mid-1990s (with lower growth in total factor productivity). Since then, the continued growth of competition has spurred further productivity gains.

Martin and Parker's findings on the importance of competition and regulation are mirrored in a number of the other studies in table 12.3—for example, those relating to the electricity industry. In electricity, competition was introduced at privatization in 1990–1991 and extended to all consumers during the 1990s.[11] Burns and Weyman-Jones (1994) in an early study concluded that the twelve regional electricity distribution companies had become more efficient after privatization, although this was a continuation of a longer-term trend. A recent review of electricity generation found that substantial cost reductions had occurred (Newbery and Pollitt 1997), and another study (Domah and Pollitt 2001) of the performance of regional electricity companies in England and Wales calculates a significant gain in social welfare, but in both cases with gains skewed to producers (in terms of higher profits) and possibly government (in terms of higher tax revenues). In electricity as in the other utility industries, these efficiency increases were a reflection of the sharp reductions in employment achieved. Employment in the industry fell from 127,300 at privatization to around 66,000 by 1996–1997. Over the same period, transmission operating costs fell by nearly 40 percent (*Financial Times* 1999). In BT employment declined from around 238,000 at privatization to 124,700 by 1999, and in British Gas from about 92,000 at privatization to 70,000 by 1994.

Turning to the water industry, where there is still very little competition, Shaoul (1997) concluded that significant efficiency gains, defined as lower costs relative to output, occurred before privatization. After privatization, at first employment in the industry rose, in 1990–1991 the average number employed in the water and sewerage companies was 45,863. By 1993–1994 this had grown to 58,270. More recently, numbers have fallen and the water regulator's price caps imposed in 2000 necessitated, for the first time, real price reductions for water and sewerage services. What appears to have happened in this industry is that lax regulation at the outset plus a lack of competition combined to keep efficiency incentives weak in the early years (Saal and Parker 2000, 2001).[12]

In the case of all of the privatizations, results may well have been affected by technical change. This is particularly so in telecommunications and electricity generation, where there have been some notable technological improvements. Changes in international prices, notably for fuel inputs such as oil and gas, have also been an important factor in the electricity sector. One way forward is to compare the performance of the U.K. utilities with those overseas and able to capitalize equally on the new technologies and affected by the same world price movements for key inputs. In this respect, O'Mahony's (1998) work on comparative productivity levels in the electricity, gas and water sectors in the United States, France, Germany, and Japan compared with the United Kingdom is of interest. Table 12.4 reproduces some of her results. It is evident that her calculations suggest that the labor and total factor productivity gap between the United Kingdom and the other

Table 12.4
Comparative productivity: Electricity, gas, and water sectors, 1979–1995 (U.K. = 100)

	Labor productivity (output per hour)			Total factor productivity		
	1979	1989	1995	1979	1989	1995
United States	474	345	245	247	190	176
France	238	255	173	101	110	99
Germany	202	156	103	149	116	97
Japan	180	155	107	117	88	73

Source: O'Mahony (1998).

countries has narrowed, but in most cases, this narrowing dates back to the late 1970s or before. That is, the catching up in comparative productivity predates privatization, a result consistent with the findings of some of the studies in table 12.3. For example, Parker and Wu (1998) found in comparing the British steel industry with a number of other steel industries around the world that the relative performance of British Steel declined after privatization. British Steel improved its performance sharply in the last few years under state ownership, when the industry was rationalized, capacity and staffing were cut, and the industry became attractive to private investors. It remains a matter of speculation whether the rationalization occurred because of the imminent threat of privatization, for which privatization can take credit, or whether it simply provided the opportunity for government to sell off the industry.[13]

12.2.2   Prices and Services

In most of the United Kingdom, public utilities prices and tariffs have fallen since privatization, reflecting gains in productive efficiency. The following examples are selected to reflect the general nature of the price changes after privatization (a more detailed account can be found in Parker 1999a). Taking telecommunications first, from 1984 to 1999, average real charges fell by around 48 percent on average, although this change certainly results from technology and competition in addition to ownership change and regulation.[14] Turning to the gas sector, the next utility to be privatized after telecommunications, domestic gas bills fell by an average of 2.6 percent a year between 1986 and 1997, again in real terms. After 1997 the gradual introduction of competition in domestic gas supplies led to further cuts of up to 20 percent.[15] Real industrial and commercial gas prices fell over the same period by about 5 percent a year.

In the electricity market, the decline in charges for domestic consumers in England and Wales between 1990 and 1999 was around 26 percent in real terms for domestic consumers; the reduction for industrial and commercial consumers was even larger, totaling between 25 and 34 percent (see table 12.5).[16] The main exception to this impressive track record on charging was registered in the water and sewerage industry. Here domestic charges rose sharply after privatization, by over 40 percent in real terms for average unmeasured water and sewerage bills (less for measured or metered services). The privatized water

Table 12.5
Price reductions for electricity suppliers in Great Britain, 1990–1999 (%)

Small users	30
Medium-sized users	34
Moderately large users	33
Large users	31
Extra-large users	25

Source: Littlechild (2000, 33). Note that Littlechild uses the term *sites* instead of *users*.

companies justified these increases in terms of the need to fund investments to modernize water and sewerage systems after years of underinvestment when in the state sector and to meet the requirements of EU water quality directives. But the scale of the increases may also reflect a lack of competition in water services since privatization.

It is also important to recognize that the above figures are averages and conceal disparities in the distribution of the welfare gains among different consumer groups (Hancock and Waddams Price 1995, Waddams Price and Hancock 1998, Markou and Waddams Price 1999, Florio 2002, Waddams Price and Young 2003). State ownership is associated with cross-subsidies and "no undue discrimination" clauses that lead to uniform pricing. Privatization, especially when coupled with competition, can be expected to lead to prices more closely related to the marginal costs of supplying different user groups, provided that the removal of cross-subsidies is acceptable to industry regulators. In practice, regulators in the United Kingdom have accepted the case for removing much of the cross-subsidy on the grounds that it distorts price signals, although they have sometimes acted to slow the removal to avoid sudden, large price adjustments. The result over the longer term has been different price changes for different user groups. Users with lower marginal costs, usually large users or industry, have tended to receive bigger reductions in charges than smaller, often poorer consumers, which are individually more costly to serve (NAO 2001). The result is that lower-income groups have received smaller welfare gains from privatization, and in some cases have lost out, especially from privatization of energy supplies.[17] In this sense, it has not proved possible for regulators to separate neatly the pursuit of economic efficiency from the social consequences of their actions (Baldwin and Cave 1999). This is something formally recognized in the Utilities Act 2000, which enables government to give guidance to the energy market regulator to take account of social and environmental as well as economic outcomes.

Service quality changes since privatization are particularly difficult to summarize because service quality is multidimensional. Nevertheless, there is no substantial evidence that lower staffing and price reductions in the public utilities have been at the expense of service quality;[18] for privatized companies operating in competitive environments, reducing service quality to the disadvantage of consumers leads to a loss of market share and therefore is not usually a commercially sensible option. In telecommunications, gas, water services, and electricity, performance targets for service quality have been introduced by the regulator, with penalties and compensation payments paid to consumers where service falls below target. Over the years, the regulators have set more exacting service standards that have delivered service improvements. The result is evidence of improved service quality since privatization across the privatized utilities, with the notable exception of the railways (for a review see Parker 1999a), to which we now turn.

The privatization of the railways in the mid-1990s was an ambitious project to introduce competition by dividing the railways into an infrastructure operator, Railtrack (responsible for lines, signaling, and major stations), twenty-five passenger train operating companies (most with monopolies of services on particular routes but with plans to introduce competition later; these plans were subsequently abandoned), six freight service companies (three were quickly merged into one to facilitate a successful sale), three companies leasing rolling stock (known as Roscos), and numerous rail maintenance businesses and other specialized activities. The result was the disintegration of the monopoly British Rail and the replacement of management control of resource use across the industry by very large numbers of legal contracts (Tyrrall and Parker 2005). Few now defend the form of this privatization and its resulting transaction costs, and pressures have developed to reintegrate parts of the industry (Pollitt 1999). The train companies were successful in raising passenger numbers, by over 30 percent in four years, but this led to train overcrowding.

Although Pollitt and Smith (2002; see table 12.3) paint a generally favorable picture of rail privatization in Britain, their analysis ends in 2000 before a significant decrease in service reliability and the financial collapse of Railtrack occurred. In October 2001 Railtrack was placed in receivership.[19] The government refused to increase its funding to the company while it remained under private ownership. In 2002 the government replaced Railtrack with Network Rail, a company limited by guarantee but effectively a new state enterprise—although government refuses to concede that this amounts to renationalization of the rail infrastructure. What is certain is that the Ladbroke Grove, Hatfield, and Potters Bar rail crashes between 1999 and 2002 and continuing (and in part consequential) delays and cancellations of train services have meant that rail privatization has damaged the reputation of privatization in general within the United Kingdom. It is interesting to note, however, that even in the 1980s, when the public was eagerly buying privatization shares with the aim of making a quick capital gain, public opinion polls often recorded a majority against the policy of privatization (Clifton, Comín, and Fuentes 2003).

12.2.3 The Distribution of Gains

Finally, a fuller analysis of the welfare gains from privatization needs to address the distribution of the economic net benefits, which seems to have been regressive in terms of impact on income and wealth (Florio 2002). Certainly the City benefited from accountancy, legal, consultancy, and flotation fees and as an investor (TUC 1985a). At least £780 million had been paid in fees and commissions by 1994 (Helm 1995). Also, profitability was buoyant in the privatized utilities, especially in the early years after privatization. For example, the rate of return on capital employed in the water industry rose from an average of 9.8 percent at privatization in 1989 to 11.1 percent by 1996–1997; in electricity the increase was larger, with average returns rising from around 4 percent in generation and 6.5 percent in distribution and supply to around 11 percent and 8.8 percent respectively, between 1990/1991 and 1995/ 1996 (Parker 1997). As a result, and because shares were sold at attractive prices, in part to encourage small investors, investors benefited from large and sometimes spectacular rises in share values. While returns have varied, on average, individual investors who bought shares in the privatized utilities at flotation obtained returns on their investment up to the end of April 1997 exceeding 10 percent per annum in real terms.[20] The average return in the water sector was 24 percent and in the electricity distribution and supply sector 38 percent a year. The latter figure was buoyed by takeover bids in the mid-1990s for distribution and supply companies in England and Wales.[21]

Table 12.6 summarizes the findings from a study of returns to investors in the privatized utilities, showing the returns obtained by investors if the shares were sold at the end of the first day of trading, after

Table 12.6
Examples of returns to investors in the privatized utilities

	% returns to investors selling after:						Still held at
	1 day	1 year		5 years			April 30, 1997
BT (1)	35	84	(+69)	20	(+6)	14	(+3)
BT (2)	5	22	(+5)	10	(−3)	12	(−2)
BT (3)	5	5	(−4)	—	—	8	(−5)
British Gas	10	24	(+20)	15	(+9)	11	(+2)
Water and sewerage (average)	20	39	(+45)	23	(+18)	24	(+16)
RECs							
Average	23	41	(+29)	40	(+27)	38	(+25)
Powergen (1)	22	29	(+26)	30	(+19)	29	(+18)
Powergen (2)	3	9	(−14)	—	—	16	(−3)
National power (1)	22	22	(+19)	28	(+17)	30	(+19)
National power (2)	4	6	(−17)	—	—	23	(+4)

Source: Parker (1997).

Figures in parentheses show gains relative to movement of the FT All Share Index over the same period. Returns are to individuals investing and are calculated as internal rates of return. Due to special incentive schemes, the return to institutional investors is slightly lower.

All returns are real returns deflated using the RPI.

One-day return is an absolute IRR (not annualized). It shows the gain from the first day's trading on the selling price. All other periods reflect annualized returns.

The lower first-day returns on second and third tranches of shares sold reflect the fact that later issues are priced close to the current market price.

one year, five years, and if the shares were still held on April 30, 1997. The gains on the first day of trading for initial share offers underline the attraction of the shares to small investors keen to make a quick profit and were generally significantly greater than usually occurs for IPOs in the U.K. stock market (Boyfield 1997, Florio 2002). Where privatization shares were bought at flotation by foreign investors, there was a net welfare loss to the United Kingdom due to underpricing; when bought by domestic investors, there was a redistribution of wealth from government or taxpayers to domestic shareholders.

Returns to investors in the United Kingdom following privatization were high, and it seems higher than government anticipated at the time of the sell-offs (otherwise presumably the government would have held out for a higher price for the shares at the time of their sale). The high profits and shareholder returns can be attributed either to the companies' exploiting their market power in the face of lax regulation or to government's underestimating the scope for cost savings following privatization. Opinion seems to be divided on which of these explanations is the more important, but probably both apply (Boardman and Laurin 1998, Dnes et al. 1998). What is clear is that the regulators have been able to respond fully only when the price caps have come up for reconsideration, at so-called periodic reviews (although some regulators, notably the water regulator, intervened earlier, and in the other industries, companies were successfully cajoled from time to time not to increase their prices by the maximum permitted under their price cap). Price cap reviews in the mid- to late 1990s reduced revenues to the privatized utilities, leading to significantly lower profitability and returns to investors closer to the cost of raising capital (or a "normal" return). It is in no small part for this reason, for example, that the privatized electricity companies, which proved such a tempting target for takeovers by foreign companies, especially U.S.-based utilities in the mid-1990s, have since been resold, often at a loss.[22]

Another obvious gainer from privatization has been senior management, many of whom kept their jobs at privatization (Cragg and Dyck 1999, Martin and Parker 1997). The introduction of stock options and profit-related bonuses has led to a large rise in the pay of senior management. This has led in turn to media and union criticism of privatization's "fat cats" (TUC 1985b). At the same time, job losses, deunionization, and changes to collective bargaining in a number of privatized enterprises (TUC 1986, Ferner and Colling 1991) have produced a widening of pay differentials between unskilled workers and skilled workers and, of course, top management. Study suggests that privatization did not lead to an obvious fall in average wages in privatized companies (Martin and Parker 1996), but differentials have widened. There has been much variation in employment trends across privatized businesses, and changes in pay and employment to a degree reflect wider changes in the U.K. economy. It is worth noting that in some cases, when large-scale redundancies occurred, as in BT in the early 1990s, many of those made redundant received generous redundancy packages. This means that in assessing the net benefits from privatization, the effect on workers is particularly difficult to assess.[23]

A further possible gainer was government, and therefore taxpayers, who substituted paying subsidies to and receiving future revenues from the nationalized industries, for the sale price plus future taxation on any higher profits earned after privatization. There is evidence that the taxpayer has been a net gainer in a number of cases (Domah and Pollitt 2001), but no means all and perhaps not overall. Shaoul (2003) provides a financial analysis of the privatization of the National Air Traffic Services, through a public-private partnership (PPP), which suggests the government faces higher financial costs to bail out the failing sale. Florio (2002) concludes that public sector net wealth declined sharply during the years of privatization, reflecting in part the underpricing of assets sold. He concludes "that underpricing was recovered through the fiscal dividend is unconvincing" (35).[24]

More generally, Florio (2002; also see Brau and Florio 2001 and Florio and Grasseni 2003), using social-cost benefit analysis, argues that British privatizations had modest effects on the efficiency of production and consumption, but that they did have important and regressive effects on the distribution of income and wealth. Overall, he concludes that privatization did not lead to an unambiguous Pareto welfare improvement.

12.3   Lessons from the U.K. Experience

By 2004 there was little left in the industrial sector in the United Kingdom to privatize, although the welfare state still remains largely untouched by privatisation. Apart from some competitive tendering for contracts, such as for cleaning hospitals and schools, and isolated examples of private companies being brought in to sort out underperforming educational and health services, the welfare state remains solidly state provided.[25] Recently the government recommended greater use of private companies and private capital in the provision of health care, but this has met with determined opposition from backbench Labour MPs and public sector trade unions.

The Conservative government backed away from privatizing the Post Office in 1994 because of the potential adverse impact on rural post offices and because of the possible loss of uniform postal charges across the country. Many Conservative MPs are elected by rural constituencies, and rural areas might expect to be losers from the introduction of private competition. The current Labour government has tried to introduce further commercialization of the Post Office, begun under the Conservatives, but similarly shows no desire (or the lack of political courage) to privatize the post. London Underground, by contrast, is currently subject to restructuring that has led to private companies' becoming responsible for the infrastructure. This project is highly controversial but promoted by the Labour government as an example of the benefits of PPP. Indeed, most privatizations under Labour have taken the form of PPPs or PFIs (private finance initiatives, a close relation). The intention is to introduce the reputedly superior project management skills of the private sector into transport, defense, the NHS, education, and other public services. By April 2003, 564 PFI deals had been agreed with a capital value of £35 billion (*Financial Times* 2003). However, the extent of the long-term cost savings to taxpayers from PPPs remains highly uncertain, especially since government may raise capital more cheaply than the private sector (*Economist* 2003, Parker and Hartley 2003).[26] Meanwhile, one major privatization under Labour using a PPP, the selling off of the Civil Aviation Authority's National Air Traffic Services (NATS) mainly to a consortium of seven U.K. airlines, quickly ran into financial difficulty,[27] and like the railways and British Energy (nuclear power),[28] it has sought financial assistance from the government.

So what are the lessons from the United Kingdom's privatization experiment for the United Kingdom and other countries? First, the empirical evidence is consistent with economic theory and suggests that competition and, in the absence of competition, effective state regulation are important if privatization is to lead to performance improvements, including lower prices and improved services. Ownership change on its own does not appear to have a significant effect in terms of improving economic performance where there is market dominance, especially in terms of welfare gains to consumers. Management in monopolies may seek an "easy life" whether in the private or public sectors, while in private sector monopolies, management can meet investors' expectations of profits by simply raising prices. Although it is dangerous to try to generalize across very different industries with different competitive conditions at the outset, nonetheless, in general the evidence here is consistent with economic theory in making competition first best in terms of reliably generating economic efficiency gains, followed in the absence of competition by effective regulation, and then privatization. At the same time, however, it would be wrong to dismiss the benefits of privatization in the United Kingdom. Without it, competition probably would not have been permitted or would have proved more difficult to produce, for example, in electricity and gas supplies, and regulatory systems would have remained highly politicized. In other words, increased competition and improved state regulation of utilities may be a direct product of the privatization process. It is educational that the United Kingdom had experimented with various reforms for its nationalized industries in the 1960s and 1970s in the face of poor performance, to little obvious advantage (NEDO 1976) and governments had continued to protect state monopolies from the threat of competition.[29]

Second, utility privatizations led to very high returns to some investors, at least until competition or regulatory pressures became effective. This meant that in the early days, generally investors rather than consumers were the main gainers from privatization of the public utilities. 'Stagging' gains in the first hours of trading in the shares of a newly floated company are commonplace in stock markets,[30] but the gains from privatization issues in the United Kingdom seem, on average, to have been exceedingly generous and beyond what was needed to ensure that the flotations were a success.

Third, although space has precluded a full discussion of the development of economic regulation in the United Kingdom, and more specifically the evolution of the powers of the regulatory offices—Oftel, Ofgas, Ofwat, Offer and ORR—it is clear from the United Kingdom's experience that where firms are privatized with considerable market dominance, developing effective regulation takes time but is essential. One of the United Kingdom's main contributions to economic policy in recent years has involved improvements in our understanding of regulatory governance and the popularizing of certain regulatory tools, most notably the price cap (Littlechild 1983, Parker 2002).

Fourth, the enterprises that were privatized fell into no set pattern, with some of the utilities remaining dominant in their sectors (for example, in spite of competition and regulation, BT still accounts for around 70 percent of domestic residential and 60 percent of all business calls within the United Kingdom)[31] and others (e.g., Amersham International) becoming indistinguishable from other private sector companies. The result is an industrial structure involving both monopolistic and competitive privatized companies. The supervision of privatized markets falls increasingly to the competition authorities, in the United Kingdom notably the Competition Commission, both to ensure alongside industry regulators that competition develops where it is absent and to protect competition once it has been established. A further lesson emphasizes the importance of parallel developments in competition policy to police the privatized markets effectively to prevent monopoly abuse and encourage new market entry. The United Kingdom strengthened its competition laws in 1998 with the Competition Act and in 2002 with the Enterprise Act. This legislation has increased the powers of the competition authorities to investigate and penalize collusive behavior between companies and abuses of market power that lead to a substantial lessening of competition. Privatization has not led to the withering away of the state, but rather to a reformulated role for government as a market regulator rather than a direct service provider (Cook 1998, Saal 2003).

Finally, the United Kingdom's experiment with privatization came after decades of relative economic decline. Thatcher's election occurred because of growing public discontent with poor economic growth, rising inflation, growing unemployment, and poor labor relations in the United Kingdom. Privatization has not proved to be an economic miracle. But as part of the wider restructuring of the economy that occurred in the 1980s, involving tax cuts, public spending caps, trade union reform, and the closure of declining industries, it has contributed to reversing the perception of the United Kingdom as "the sick man of Europe"—albeit that the United Kingdom's GDP growth rate has not noticeably increased as a result. In particular, privatization has played an important part in reducing the burden of the state in the U.K. economy. Whereas in 1979 nationalized industries accounted for 10.5 percent of GDP, by 1993 the figure had fallen to 3 percent and public sector employment fell by 1.5 million as a result of the sale of the industries (Talbot 2001). Whereas the precise economic effects of U.K. privatization remain uncertain and will continue to be debated, as part of the wider restructuring of the economy undertaken in the 1980s the outcome appears less controversial.

Acknowledgments

I thank Ingo Vogelsang, the editors, and an anonymous referee for their helpful comments on earlier drafts of this chapter. The usual disclaimer applies.

Notes

1. A fuller listing, including 119 organizations, can be found on the HM Treasury Web site: ⟨www.hm-treasury.gov.uk/documents/enterprise_and_productivity/public_enterprise⟩

2. Under fixed-price offers for sale, the sale price is set and publicized in advance, whereas under sale by tender broadly, the price is set by demand and supply during the sale. Offers for sale provide more certainty regarding the purchase price and therefore are more attractive to small investors. They also offer the best prospects for a quick capital gain on selling the shares shortly after privatization.

3. A small percentage of shares were reserved for employees of BT. This was a model copied for a number of subsequent privatizations.

4. Today Ofgas and Offer have merged to form Ofgem (Office of Gas and Electricity Markets). The railways have another regulator, alongside the ORR: the Strategic Rail Authority (SRA), although the government has now announced that this is to be abolished.

5. Nigel Lawson, chancellor of the Exchequer from 1983 to 1989, notes in his memoirs (Lawson 1992) that the government stumbled by accident on the popularity of selling shares at a discount to the public when it inadvertently underpriced the sale of Amersham International in 1982.

6. British Energy owns eight nuclear stations, excluding the older Magnox stations, which remain state owned.

7. Bus services in London were put out to tender more gradually between 1985 and 1994.

8. By 1999 five operators—FirstGroup PLC, Arriva PLC, Stagecoach Holdings PLC, The Go-Ahead Group PLC, and the National Express Group PLC—accounted for an estimated 69 percent share of the local bus service market ⟨www.researchandmarkets.com⟩.

9. An extension of DEA analysis is the Malmquist indexes to reflect productivity growth.

10. In the 1970s the term *property rights theory* was used, but today the term *principal-agent theory* is preferred in the literature.

11. Except in Northern Ireland, which has its own electricity system.

12. In the water and sewerage industry, the need to raise capital investment also led to real price increases (see the discussion of funding needs below). Saal and Parker attempt to control for environmental and water quality improvements in their econometric studies of productivity and costs in the water sector.

13. Nigel Lawson (1992) is in no doubt that privatization deserves the credit: "It was the process of preparing State enterprises for privatization, and the prospect of privatization, that initially enabled management to be strengthened and motivated, financial disciplines to be imposed and taken seriously, and costs to be cut as trade union attitudes changed" (239–240).

14. Within this average, line rental charges rose in nominal terms and remained broadly constant in real terms over the period. There was a sharp fall in call charges, especially long-distance and international charges.

15. After the domestic market was liberalized, around one in four domestic consumers switched from the former monopoly supplier, British Gas, to a new supplier. Similarly, by June 2000 one in four customers had exercised their new right to change their electricity supplier (NAO 2001).

16. The electricity industries in Scotland and Northern Ireland are separately structured, and competition has been less intense. In Scotland the reduction in domestic charges up to 1997 was about 7 percent and in Northern Ireland a miserly 0.4 percent.

17. It is, of course, possible that this loss has been at least in part offset where businesses benefiting from lower input costs have been able to lower the prices of their products to low-income consumers. I thank Jonas Prager of New York University for drawing this possibility to my attention.

18. Perhaps the most publicized example of a decline in service quality outside the railways occurred in telecommunications in 1987, when the number of functioning public telephone boxes fell sharply. The regulator quickly persuaded BT to increase maintenance spending.

19. This High Court action meant that administrators appointed by government became responsible for running the company. The train operating companies have also turned to public subsidies, contrary to the plans for sharp year-on-year reductions in public financing at the time of privatization. More than half have had to be rescued from increasing losses. The train operating companies are now benefiting from fewer but larger franchises and longer franchise periods. The result is to replace competition for franchises ("competition for the market") with longer-term investment incentives.

20. May 1997 saw the election of a Labour government. This government imposed a £5.2 billion windfall profits tax on the utilities, including the privatized airport operator BAA, in an attempt to recoup some of the large profits made.

21. The figures quoted are internal rates of return based on capital gains, dividends, and amounts invested; for the method of calculation, see Parker (1997).

22. A more recent factor has been the introduction of the New Electricity Trading Arrangements for wholesale power that have reduced wholesale electricity prices and therefore profitability in generation. These new arrangements were introduced in March 2001 and replaced the power pool introduced at privatization and which had been subject to alleged gaming by the major generators.

23. Also, many redundancies in privatized companies have been 'voluntary'.

24. The windfall profits tax introduced by the Labour government shortly after its election in 1997 was intended to recover some of the rents from asset underpricing.

25. The 1980s and 1990s saw an expansion in private sector provision of care homes for the elderly. However, more recently, many have closed following a tightening of state financing.

26. The extent to which the state really does have a lower cost of capital than the private sector remains controversial. Critics argue that the government raises capital more cheaply only by transferring default risk to taxpayers who are undercompensated for the risk.

27. NATS was privatized in 2001, and the state retains a 49 percent shareholding and a golden share. Golden shares have been introduced in a number of privatizations and enable the government to protect the company from unwelcome takeover bids. However, in a number of cases, the golden shares have been abandoned, and recently the European Commission signaled its unhappiness at the use of golden shares and challenged their legality.

28. British Energy's problems have been exacerbated by falling wholesale electricity prices under the New Electricity Trading Arrangements.

29. In the early 1980s, the U.K. government attempted to encourage new entry into the electricity and gas markets without privatization. The results were very disappointing in the face of the market dominance of the state-owned firms, which ultimately had recourse to taxpayer support.

30. *Stagging* is a commonly used term in stock markets for buying new issues and selling quickly for a profit.

31. The figures are lower for international calls (residential 58.6 percent and business 40 percent). For a detailed breakdown, see Oftel (2002).

References

Baldwin, R., and Cave, M. 1999. *Understanding Regulation: Theory, Strategy and Practice*. Oxford: Oxford University Press.

Berry, S. 2002. "Thatcherism Is Dead. Long Live Thatcherism!" ⟨www.libertarian-alliance.org.uk⟩.

Bishop, M., and Green, M. 1995. *Privatisation and Recession—the Miracle Tested*. London: Centre for the Study of Regulated Industries.

Bishop, M., and Thompson, D. 1992. "Regulatory Reform and Productivity Growth in the UK's Public Utilities." *Applied Economics* 24, 1181–1190.

Boardman, A. E., and Laurin, C. 1998. "The Performance of Privatized British Public Utilities and the Windfall Profits Tax." Mimeo. Faculty of Commerce, University of British Columbia.

Bös, D. 1991. *Privatization: A Theoretical Treatment*. Oxford: Clarendon Press.

Boycko, M., Shleifer, A., and Vishny, R. W. 1996. "A Theory of Privatisation." *Economic Journal* 106, 309–319.

Boyfield, K. 1997. *Privatization: A Prize Worth Pursuing*. London: European Policy Forum.

Brau, R., and Florio, M. 2001. "Privatisations as Price Reforms: An Analysis of Consumers' Welfare Change in the U.K." Working paper no. 19.2001, Dipartimento di Economia Politica e Aziendale, Universita degli Studi di Milano, Milan.

Buckland, R. 1987. "The Costs and Returns of Privatisation of Nationalised Industries." *Public Administration* 65, 241–257.

Burns, P., and Weyman-Jones, T. 1994. "Regulatory Incentives, Privatisation and Productivity Growth in UK Electricity Distribution." CRI technical paper 1, Centre for the Study of Regulated Industries, London.

Burton, J., and Parker, D. 1991. "Rolling Back the State? UK Tax and Government Spending Changes in the 1980s." *British Review of Economic Issues* 13(31), 31–66.

Clifton, J., Comín, F., and Fuentes, D. D. 2003. *Privatisation in the European Union: Public Enterprises and Integration*. Dordrecht: Kluwer.

Cook, P. 1998. "Privatization in the UK." In D. Parker, ed., *Privatisation in the European Union: Theory and Policy Perspectives*. London: Routledge.

Cox, A., Harris, L., and Parker, D. 1999. *Privatisation and Supply Chain Management: On the Effective Alignment of Purchasing and Supply after Privatisation*. London: Routledge.

Cragg, M., and Dyck, I. J. A. 1999. "Management Control and Privatization in the UK." *RAND Journal of Economics* 30, 475–497.

Dassler, T., and Parker, D. 2003. "Harmony or Disharmony in the Regulation and the Promotion of Competition in EU Telecommunications? A Survey of the Regulatory Offices." *Utilities Policy* 12, 9–28.

De Alessi, L. 1980. "The Economics of Property Rights: A Review of the Evidence." *Research in Law and Economics* 2, 1–47.

Dnes, A. W., Kodwani, D. G., Seaton, J. S., and Wood, D. 1998. "The Regulation of the United Kingdom Electricity Industry: An Event Study of Price-Capping Measures." *Journal of Regulatory Economics* 13, 207–225.

Domah, P., and Pollitt, M. G. 2001. "The restructuring and Privatisation of Electricity Distribution and Supply Businesses in England and Wales: A Social Cost-Benefit Analysis." *Fiscal Studies* 22, 107–146.

Economist. 2003. "Low Marks for PFI." January 18, 31.

Ernst & Young. 1994. *Privatization in the UK: The Facts and Figures*. London: Ernst & Young.

European Commission. 1990. *Amending Directive 38/EEC with Regard to the Implementation of Full Competition in Telecommunications Markets, 96/19/EC*. Brussels: European Commission.

European Commission. 1996. *Electricity Directive 92/EC*. Brussels: European Commission.

Farrell, M. J. 1957. "The Measurement of Productive Efficiency." *Journal of the Royal Statistical Society* A120, pt. 3, 253–281.

Fawkner, J. 2003. "Lessons from UK Experience in the Privatisation of Public Transport." ⟨www.leipzig-conferences.de/april/pdf/speeches⟩.

Ferner, A., and Colling, T. 1991. "Privatisation, Regulation and Industrial Relations." *British Journal of Industrial Relations* 29, 391–409.

Filatotchev, I. 2003. "Privatization and Corporate Governance in Transition Economies: Theory and Concepts." In D. Parker and D. Saal, eds., *International Handbook on Privitisation*. Cheltenham: Edward Elgar.

Financial Times. 1999. "Competition Remains the Top Priority." October 18, 23.

Financial Times. 2003. "Big Expansion Planned in PFI Projects." June 11, 6.

Florio, M. 2002. "A State without Ownership: The Welfare Impact of British Privatisations 1979–1997." Working paper no. 24.2002, Dipartimento di Economia Politica e Aziendale, Università degli Studi di Milano, Milan.

Florio, M. 2003. "Does Privatisation Matter? The Long-Term Performance of British Telecom over 40 Years." *Fiscal Studies* 24, 197–234.

Florio, M., and Grasseni, M. 2003. "The Missing Shock: The Macroeconomic Impact of British Privatisation." Working paper no. 21.2003, Dipartimento di Economia Politica e Aziendale, Università degli Studi di Milano, Milan.

Hancock, C., and Waddams Price, C. 1995. "Competition in the British Domestic Gas Market: Efficiency and Equity." *Fiscal Studies* 16, 81–105.

Harris, L., Parker, D., and Cox, C. 1998. "UK Privatisation: Its Impact on Procurement." *British Journal of Management* 9, special issue, S13–S26.

Haskel, J., and Szymanski, S. 1993. "The Effects of Privatisation, Restructuring and Competition on Productivity Growth in UK Public Corporations." Department of Economics working paper no. 286, Queen Mary and Westfield College, London.

Helm, D. 1995. *British Utility Regulation: Principles, Experience and Reform.* Oxford: Oxford University Press.

Hutchinson, G. 1991. "Efficiency Gains through Privatization of UK Industries." In K. Hartley and A. F. Ott, eds., *Privatization and Economic Efficiency: A Comparative Analysis of Developed and Developing Countries,* Aldershot: Edward Elgar.

Kay, J., and Thompson, D. J. 1986. "Privatisation: A Policy in Search of a Rationale." *Economic Journal* 96, 18–32.

Lawson, N. 1992. *The View from No. 11: Memoirs of a Tory Radical.* London: Bantam.

Lipsey, R., and Lancaster, K. 1956. "The General Theory of Second Best." *Review of Economic Studies* 24, 11–32.

Littlechild, S. C. 1983. *Regulation of British Telecommunications' Profitability.* London: HMSO.

Littlechild, S. C. 2000. *Privatisation, Competition and Regulation.* London: Institute of Economic Affairs.

Markou, E., and Waddams Price, C. 1999. "UK Utilities: Past Reform and Current Proposals." *Annals of Public and Cooperative Economics* 70, 371–416.

Martin, S., and Parker, D. 1996. "The Impact of UK Privatisation on Employment Profits and the Distribution of Business Income." *Public Money and Management* 16, 31–38.

Martin, S., and Parker, D. 1997. *The Impact of Privatisation: Ownership and Corporate Performance in the UK.* London: Routledge.

Mitchell, W. C. 1988. *Government As It Is.* London: Institute of Economic Affairs.

NAO. 2001. *Giving Domestic Customers a Choice of Electricity Supplier.* London: Stationery Office.

NEDO. 1976. *A Study of UK Nationalised Industries: Their Role in the Economy and Control in the Future.* London: National Economic Development Office/HMSO.

Newbery, D., and Pollitt, M. G. 1997. "The Restructuring and Privatisation of the CEGB—Was It Worth It?" *Journal of Industrial Economics* 45, 269–304.

Niskanen, W. A. Jr. 1973. *Bureaucracy, Servant or Master?* London: Institute of Economic Affairs.

Oftel. 2002. *Protecting Consumers—Oftel's New Price Control Proposals.* London: Office of Telecommunications.

O'Mahony, M. 1998. *Britain's Competitive Performance: An Analysis of Productivity by Sector, 1950–1995.* London: National Institute of Economic and Social Research.

Parker, D. 1994. "A Decade of Privatisation: The Effect of Ownership Change and Competition on British Telecom." *British Review of Economic Issues* 16, 87–113.

Parker, D. 1997. "Price Cap Regulation, Profitability and Returns to Investors in the UK Regulated Industries." *Utilities Policy* 6, 303–315.

Parker, D. 1998. "Privatisation in the European Union: An Overview." In D. Parker, ed., *Privatisation in the European Union: Theory and Policy Perspectives.* London: Routledge.

Parker, D. 1999a. "Regulating Public Utilities: Lessons from the UK." *International Review of Administrative Sciences* 65, 117–131.

Parker, D. 1999b. "The Performance of BAA before and after Privatisation." *Journal of Transport Economics and Policy* 33, 133–146.

Parker, D. 2002. "Economic Regulation: A Review of Issues." *Annals of Public and Cooperative Economics* 73, 493–519.

Parker, D., and Hartley, K. 2003. "Transaction Costs, Relational Contracting and Public-Private Partnerships: A Case Study of UK Defence." *Journal of Purchasing and Supply Management* 9(3), 97–108.

Parker, D., and Saal, D. (eds.). 2003. *International Handbook on Privatization*. Cheltenham: Edward Elgar.

Parker, D., and Wu, H. S. 1998. "Privatization and Performance: A Study of the British Steel Industry under Public and Private Ownership." *Economic Issues* 3, 31–50.

Pollitt, M. G. 1999. "A Survey of the Liberalisation of Public Enterprises in the UK since 1979." In M. Kamagami and M. Tsuji, eds., *Deregulation and Institutional Framework*. Tokyo: Institute of Developing Economies, External Trade Organisation.

Pollitt, M. G. 2001. "The Restructuring and Privatisation of the Regional Electricity Companies in England and Wales: A Social Cost Benefit Analysis." *Fiscal Studies* 22, 107–146.

Pollitt, M. G., and Smith, A. S. J. 2002. "The Restructuring and Privatisation of British Rail: Was It Really That Bad?" *Fiscal Studies* 23, 463–502.

Saal, D. 2003. "Restructuring, Regulation and the Liberalization of Privatised Utilities in the UK." In D. Parker and D. Saal, eds., *International Handbook on Privitisation*. Cheltenham: Edward Elgar.

Saal, D., and Parker, D. 2000. "The Impact of Privatisation and Regulation on the Water and Sewerage Industry in England and Wales: A Translog Cost Function Model." *Managerial and Decision Economics* 21, 253–268.

Saal, D., and Parker, D. 2001. "Productivity and Price Performance in the Privatised Water and Sewerage Companies of England and Wales." *Journal of Regulatory Economics* 20, 61–90.

Saundry, R., and Turnbull, P. 1997. "Private Profit, Public Loss: The Financial and Economic Performance of U.K. Ports." *Maritime Policy Management* 24, 319–334.

Shaoul, J. 1997. "A Critical Financial Analysis of the Performance of Privatised Utilities: The Case of the Water Industry in England and Wales." *Critical Perspectives on Accounting* 8, 479–505.

Shaoul, J. 2003. "A Financial Analysis of the National Air Traffic Services PPP." *Public Money and Management* 23, 185–194.

Talbot, C. 2001. "UK Public Services and Management (1979–2000)." *International Journal of Public Sector Management* 14, 281–303.

Thatcher, M. 1993. *Margaret Thatcher: The Downing Street Years*. New York: HarperCollins.

TUC. 1985a. *Stripping Our Assets: The City's Privatisation Killing*. London: Trades Union Congress.

TUC. 1985b. *Privatisation and Top Pay*. London: Trades Union Congress.

TUC. 1986. *Bargaining in Privatised Companies*. London: Trades Union Congress.

Tullock, G. 1976. *The Vote Motive*. London: Institute of Economic Affairs.

Tyrrall, D., and Parker, D. 2003. "The Fragmentation of a Railway: A Study of Organisational Change." *Journal of Management Studies* 42, 507–537.

Vickers, J., and Yarrow, G. 1988. *Privatization: An Economic Analysis*. Cambridge, Mass.: MIT Press.

Waddams Price, C., and Hancock, R. 1998. "Distributional Effects of Liberalising UK Residential Utility Markets." *Fiscal Studies* 19, 295–319.

Waddams Price, C., and Weyman-Jones, T. 1996. "Malmquist Indices of Productivity Change in the UK Gas Industry before and after privatisation." *Applied Economics* 28, 29–39.

Waddams Price, C., and Young, A. 2003. "UK Utility Reform: Distributional Implications and Government Response." In C. Ugaz and C. Waddams Price, eds., *Utility Privatization and Regulation: A Fair Deal for Consumers?* Cheltenham: Edward Elgar.

Contributors

Pablo Arocena
Universidad Publica De Navarra,
Spain

Sean D. Barrett
Trinity College Dublin, Ireland

Ansgar Belke
Universität Stuttgart-Hohenheim,
Germany

Michel Berne
Institut National des
Telecommunications, France

Henrik Christoffersen
AKF, Institute of Local
Government Studies, Denmark

Eric van Damme
CentER for Economic Research,
Tilburg University, Germany

Andrea Goldstein
Organisation for Economic Co-
operation and Development
(OECD), Paris

Günter Knieps
Albert-Ludwigs-Universität
Freiburg, Germany

Marko Köthenbürger
CES, University of Munich,
Germany, and CESifo

David Newbery
Cambridge University, United
Kingdom

Martin Paldam
Aarhus University, Denmark

David Parker
Cranfield University, United
Kingdom

Gérard Pogorel
GET/ENST, Paris

Friedrich Schneider
Johannes Kepler University of
Linz, Austria

Hans-Werner Sinn
CESifo

Ingo Vogelsang
Boston University, United States

John Whalley
University of Western Ontario,
Canada

Johan Willner
Åbo Aakademi University,
Finland

Index